P9-BXZ-083

State and Local Government

State and Local Government

Sustainability in the 21ˢᵗ Century

Christopher A. Simon
University of Utah

Brent S. Steel
Oregon State University

Nicholas P. Lovrich
Washington State University

New York   Oxford
Oxford University Press
2011

Oxford University Press, Inc., publishes works that further Oxford University's
objective of excellence in research, scholarship, and education.

Oxford New York
Auckland Cape Town Dar es Salaam Hong Kong Karachi
Kuala Lumpur Madrid Melbourne Mexico City Nairobi
New Delhi Shanghai Taipei Toronto

With offices in
Argentina Austria Brazil Chile Czech Republic France Greece
Guatemala Hungary Italy Japan Poland Portugal Singapore
South Korea Switzerland Thailand Turkey Ukraine Vietnam

Copyright © 2011 by Oxford University Press, Inc.

Published by Oxford University Press, Inc.
198 Madison Avenue, New York, New York 10016
http://www.oup.com

Oxford is a registered trademark of Oxford University Press

All rights reserved. No part of this publication may be reproduced,
stored in a retrieval system, or transmitted, in any form or by any means,
electronic, mechanical, photocopying, recording, or otherwise,
without the prior permission of Oxford University Press.

Library of Congress Cataloging-in-Publication Data

Simon, Christopher A., 1968-
State and local government : sustainability in the 21st century / Christopher A. Simon, Brent S. Steel,
Nicholas P. Lovrich, Jr.
   p. cm.
Includes index.
ISBN 978-0-19-975200-3 (alk. paper)
1. State governments—United States. 2. Local government—United States. 3. Federal
government—United States. 4. Sustainability—United States. I. Steel, Brent. II. Lovrich,
Nicholas P. III. Title.
JK2408.S49 2010
320.473—dc22   2010019932

9 8 7 6 5 4 3 2 1

Printed in the United States of America
on acid-free paper

DEDICATIONS

To my parents, Raffi G. and Susan M. Simon.
–CAS

To my late grandparents, Pearl and Arnold Shaffer.
–BSS

To my daughter Nichole and her generation — may they make the
changes needed to preserve the planet for their children.
–NPL

Brief Contents

Contents

CHAPTER 9

State and Local Bureaucracy and Administration • 206

CHAPTER 10

Budgeting and Sustainability • 230

Preface

Sustainability is about improving the odds of continued existence under preferred conditions. *Preferred conditions* can entail many things. Nineteenth-century writer Henry David Thoreau presented a rather succinct glimpse of a very personal journey to discover the meaning of life lived under *preferred conditions.* In one of his most insightful chapters, "Where I Lived and What I Lived For," in the classic account *Walden (or Life in the Woods)*, Thoreau vowed to confront the "essential facts of life" in terms of modes of living and principles by which to live well.

While Thoreau's soul-searching journey was a highly personal one carried out in a bucolic setting, in a modern society composed of billions of individuals sharing a planet newly aware of its own fragility the generally accepted political, social, and economic institutions and guiding principles defining society as a whole would seem to require the same process of careful soul-searching by the next generation of college-educated persons. As our global society evolves, decisions about what principles and practices should continue to be accepted and what changes should be made ought to result from a sustained, open, and easily accessible dialogue about our individual and collective preferences. It is our hope that this book contributes to that dialogue.

In the larger societal sense, sustainability might be easily confused with the concept of "hanging on." Clearly, many great nations and civilizations have experienced both long and painful declines and have sought to remain sustainable despite a growing sense of the inevitable. More positively, sustainability could serve as recognition that without general guidelines for existence an upward societal trajectory and an improved future is unattainable. Rather than drive society towards eventual disaster, perhaps it would be better to alter course and avoid trouble.

This book is a collective effort to understand and apply current conceptualizations of sustainability to a study of state and local government. It is an attempt to focus our attention on a basic understanding of the time-tested institutions and guiding principles likely to take society and governance towards greater advancement. Our work is, however, tempered by a developing understanding of *smart growth*—growth in productive capacity, quality of life, and social justice that does not necessitate large-scale destructive or extractive activity. The growth sought produces widespread mutual benefit and is prudent in design and thoughtful in execution. The growth in question here is mindful of the past, yet builds better lives and futures for our posterity.

It is important to recall that sustainability is neither a conservative nor a liberal concept. Rather, it is built around a basic human need to maintain our collective and individual bearings in an ever-changing world. Throughout time, humans have found their collective and individual bearings through institutional memberships and shared principles. While conservatives and liberals may place varying emphases on aspects of institutions and principles, conservatives and liberals alike desire to maintain core democratic values and are eager to sustain the institutions that give life to those values.

As authors, we seek to provide a book that will help students understand a current conceptualization of sustainability and how it plays out in the governance of the states and localities in the nation. It is a dialogue built on the ideas, experiences, and events of many cited scholars and their works, as well as the personal research experiences of the authors themselves.

Our book represents a unique opportunity for three generations of scholars to reflect upon and collectively consider their decades-long research, and the meaning of that research to both the broader society and to students of contemporary politics. Nicholas Lovrich served as a graduate-school mentor to Brent Steel, and Brent in turn mentored Christopher A. Simon as an undergraduate and guided him to study with Lovrich. Steel and Lovrich have collaborated on research for over 30 years, while Simon has frequently collaborated with Steel and Lovrich for nearly 20 years.

Research experience was not the only guide or source of our inspiration, of course. For Christopher A. Simon, his years of alternately living on a sailboat and a farm brought him close to issues of survival and the wise use of the resources available to both him and his parents, Raffi G. and Susan M. Simon. Along with his youthful experiences sailing the Pacific Ocean and working the tilled farmland of Central Oregon, his parents instilled in him the importance of studying history and philosophy. For Brent Steel, growing up traveling and camping with his grandparents in locations ranging from Alaska, to northern and western Canada, and to the mountains of the American West, he learned a deep appreciation for the environment and our need to be sound stewards of our environment so that future generations can enjoy and "soul search" just as Thoreau had done. For Nicholas Lovrich the experience of growing up in an immigrant family in a multicultural social setting provided an opportunity to see American society from a slight distance. Viewed from that perspective, it was possible to see the great value present in the inventive and adaptive capacities of Americans in every state and hamlet across the country as they manage the changes brought on by their powerful economic system, drawing upon access to vast natural resources and benefitting from wise investment in the education of the nation's youth.

We would like to express our deep gratitude to Jennifer Carpenter, Politics Editor at Oxford University Press. Jennifer helped us move through the many excellent editorial reviews with uncommon insight, and her suggestions for modification were uniformly of enormous help. Editorial Assistant Maegan Sherlock was ever-available to help us with the many critical details that turn a manuscript into a finished published work. We appreciate the enthusiastic encouragement of Raymond Tatalovich, Professor of Political Science at Loyola University (Chicago), longtime friend and adviser to Simon, Steel, and Lovrich alike. The diligent work of Brent's student research assistants was of great importance to the successful completion this book, including Monica Hubbard, Kristen Chatfield, Yao Yin, and Kirsten Winters (who wrote the glossary for this book). Special thanks are due to the anonymous reviewers who guided us through several careful revisions of this text.

CHAPTER 1

Introduction and Themes

Introduction

State and local governments are the most visible levels of government in the United States. As you leave your family house, apartment, or school dormitory you encounter state and local government services, programs, and infrastructure. From traffic lights, streets and highways, water and sewer services, K–12 education, higher education, parks, mass transit, law enforcement, utilities, communications and mass media, and many other activities, state and local governments are either directly involved in offering these services or in regulating organizations hired to provide such services. From the 50 states to the 3,033 county, 19,492 municipal, 13,051 school district, 16,504 town or township, and 37,381 special district governments (which could include hospital districts, rural fire districts, soil conservation districts, irrigation districts, regional transportation districts, and many more), the typical citizen encounters state and local government services and programs on a daily basis.

While state and local governments are the most visible and potentially most important on a daily basis for most citizens when compared to the federal government, the generally low levels of interest in and knowledge concerning these governments and the often high levels of cynicism regarding their leaders among citizens is of great concern to many political scientists.[1] Given the importance of civic knowledge to effective participation and democratic institutions, how many states require students to take civics and government education? As of 2007, only 29 states require a government or civics course in high school. However limited this coverage may seem, this is a much higher proportion than is present at the university level: only nine U.S. states require some study of American government, with five of these also requiring study of their respective state governments as well.[2] Of course, universities and political science departments

may require such courses on their own, but courses on state and local government tend to be optional in most colleges and universities. The purpose of this
book is to provide an accessible overview and guide to state and local government for students with little to no exposure—and possibly limited interest—in
order to encourage lifelong democratic participation and what Russell Dalton
calls "engaged citizenship."[3] In an attempt to achieve this purpose, we will present state and local government in a contemporary context by examining the
many forces that either promote or threaten social, economic, institutional, and
environmental sustainability. In using the term *sustainability*, we make use of
the 1987 **Brundtland Report** definition (also known as *Our Common Future*):
*development that meets the needs of the present without compromising the ability
of future generations to meet their own needs*. The book will make note of where
students can go to find additional information on state and local governments,
and how citizens can follow the developments of—and even become actively
involved in—the unfolding of state and local governance issues that affect their
own daily lives.

Each chapter in this book incorporates some of the most important recent
research available and identifies key concepts that are important to deepen our
collective understanding of state and local government and sustainability. These
concepts are highlighted in **boldface** in the text and are included in the glossary at
the end of the book.

The major topics to be discussed in this introductory chapter include:

- Changing socioeconomic, demographic, and technological forces and
  how they affect state and local governments
- How many states and communities have responded successfully to these
  forces to promote sustainability
- A final summary of the book's themes, and how the book's chapters are
  organized

Forces Facing State and Local Governments

State and local governments currently face many ongoing and numerous new challenges that complicate their task of sustaining current public services and programs.
How public officials adapt or do not adapt to these changes will affect the long-term
viability of virtually each and every state and local government in the country. As
the United States has developed from a rural and agricultural-based economy in the
1700s into an industrial powerhouse in the 1800s, and now as it becomes increasingly a **postindustrial society** with a knowledge-based economy and the majority
of citizens employed in service sector jobs instead of the agricultural and industrial
sectors, state and local governments have had to cope with a wide array of socioeconomic and political changes (Table 1.1). Needless to say, the dramatic events of the
nation's first major experience with foreign terrorism on September 11, 2001 have

added to concerns for homeland security that were scarcely considered prior to that horrific historic event.

A substantial literature has developed examining the social, economic, and political implications of postindustrialism.[4] While some degree of definitional disagreement is present among scholars writing in this area, a few commonly agreed upon central features of this new type of society can be identified that help us understand the dynamics of state and local government today. Postindustrial societies—such as the United States, Canada, the nations of the European Union, Australia, and Japan—are characterized by the following traits:

- Economic dominance of the service sector over those of manufacturing and agriculture
- Complex nationwide communication networks
- A high degree of economic activity based upon an educated workforce employing scientific knowledge and technology in their work
- A high level of public mobilization in society (including the rise of historically new social causes such as the civil rights movement, the women's rights movement, the anti-nuclear movement, the anti-globalization movement, the environmental movement)

Table 1.1. Socioeconomic and Political Characteristics of the United States

	Preindustrial	Industrial	Postindustrial
ECONOMIC FEATURES			
Sectoral dominance	Agriculture	Manufacturing	Services
Systemic character	Labor intensive	Capital intensive	Knowledge intensive
Technical change	Slow	Rapid	Exponential
Material condition	Poverty/ subsistence	Rising productivity	Affluence
SOCIAL FEATURES			
Population	Rural	Urban	Megalopolitan
Population growth	High	Moderating	Low or negative
Community	Intimate	Eroding	Impersonal
Literacy	Low	Medium	High
Dominant values	Basic/survival needs	Material security	Post-materialist values?
POLITICAL DIMENSIONS			
Central issue	"Who shall rule?" (political order)	Economic growth (economic order)	Sustainable development
Object of conflict	Office/power	How to distribute expanding wealth	Both quantity-of-life and quality-of-life issues
Attitude toward authority	Deferential	Supportive (elite directed)	Challenging (elite challenging)
Governability	Variable	High	Declining—"crisis of confidence"

- Population and employment growth in urban areas (and subsequent decline in rural areas)
- Historically unprecedented societal affluence[5]

As the United States developed from a small preindustrial nation of a few small settlements and many farmers and artisans into a modern, continent-spanning postindustrial economy connected to a knowledge-based global economy, different sets of concerns and issues have assumed priority in our collective consideration of public affairs. In the early years of the young country's history the principal issues of concern were such matters as basic nutrition, shelter, access to water, safe routes of travel, safety of person and property, and so forth. Because of such immediate survival and infrastructure concerns, American state and local governments—which were generally small in scale and limited in capacity—accorded little attention to such contemporary issues as environmental protection or other **higher-order needs** such as gender equity and global economic justice.

As the United States moved into extensive mining and natural resource extraction and the large-scale fabrication and manufacturing of durable goods, many issues relating to industrialization became important for American state and local governments. Highly troublesome issues such as unsafe workplaces, unrestrained child labor exploitation, uncontrolled urbanization, inadequate local transportation systems, poor public health services, toxic waste disposal, and inadequate public education systems arose as the industrialization process proceeded. All of these issues were addressed by state and local government regulation in due course, with federal government action coming only after state and local governments took the initiative to address these adverse consequences of industrialization.

With the ultimate development of a more affluent postindustrial economy and more adequate systems of public regulation, new issues have emerged that reflect a profound concern for global sustainability. This historically unprecedented concern for our collective global future translates into particular issues of great importance for contemporary state and local governments in the United States. Issues regarding water resource protection and conservation, **smart growth** and environmental stewardship-oriented land use practices, the enforcement of energy-efficient building standards, the implementation of air quality protection measures, and the reduction of the impact of carbon emissions on global climate change are all directly involved in promoting sustainable economic development in state and local governments in the United States today.

State and local governments in many areas of the nation face additional challenges in the areas of dramatic demographic shifts (aging populations, racial and ethnic diversification, and the influx of large numbers of immigrants), continued urbanization, economic globalization, ongoing technological change, changing social norms, and growing environmental awareness. Thoughtful observers taking note of these changes, such as Roger Kemp, have argued that state and local governments will be affected directly in a number of ways in the 21st century. He

Photo 1.1. An example of child labor: boys working in a glass factory. Source: Bettman/Corbis.

has observed the following in this regard: "Evolving societal conditions and public perceptions have created trends that *require communities to change* in order to meet the public's expectation for effective and equitable governance" [emphasis added] (2001: 1).[6] These historic changes, closely associated with the advent of postindustrial society, are discussed below to provide a suitable backdrop to our exploration of state and local government in contemporary America.

Demographic Change

People are living longer than ever before, a fact that affects a host of government services, including: (1) increasing costs associated with retirement pensions, healthcare, and other social services such as independent, assisted, and dependent living arrangements for the aged; (2) increasing demand for senior citizen recreational and leisure activities, including parks, libraries, and exercise opportunities; and (3) higher rates of political participation in state and local affairs by senior citizens. Seniors exhibit high rates of political participation when compared to younger cohorts, which means the public policy preferences of seniors may disproportionately affect state and local community decisions (e.g., preference for lower taxes because of fixed retirement incomes, preference for robust spending on public safety and meager spending on education).

Another important demographic change taking place in much of the country is large-scale immigration from Mexico, Central America, and South America. Such immigration creates new public issues for many communities, including the need for bilingual government services in education, justice, and social spheres, new cultural diversity programs, new approaches to housing and transportation services, new types of law enforcement issues arising from claims of biased policing, and so forth. Hispanics or Latinos are now the largest minority group in the United States and their proportion of the population continues to grow at a rapid rate. In Florida, New York, Illinois, California, and most Southwestern states powerful new political voices and advocacy groups articulating Latino demands for state and local government programs and services are adding to the challenges of those governments.

Another demographic trend that has been in stark evidence is the increasing presence of women in the workforce and in state and local government leadership roles. This enhanced presence of women in the workforce and in leadership roles has led to increased emphasis on such issues as family leave policies, daycare provisions, equal employment opportunities, comparable worth compensation policies, sexual harassment, and domestic violence. Due to a variety of factors, including rising educational levels as well as higher percentages of women working outside the household, average family size is declining, potentially leading to more high-density residential areas (e.g., townhouses, condominiums) being created in urban areas. This type of residential settlement pattern places different demands on existing state and local service infrastructure than those associated with the traditional "suburban sprawl" pattern of housing settlement.

Urbanization

The United States has been transformed from a rural nation of 3,929,214 people in 1790 (our first census of population) to an urban society of an estimated 305,529,237 people as of 2009. After a relatively slow rate of urban growth in the 18th century, the pace of urbanization picked up dramatically during the 19th and early 20th centuries (Table 1.2). During the 20th century the urban population continued to increase and suburban areas started to develop and grow as well. During the 1980s and 1990s a substantial number of rural counties in the United States lost population, while urban and suburban counties grew at a rapid rate. The migration of people from rural to urban/suburban counties was driven by the most highly educated and/or skilled younger cohorts leaving rural areas to seek jobs or further education in urban core areas.[7] These migration patterns have led to the acquisition of increased economic and political power on the part of urban and suburban centers vis-à-vis rural areas, and contributed to the political

Photo 1.2. Sustainable communities and equality: Chicana woman at an antidiscrimination rally. Source: Bettmann/Corbis.

and economic decline of communities whose local economies are based in the rural periphery.[8]

Urbanization has had a pronounced social, economic, and environmental impact on communities throughout the country. A visitor to a major city in the United States will likely experience traffic congestion arising from our love of automobiles, be greeted by smoggy air and haze in the summer, witness municipal sewage being dumped into rivers, and be shocked by the enormous amounts of trash produced by our mass consumption society.[9] Viewed from a regional perspective, that same visitor to a major metropolitan population center might be saddened by a sense of loss of once-prime agricultural lands, forests and woodlands, wildlife habitat, and wetlands due to urban sprawl.[10] In fact, some of the most divisive political issues in U.S. state politics result from urban areas encroaching on rural communities and their land-based economies.[11]

The phenomenon of suburban sprawl has led to the growth of geographically vast metropolitan areas where cities have literally grown into each other, often swallowing up prime agricultural areas and natural landscapes in the process. For example, there are huge continuous urban areas between San Diego and Los Angeles in California, and "the eastern seaboard of the USA, where one quarter of the national population reside on less than 2% of the nation's land."[12] These vast metropolitan areas universally succumb to serious traffic congestion and harmful air quality problems, not to mention the dependence they breed for the consumption of great amounts of petroleum products.[13]

Continuing growth and geographical dispersion of urban and suburban areas in the United States, along with the decline in natural resource and agricultural sectors of the economy, has led to the service sector employment accounting for over 70% of the U.S. economy. Employment in the agricultural and natural resource extraction sectors has declined to less than 2% of the contemporary labor force.[14] In addition, unemployment and poverty rates are typically higher and wages lower in the rural periphery compared to the metropolitan areas.[15] Substantial economic decline in rural communities can contribute to a felt imperative among its residents to increase natural resource extraction in order to sustain community viability,

Table 1.2. **Urban and Rural Population Change in the United States**

Year	Percent Urban	Percent Rural
2000	79	21
1990	75	25
1960	70	30
1930	56	44
1900	40	60
1870	26	74
1840	11	89
1810	7	93
1790	5	95

Source: U.S. Department of the Census Web site (www.census.gov).

while continued growth in the urban service industry creates a contrary imperative toward nonmaterial uses of natural environments such as recreation and provision of wildlife habitat.[16]

Other issues often confronting communities arising from urbanization include escalating land prices due to the **gentrification** of neighborhoods (i.e., the displacement of low-income residents living in inexpensive housing by high-income residents living in high-cost housing); traffic congestion leading to demands for more freeways, parking lots, and possibly mass transportation such as buses and light-rail systems; more expensive construction costs due to the development in densely populated areas; and more demands for inner-city services, which could include social, educational, public health, public safety, recreation and open space, and economic security issues.

Globalization and Economic Change

Globalization is a concept used to describe, among other things, the current worldwide expansion of economic markets in a very broad range of goods and services. The creation of the current global free market economy was facilitated by a variety of "international regimes" (i.e., treaties and multilateral agreements) such as the GATT (General Agreement on Tariffs and Trade) and institutions such as the World Trade Organization, the World Bank, and the International Monetary Fund. Globalization is based on the economic theory of **neo-liberalism**, a worldview perspective that promotes free trade, continuous economic growth, free domestic markets, maximal individual choice in consumption, reduced government regulation of the economy, and "the advocacy of an evolutionary model of social development anchored in the Western experience and applicable to the entire world."[17]

In general, neo-liberalism and globalization view economic growth as the primary expression of human progress and believe that the expansion of free trade and the promotion of Western consumerism are the proper public policy goals for nations and local communities alike. Critics of globalization, however, point to the phenomenon of international homogenization in culture, lifestyles, and technology that accompanies globalization. This phenomenon is referred to by some opponents of globalization as the **McDonaldization effect**.[18] An example of this phenomenon would be the increasingly similar types of suburban shopping areas emerging across communities in the United States, each featuring similar restaurants, clothing stores, coffee shops, superstores, and the like. Critics point to diminishing local control and loss of cultural diversity, while the advocates of "mall development" point to the sales tax revenue and employment benefits to local communities that are associated with such ubiquitous and uniform contemporary commercial land use development practices.[19]

The globalization of the economy creates special problems with states and local communities as they seek to attract and retain businesses and generate employment in an international and national context. Many states and local communities find themselves in a situation where, in order to attract potential employers, they must offer various tax concessions and economic development subsidies such as infrastructure and targeted worker-training programs. The influx of new chain stores and nationally (or even internationally) franchised businesses causes locally owned businesses to struggle to survive, often bringing adverse effects on local community culture and resulting in less local influence over investment in local, community-based enterprises.

Compounding these global changes are generally constrained state and local government budgets. Unlike the federal government, the ability of the state and local governments to engage in deficit spending is extremely limited, and "balanced budgets" with respect to anticipated revenues and budgeted expenditures are very much the norm across the country. State and local government fiscal capacity is generally highly constrained due to the following factors: widespread use of economic incentives (tax concessions and targeted expenditures) for the promotion of economic development; widespread public hostility to raising taxes to support public services and programs;[20] the increasing cost of many essential services and entitlements such as healthcare facilities and services, fire protection, police protection, corrections facilities, transportation infrastructure (e.g., streets, roads and bridges), and education; and the increasing demand and cost for new amenities and services characteristic of postindustrial societies, such as cultural (visual and performing arts) programs, access to broadband Internet services, public libraries, park and recreation programs, walking and bike trails, museums, and so forth. To provide these services states and communities have come to rely heavily on a variety of user fees and charges and other non-property, non-sales, and non-income tax revenues. Steger reminds us in this regard:[21]

> Citizens don't mind paying for those services they use, but they will increasingly demand that other taxpayers pay their fair-share of taxes for the cost of providing those "other" services that "they" do not use. This will pose a political problem, since everyone uses selected services but no one uses every public service.

Technological Change

The growing role of a ceaselessly changing information technology is particularly important to understanding some new issues facing state and local government in our contemporary postindustrial, highly knowledge-based society. The technological infrastructure of communities plays an important role in attracting the knowledge-based businesses characteristic of postindustrial countries, and this modern information technology infrastructure is becoming an important component of state and local government governance as citizens grow increasingly comfortable with the use of the Internet to access government information, to file required forms, to renew their driver's licenses, to register to vote, to reserve summer campgrounds, to pay taxes, and to communicate with their elected and career service public officials.

Most state and local governments are heavily reliant on computers and electronic communication, both large servers and desktop computers, to conduct their work. This development has been referred to in a number of ways, including **e-government**, online government, and transformational government. State and local governments are increasingly exchanging information and providing services to businesses and citizens alike in an effort to promote efficiency and increased accountability. A 2002 survey of local governments conducted by the International City/County Management Association found that over 85% of municipalities had active Web sites, providing a large variety of services and information for citizens.[22] For example, citizens in many states can now acquire their fishing and hunting licenses by using the Internet, they can pay local property and state income taxes online, and they can get transportation updates concerning weather, road and bridge construction projects, or traffic congestion from state and local government Web sites on their personal computers or web-enabled cellular phones. Many local governments are even now monitoring their high-crime areas and mass transportation corridors with the use of digital video cameras to provide greater protection for citizens—in some areas even monitoring traffic intersections and roads for traffic violations (e.g., speeding or running a red light) in order to issue electronic citations to violators and notices of violations to prosecutors and courts.

Many state and local governments across the country are also using the Internet to engage citizens in the policymaking process, and some are even implementing electronic voting technologies as part of this process. This innovation has been called **e-democracy**. Most state governments have established Web sites that include extensive information concerning all branches of government and various departments and agencies, and information on how and where citizens may contact their elected and career service officials.[23] Similarly, new electronic voting technologies are being implemented to speed the counting of ballots as well as providing more user-friendly access for disabled voters. However, e-democracy has also generated considerable controversy because its critics argue that election fraud can occur through difficult-to-detect software malfunctions or even the electronic manipulation of vote counts.

While e-government and e-democracy are important new technologies consistent with the advent of postindustrial society, important social justice concerns can arise about selectivity in access. For example, recent research has found that the young, the highly educated, the urban, the middle and upper-middle class, and the nation's white citizens are the most likely to use the Internet.[24] In addition, in a recent study of municipal Web sites research found that "city size and scale matter in achieving overall web site quality."[25] Smaller and more rural local governments have far fewer resources and more limited expertise to develop and maintain Web sites and Internet services, thus resulting in another type of access gap. Thus, the ability of e-government and e-democracy to deliver on the promise of enhanced service efficiencies and enhanced democracy and social equity remains somewhat in question.

Another related concern that arises from rapid technological innovation in the United States has been referred to by some scholars as the troublesome **democracy versus technocracy quandary.**[26] Operating in a postindustrial setting, state and local governments face many policy problems that are highly technical in nature and

Photo 1.3. Electronic voting is a visible form of electronic democracy. Source: © Lisafx | Dreamstime.com

require scientific knowledge to manage effectively. As Frank Fischer in *Citizens, Experts, and the Environment* aptly observes: "The tension between professional expertise and democratic governance is an important political dimension of our time. Democracy's emphasis on equality of citizenship, public opinion, and freedom of choice exists in an uneasy relationship with the scientific expert's rational, calculating spirit."[27]

While there are considerable geographical, cultural, and economic differences among state and local governments, they all feature democratic systems of governance that have experienced a noteworthy decline in public trust of government (both elected representatives and governmental bureaucracies).[28] Along with this diminished trust have come forceful demands for increasing citizen involvement in governance (Inglehart, 1997; see note 5). The concern that arises in this context is that the demand for the enhancement of direct citizen participation (democracy) and the need for scientific expertise (technocracy) to frame issues and develop appropriate policy options in complex areas of public policy may well come into direct conflict.[29] On the one hand, placing too much emphasis on science and technical expertise as the ultimate determinants of policy outcomes risks the erosion of democracy and the progressive diminishment of active engagement of the citizenry.[30] On the other hand, excessive democracy in the form of the direct involvement of ill-informed citizens in policymaking and program implementation may relegate technical and scientific information to such a peripheral role that complex problems will be inadequately addressed by the adoption of "political" solutions reflecting the relative power of a narrow set of intensely interested parties.[31]

Value Change

As discussed above, in the decades following World War II a number of fundamental changes transpired in the United States that have fundamentally changed politics from what had existed in previous years. The shift from an agricultural to an industrial society and then a postindustrial society has led to substantial **value change** (fundamental cultural realignment) in the United States, and this value change has direct implications for state and local governments. Personal value structures among citizens (particularly younger cohorts) are developing in ways that involve what the widely read psychologist Abraham Maslow termed "higher order" needs (e.g., social affiliation, quality of life concerns, connection to transcendent values) supplanting more fundamental subsistence needs (e.g., health and safety concerns, material acquisition) as the motivation for much individual and societal behavior.[32] Value changes entailing greater attention to **post-materialist needs** are thought to have brought about changes in many types of personal attitudes and public policy preferences, including those related to environmental protection, to gender equity, and to global justice and other similar philosophical or worldview issues.[33] Some careful observers of societal change in postindustrial societies suggest that the development of social movements in the United States relating to consumer protection, women's rights, gay rights, and environmental protection are a clear reflection of societal value change.[34]

The development of new values and social movements among citizens has resulted in the questioning of many traditional state and local government institutions and long-established policies. Many scholars believe this is most pronounced among what has been labeled the "millennial generation" (born after 1982). When compared to older cohorts, Millennials have been found to be: (1) very optimistic about their own lives and the role of government in their lives; (2) believe that special interest groups currently have too much influence; (3) are more involved in local community based civic activities; (4) more tolerant of gays, race and ethnic diversity; and, (5) very supportive of nontraditional roles for women.[35] Millennials also have been heavily influenced by new communications technologies (e.g., smart phones) and are very comfortable and adept users of social networking sites such as MySpace, Facebook, Twitter and YouTube.

Environmental Change and Concern

As with the other factors affecting state and local governments, new environmental issues and concerns also reflect the nation's transformation from a preindustrial agricultural nation in 1776, to the coming of the Industrial Revolution in the late 1800s, and then to the development of a postindustrial society in the latter half of the 20th century.[36] From colonial times to the beginning of the 20th century, environmental policy was primarily framed by **anthropocentric concerns** such as the impact of pollution on human health and the need for the careful conservation of natural areas for future extraction of economically desirable products. The natural environment was seen primarily as something to either conserve or conquer, depending on the uses to be made of it, to improve the quality of human life; apart from the needs of human beings, the environment *per se* had no particular value.

The start of the 20th century witnessed rapid growth in the number of citizens and organized groups interested in the conservation of natural resources. Interest in conservation often arose in reaction to the highly visible widespread abuse and even destruction of public forests and waterways. A new approach to the stewardship of natural resources was adopted in the United States over time, based largely on the writings of the visionary Gifford Pinchot. He was a highly respected figure who argued for the development of scientific expertise leading to the intelligent use and development of natural resources and the protection of natural resources for the benefit of future generations. This approach to the natural environment was based on a premise of anthropocentrism—that is, a human-oriented view of nature where human needs, wants, and desires are given preeminent priority in the managing of natural resources. Moreover, it assumes that the nonhuman part of the environment is to be seen as little more than a fund of raw materials for humans to make use of as they see fit. It follows from this premise that providing for human uses and benefits becomes the primary aim of any environmental policy, whether those uses are for commodity benefits (e.g., lumber, food or energy) or for aesthetic or spiritual benefits (e.g., wilderness preservation and outdoor recreation).

By the late 1960s, however, a new environmental policy orientation emerged in some U.S. states and many communities, one that is more **biocentered** or "eco-centered" in its premises[37] and in its philosophical character.[38] The biocentric approach elevates the requirements and value of all natural organisms, species, and ecosystems to center stage and, in some versions, makes the earth or nature as a whole the focus of "moral considerability." Advocates of this orientation do not ignore human needs, but rather they place such needs in a larger, natural, or ecological context. In addition, adherents to this view of the natural world tend to assume that environmental assets such as mountain ranges, free-running streams, pristine ecosystems, wilderness areas, wildlife, and nonedible animals and plants all have value in and of themselves as biodiversity assets. This perspective has become an important component of the new social movement advocating the adoption of sustainability-promoting policies and programs in American communities, a topic which we take up next.

Sustainable and Resilient States and Communities

The advocacy for sustainable states and communities in postindustrial America has become one of the major social movements of our time.[39] Widespread concern with the long-term carrying capacity of our conventional economic, social, and ecological processes and with the institutions required to manage them has led many state and local government officials and civic-engaged citizens to conceive and implement a wide range of innovative policies in pursuit of sustainability. The concept of **sustainability** refers to the manner in which the social, economic, institutional, and environmental needs of a community are met without compromising the ability of future generations to meet their own needs.[40] Early approaches to addressing sustainability have placed rather differing emphases on these various needs,[41] but in general the four core dimensions of sustainable communities are:

- Social objectives: systematic investment in *human capital*, featuring lifelong education promoting environmental sensitivity and adaptability to change, and *social capital*, enabling the widespread co-production of public goods through both coordinated individual action and enhancing the capacity for effective collective action on behalf of environmental protection[42]
- Economic objectives: through public law and policy, and through public–private partnerships, bring about a shift towards "sustainable economics" featuring equitable and competitive arrangements in the marketplace supplying high-quality (e.g., nontoxic, organic, nonexploitive), reasonable-cost goods and services produced with minimum damage to the environment[43]
- Environmental objectives: protection of the global ecosystem, enhancement of local biodiversity, protection of endangered species, and systematic preservation of natural areas from harm resulting from unsustainable economic exploitation or unwise uses
- Institutional objectives: structural change to promote greater population density as opposed to urban sprawl, promote greater social equity among economic classes and racial/ethnic groups, promote greater attention to intergenerational justice, promote global justice, and enhance mechanisms for civic engagement at the local government level

Many contemporary sustainability efforts being undertaken by state and local governments are directed at meeting pressing environmental concerns, especially those that entail health-threatening deterioration of water or air resources or that involve the pending depletion of natural resources upon which the quality of public life of local communities depend.[44] At the same time, however, the sustainability efforts taking place in some communities address important issues related to population-based conditions, such as public health epidemics,[45] social and economic inequities leading to violence,[46] and the promotion of greater civic engagement in the process of monitoring quality-of-life conditions in local communities.[47] The principal assumptions underlying the sustainability movement are that the preservation of a quality environment, the use of renewable or highly efficient energy resources, the maintenance of a healthy population with ready access to preventive care and emergency health services, the presence of economic and social equity, and the maintenance of an engaged citizenry will lead to urban areas having sustainable futures in a world where global climate change, environmental degradation, and natural resource scarcities serve as warning signs that we must change our way of life in many ways to ensure a sustainable future for the next generation.[48] As noted by the Development Assistance Committee of the Organization for Economic Cooperation and Development:[49]

> …we have learned that successful development strategies must integrate a number of key elements: they require a sound and stable policy framework; an emphasis on social development; enhanced public participation by the local population, and notably by women; good governance, in the widest sense; policies and practices that are environmentally sustainable; and better means of preventing and resolving conflict and fostering reconciliation.

The proper balance among what is often referred to as the "three Es"—environment, economy and equity—is widely seen as being central to the achievement of a sustainable future.[50] There are, of course, inevitable tradeoffs associated with seeking to achieve these goals simultaneously.[51] The tension between promoting economic growth and the equitable sharing of opportunities that arises from the claims on the use of property as both a private resource and public good creates property conflict. The tension that arises from the competitive claims on the use of natural resources creates a resource conflict. And the challenge of improving the situation of the poor through economic growth while protecting the environment creates a development conflict. Resolving these tensions and conflicts is an ongoing process for virtually all state and local governments in the contemporary United States.

Understanding state and local government sustainability issues and the ability of state and local governments to adapt to change (i.e., display **adaptive capacity** or "resilience") means understanding the dynamics of the key sociocultural, bio-ecological, and governance systems within which American states and their respective communities operate (see Fig. 1.1). A growing body of literature now exists that identifies some of the specific aspects of community affecting adaptive capacity. Infrastructure, diversity of economic activity, dedicated community leadership, access to physical and knowledge resources, levels of social trust and interaction, broad distribution of informal power, and linkages to outside centers of political power all emerge as important factors in promoting sustainability.[52] Community size, degree of geographic isolation, attractiveness of natural features, and past experiences in responding to change further affect a community's vulnerability and/or adaptive capacity.[53] When a community faced with change displays a greater level of adaptive capacity, outcomes can include greater economic well-being (including reductions in poverty and wealth inequality among groups), more effective decision-making processes through improved institutional capacity and efficiency, and more active participation by concerned parties to ensure that governmental actions match local needs and resources.[54]

For example, rural communities are particularly vulnerable to developments such as climate change because their internal capacity and infrastructure available to deal with large-scale change are generally quite limited. As the participants in the U.S. Global Change Research Program concluded in a recent study: "Because rural populations and their communities are highly dependent on the area's natural resources…they are at risk from climate change and from potential increases in climate variability. Rural economies…are economically vulnerable due to lower profits and tax bases, fewer resources, and their reliance on livestock and cropping systems that are often stressed."[55] It follows, as a consequence of these several considerations, that our nation's rural communities may need to approach adaptation to global climate change much differently than do more well-resourced and expertise-rich urban jurisdictions.

General determinants of adaptive capacity and sustainable communities can also include the following considerations:[56]

- Improved access to resources
- Reduction of poverty
- Lowering of inequities in resources and wealth among groups
- Improved education and information
- Improved infrastructure
- Diminished intergenerational inequities
- Respect for accumulated local experience
- Assurance that responses are comprehensive and integrative, not just technical
- Active participation by concerned parties, especially to ensure that actions match local needs and resources
- Improved institutional capacity and efficiency

Institutional resiliency, or the ability for local governmental and community-based institutions to withstand or react to major stressors, is affected by institutional "legitimacy, how well they maintain [institutional] capital, and whether their agenda is in line with risks."[57] The presence of established and effective governmental and community-based institutions increases adaptive capacity as these institutions facilitate management and help community stakeholders deal with various risks to sustainability (e.g., economic transformation and climate change). Also, such institutions increase adaptive capacity of a community to the extent they are participatory, proactive, and representative of the population.[58] Proactive institutions increase adaptive capacity by planning ahead through such measures as mitigation of the problem, strategic planning, and the formulation of emergency management plans.[59] There-

Photo 1.4. Farmer inspecting his drought-stricken crop. Rural areas are highly vulnerable to climate change. Source: © Lenice | Dreamstime.com

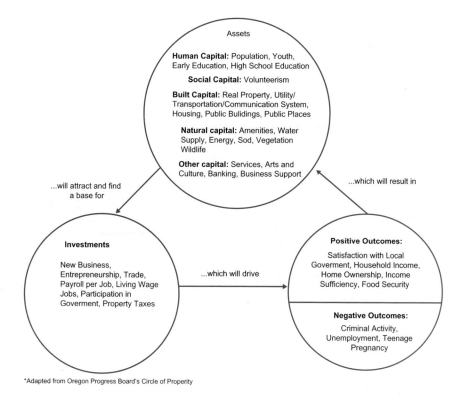

Figure 1.1. Indicators of Community Vitality and Sustainability

fore, as we proceed through this book, we will identify factors that promote and those that inhibit economic, social, environmental, and institutional sustainability in states and in local governments across the United States.

Summary and Book Outline

State and local governments in postindustrial America are facing many long-term and numerous newly emergent demographic, social, technological, and environmental changes that challenge their long-run social, economic, ecological, and institutional sustainability. In addition to these macro-forces, the recent near-total collapse of the U.S. financial system and the poor performance of the general economy in 2009 pose a serious challenge to sustainable state and local governance—perhaps the greatest challenge since the Great Depression of the 1930s. This introductory chapter has briefly discussed some of these long-term changes and more recent challenges that have arisen, as well as noted some things that American state and local governments can do to meet their respective sustainability challenges. As we discuss different aspects of state and local government in this book, we will identify both potential bar-

Photo 1.5. Hurricane Katrina: Army performs search and rescue. Sustainability means planning ahead for unexpected emergencies. Source: David Howells/Corbis.

riers to and opportunities for the promotion of sustainability and the achievement of resilience through the development of adaptive management capacity. This particular discussion will typically appear toward the end of each of the following chapters.

The first section of this book focuses on the diversity of state and local governments in our federal system (Chapter 2) and the rapid proliferation and diversity of sustainability-promoting practices and policies in state and local governments (Chapter 3). Chapter 4 discusses the various actors affecting state and local policy processes.

The second section of the book (Chapters 5 through 9) focuses on the framework and principal institutions of state and local government, what we call **linkage mechanisms**. A central theme in each of these chapters is how these institutions and their associated governmental processes affect all of our lives in many ways, only some of which we are typically aware. In addition, we will identify where students can access these processes and/or learn more about topics at hand. The final section of the book (Chapters 10 through 12) will focus on important policy developments in state and local government, including the expansion of social programs, changes in education policy, developments in criminal justice (courts, police, and corrections), and trends in taxes and government expenditures.

While the general level of knowledge citizens and students have about state and local government can be somewhat limited, our hope here is to engage readers and promote thoughtful lifelong **engaged citizenship** with state and local governance. Dalton has defined this type of citizenship as emphasizing "a more assertive role for the citizen and a broader definition of the elements of citizenship to include social concerns and the welfare of others" (2008: 5).[60] The growing literature on sustainability suggests strongly that this engagement is among the most important components of resilient and sustainable communities (Walker and Salt, 2006; see note 60). With American youth volunteering at near-unprecedented levels for community service in America, and now a historic level of engagement by youth in the 2008 general election, the time for learning about and engaging actively with state and local governments has never been better.

Key Terms

Adaptive capacity	Higher-order needs
Anthropocentric concerns	Institutional resiliency
Biocentered	Linkage Mechanisms
Brundtland Report	McDonaldization effect
Democracy versus technocracy quandary	Neo-liberalism
E-democracy	Postindustrial society
E-government	Post-materialist needs
Engaged citizenship	Smart growth
Gentrification	Sustainability
Globalization	Value change

Discussion Questions

1. Based on your reading, list and discuss four characteristics of postindustrial society commonly found in the United States, Canada, Australia, and many nations in the European Union.
2. Based on your reading, list and discuss three particular issues of great importance for contemporary state and local governments in the United States in terms of promoting sustainable economic development.
3. According to the chapter, list and discuss four core dimensions (objectives) of sustainable communities.

CHAPTER 2

Federalism

Introduction

More than any other aspect of U.S. government structure, federalism contributes significantly to innovation in local, state, and national government alike.[1] However, it is unlikely that the contemporary impacts of federalism in postindustrial America were fully anticipated by the framers of the U.S. Constitution. The Founders were driven to a much greater extent by a desire to strike a balance in political power between a nascent national government and the several pre-existing state governments than in promoting innovation and the capacity to adapt to ever-changing socioeconomic and environmental circumstances. The adoption of a federal form of government at the outset of our nation's history reflected an appreciation for the cultural heterogeneity that characterized the original 13 states.[2] As the intergovernmental relationships between the federal government and the states have evolved over time, however, federalism in America has repeatedly proven to serve as an important institutional asset in the service of sustainability.

This chapter will demonstrate how a variety of incentive structures propel state and local governments toward greater open-mindedness, experimentation, and learning from experience than is generally the case with the national government. Unlike the more insulated national government, the states and their many local governments face increasingly vexing and complex social and economic challenges that cannot be brushed aside in favor of engagement in the rough-and-tumble of global politics and national partisan competition; citizens in our towns, cities, counties, and states frequently demand that action be taken to address their immediate concerns for the quality of life where they live, and they tend to expect tangible results from their state and local governments.

Law enforcement services and community safety are good examples of such concerns for immediate tangible results. When criminal activity increases in a state or local jurisdiction, citizens often call for stricter laws, stiffer penalties for violations, and more robust enforcement; the sidestepping of issues and the shifting of blame to others are generally not acceptable dodges of responsibility to citizens calling for effective action. The heightened visibility of problems at the state and local level and the demand for quick solutions to those problems commonly place a heavy burden on state and local governments for timely action. While the often-intense atmosphere can be quite stressful for state and local policymakers, some of the very best and most innovative solutions to tough problems emerge from this setting, leading to the development of solutions that promote the sustainability of states and local communities in one location that are often copied, modified, and implemented in other state and local government settings across the nation.

The term *federalism* refers to a formal legal relationship between one or more levels of government *vertically organized*, and a whole host of relationships between similar levels of government *horizontally organized*. As Watts notes, the highly regarded late scholar of federalism Daniel Elazar viewed federalism as a complex contractual arrangement; for Elazar, federalism represents a form of "shared rule plus self rule—and a balance between cooperation and competition among the general and constituent governments."[3] The structure of American federalism was initially intended to protect preexisting units of government (the states) and to serve as an authoritative method of assigning or dividing responsibilities among the levels of government. In contrast, contemporary approaches to American federalism—the result of over a century of change—clearly emphasize collaboration among and across units of government while continuing to respect the distinctive priorities and needs of populations in different state and local jurisdictions. Today, an expansive and flexible understanding of American federalism represents a clear opportunity for innovation rather than representing a strict limitation on what actions any particular level of government is allowed to take.

This chapter will:

- Explore the historical evolution of federalism
- Discuss different models of federalism that have evolved over time
- Outline a model of intergovernmental relations that promotes sustainability in state and local government
- Consider the future of American federalism

Units of Government

While most of us are aware that there is one national government and there are 50 state governments, we often lose sight of the fact that there are other units of government that serve our everyday needs. As of 2007, in the United States there are 89,476 units of government beyond the national government and the 50 state governments. Each of these units of government offers some degree of opportunity for citizens to make their priorities known and to make demands upon government. The existence of such a multitude of governmental bodies provides Americans with myriad opportunities to become involved in the political process and to "make a difference" in the quality of life in their respective communities.

Beyond the prominent national and state governments of which most of us are well aware, there are several additional important types of government that are prominent: counties, municipalities, townships, school districts, and special purpose districts. As of 2007, there are 3,033 counties in the United States. Some states have very few counties (Delaware contains only 3) while some states have many counties (Texas has 254). The number of municipalities (incorporated cities) has increased by more than 8% since 1962, while the number of townships (small communities) has decreased by approximately 4% during the same time period.

Illinois has the greatest number of municipalities within its boundaries, while Minnesota has the greatest number of townships. Several states do not permit the township form of government, while the state with the fewest municipalities is Hawaii, with only one incorporated city (Honolulu). As noted in Figure 2.1, school districts, a highly recognizable unit of local government in every state, are rapidly decreasing in number, with many small districts in rural areas merging to form a smaller number of larger districts. Between 1962 and 2007 the number of school districts in the United States decreased greatly, by more than 60%. California has the most school districts, while Virginia has only a single district for the entire state.

While the growth of the national government is a frequent topic of discussion in the news media, the fact of the matter is that local government is the more

Photo 2.1. El Paso County Courthouse. Texas has the most counties in the United States.
Source: © Aneese | Dreamstime.com

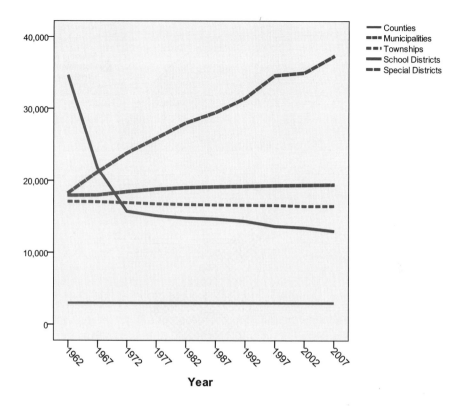

Figure 2.1. Units of Government Historically (1962–2007)

dynamic component of public sector growth by quite a margin. Special purpose
districts are one of the biggest areas for growth in this regard. There are over 37,000
special purpose districts in the United States at this time. The U.S. Bureau of the
Census places special purpose districts into four major categories: natural resources,
fire protection, housing and community development, and "other" special districts.
Such "other" special districts relate to water districts, irrigation districts, sewer dis-
tricts, road districts, public utility districts, port districts, cemetery districts, and
so forth. One unique aspect of American federalism is the ability of state and local
governments to create special purpose districts. We will see in this chapter how this
aspect of American government plays a substantial role in the promotion of community sustainability.

Figure 2.2 breaks down the proportion of special purpose districts that fit within each category used by the U.S. Census Bureau. Over half of all special purpose
districts fit within the "other" category, covering a myriad of policy issues critical to
particular state and local governments. Of the special purpose districts specifically
categorized by the U.S. Census, natural resource districts are the most common, followed by fire districts. With interest in community sustainability growing throughout the country, it is likely that the number of community development districts

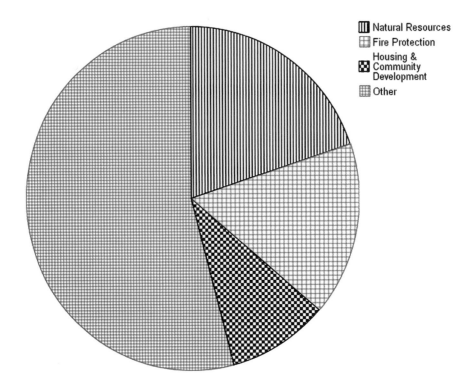

Figure 2.2. Types of Special Districts, 2008

will increase in the 21st century and their activities will reflect an active promotion of sustainability themes. Resources from both national and state government in the form of grants and technical assistance aid small communities in a number of areas of physical infrastructure and social services, and many of the innovations found at the local level of government have been replicated, modified, and implemented countrywide.

Historic Roots of Federalism

The origin of American federalism offers great insight into the values that define American culture and that have guided the development of our public institutions. As a governing arrangement, federalism occupies a space somewhere between **confederal** systems and unified systems.[4]

The first governing relationship in the "breakaway" colonies of former British North America was confederal. Following the achievement of independence in the Revolutionary War, the former colonies operated as sovereign governmental powers. The term *sovereignty* means that a political authority (in this case each colony) recognizes no higher power as a rightful restraint upon its action, and maintains the full right to agree or desist from any collective action with other political authorities of equal status. Under the Articles of Confederation,[5] state sovereignty was duly recognized. The Articles bound the states to little more than a promise to engage in mutual armed defense. The Confederation rather quickly proved to be ineffective at coordinating goals or developing cooperative relationships among and between the 13 state members.

The confederal governing arrangement was the exact opposite of the form of government from which the colonies had separated—namely, the unitary form of government. Under unitary government, political power is concentrated in a single location in the hands of a single office (the sovereign) or among a centralized national elite (elected or otherwise). All units of government at the sub-national level exist entirely at the mercy of the national government, and they exercise only those powers expressly delegated by the sovereign authority. Lacking sovereignty, in unitary forms of government all sub-national units of government can be created and abolished at the will of the sovereign national government.

Under the second American constitutional arrangement—the U.S. Constitution (1787)—the Founders shared the belief that the confederal system had not been effective and that a governmental arrangement somewhere between confederal and unitary government would more effectively meet the needs of the new nation.[6] American federalism creates some elements of national sovereignty in particular areas of law and governance, while embedding strong protections for state government in many other areas of public life.[7] Over the years the U.S.

Photo 2.2. Constitutional Convention, Philadelphia, 1787. Source: Howard Chandler Christy, Architect of the Capitol.

Supreme Court has had frequent occasion to adjudicate disputes concerning the relative powers of the federal and state governments under the U.S. Constitution, and for the most part those decisions have permitted the national government to extend its powers considerably while at the same time keeping state sovereignty principally intact.

Advantages of Federalism

Over the course of the nation's history, it has become clear that there are many advantages to federalism. There are also some noteworthy disadvantages, and these will be identified later in this chapter; for the time being the focus rests on advantages. Six particular advantages merit some discussion here:[8]

1. *Myriad of governmental units.* Many opportunities exist for citizens to directly influence policy decisions in their respective states or communities.
2. *Competition between units of government.* Competition between jurisdictions for citizens, business investments, and talent may lead to government efficiency. State and local governments tend to become entrepreneurial, offering greater benefits for the tax dollar[9] or reducing tax burdens to attract citizens and businesses seeking to reduce their fixed costs of operation.
3. *Incentives to prevent growth in government and promote efficiency.* The competitive nature of federalism is comparable to many aspects of free market capitalism. When government is a monopolistic provider, it is more likely to overproduce goods and services.
4. *Responsiveness to citizens is enhanced.* If a unit of government becomes too costly, citizens can either demand improved services or move elsewhere.
5. *Federalism is correlated with local government efforts to support private economic growth.* The provision of competitively priced infrastructure resources (e.g., roads, utility services, schools, medical services, recreational amenities) is a critical ingredient in any model of economic growth. Economic development, in turn, generally creates jobs and enhances household incomes.
6. *Federalism stimulates public and private innovation, often in active partnership.* The existence of federalism in the United States facilitates the systematic "reinvention of government."[10] The speed with which creative solutions to local problems are replicated is enhanced by the progressive professionalization of state and local government employees and the use of the Internet to capture, store, and disseminate information on a national (and even global) scale.

Potential Challenges Facing Federalism

While the advantages of federalism almost certainly outweigh the costs for most scholars writing in this area, federalism does face some potential challenges in application in many circumstances. Three such challenges are:

1. *Federalism can produce unequal outcomes between states, across communities, and for individuals living within these different jurisdictions.* Unequal outcomes are often associated with economic inequalities due to different levels of economic growth across states, and even within states and local communities. When traveling from city to city, state to state, observe the differences in wealth and opportunity that exist within each location. At times, these differences are a function of the city or state's capacity to sustain an economic base or to evolve with and adapt to changing economic conditions.

   Historically, states and cities differed considerably in their level of political and social equality. For decades in many parts of the South, for instance, individual opportunity was systematically biased to benefit whites over persons of color. A devastating Civil War, major amendments to the U.S. Constitution, and a series of landmark statutes and watershed decisions of the U.S. Supreme Court have all worked to overcome the serious inequalities brought about by a malevolent manifestation of state's rights in service to racial discrimination—all permitted by the institution of federalism.

2. *Federalism potentially produces inefficiency through policy replication.* Each state and local government independently formulates, finances, and implements public policy. In many ways this is a good thing because each state and local government has its own special set of circumstances and cultural values encoded in its public policy. However, there are added costs to having each state and local government essentially replicating many policy choices. In many cases it would be more efficient to have one uniform policy that efficiently and effectively meets all citizens' needs in a particular area of public life.

3. *Federalism can, at times, cloud our understanding of who is responsible for public policy outcomes.* In federalism, many units of government overlap, and at times the policy preferences of different levels of government collide—that is, their goals might be diametrically opposed. When policy failure results, constituents often want to know why things are either not being accomplished or not being managed in a manner reflecting their preferences. The spectacle of finger-pointing across different levels and units of government leaves citizens confused and, at times, upset with government overall.

Models of Federalism

Political scientists have developed a number of ways to describe and study federalism. In their highly regarded synthesis of prior research in this area published as an article in *Publius: The Journal of Federalism*, Donald Rosenthal and James Hoefler[11] identify a condensed list of models of American federalism featuring the following core concepts:

- Dual federalism
- Cooperative federalism
- Pragmatic federalism
- Non-centralized federalism
- Nation-centered federalism

Dual Federalism

According to Lord James Bryce,[12] a perceptive British observer of early American political life, the U.S. Constitution represents primarily an attempt to "build a more perfect Union" between the national and state governments. Strengthening the national government provides for a nationwide common market free of tariffs and barriers to commerce, a condition from which all states would benefit. Such a national government could also "provide for the common defense" more effectively than was possible under the Articles of Confederation. While certain governmental powers were expressly enumerated for the national government, the U.S. Constitution recognizes that state sovereignty should be carefully provided for in law. For the advocates of "states' rights" the Tenth Amendment to the Constitution served—then as now—as the guarantee of a balanced relationship between national and state government; that provision of the constitution is known as the **reserved powers** amendment, which holds that all governmental powers that are not explicitly granted to the national government in the constitution are reserved to the states and their people.[13]

In his major work, *The American Commonwealth*, Lord Bryce noted that even in the post-Civil War period state sovereignty and the notion of **dual federalism**—namely, two systems fulfilling distinct purposes without any significant overlap in function[14]—was maintained. States could not be taxed to finance the national government, which is a principle that remains to this day. American states were afforded a significant amount of autonomy in creating their own legal systems and governmental institutions. As long as the authority of the national government was not challenged or constrained in those areas where it was constitutionally authorized to act, states retained a significant degree of sovereignty, in some cases exercising powers concurrently shared with the national government. For Bryce, dual federalism was feasible in the 18th and 19th centuries largely because the scope of government action was rather restricted and far less complicated than it is today; both levels of government had a strong sense of enumerated, retained, and concurrent powers being exercised within a workable constitutional legal framework.

The federal–state relationship was fairly simple in the early years of the Republic in part because citizens looked primarily to their local communities to provide the basis of a sustainable existence. Until the early part of the 20th century, most Americans resided in rural settings, primarily in farming communities or small towns. There was relatively little overlap in government units, reducing the probability of conflict over resources, or in terms of the impact of public or private choices.

While the dual federalism model was well suited to its times in preindustrial America, it suffered from limitations that proved to be insurmountable in due course. Most importantly, the dual federalism model was largely silent on the key issue of the protection of individual rights. A focus on community-derived notions of a good society within a state can have the deleterious effect of restricting individual rights and liberties, particularly those of vulnerable minorities. In reflection of the dual federalism concept, in the case *Barron v. Baltimore, Maryland* (1833) the U.S. Supreme Court narrowly defined the national government's role in protecting the basic liberties and rights of citizens, leaving to the states and their respective constitutions the lion's share of responsibility in this area of American law. The Court ruled that those rights set forth in the Bill of Rights (the first ten amendments to the U.S. constitution) applied to the relationship between states and the national government rather than the relationship between citizens and the national government. The Court left it to the states to decide matters such as what constitutes freedom of speech, the right to counsel, a jury of one's peers, and due process of law in criminal cases.

Some of the Founders had argued that dual federalism was an unworkable idea, but it took over a century before the social inequities associated with the dual federal model became widely recognized.[15] In looking back over the history of American federalism, one could conclude that much of our history has been spent trying to maximize both the exercise of "freedom and the pursuit of happiness" by citizens and provide for the welfare of the nation, its states, and the communities within which our citizens reside. This simultaneous pursuit of individual liberty and collective welfare has always been a challenge for our nation, and it continues to demand the best of our thinking. In the contemporary setting many of our states and local communities endeavor to build a sustainable foundation for life for both present and future generations of Americans.

Cooperative Federalism

The dual federalism model survived the Civil War and remained fairly prominent up until the final decades of the 19th century. The emergence of **cooperative federalism**—the notion that the presence of urgent shared goals required concerted effort by all levels of government—was, in part, the result of:

- The growth of urbanism and demise of intimate small communities
- Large-scale industrialization and rapid population growth through mass immigration
- The expansion of the role of the national government as the guarantor of individual rights and liberties

These changes in American society inspired many reformers within cities and in some of the states (i.e., Progressives) to press for government "regulation in the public interest." The growth of corporate capitalism led to major excesses in the use of private power to the detriment of the public good and the exploitation of the most disadvantaged, and in time gave rise to unionization, social regulation, and political reform of machine politics arising from the corruption of public institutions. From a sociological perspective, industrialization and urbanization have led to a dispersal of community members so that people are more likely to be highly mobile. Ironically, Americans tended to adopt a lifestyle of personal independence from family and kin and neighbors alike, becoming more distant from one another in terms of private choices. This impermanency created a false sense of independence even though societal interdependence actually increased with innovation with respect to what forms of transportation are used, what forms of energy are consumed, and what food products are consumed.

During this period social inequities grew, both in terms of the stratification of wealthy and impoverished classes and in terms of inequities associated with the status of women, unorganized labor, and racial and ethnic minorities. Many influential writers and prominent decision-makers of the time contributed in different ways to the progressive vision for the United States, one that relied heavily on a cooperative relationship between all levels of government responding in a coordinated way to rapid social change. In many ways, the aforementioned changes challenged the capacity of American democracy in general, and federalism more particularly, to respond to modern dilemmas using an 18th-century model of governance.

The Progressive reformers of this period believed that many of the positive communitarian aspects of American community and society—the obligation to help neighbors in need, reciprocating a kindness with a kindness in return, volunteering one's time to civic projects, participating in local governance—as described in the historical writings on America penned by the foreign observers Alexis de Tocqueville[16] and Lord James Bryce were in peril. Progressives were at once reflective and visionary in their thinking, embracing an idealized vision of an American past but taking a pragmatic approach of action, free of the constraints created by partisan ideology. The concept of cooperative federalism was developed to expedite the process of addressing serious social and economic problems through forceful governmental action. The combined use of local, state, and national government authority in addressing public health and safety was commonplace, with the guiding principle being "use what works best" in the best sense of pragmatism.[17]

Some critics of cooperative federalism have argued that this model of federalism represents an attempt on the part of national government to pull power away from the state and local governments. In fact, the roots of **Progressivism** can be traced directly back to state and local government; it was an idea born at the local level, not at the national level of public political dialogue. Progressivism recognized many of the very serious social and economic dilemmas that had been largely unaddressed for quite some time: women's rights, minority rights, public health and sanitation problems, food and water safety and availability, homelessness, community planning, open and fair government and elections, and accessible and equitable public education, to name but a few of the major issues—issues that remain important and yet today are not addressed as fully as they should be. How these issues are addressed constitutes the foundation of community sustainability, and affects group and individual rights alike.

On the state and local level, Progressivism accomplished a great deal in relation to the aforementioned goals. It is fair to say that many national government efforts were noteworthy, but overall they were less pronounced than those witnessed at state and local government levels. President Theodore Roosevelt made important inroads in efforts to promote food and drug safety. He also challenged the growth of corporate capitalism, which was central to the complex relationship of the individual, the private market, and the public forum. President William Howard Taft's Commission on Economy and Efficiency served as the foundation of the modern bureaucratic systems needed for national government response to progressive demands. Finally, Governor Robert LaFollette (R-Wisconsin) and Governor (and later U.S. President) Woodrow Wilson (D-New Jersey) both campaigned and advanced Progressive agendas for political campaign and election reform. However, large-scale national Progressive reform was not realized until President Franklin D. Roosevelt's New Deal. While critics might claim that many aspects of FDR's efforts were nation-centered, the outcomes of FDR's programs have demonstrated over time that many New Deal programs were, in effect, a reflection of cooperative federalism operating under dire socioeconomic conditions.

Photo 2.3. Senator Robert M. La Follette (R-Wisconsin). Source: Robert Chester La Follette, U.S. Senate Collection.

Cooperative federalism occurs on many points along a continuum of varying locus of action. Top-down models are generally characterized by considerable national government influence in relation to the states. An example of top-down federalism might be seen in the area of environmental policies, which are designed to establish national guidelines for environmental quality for the benefit of all citizens. Conversely, bottom-up federalism often entails innovations originating at the state and local level that, in time, reach national-level policy agendas. Welfare reform, for instance, originated at the state level in

Photo 2.4. President Franklin D. Roosevelt.
Source: ABCU Photo Bank via AP Images.

Wisconsin. The innovation was touted as a policy success and became a focus of national policy with the national Welfare Reform Act of 1996. Over the long run, bottom-up and top-down types of federalism necessitate a cooperative framework; at the very least, government agencies must accede to the concurrent power and authority of another level of government.

Given the examples above, it is tempting to fall into the trap of associating top-down with "liberal" and bottom-up with "conservative" political ideologies. In reality, both political liberals and conservatives alternately see value in both ends of the ideological continuum. Although a shift away from the strong nation-centered federalism of the Johnson years (1963–1969) occurred primarily during the Reagan presidency (1981–1989), that shift tended to slow and retreat during the George H.W. Bush presidency.[18] Federalism scholar Paul Peterson has pointed out that many of President George W. Bush's policies moved the Republican agenda towards a more top-down model of federalism.[19] Homeland security[20] and education reforms such as No Child Left Behind have increased the national government's influence over state and local government priorities and, to some degree, led to structural changes in the way services are delivered at the local level.[21] Natural disasters such as Hurricanes Katrina and Rita illustrate the limits of the national government to solve local problems of substantial scope and scale.[22]

By themselves, shifting social and political institutional values do not fully explain the nature[23] of cooperative federalism in the United States. Evolving legal theories established by the Supreme Court were critical not only to the constitutional legitimacy of cooperative federalism, but also to the initiation of movement along the top-down/bottom-up federalism continuum.

Pragmatic Federalism

Rosenthal and Hoefler[24] indicate that pragmatic federalism was in part born out of disenchantment with cooperative federalism. The latter approach was premised on the notion that the behavioral science of the 1950s and 1960s could be used to guide national-level policy choices, identifying target populations and meeting needs.

Social science would guide policymakers at the national government level to tailor policy responses and interactions with state and local policymakers—in essence, the concept entailed the creation through social science of a cooperative intergovernmental relationship. Unfortunately, many policy prescriptions guided by the behavioral approach failed because the model often ignored many unquantifiable aspects of the policy process, such as the interaction between policy, institutions, values, preferences, and effective solutions.

Pragmatic federalism is characterized by two unique qualities: (1) flexibility—it is outcome-driven rather than process-driven; and, (2) the downplaying of the philosophy of government, meaning the set theories about the proper relationship between the national government and state governments are of limited interest in this model.[25] *Ad hoc* network relationships are considered more important than *ex ante* approaches (i.e., build the relationship around the problem to be solved rather than make the problem fit around a preconceived notion of the relationship).

Several Democratic state governors began to take a significant role in both the identification and advancement of this new approach to federalism. A political scientist, former county administrative officer, and later a two-term Maryland governor, Parris Glendening (and his co-author Reeves) wrote one of the earliest accounts of this new model of federalism in a 1984 book entitled *Pragmatic Federalism: An Intergovernmental View of American Government*. In his various roles as a local and state official, Glendening's account of pragmatic federalism is built on both theory and practice as he experienced it.

When Glendening and Reeves developed their approach in the mid-1980s, it was in response to a growing interest in the centralizing tendencies on the part of American national government.[26] At a time when President Ronald Reagan, a champion of smaller national government, was riding high in the opinion polls, Glendening and Reeves argued that a reversal of the centralizing trend, if it occurred at all, was unlikely to become part of a long-term trend. They argued that the concentration of authority in a centralized government structure was an historical trend that would continue, but that the nature of the trend must be considered and shaped in a manner most beneficial to all stakeholder governments and to public service recipients.

Glendening and Reeves tied three very important phenomena together in their effort to explain the value of pragmatic federalism. First, following on a strong tradition in the academic literature of questioning rigid bureaucratic approaches to policy formulation and implementation, Glendening and Reeves argued for greater reliance on informal relationships between policy actors who are guided by circumstance rather than organizational structure. Second, they favored movement towards proactive street-level policymaking and analysis whenever possible. Finally, a growing trend towards public–private partnerships in solving problems and a shared-governance movement played an important role in shaping Glendening and Reeves' innovative approach to thinking about American federalism.

At the time Glendening and Reeves were writing their account of federalism, Governor Bill Clinton (D-Arkansas) was promoting a similar new governance model. Interestingly, both Glendening and Clinton were raised in relative poverty, in Florida and Arkansas, respectively. In both cases, they had witnessed first-hand the positive role of government in shaping the lives of the least fortunate members of American society. Both men had gone on to become prominent state-level politicians in the 1980s. Importantly, neither forgot the role of government in their lives. They also felt that public sentiment regarding the size of the national government had more to do with the outcomes of government operations and less to do with the government's process and policy goals.

The decline of the cooperative federalism model was fueled in part by significant changes to methods of funding programs. Discussed later in this chapter, funding in the form of grants-in-aid emanating from the national level to meet program goals was increasingly made in the form of block grants—revenue transfers that gave state and local governments considerable flexibility in determining specific policy goals and methods of meeting those goals. During the Reagan years, the national government retreated in its support of many policy areas; the public need was still present, but solutions and funding were left up to leaders in state and local governments.

Entrepreneurial-minded state and local government leaders, such as Glendening and Clinton, provide sterling examples of the practicality of pragmatic federalism, which can be considered an innovation in public management that refines our evolving federal system.[27] The success of Democratic and Republican policy leaders alike at the state and local level in the last two decades of the 20th century offers time-tested support for a pragmatic approach to federalism—a model in which resources, goals, and public–private stakeholders and entrepreneurs are brought together to craft solutions to priority public concerns.

Non-Centralized Federalism

Non-centralized models of federalism can be traced to a growing skepticism over the dominant role of Congress and the national government in intergovernmental relations. In the 1960s, Daniel Elazar wrote his now-classic account *Federalism: A View from the States*, in which he illustrated the considerable and persisting political and social diversity present in the United States.[28] In the 1950s and 1960s, a period where cooperative and nation-centered federalism held sway, Elazar's analysis was in contradistinction to commonly held views of federalism that downplayed long-standing state and regional diversity.

Non-centralized federalism tends to look to historically chronicled analysis and community-based approaches for understanding American federalism. Working from the premise that strong democracy relies most immediately on stalwart local communities and robust public and/or private institutions, advocates for non-centralized federalism argue for a more individual-focused approach, relying on the individual consumer acting in market transaction to solve his or her own dilemmas rather than with the community through collective decision-making. The former approach—built on the principles of **communitarianism**—is closely tied to pragmatic federalism and to an historical interpretation of community-level decision-making capacity, while the latter approach is often built on **classical liberalism**, which emphasizes a limited role for government.

Advocates for non-centralized federalism share a common desire to ensure that the citizen-stakeholder plays a critical role in decision-making. In *Democracy in America*—a book often quoted by non-centralism advocates—Alexis de Tocqueville expresses similar concern regarding the possibility of unwisely limiting the roles of citizen and community as decision-making is centralized in the hands of professional administrators.

Not all communities possess an equal capacity for extensive citizen-stakeholder participation. Over decades, in some cases centuries, political and social traditions slowly evolve, producing norms of participation and views about the role of citizens and government and the interchange between the two. Elazar places these different traditions under the rubric known as **political culture**. In his analysis, Elazar identifies three major categories of political and social relationships: **individualistic**, **moralistic**, and **traditionalistic**.

Individualistic political culture fits well within the classical liberal tradition of non-centralized federalism. Within individualistic political cultures, most problems are seen in terms of individual solutions: communal solutions are not highly valued. Individualistic traditions look at most problems in terms of private property rights dilemmas. Solutions, therefore, are viewed as being best identified through the proper transfer of rights. For example, the individualist would see poverty as being best solved through the exchange of property: a person's labor (property) for a salary (property) to be used to purchase food (property). In individualistic political cultures, non-centralized federalism would largely mean limited government at all levels and reliance on the marketplace to meet demands or solve problems.

In moralistic political cultures, problems and solutions are viewed quite differently. Moralists tend to see problems in terms of community dilemmas that must be identified through interchange and community choice. Solutions are proffered in an open public forum and agreement on solutions is generally seen as best determined through widespread mutual agreement. The New England town hall meeting is often held up as a classic example of governance in a moralistic political culture. Non-centralized federalism, therefore, is more likely to be viewed as the optimal method of creating an inclusive public dialogue about government and governing. Moralistic political culture is horizontally organized, placing significant emphasis on the role of all individuals regardless of their social status or economic position within society.

Traditionalistic political culture is vertically organized, which means that individuals in positions of power have greater influence in the decision-making process than individuals who hold lower political, social, or economic status. In traditionalistic political cultures, a limited view of collective decision-making excludes most citizen-stakeholder voices in the governance process. Citizens in a traditionalistic political culture tend not to expect to play a role in governance at the state and local level—they tend to defer to the aforementioned elites. In traditionalistic political culture, non-centralized federalism may work to the disadvantage of the mass while benefiting elites and their allies.

According to Elazar, traditionalistic political cultures are most prominent in the American South. While conditions have changed a great deal over the past several decades, poverty in the South and responses to poverty provide a solid example of the negative impact of traditionalistic political culture. President Lyndon Johnson's War on Poverty in the 1960s uncovered the extent of political, social, and economic disparity. Traditionalistic elites in the rural South chose to ignore poverty as an issue for reasons related to racial discrimination and contempt of elites for the lower social classes. National government intervention was the first major step towards alleviating poverty in the South; however, the issues of institutionalized racism and endemic poverty have not entirely faded from the political scene, either in the South or in many other areas of the country.

Based on compelling evidence produced through political culture theory and considerable social science, moralistic political culture presents the greatest opportunity for equal access and broadly inclusive dialogue, and widely accepted choices and outcomes. When considering conflict in relation to the non-centralized federalism model, an underlying assumption is that the scope of conflict will be largely contained to the state or local level. In moralistic political cultures, governance is constructed in a way that support for public solutions to identified collective dilemmas is initially strong and remains strong on a consistent and prolonged basis. Individualistic political cultures are less likely to identify problems as requiring collective action: the marketplace is seen as the provider of solutions to individual wants and needs and property rights exchange. As a consequence, a strong central government is not a likely solution for the individualist. Conflicts in an individualistic political

Reflections on Government in the Old Days

Stepping into a county clerk's office only a generation ago for voter registration, the author found a single employee with index cards and two typewriters—an old manual version and the new electric model. The sheriff's office was not dissimilar. A Polaroid camera and flashbulbs lay on the counter for mug shots, there was a teletype machine for important information coming from the state or national level regarding criminal activity, and an enormous vacuum-tube contraption called the dispatch center: you didn't dial 911, you dialed "O" and asked the operator to be transferred to the police department. Nobody really sat at the dispatch center, but a burning cigarette in an amber-colored glass ashtray indicated that someone was around occasionally. There was "The Computer" over in the corner, but nobody really knew how to use it except for the sheriff's young daughter—she played video games on it while she waited for her father to drive her home after school.

culture will arise over issues related to property rights exchange and are less likely to be contained at the local level. Non-centralized federalism leads to highly biased governance choices and outcomes. Potentially, non-centralized federalism could increase conflict as citizens actively seek redress at "higher" levels of government when demands or needs are not addressed in local or state governance processes.

21st-Century Network Approaches to Federalism

Two major conditions led to dramatic changes in the character of federalism in the United States. First, as discussed in Chapter 1, *technology* has forever changed the way in which governance occurs.

Computers are a central part of the governance process at all levels of government today. Initially, computer networks were within a single office and were not connected to other networks. With the advent of the Internet, inter-office networks have expanded exponentially and are increasingly complex—a web of communication connects the government to individuals and to the private sector. Technology has made it relatively inexpensive and rather easy to transmit large quantities of information very quickly between decision-makers in various government offices, in the process influencing choices and creating opportunities for coordination and collaboration across jurisdictions. Inter-state and inter-local partnerships (or compacts) and agreements of understanding to coordinate efforts and goals have become a prominent aspect of 21st-century federalism.[29] Building on the idea of pragmatic federalism, the rise of network-based federalism means that day-to-day governance is often circumstance-based and informal, with networks forming around problems and then quickly dissipating after solutions have been arrived at and implemented.

A second major condition that has led to a greater reliance on network approaches to federalism is the *post-9/11 policy environment and the War on Terrorism*. Events related to terrorism and terrorist plots do not honor jurisdictional boundaries. In attacking enemies, terrorist organizations often use the same technological tools that have made our lives easier—the Internet, rapid forms of transportation, and the ability to network globally. Homeland Security policies require interagency communication and collaboration as a condition of the receipt of federal funding. Of course, delays in communications posed by jurisdictional squabbles can significantly reduce the ability of government at all levels to plan for and react to emergencies in a timely and effective manner.

A related condition has been the decline of the traditional fiscal federalism relationship. In the 1950s and 1960s, policy goals of the national government—in cooperation with state and local government—were supported with financial resources received from the federal government. This **fiscal federalism** relationship meant that new policy goals were not as burdensome to state and local government in cost terms as they had been in the past. Beginning with the Reagan and G.H.W. Bush presidencies, and moving forward into the Clinton and G.W. Bush era, the monetary taps of fiscal federalism have decreased: federal resources are now in much more limited supply. Given these conditions, it becomes clear to state and local government leaders that network federalism is a natural solution to reducing costs—essentially, it expands the information and expert "pool" as well as places greater reliance on mutual assistance.[30]

How is network federalism different than other forms of federalism? First, network federalism arrangements are often decentralized to the level of the individual or informal team. Individuals may be assigned to formal organizations, but most of their work is based on highly situational informal relationships or teams that respond to circumstances. For example, law enforcement response to riots and natural disasters is often a function of changing circumstances. Second, the strength of coupling or formal control within and between levels of government or agencies is very limited. Third, power is informally distributed and redistributed depending upon need rather than convention, which had been based on formal vertical power distribution.

There are at least three advantages to the newly emerging model of network federalism:

- *Reduced cost*—While governmental units continue to overlap, collaboration means that wasteful stand-alone efforts are limited.
- *Increased effectiveness*—Network federalism means that individuals converge around a problem based on the nature of a problem at any given moment.
- *Increased unity of purpose*—As governmental units begin to work together to create mutually beneficial successes, there is a greater sense of unity and less jurisdictional squabbling and miscommunication.

While network federalism sounds like a laudatory solution, there are at least three potential challenges that must be considered in the years to come:

- *Diminished accountability*—Accountability at all levels of government has posed a challenge. Informal intergovernmental relationships in network federalism mean that discovering and rectifying problematic sources of dysfunction is nearly impossible.
- *Groupthink*—As intergovernmental or interagency teams become more common, group members are more likely to begin to see problems and solutions in a similar manner, essentially eliminating the necessary arguments that furnish information about all sides of a problem. Groupthink can also lead to elitist and exclusionary governance processes and outcomes.
- *Centralizing trends*—Network federalism does not mean that all levels of government have equal resources and capacity to respond to governance issues. The national level of government is often thought to be well funded and highly professional in terms of personnel training and leadership. Networks tend to form around resource providers and leaders as well as network points where information is most effectively

gathered and disseminated. In many instances, it is likely that networks will form around national government actors, while state and local actors might serve in a supporting capacity.

Conditions for Sustainable Federalism

Federalism can, and frequently does, work towards the accomplishment of the core goals of sustainability. Each unit of government is interconnected to other units of government and, as cooperative and network federalism illustrate, there is a need for all of units of government to face the enduring truth: "we're all in it together!" In other words, while each unit of government must consider its own capacity to achieve sustainability, there is a clear sense that working together makes sustainability more likely. In the U.S. federal system, the *social objectives* dimension of sustainability is achieved through the porosity of government institutions and the multiple points of contact between citizens and overlapping units of government. Strong social capital and the collective action of civic-minded communities are often associated with effective and adaptable government. The *economic objectives* dimension of sustainability is also served by federalism. Sustainable economics means managing resources at the local level, where citizens are more likely to witness the production process at work and can better scrutinize the sustainability of the economic process in relation to negative environmental impacts produced. Understanding the true costs and benefits of achieving

Photo 2.5. Shaping the agenda often means getting involved. Source: © Dragon_fang | Dreamstime

what is wanted may refocus local consumer attention on which goods and services really do contribute to sustainability.

The *environmental* dimension of sustainability can benefit from federalism as well. With multiple points of citizen–government interaction, federalism offers a greater opportunity to raise awareness of policies that could damage environmental quality. Local management of the environment and common resources may also give citizens greater responsibility for the resources from which they collectively derive benefit—good stewardship practiced by multiple actors in a federal system of governance may serve to remind all parties involved of the many different stake-holders who benefit from well-protected environmental resources.

Finally, the *institutional* dimension of sustainability is well served by feder-alism. Institutions operating in a sustainable future government may look and operate differently than the nation's current paradigm built around 18th- and 19th-century public and private institutions constructed in far simpler times. While the desirable values undergirding those institutions might be known (e.g., social and political equity; racial, ethnic, and gender equality; intergenerational

Federalism: What Can I Do?

According to public opinion polls conducted by Gallup, a major-ity of Americans are unaware of the role of the federal government in their local school districts, know-ing little if anything about important laws such as the No Child Left Behind Act of 2002 (http://www.gallup.com/poll/1612/Education.aspx).

Because education is such an im-portant and expensive function, with federal, state, and school district lev-els of governance involved through regulation and finance, informed par-ticipation in school board meetings and voting on school funding neces-sitates some investigation.

1. Contact your local school district to see how federal, state, and local governments are involved in financing education.

2. Attend your local school board meeting to learn about pressing issues facing the school district.

3. Contact your state legislators and state department of education to learn how federal government regulations, such as the No Child Left Behind Act, affect state education policy.

4. Contact a K–12 teacher in your local school district to discuss how federal, state, and local policies affect how he or she teaches in the classroom.

For general information go to "Edu-cation and Federalism," The Nelson A. Rockefeller School of Government, State University of New York: http://www.rockinst.org/education/federal-ism.aspx

justice), effective institutional designs may be less well understood. For example, network federalism promises to take governance in new and exciting directions, yet the exact nature of those new and exciting directions will be shaped by the technology of tomorrow. Federalism offers the opportunity to experiment with different institutional designs, to determine what works best, when, and for what purpose.

Conclusion

Readers of this book who are preparing for careers in state or local government or who will work closely with government in one capacity or another will likely deal directly with intergovernmentalism. Intergovernmental relationships are important in the United States because the federal model is not clearly defined. In a political system where powers are separated between governmental units at national, state, and local levels, questions of proper jurisdictional authority will certainly arise in the course of carrying out one's duties or conducting one's business affairs. One noteworthy strength of the U.S. model of federalism lies in the overlapping responsibilities shared by a whole host of governmental units, entities that must cooperate in order to address localized and/or regional problems affecting their constituents. The overlapping responsibilities and duties can be both a source of angst and a source of strength, bringing a diversity of experience and resources with networks of contacts. Network federalism has proven to be the more accepted view of U.S. federalism and is the source of cooperative federalism or intergovernmentalism.

According to research on sustainable federal systems carried out in the international context, federal systems that are based in constitutionalism (see Chapter 5), feature defined powers of each layer of government, are reflective of cultural and geographic diversity, have democratic institutions, and provide adequate resources for governance are the most institutionally sustainable systems.[31] One of the most important elements of successful intergovernmental relationships in the U.S. context pertains to resources. Approximately 70% of a typical public agency's budget goes to salaries for employees. If proportional weight is any guide, then the most important resource that money buys is people's time, knowledge, skills, and abilities. Another important resource purchased by money is the infrastructure of a governmental body and the tangible goods and services needed to produce a desired governmental outcome. When a county wishes to establish a public health office, money will purchase the time and professional skills of physicians, nurses, and medical supplies needed to accomplish the public health function. If, however, the state or national government mandates certain health practices—such **mandates** frequently shape the relationship between governmental entities—then commensurate resources are required to meet the expectations established by those mandates. A successful intergovernmental relationship often requires the transfer of funds from one unit of government to another. That being said, some careful observers of American government and some state officials question the amount of federal spending and aid they receive in relation to the amount of federal taxes paid by the citizens and businesses of their state.

The data reported in Table 2.1 indicate wide disparity among states with respect to how much is paid in federal taxes versus how much is returned in federal spending and aid. Of course, the amount of money collected and spent by the federal government is related to many factors, including but not limited to the salary levels of workers in high-income states leading to higher federal govern-

Table 2.1. Federal Tax Burden and Expenditures by State, 2004

State	Federal Tax Burden per Capita	Percentage of State Revenue from Federal Government	Federal Spending in State per Dollar of Taxes Paid
Alabama	4,694	26.7	1.71
Alaska	6,425	28.4	1.87
Arizona	5,240	25.1	1.30
Arkansas	4,437	29.0	1.47
California	7,012	21.6	0.79
Colorado	7,002	18.5	0.79
Connecticut	10,570	17.4	0.66
Delaware	6,862	17.5	0.79
Florida	6,290	18.7	1.02
Georgia	5,723	20.9	0.96
Hawaii	5,585	22.3	1.60
Idaho	4,646	24.2	1.28
Illinois	6,999	20.5	0.73
Indiana	5,488	20.6	0.97
Iowa	5,319	23.4	1.11
Kansas	5,595	19.3	1.12
Kentucky	4,833	27.2	1.45
Louisiana	4,587	27.3	1.45
Maine	5,419	28.1	1.40
Maryland	7,404	19.7	1.44
Massachusetts	8,916	21.3	0.77
Michigan	6,044	23.1	0.85
Minnesota	6,920	20.3	0.69
Mississippi	4,046	33.4	1.77
Missouri	5,604	25.1	1.29
Montana	4,807	32.4	1.58
Nebraska	5,693	21.7	1.07
Nevada	6,550	14.5	0.73
New Hampshire	7,521	21.1	0.67
New Jersey	8,999	16.1	0.55
New Mexico	4,927	30.5	2.00
New York	7,940	25.5	0.79
North Carolina	5,306	24.4	1.10
North Dakota	5,133	30.2	1.73
Ohio	5,568	22.6	1.01
Oklahoma	4,685	25.1	1.48
Oregon	5,613	22.7	0.97
Pennsylvania	6,339	23.0	1.06
Rhode Island	6,557	27.4	1.02
South Carolina	4,767	25.1	1.38

Table 2.1. Continued

State	Federal Tax Burden per Capita	Percentage of State Revenue from Federal Government	Federal Spending in State per Dollar of Taxes Paid
South Dakota	5,358	31.0	1.49
Tennessee	5,323	30.1	1.30
Texas	5,841	22.3	0.94
Utah	4,533	22.3	1.14
Vermont	5,971	30.0	1.12
Virginia	6,792	16.1	1.66
Washington	7,128	19.5	0.88
West Virginia	4,248	28.8	1.83
Wisconsin	6,000	20.4	0.82
Wyoming	7,105	35.0	1.11

Adapted from *The Book of the States—2006* (Lexington, KY: Council of State Governments, 2006).

ment revenues through income taxes and other fees (e.g., 2006 mean wage for Connecticut was $45,970, while in Mississippi it was $30,460); the presence of higher levels of poverty leading to more federal spending on poverty programs (e.g., the percentage of the population living in poverty in New Hampshire in 2006 was 5.5% compared to 16.0% in Alabama); and, of course, the presence of strong and influential senior elected officials in Congress steering resources back home to their own state (e.g., **pork barrel** projects and the inclusion of earmarks in agency allocations).

People themselves are important resources; however, the structure of the institution for which people work and the working environment and location do more to shape the effectiveness of workers. Individuals working in the Federal Bureau of Investigation, for instance, are often used to working in a particular agency setting with a unique **organizational culture**. The culture of an agency affects the disposition of individuals. Professionalism is also an important element in intergovernmental relationships. In terms of elected officials, professionalism is reflected in the level of knowledge, experience, and personal and administrative staff support available. Administrative staff at different levels of government may vary in terms of their experience, level of education, salaries, and training; these are all quite important characteristics of public sector administrative professionalism.

Finally, as the literature on sustainable communities suggests, the social and economic conditions under which a particular level of government or an agency of government operates has a significant impact on intergovernmental relationships. When the U.S. Army Corps of Engineers arrives in a local area intent on building a dam for flood control or power generation, the conditions under which state or local governments operate will have an impact upon their relationships with the Army Corps of Engineers.

While conditions cannot be made uniform across levels of government or jurisdictions, successful federalism requires that political and administrative entities engaged in intergovernmental work come to terms with these differences in working conditions in order to maintain effectiveness and professionalism. Often, variations in these elements of difference become a source of strength in the intergovernmental enterprise as creative synergies are discovered and innovative solutions to difficult problems are crafted. Alternatively, intergovernmental relationships that ignore these differences or develop a mistrusting or intensely competitive relationship often produce intergovernmental failure.

Key Terms

Classical liberalism

Communitarism

Confederal systems

Cooperative federalism

Dual federalism

Fiscal federalism

Individualistic political culture

Mandates

Moralistic political culture

Political culture

Pork barrel

Progressivism

Public goods

Organizational culture

Reserved powers

Traditionalistic political culture

Discussion Questions

1. Why was federalism adopted in the United States? Are the reasons leading to its adoption still relevant in the 21st century?
2. Based on your reading, what are the various models of federalism that developed over time, and what are some of the advantages and disadvantages of each type?
3. In what policy areas should states have more authority vis-à-vis the national government (e.g., social policy such as medical marijuana, abortion, death penalty, K–12 education standards)? In what policy areas should the national government have more authority vis-à-vis the state governments?

CHAPTER 3

The New Margins
Sustainability

Introduction

As noted in Chapter 1, American state and local governments face very difficult challenges involving both issues that have evolved slowly over a long time, as well as issues that are newly salient due to the advent of postindustrial society and the globalization of commerce and industry. Both domestic migration and immigration by foreigners contribute to a shifting population and change in community demographics in many areas of the country. In a trend of considerable duration in the United States, rural residents are continuing to move to the nation's major cities; this is particularly the case for single young professional men and women who have acquired some degree of higher education. Immigration issues relate to both documented and undocumented individuals entering U.S. cities in a number of states in search of employment and the opportunity to enjoy the benefits of the American quality of life.

As a consequence of these changes, state and local government public agencies in many areas are struggling to meet the social and economic needs of an ever-changing population. Infrastructure development, including broadband access to the Internet, and the maintenance of the built environment have become growing concerns in many communities across the nation. As local communities evolve, it is clear that the governmental response to global societal change and changing local conditions must match the new perspective of community sustainability. One dimension of changing circumstances for state and local government entails private-sector firms no longer maintaining their loyalty and reliable ties to local communities. Globalization has meant that worldwide markets greatly affect business location and tenure in particular locations. The business sector itself is more fluid, dynamic, and "virtual" due to telecommuting and the Internet. Business owners increasingly work with consultants, contractors, and employees in Asia, the Indian Subcontinent, Latin America, Europe, Africa, or the Middle East rather than pay salaries to local workers for the desired services rendered. The private sector is more *ad hoc* than ever before in human history; this fact greatly affects the insularity associated with traditional notions of development.

Finally, the long-standing American tradition of the active promotion of civic life has diminished dramatically. As noted by Harvard political scientist Robert Putnam and many other scholars, long-standing civic institutions are clearly on the decline. Some new institutions have arisen, to be sure, but they tend to be quite different from the social institutions whose benefits historically contributed to a small-scale, local quality of life and public welfare. Some of these new forms of interaction among people are based in ephemeral Internet spaces—chat rooms and the like—while others entail only the most superficial interpersonal engagement and/or revolving-door memberships that grow or recede largely based on the nature of the times.

In summary, among the transitions that state and local governments must adapt to are often-dramatic population shifts, the growing presence of the private sector in civic life, and the relative lack of sustained human interaction in contemporary American culture.

So, how do American state and local governments tend to operate under these rapidly changing circumstances? Earlier notions of state and local government responsibility and scope of influence must be considered as a starting point for our discussion. Of course, in times of change the treasured values of stalwartness and loyalty to tradition must give way in some important areas of activity to the recognition of the need for continual and timely innovation if public institutions in state and local government are to remain relevant to the people they serve.

Against these background developments causing a broad range of societal changes in American society, this chapter will discuss the following specific topics:

- A basic model of public policy innovation
- Infrastructure renewal issues present at the state and local government level
- Resource identification and development/conservation issues
- Livability issues to be addressed at the state and local government level

Basic Model of Public Policy Innovation

Historically, one of the greatest strengths of U.S. democracy has been its ability to remake itself when circumstances require adaptation to change. Government institutions and American society as a whole at critical junctures have faced up to changing conditions requiring the development and implementation of effective policy innovations. Public policy innovation, after all, is clearly in keeping with the spirit of optimism and belief in progress so common in U.S. democracy. The federal system of governance has inspired a propensity to experiment with new approaches to both old persisting problems and new challenges when they arise. Such ongoing experimentation and the frequent replication of successful innovations are important additions to the adaptive capacity of American state and local government. It is certainly no mere accident that the vast majority of the nation's national political leaders began their public service careers at the state and local level of government, where great opportunities and clear need for innovation present themselves.[1]

Public policy innovation in the United States is seldom, if ever, a function of one person's abilities or efforts, as might be the case in other more centralized and autocratic regime types. Innovation in U.S. state and local governments is most nearly always a function of the openness to change and willingness to risk the unknown consequences of the adoption of new approaches to old and new problems alike by political, social, and economic institutions in which elected and appointed leaders and citizen stakeholders live, work, make choices, and express their policy preferences.

Research conducted in this area is quite plentiful, and this body of research clearly suggests that there are several common preconditions or factors that tend to facilitate public policy innovation. Of paramount importance in this regard is the issue of **political trust**. Political trust relates in part to the process of governance and to the public institutions within which public decisions are made. Key questions to consider are the following: Are the institutional rules and decisional practices derived from public institutions viewed as fair and unbiased? Do these institutional rules and procedures encourage innovation and produce outcomes that improve governance and society? **Social trust** is of equal importance, and this condition relates to the ways in which people interact with one another, publicly and privately; this is often a function of our individual experiences as well as the institutions through which we interact with others.[2]

Photo 3.1. Intergenerational social trust is very important in sustainable communities.
Source: © Milkos | Dreamstime.com

A concern in contemporary American culture is the growing isolation of the individual and a related decline in the social trust and political trust that follow from that social isolation. The overarching theme of these studies of **political culture** is the critical role of **social capital**—the values and norms held by citizens that reflect trust in others, the active pursuit of engagement in networks of interpersonal

Photo 3.2. Cesar Chavez led the farm worker movement in a fight for equal rights. Source: Bettman/Corbis.

relations of a wide variety, and standards of interchange among people involving the principles of reciprocity (return a favor with a favor) and mutual respect. As highlighted in Chapter 2, the noted scholar Daniel Elazar found that political culture varies greatly across American state and local government settings, and this variation helps shape the capacity for and nature of public policy innovation across the American governmental landscape.[3]

Demographic characteristics of the settings within which American state and local governments function are also of particular importance in the study of public policy innovation and the capacity of state and local governments to adapt to societal change. Demographics include such things as socioeconomic conditions, the racial and ethnic composition of a community, geographical location, and size of area (population as well as geographic concentration and dispersement). Socioeconomic conditions relate not only to the relative wealth or poverty present in a state or community, but also to the distribution of wealth. Relevant socioeconomic factors also include the education level and type of employment of residents.

Wealth, health, and level of education greatly influence the capacity of citizens to participate in the governing process to express their policy preferences and assess proposed policy innovations. Innovation usually means doing something new for the first time, or doing something of long-standing practice somewhat differently, and in the process accepting some element of risk in the hope of producing a better future. Clearly, without some degree of wealth the capacity to assume the risks of innovation is limited. Without health and education, it is difficult to summon the energy and comprehend the need to be innovative; also, lack of health and education often leads to extreme caution and fear of change, usually among the very people for whom innovation would be most beneficial.

The racial and ethnic composition of communities plays a very significant role in public policy and policy innovation in the United States. In his recent widely discussed book *Faces of Inequality*,[4] Rodney Hero argues persuasively that racial and ethnic diversity not only shape citizens' perspectives of many policy dilemmas, but also influence how state and local governments come to adopt, or avoid considering, timely innovative policy solutions. In short, innovation tends to occur more often in communities where the diversity of public views of stakeholders is actively incorporated into the public policymaking process. For example, the changing demographic composition of many states and communities across the country requires considerable innovation to meet the needs of increasingly complex local communities. There is strength in the range of perspectives on a problem afforded us by diversity, and public policy innovations that build on this strength are much more likely to succeed than those that take a narrow focus on the problem to be addressed.

There is an old saying in the real estate business world: three things, "location, location, and location," determine success. Somewhat the same observation may be made about public policy innovation. Some locations are considerably more amenable to innovation than are others. However, nearly every place in the world has one noteworthy limitation or another, and some have many apparent limitations. Successful policy innovators are able to identify the assets of nearly any location—that is, place-based strengths upon which successful innovation can be built.[5] For example, many Midwestern, Northern Plains, and Rocky Mountain states and local rural areas within them have lost substantial population due to the decline in family farming; nonetheless, public and private policy entrepreneurs, often working in partnership, have developed innovations that have slowed economic decline in many agrarian areas and strengthened community-based social and economic benefits. This is the case in places where wind turbines have appeared on the same plains where the nation's grains are still produced, supplementing the incomes of local farmers and building a clean, renewable energy future for forthcoming generations.[6] Some locations require more sophisticated solutions to difficult problems, but identifying the inherent strengths and assets present in any particular setting is universally important to the policy innovation process.

The population size and the extent of the geographical area are also generally important considerations in policy innovation. Metropolitan areas have the advantages of being concentrated in terms of population and infrastructure, conditions that make the implementation of some types of policy innovations somewhat easier than would be the case in sparsely populated areas. Many rural areas, in contrast, face a number of major challenges with respect to innovation. Not only are many rural areas becoming increasingly diverse, as are metropolitan areas, but the physical distances between small communities that are typical in rural areas makes innovation difficult to formulate and difficult to implement.

The dispositions of political and social leaders clearly shape policy innovation formulation and determine the likelihood of success as well. As noted, innovation involves moving in new directions, often into a somewhat unknown future. Leadership is a key element in innovation because not only is an effective leader capable of conceptualizing future conditions, but a leader also can identify policy innovations that will create desirable future outcomes. For example, Wisconsin Governor Tommy Thompson played a significant leadership role in shaping welfare reform—a policy innovation that led to similar reforms in other states as well as national-level reforms enacted by a Republican Congress and signed into law by the Democratic President Bill Clinton in 1996.

In many policy arenas, innovation involves more than elected leaders taking the initiative; innovation often also requires that local social and business leaders play a significant role in developing and implementing innovation.

Finally, policy innovation is facilitated to a considerable degree by **bureaucratic capacity**. The administrative agencies of state and local government play a significant role in formulating and implementing policy innovations. Bureaucratic capacity involves well-trained professionals working in public organizations to meet political and social goals through the timely development and effective implementation of public policy. To attract and retain professional, experienced, and well-educated people to key positions in public agencies, those agencies must be adequately funded, professional in operation, and effectively organized to meet ever-changing needs and ambitious goals set out in the policy innovation enterprise.

One example of bureaucratic capacity that is currently widely discussed relates to education policy. Most of you reading this book have experienced in your pre-college education the effects of No Child Left Behind, a national-level innovation relating to raising standards for elementary and secondary school instructional performance and high school graduation and the use of high-stakes tests. This federal policy innovation is shaped very heavily by state and local policy choices. Many state and local education officials and state legislators view this federal legislation as an "unfunded mandate"—that is, a requirement established by one level of government (the federal government in this case) that other levels of government must meet at their own uncompensated expense.[7]

Infrastructure Renewal

The United States is without question a land of vast natural resources. In the past, these seemingly abundant resources were taken largely for granted by Americans. Beginning in the 1960s and 1970s, however, circumstances began to change as access to natural resources such as fossil fuels, water, fertile farmlands, forest stands, and wildlife habitat began to tighten appreciably.[8] There was a growing sense that the pursuit of sustainability meant more than building and maintaining durable infrastructure that could last for long periods of time. Conservation, historic preservation, and environmental protection all became increasingly important aspects of the policy landscape at the local, state, and national level alike, affecting the way planning was done at all levels of government. At this point, some public policy areas featuring clear themes of environmental sustainability are making a favorable difference in the promotion of sustainability at the state and local level of government.

Water and Waste Systems

Clean water and sanitary wastewater processing and removal are very important functions of government, dating back virtually millennia. In antiquity, population centers were nearly always established near a water supply for purposes of human food production as well as for direct use (i.e., drinking, cooking, and washing). Waste systems were of equal importance; in this regard, contemporary forensic anthropologists provide ample evidence of how waste mismanagement contributed to a reduction in public health, with the introduction of preventable risks such as the stagnant water-related diseases like malaria and typhoid fever (for historical background, see Rosen, 1993, note 16; Diamond, 1997, note 37).

In 19th-century U.S. cities, untreated effluent typically ran in the street gutters and trash was periodically disposed of by open burning. The potential for water and airborne disease was quite high given these conditions and practices. Highly communicable diseases such as typhoid and tuberculosis were not uncommon under these conditions. In the 1830s, New York City suffered a widespread cholera outbreak that led to the deaths of more than 3,000 people. A similar epidemic in the 1860s led to the death of over 1,000 residents. The New York epidemics were not dissimilar to cholera outbreaks in other urban areas in the United States. Municipal sanitation laws were in place and were enforced, particularly during the epidemics, and this was indeed a good thing. However, insufficient resources were available to the public health authorities of the day to cope with a growing population and a large immigrant class in many cases bringing with them diseases contracted in other regions of the world or contracted during travel to the United States in confined ship's quarters.

Unfortunately, state and local governments in the past often made social and economic choices that were beneficial to their citizens in the short run but had some unintended long-term negative consequences and created externalities (the transferring of costs to others) for other jurisdictions. Spilling wastewater into a river downstream from a town, for instance, is one inexpensive way of removing waste for the upstream party, but this practice has the effect of polluting water for other users downstream, who bear the costs of cleaning up the water to make use possible.

Powerful economic interests at the state and local level often have the capacity to influence policy choices in ways that are personally beneficial but are inimical to community sustainability and long-term public health. For example, in many of our cities industrial waste disposal in the streets was quite common in the 18th and 19th centuries; to make matters worse, during this era the dominant mode of transportation—horse-drawn carriages—deposited virtual mountains of animal waste in the streets of our cities.

In the 19th century, sanitation and water services were frequently provided by private businesses operating for profit. For much of the 19th century, sanitation was a luxury few households could afford;[9] the underclass continued to rely on community wells and often remained at high risk for water-borne disease. Yet, as history clearly indicates, the absence of uniformly provided water and waste removal services for all households, once epidemics begin, leads to patterns of illness that do not discriminate as to socioeconomic class.[10]

During the Progressive Era (c. 1890s–1920s), a concerted effort was made to promote improved sanitation and clean water resources, the cornerstone of public health sustainability.[11] An important breakthrough in water provision and waste management services came with the widespread establishment of public utility commissions (PUCs) at the municipal or county level, and at the state level in some states.[12] The principal purpose of PUC management was, in the words of one typical statute, to provide "service and facilities as shall be safe, adequate, and sufficient."[13] PUCs often both regulate the quality of service as well as fix stable prices and provide equitable access to public utilities.[14] The establishment in the 1860s of public health departments in New York and other states[15] were examples of further water quality and effective waste removal public policy innovations.[16]

While the regulation of water quality and waste management has generally become an accepted part of state and local government function, the methods by which these services are delivered have been the subject of some debate. In retrospect, it remains unclear whether the public provision—through public utility corporations—of water and waste services led to improved public health outcomes beyond those that might have resulted from the private provision of such services.[17] Some academic studies have concluded that the private provision of water and waste management services did not produce outcomes dissimilar from public provision. Critics of publicly provided water and waste management services charge that by centralizing the functions of water provision and waste management, local government became the sole consumer of a good—essentially, a monopoly—which resulted in economic distortion and loss to both taxpayers as well as wage laborers working in utilities enterprises.[18] While these critics have not persuaded many state and local governments to abandon their reliance upon waste management and water provision monopolies, there has been a marked effort to increase resource supplier competition in states and local governments and provide for a more active governance role for utility service consumers.[19] In the 1990s, policy entrepreneurs at the state and local level made a pronounced effort to use competition to improve service delivery, in the process often reducing costs to consumers.[20]

National policy has an impact upon water quality and waste management, both domestically and internationally.[21] Clean water standards are the principal means by which the federal government becomes involved in water and waste management issues. These two universally present local area services are important aspects for quality of life for existing residents and businesses, and for prospective new residents and businesses. Innovative communities will be wise to invest in the building and maintenance of superior-quality water systems.[22]

While states and their local governments began many of their public health sustainability efforts in the mid- to late 19th century, the national government stepped up its role in this area substantially in the 1960s and 1970s. The National Environmental Policy Act of 1969 (NEPA), the Clean Air Act of 1970, and the Clean Water Act of 1977 (CWA) gave federal regulatory agencies strong powers to establish standards in the area of water quality and waste management practices. Emerging from the CWA, the National Drinking Water Clearinghouse provides important information on water resources and waste management issues facing state and local governments and many individual property owners across the country. Without stifling state and local policy innovation in this area, federal action on water and waste management issues does serve as a tool to promote a considerable degree of equity of conditions across the nation.

Government Buildings

Government buildings are a very important consideration in state and local government innovation in the 21st century. Unknown to most citizens, government infrastructure investments (including the initial design and construction, the operation over time, and the long-term maintenance) consume a significant portion of all U.S. governmental budgets; these costs increase in relation to both energy costs and building age. Older buildings are becoming increasingly problematic due to risks associated with dangerous (even toxic) materials used in their original construction. Unhealthy wallboard and insulation materials, synthetic carpeting emitting noxious fumes, and poor air filtration and circulation systems found in many older buildings increase public health risks to the building occupants and the workers who maintain the aging structures. The increased costs in areas such as disability and healthcare benefits paid to these people exposed to unhealthful environments often outweigh the costs associated with new construction.

In addition, older government buildings are often inaccessible to individuals with disabilities, and they feature antiquated wiring systems that cannot accommodate modern information technology. If you have visited older government buildings, these structures tend to be imposing and project a paternalistic relationship between the citizen and government workers that is unlikely to serve the needs of either party very well. The physical structure limits the ability of a public agency to meet the needs of 21st-century highly networked organizations, thereby constraining government's ability to respond to an ever-changing technology and be sensitive to ever-evolving citizen needs.

Innovative state and local governments across the country are increasingly seeking to reduce building construction, maintenance, and ancillary costs and improve customer service accessibility and service delivery in their jurisdictions. In many instances, state and local governments are opting out of taking on some permanent infrastructure costs by entering into limited-term lease contracts with private office space suppliers. Through long-term renewal lease options, the needed space can be chosen and designed so as to be accessible to a customer base while avoiding the costs of land acquisition, construction bidding, and long-term building maintenance. The final point is especially important in state and local government because of the extent of population growth and migration taking place in many areas. In these circumstances public service providers in many cases must be located in close proximity to customers if public goods and services are to be delivered effectively in many public service areas.

In the case of new public structure construction, the federal Office of Energy Efficiency and Renewable Energy (EERE) promotes the concept of the **whole building design** approach. The EERE approach to building practice is advocated for residential and commercial buildings as well as for government structures. In essence, building design is viewed holistically; architects and engineers are asked to consider the building's purpose, workforce, future, and operations and maintenance costs as a comprehensive whole. In the past, productivity was seen as a function of the individual worker operating within an organization; the whole building design approach views productivity as a function of the physical structure of the workplace as well as of the individuals working there. Customer satisfaction is also related to the physical location of goods and service delivery, and this goal of design also must be factored into building layout and construction in order to comply with the strictures of the whole building design approach. Finally, this integrated approach to infrastructure building plan development calls for maximal energy efficiency and the maximum use of renewable energy systems, both for the purpose of cost reduction and for the promotion of regional and global environmental sustainability.

The Energy Policy Act of 2005, presidential Executive Order 13101 ["Greening the Government through Waste Prevention, Recycling, and Federal Acquisition" (1998)], and Executive Order 13123 ["Greening the Government through Efficient Energy Management" (1999)] are three examples of federal government innovation related to innovative government building design. Similar derivative policies exist at the state level in most American states, and many larger governments at the county and municipal local government level have adopted comparable policies. Currently, 24 states have adopted quite stringent energy standards for existing public buildings and for newly constructed commercial buildings. It is fair to say that sustainability-promoting guidelines are in place in most of the nation's population centers for the "greening" of government buildings, and that this action qualifies as a timely innovation for the 21st century as state and local governments seek to address global climate change and promote sustainability.

The Pacific Northwest National Laboratory (PNNL), operated by Battelle Corporation for the U.S. Department of Energy, contracted with the federal government's General Services Administration (GSA) to conduct a comprehensive analysis of green building innovations, which are a key component of whole building design for the 21st century. The PNNL report concluded that the U.S. Green Business Council's Leadership in Energy and Environmental Design (**LEED**®) criteria constitutes the prime approach to government (and private sector) building design innovation. "LEED® is not only the U.S. market leader, but is also the most widely use[d] rating system employed by federal and state agencies." The existence of this standard makes it possible "to communicate a building's sustainable design achievements with others."[23]

LEED® provides six criteria for achieving sustainable government building design: sustainable sites; water efficiency; energy and atmosphere; materials and resources; indoor environmental quality; and innovation and design process:

Figure 3.1. States with Government Building Energy Standards Requirements.
Data Source: Energy Standards for Public Buildings, http://www.dsireusa.org, accessed
January 6, 2007.

- A *sustainable site* is studied in terms of land use impacts of development;
  accessibility of buildings using alternative transportation systems (e.g.,
  mass transit, bicycles, alternative fuel vehicles); the building location
  and design in relation to urban renewal project planning; and the
  reduction of light pollution.
- *Water efficiency* relates to the use of efficient landscaping to include
  xeriscape design. Water efficiency also relates to the use of low-flow
  utilities that reduce water consumption and innovative wastewater
  management systems.
- The *energy and atmosphere* dimension involves renewable energy and
  the reduction of ozone-depleting emissions. Energy demand reduction
  is an important consideration that can be maximized using natural
  lighting designs and low-energy-demand light fixtures and office
  equipment.
- *Materials and resources* relates to the use of recycled content materials,
  local or regional materials, and efficient building material waste
  management (separation of waste from recycled materials).
- *Indoor environmental quality* issues include such things as carbon
  dioxide monitoring, ventilation, and low-emitting construction and
  design materials. Temperature and light control factors are also critical
  to indoor environmental quality, with a high priority placed on natural
  lighting.

Photo 3.3. New "green" building near Ground Zero, New York. Source: Richard H. Cohen/Corbis.

• LEED® methodology places special emphasis on inclusive planning processes and innovative multidisciplinary design exercises, recognizing that new ideas can be developed in some cases and the adoption of best practices can be actively encouraged within a broadly inclusive planning process.

Government building design innovation is important for at least two reasons. First, state and local government buildings are expensive to design, to build, and to maintain. Constructing next-generation structures may reduce long-term costs to taxpayers and make government more efficient, effective, and satisfying to citizens or prospective citizens. Second, government acting as a policy innovator can demonstrate a commitment to next-generation building design and thus encourage partnerships between state and local government and private sector enterprise. Commitment to local solutions and material providers means that government creates a local demand for next-generation materials and equipment that may lead to spin-off sustainable economic development in states and local communities where such development had not yet been contemplated.

Urban Redevelopment

In the 1960s and 1970s urban redevelopment was often driven by multiple concerns—for public safety, for racial equality, and for aesthetic appeal. The post-Second World War era witnessed a tremendous migration to both the cities and the newly created suburbs. Infrastructure renewal in our major cities was desperately needed in the postwar period, but the new development of suburbia competed for capital, for human resources, and for public and private investments alike.

One of the biggest challenges faced by American states and their major cities is the rapid development of urban areas in developing nations, which collectively are on course to surpass the United States in capacity on many critical dimensions within the span of a decade. For example, new suburbs in Indian cities are attracting young professionals from around the globe. In the past decade, China's cities have been consumed with major efforts at redevelopment; building plans in Beijing, for instance, cover an area several times larger than Manhattan. In short, the challenge facing U.S. urban redevelopment innovators is of global dimension.[24] If economic and social sustainability is to be achieved, then American cities and states must strive to do at least their fair share to promote sustainability.

The 21st century faces any number of demographic changes and demands. Demographically, contemporary cities in much of the country are faced with a growing gentrification process. Young urban professionals, prosperous retirees, and the well-educated new immigrant class all are seeking succor in urban living. The cost of housing is certainly one critical factor faced by 21st-century urban planners. The quality-of-life demands of the new urban class require considerable public policy innovation on the part of state and local government. Many standards associated with pollution, for instance, have less to do with federal clean air standards and regulatory requirements than with aesthetic appeal that either draws or repels such fairly affluent people to or from city living. Open-air plazas and increased access to natural light are very important to the new prosperous urbanite. Easy access via public transportation is important, as is access to Internet technology and contemporary cultural and educational **amenities**. The young professional living in U.S. cities today is faced with an ever-changing, highly competitive economic and social environment. The knowledge-based tools needed to navigate contemporary life must be readily available.

At a deeper level, urban and suburban redevelopment faces several new challenges in many areas of the country. Lack of community cohesion and sense of place, property rights conflicts, site-specific pollution issues, and access to technology are among the common concerns. In each case, the success of redevelopment efforts hinges on the effective management of a set of relatively new issues for local government officials. These issues are critical to effective redevelopment efforts, requiring innovative thinking and actions in order to maintain effective democratic governance while promoting state, regional, and local sustainability and relevance in a global society featuring an ever-increasing range of geographic choices for living and working for what the economist Richard Florida calls "the creative class."[25]

Neighborhood and community cohesion is a critical part of maintaining the social capital networks so vital to the good society, and to the good life. In rural areas as well as highly urbanized regions, it has been shown in a wide range of public service areas that effective government and social institutions require a minimal degree of social interconnectedness,[26] and in the highly itinerant 21st century, local government cannot assume stable long-term civic networks. There is some question as to how local neighborhoods and the wider community relate; is the relationship oppositional or complementary? Evidence tends to indicate that in most cases individuals are more likely to form bonds at the neighborhood level than at a broader community level. The issue becomes especially important in state and local policy innovations intended to restructure society for the future. The new demands for social interconnectedness clearly point to a need to cultivate durable neighborhood network development. This development work must be done, however, in a manner that reduces the time costs to individuals seeking to broaden their network connections upward to the community level.

While civic networks are seen as an important aspect of urban and suburban redevelopment, other forces tend to divide and separate individuals in economic terms. The **developed community** phenomenon is a good example of this dilemma. Developed communities can be freestanding homes, condominiums, or even entire apartment complexes. Relationships among residents and between residents and developers within **gated communities** are focused more on economic status homogeneity than on other, more socially beneficial forms of community that reflect a bridging of differences in social class and racial and ethnic cultures.

While air and water quality standards are increasingly a function of federal Environmental Protection Agency (EPA) guidelines, other site-specific air and water issues are more often guided by state and local policy innovation. One particularly important example is the issue of noise pollution.[27] The issue of noise pollution becomes a concern due to a number of factors in modern communities. First, whether in rural, suburban, or urban areas, American communities are increasingly heterogeneous. Also, population is becoming denser, bringing individuals into closer proximity to one another. With the changing nature of work and the rise of home-based offices and telework, residential areas are *de facto* mixed-use areas; a residence may be a workspace at various times of the day or night and simultaneously serve as home. Transportation corridors often increase ambient noise in residential areas. Particularly in the areas of the United States where peri-urban areas are developing, the suburban fringe may abut traditionally agrarian functions such as farms, dairies, and livestock feedlots; the noise (and odor) of livestock, chemical fertilizers, fungicides and herbicides, and heavy machinery will be in evidence in these areas. Demographics may bring young socialites into close proximity with young families or retirees who have quite different lifestyles and tolerance to noise.

Several studies have shown that noise pollution is strongly related to problems of social cohesion, and may lead in some cases to public health and even criminal justice problems. Innovations focused on noise pollution relate to more than simply the decibel level of noise in a given community. European researchers have found that one of the best ways to manage noise in the residential environment is to begin by listening to residents and determining the character of the noise present in a community before making decisions about how to manage that noise. Nevertheless, noise is a form of pollution that must be managed, as are other harm-causing pollutants. A sustainable community model for state and local policy innovators must carefully take into consideration the role of noise in the development of urban redevelopment plans.

A fourth area of importance in urban redevelopment is related to technology access and use.[28] Technology, particularly computer-based data processing applications and communications technology, has often been thought of as the foundation of a new age in the U.S. economy and society. Policy innovations that have sought to improve access to communication tools are likely to continue to be at least one generation behind current use and demand patterns. Terminal-based e-mail and Internet access has been surpassed by mobile wireless technologies that significantly change the networks of communication. Access and use, for instance, are done entirely at the user's discretion, allowing people to select which information and which types of communication networks will become part of their social, political, and economic virtual world. Such network relationships are so individualized and also quickly obsolete that would-be policy innovators will have to manage a diversity of tastes in the future rather than design environments with a "typical family of four" in mind. In many respects, creating or encouraging the development of a very broadly based and interactive communication network may be a precondition to virtually all other innovations in urban redevelopment beyond the provision of a very basic essential needs infrastructure.

It is important to note that not all persons are equally capable of taking advantage of the opportunities for engagement and exploration of personal tastes made possible by the wireless technologies and the increasingly accessible Internet. The millions of Americans in our states and local communities who can be classified as *aged* and *poor* are the least likely to be enjoying the benefits of this technology, and regional and urban planning innovations related to technology will require continued efforts to "bridge the digital divide" of accessibility to broadband services and computers. Without such efforts the social equity element of sustainability is not addressed and political, social, and economic divisions may deepen rather than lessen. Such divisions, in turn, threaten the adaptive capacity of societies to "rally to a common cause" of sustainability-promoting change to confront and overcome the challenges of a planet in peril of human-induced global climate change and natural resource scarcities. In the coming decades, broadened access to information technology and computers in our nation's states and local communities must become a source of adaptive capacity for mobilizing collective action to address our sustainability challenges, not yet another source of political and economic division.

Resource Management and Development: Energy and the Environment

One resource that is critical to modern conceptions of the good life is the availability of energy, both electrical and thermal, for use in private residences and commercial enterprises. In recent years it has become increasingly clear that the major contemporary sources of energy such as fossil fuels (oil and coal) present such a high cost to the health of the environment that we must rethink our energy future and be prepared to make significant changes in how we travel, how we produce goods and services, and how we design our homes and workplaces. Virtually all state and local governments are facing hundreds of policy decisions precisely in this area of energy provision, patterns of consumption, sources of supply, choice of products, and design of workplaces and commercial and residential zoning and building regulations. Far beyond the reach of state and local governments, the U.S. federal government, international commodity cartels, and multinational energy firms play a major role in shaping energy markets, thereby affecting environmental policy choices available to governments.

Within those broad constraints of these major actors, however, state and local governments in the United States do have a great deal of room to shape local decision-making about the recycling of reusable products, about the patterns of energy use and conservation in their jurisdictions, about alternatives to auto-based transportation, about the use of LEED® construction processes and structures, and about similar measures adopted by state and local governments around the nation to promote sustainability.[29]

Energy Policy

For over a century our nation has been heavily focused upon fossil energy production and use because of our easy access to coal and oil. In the late 1850s the first successful oil well began extracting petroleum in Pennsylvania. Since that time, some states and many local communities in the United States, and elsewhere in the world, have developed entire industries and associated financial systems around the fossil energy paradigm. Early views on the sustainability of a world economy "fueled" by coal and oil resources was built on the faulty premises that the supply of cheap and easily accessible fossil energy would last forever, and that no significant damage was being done to the planet by the burning of these fossil fuels to provide energy for homes, for commercial offices, for transportation, and for industrial production. In the early 1970s, however, that very commonly shared viewpoint of the long-term sustainability of petroleum supplies in particular began to change in very significant ways:

- Social and political values at the grassroots community level in many regions of the nation began to focus greater attention on "green" or pro-environment policy initiatives, and public interest groups promoted new conservation-oriented and ecologically sensitive views of sustainability; this was particularly strong among younger generations.
- In an effort to address social equity concerns, some PUCs placed increasingly greater emphasis on equitable energy distribution to privileged and underprivileged households and businesses alike (e.g., in California, the Miller-Warren Energy Lifeline Act of 1972), and some PUCs began to explore the potential role of alternative renewal energy supplies.
- Some environmental interests identified alternative modes of living (e.g., "next generation" building design and reduced toxic emissions)

intended to enhance the quality of life in communities in ways that were not injurious to the environment.

- Land use planners focused increasingly on the role of mass transit development in metropolitan areas (e.g., Bay Area Rapid Transit), where burgeoning urban and suburban areas produce insufferable traffic congestion.

While alternative energy slipped from the national policy radar screen for much of the 1980s, a number of states and many local communities continued to explore energy policy innovations. In California, renewable energy systems were encouraged by state tax incentives. Geothermal energy was developed in the Imperial Valley, along the U.S.–Mexico border. Wind energy was harnessed in the Altamont Pass[30] region in Northern California. California researchers conducted research on clean coal and "fluid bed" combustion chamber technology for electric generation plants.[31w]

In the post-September 11 policy environment, during a period of relatively high petroleum prices and at a time when supply futures are questioned,[32] the value of state and local energy innovation is now more fully recognized and continues to be actively promoted. Currently, state and local energy innovation is primarily advanced through three principal mechanisms. First, states create markets for renewable energy through **renewable energy portfolios** (RPSs). RPSs are benchmarks for the portion of energy used by state consumers that must be supplied by renewable sources. In the 23 states with RPSs, either PUCs or state regulatory offices monitor the standards. RPS standards can be met either through direct use

Photo 3.4. Bay Area Rapid Transit (BART) in Oakland, California. Source: © Rramirez125/ Dreamstime

of renewable energy by consumers, or through the use of **green tags.** Green tags represent a validation that renewable energy was produced and made available on the electrical grid. Except for the direct impact of emissions at a particular use or production site, green tags have the same effect: committing energy producers and consumers alike to renewable zero-emission energy. Green tags can be used for tax credit purposes as well.

Second, states and local governments encourage renewable energy innovation through the use of **price subsidies** or inducements to renewable energy consumers. During periods of transition to new sources of "clean energy," the market price for green energy tends to be higher than conventional fossil fuel energy; to promote further development of clean energy sources and in time to reduce the cost of those sources, those responsible parties who generate renewable energy for grid-use or who use renewable energy sources are offered financial incentives to encourage their sustainability-promoting economic choices.

Finally, the third form of encouragement that state and local governments use is research money to underwrite applied research in science and engineering for the development of practical sustainable energy infrastructure.

Core Dimensions of Sustainability

The first chapter outlined four core dimensions of sustainability. In this chapter, we find that policy innovations focusing on sustainability can be characterized as *the new margins.* Local and state government leaders who understand the central role of sustainability concepts in contemporary public management are better able to respond to impending social, political, economic, and environmental change. Sustainability entails maintaining values while adapting to changing conditions. In terms of social objectives, a continued and growing commitment to human capital is critical to sustainability. Historically, modern society has identified certain types of knowledge, particular skills, and specific abilities associated with some types of employment to be essential to promoting "progress." This sort of progress often demands highly specialized divisions of labor, and books such as William Whyte's *Organization Man* and David Riesman's *The Lonely Crowd* provide moving descriptions of the socially isolating communities created by the type of consumption-driven modernism we have taken to be progress.

Sustainability, however, demands that we rely much more heavily on socially connected and highly inclusive communities and develop the capacity for adapting to change. Preparation for narrowly defined employment will give way to the need for highly skilled yet highly adaptable individuals who can communicate and work with individuals with a wide variety of skill sets from highly varied social and educational backgrounds. In no small measure, the educational systems of our nation, from K–12 elementary schools, through secondary schools, and including our higher education institutions, will have to adapt to the knowledge and training needs of these boundary-spanning experts of the future.

As for economic objectives, sustainability demands that we create deeper social and economic relationships focusing on collective benefits rather than focusing too heavily on the stimulation of economic motivation based on the maximal accomplishment of rational self-interest. Individual economic benefit can emerge when equitable market structures reward individual market innovation and hard work. Sustainability is promoted most effectively, however, when individual economic success leads to community benefit in the form of jobs, infrastructure development, and renewal and the nurturing of a stable tax base to support public programs which can address social equity goals.

In much the same way, the environmental objectives of sustainability are advanced when effective social and economic structures are in place and state and local governments can appeal to what psychologist Abraham Maslow refers to as "higher order needs" for beauty and justice. Appealing to consumers as individuals seeking to promote their own self-interest within their broader roles as community residents will more likely than not serve to incorporate environmental sustainability into the decision-making process of citizens. Citizens with an active concern for the environment would likely translate into a strong market demand arising

Sustainability: What Can I Do?

Here are some everyday things individuals can do to promote sustainable lifestyles and communities:

1. Print your class assignments and papers double-sided, or ask your professor if you can submit electronic versions.
2. Unplug computers and appliances if possible while not in use. This will decrease your energy use and power bill.
3. Turn off lights in rooms when not in use.
4. Bring your own reusable cloth tote bag to the grocery store or university bookstore and avoid using paper and plastic bags.
5. Bring your own mug to the coffee shop.
6. Replace incandescent lamps with compact fluorescent lamps.
7. Wash your clothes in cold water.
8. Try walking, biking, carpooling, or using mass transportation to commute to campus.
9. Go to the Environmental Protection Agency's Web site "Window to My Environment" to learn about sustainability and environmental issues in your community (http://www.epa.gov/enviro/wme/).

For general information, go to the Environmental Protection Agency's Sustainability Web site: http://www.epa.gov/Sustainability/basicinfo.htm#epa

for products that would be manufactured locally and marketed in environmentally sound ways.

Finally, institutional objectives require that sustainability become an almost "infectious" concept across state and local government jurisdictions. By means of inter-institutional networking, each sustainable state and local community would serve as a model for other communities and states seeking to accomplish similar goals for their residents. While sustainability is currently widely seen as the "new margin" for successful community and state development, it cannot be viewed in these zero–sum terms, where each successful community or state competes to gain population and resource share at the expense of others. Instead, the dynamic must become one of the contagion of best practices, with strong demand from well-informed citizens that effective practices observed elsewhere need to become part of their particular state and local government institutional and policy structure.

Environmental Protection

The National Environmental Protection Act of 1969 (NEPA), which became effective on January 1, 1970, served as the initial impetus for much state and local policy innovation. State environmental policy agencies (SEPAs) were created in most U.S. states in the 1970s to provide an interface with the EPA and to help enforce state environmental quality standards. The primary purpose of NEPA was to limit the impact of human action on the natural environment. Under NEPA, all applicable federal agency actions, or the actions of private contractors working with federal agencies, must be evaluated prior to initiation in terms of potential environmental impacts. If such impacts are anticipated, plans must be outlined for how they will be either prevented, significantly reduced, or compensated for in some appropriate way.

NEPA was the first comprehensive environmental policy legislation in the United States and provided a major impetus for the development of a deeper understanding of environmental health throughout the country. With growing concern for environmental quality issues relating to air and water and wildlife habitat, many state policy innovators saw NEPA and state analogues as presenting an opportunity to consider more carefully the quality of the environment within their own jurisdictions. Using NEPA as a blueprint, state environmental quality standards are in many cases more stringent than federal requirements. Currently, 18 U.S. states have "NEPA-like" requirements being enforced by so-called mini-NEPA state agencies.

Environmental quality innovations are an important part of promoting sustainable development in states and communities, and they are related to other state or local goals directed toward promoting a clean environment, providing good public health services, and providing strong public safety services to be called upon in the event of natural disasters. Economic vitality is clearly necessary to sustain all of these environmental and community protection efforts, but the recognition is now rather widespread that such commercial and manufacturing activities as take place to provide employment and income and tax revenue to state and local government must be carried out in an environmentally sensitive manner.[33]

Livability

As noted above in the discussion of energy resources, the term *sustainability* has meant different things to different people at different times. Currently, American states and local communities face significant challenges in how that term—understood as entailing the simultaneous achievement of economic vitality, environmental protection, and social equity promotion without diminishing the prospect of future generations—is translated into practical policy goals and programs. The goals of state and local government must simultaneously maintain economic success in various markets, local and global, as well as provide for equal opportunity for healthy living. In the past these goals have been at odds with each other. While no single state or local community can say it has achieved fully all of these goals, and done so in a way to leave the same or better conditions for the next generation, many state and local governments have made noteworthy simultaneous progress toward these goals. The following section seeks to address emergent livability issues in the United States and to discusss the role that state and local governments will come to play in addressing those issues.

Eldercare

As the Baby Boom generation reaches retirement age, the percentage of the population 65 years of age and older is expected to grow rather substantially, increasing to nearly 17% by the year 2015. The nation's changing social and economic demographics mean that many older Americans will either have no children or only one child to help them address their needs for care in their old age, increasing the burden on society and individuals trying to balance work with caregiving activities.[34] Countless working hours will be devoted to eldercare, reducing productivity and earnings for many young and middle-aged adults. Communities in which is it difficult for the infirm to navigate and where caregiving facilities and services are lacking will likely suffer in terms of attracting workers and retirees alike. Also, to build an

Photo 3.5. Environmental protection and sustainability. Source: Marnie Burkhart | Corbis.

effective caregiving community, state and local governments must be mindful of the diverse nature of the aging population.[35]

At the federal level, several agencies deal directly with issues related to elder-care. The three most prominent such agencies are:

- Administration on Aging
- Centers for Medicare and Medicaid
- Social Security Administration

The Older Americans Act (OAA) of 1965 (reauthorized 2006) is a federal law that serves as the foundation of many state and local efforts to respond to the dramatic demographic change facing the nation in the coming decade. The OAA established the Administration on Aging and led to the creation of the National Aging Network (NAN), a large network of eldercare service providers. The OAA also promotes the development of senior centers and programs for traditionally underserved populations, such as Native Americans.

Treating the elderly with respect and dignity requires a wide range of services and a great deal of thoughtful planning. Community sustainability in an era of an aging population requires more than just providing basic necessities; it entails promoting the ability of seniors to maintain quality relationships with others, both of their own age and those younger than themselves. Along with state and local resources and community-based organizations (religious and secular), the OAA offers grants-in-aid to states and local communities attempting to serve the needs of the elderly. Innovations in the eldercare area include nutrition programs, employment programs, and disease prevention programs. Intergovernmental co-operation has helped to build the National Family Caregiver Support Network and Eldercare Network; the former is designed to help caregivers cope with issues related to eldercare and life management. National law has also sought to reduce elder abuse and to promote elder rights. The latter organization is of help to both the elderly and their caregivers, providing information about services near an elderly person's home. The Eldercare Locator is also helpful in linking an elderly person's work skills with particular jobs; this is of growing interest to Baby Boomers. Many of these new retirees discover that they have not saved sufficiently for their retirement years, that the costs of living in retirement are higher than they expected, and that they will require further years of employment. Of the nearly $1.5 billion enacted for the Administration on Aging in 2010, $1.4 billion of the federal allocation was allocated to programs designed to support both state and local government eldercare programming.

Social Capital and Civic Life

In the timeless historical treatise entitled *Democracy in America*, the French visitor of aristocratic heritage Alexis de Tocqueville described the rather idyllic **community-focused** existence that he observed during a prolonged visit to the United States in the 1830s. Americans throughout the country were witnessed working side-by-side in local communities, with neighbors helping neighbors and citizens generally doing their fair share to address shared problems. Volunteerism was common and was even relied upon in many situations to provide essential governmental services such as firefighting and road maintenance. In his books *Making Democracy Work* and *Bowling Alone*, contemporary Harvard political scientist Robert Putnam reported strong correlations between successful robust democratic institutions, high rates of civic volunteerism, and strong social institutions.[36] Putnam also pointed out, however, that when civic life declines, democratic institutions show a similar decline. Without dynamic civic institutions and without the active engagement and support of citizens (young and old, well-off and of modest means), state and local government's ability to maintain livable communities in which sustainability is being pursued is severely constrained. Maintaining civic involvement among a diverse set of citizens, encouraging grassroots volunteer-driven efforts to solve problems, and cultivating discussion regarding the future desired condition of a community are all important ingredients in successful governance and the pursuit of sustainability.

Several national-level programs being implemented at the state and local government level are designed specifically to help promote civic engagement and encourage community involvement. The Corporation for National and Community Service, a federally sponsored nonprofit corporation, manages AmeriCorps, Learn and Serve America, America Reads, and Senior Corps. By volunteering in these programs citizens become more aware of their communities and come to understand the problems that government, the nonprofit sector, and the private sector are seeking to address as they pursue global, national, regional, state, and local sustainability. Volunteerism not only serves the public interest, but also gives the individual volunteer a sense of self-efficacy and personal fulfillment and generally leads to higher levels of active participation in other dimensions of civic life.

Existing nonprofit religious institutions such as synagogues, churches, temples and mosques also serve a long-standing and significant role in U.S. states and local communities. Houses of worship often draw people from all walks of life into an atmosphere of mutual trust for the pursuit of common goals. Communality is the primary basis of community in these religious groups; similarities in terms of beliefs, needs, and often worldviews provide the social cement for these aggregations of co-religionists. Civic clubs such as Rotary, Kiwanis, Lions, Moose, and Elks may draw individuals together on the basis of other forms of communality, most frequently a mutual commitment to help the less fortunate members of society. Other civic associations include the League of Women Voters, the American Civil Liberties Union, municipal and county historical societies, and Chambers of Commerce offer venues for those interested in community betterment and the camaraderie that comes from volunteerism.

Another form of civic engagement is participation in the cultural arts. The arts might include local or regional museums focusing on a much broader swath of literary, visual, and performing talent. Musical societies and orchestras are also important in drawing together individuals from the community. Policy innovations in terms of the promotion of the arts are often overlooked in terms of their significant impact in terms of building sustainable states and local communities. The ability of state and local government to operate effectively and accomplish significant goals through innovation may hinge on something as apparently unrelated as the arts; one often sees political leaders gathering at artistic events and mingling and interacting with other citizens outside the setting of formal political institutions, adding to their value.

Conclusion

Extensive policy innovation in pursuit of a sustainable future in an age of global climate change and pending shortages of critical natural resources will be a necessity in the coming decades. State and local government, just as much as the federal government, will have to rise to the challenges to be faced in addressing the three "Es" of sustainability: promotion of economic vitality, protection of the environment, and promotion of social equity.[37] This book documents how innovations at the state and local government level have often led the way for national movements addressing the difficult transitions made by Americans from an agricultural society to an industrial society, and finally from an industrial society to a postindustrial society. American federalism, the flexibility of state constitutional processes, and the wellsprings of social capital in communities throughout the country have in combination given rise to considerable innovation in public policy and in governance practices. We are optimistic that these major elements of state and local government in America will lead to the next set of innovations that will bring us closer to a sustainable future wherein we can carry out our obligation to future generations to leave the planet no worse off than we found it.

Given the realization worldwide that space, natural resources, and seemingly inexhaustible energy supplies are actually limited, and that development has led to the serious risk of irremediable damage to our planet, our newest challenge is to discover what innovations in public policy and private actions need to occur to provide for a sustainable future. One hope for the future is for all to live in sustainable local communities that are inclusive of persons of diverse background, that nurture citizens young and old, that enrich those of high and pedestrian tastes alike, and that treat all equitably with respect to the free pursuit of life, liberty, and happiness in a healthful environment. The role of state and local governments in meeting this challenge is certainly great, but the men and women serving in leadership roles in these governments, the public servants serving citizens in the public agencies maintained by these various governments, and the many nonprofit and private sector partners of these governments are up to that challenge. If this book hits its mark, we should have new recruits to the cause of sustainability in the years ahead.

Key Terms

Amenities

Bureaucratic capacity

Community-focused

Developed community

Gated community

Green tags

LEED®

Political culture

Political trust

Price subsidies

Renewable energy portfolios

Social capital

Social trust

Whole building design

Xeriscape design

Discussion Questions

1. Discuss three important preconditions or factors that facilitate public policy innovation.
2. Summarize both the proponents' and critics' positions on the relative benefits (or lack thereof) of the development of PUCs.
3. According to the chapter, what are four ways in which views of sustainability of petroleum began to change in the 1970s?

CHAPTER 4

Key Actors and the Policy Process in State and Local Governments

Introduction

In this chapter we describe state and local government policy processes and the various actors and interests that typically seek to influence those processes. Public policy and the policy process have been defined in the following way by most social scientists that study these phenomena:

> Policy is what the government says and does about perceived problems. Policymaking is how the government decides what will be done about perceived problems. Policymaking is a process of interaction among governmental and non-governmental actors; policy is the outcome of that interaction.[1]

From this definition it is clear that a diverse set of actors can become involved in the making of state and local public policy. Beginning with the perception of a problem, making it an issue for government action, getting it on the government's agenda for consideration, and finally securing relevant government action all entail the involvement of many parties sharing a stake in the form of government action taken.[2] For many state and local governments the process can become rather complex, featuring a multitude of actors engaged in one or more aspects of policymaking. Broadly speaking, one can place the actors in the state and local government policymaking process into one of two distinct broad categories: **institutional actors** and **non-institutional actors**.

The institutional actors involved in the public policy process are governments and governmental agencies that deal with public affairs—namely, the subjects of many other chapters in this book, including legislative bodies, executive departments, and the judicial branch. Depending on the policy issue in question, there are often state and local as well as national-level institutions involved in policy issues arising in our federal system of government. As discussed in other chapters, the United States has a very large number of such agencies and governments due to the federal (as opposed to unitary) nature of the U.S. political system. The separation of powers provided for in both our federal and state constitutions keeps our governmental system decentralized; in countries such as Japan, Great Britain, or France, where governmental power is more centralized, far fewer such institutional actors become involved in regional and local policymaking.

The non-institutional actors involved in the policy process, a principal focus of this chapter, are diverse and can include political parties (e.g., Republicans and Democrats), interest groups (e.g., National Rifle Association, Sierra Club, National Organization for Women), social movements (e.g., civil rights movement, environmental movement), non-governmental organizations (NGOs) (e.g., League of Women Voters, Project Vote Smart), the mass media (e.g., newspapers, radio, television, the Internet), and individual citizens. These potential actors are fiercely independent of the government, have different types of resources at their disposal, and employ varying strategies in their efforts to influence state and local public policy. This chapter will discuss each of these sets of actors and describe how they may exercise influence over state and local policy processes. More specifically, this chapter will accomplish the following goals important for a sound understanding of state and local government and politics:

- Review the changing nature of the policy process in postindustrial society
- Examine how citizens can get involved in state and local government policy processes
- Discuss the role of political parties and elections in state and local politics and policymaking
- Discuss the types of interest groups present and the strategies these groups typically use in state and local policy processes
- Review the role of the mass media in policy processes
- Examine how industry and business can often exert significant influence in state and local politics
- Discuss the role of social movements in shaping state and local politics and policy processes
- Compare how policymaking processes differ between various systems, including the separation of powers political system found in the United States and the integration of powers (parliamentary) political systems found elsewhere

- Briefly present models of how the policymaking process occurs in state and local governments
- Offer suggestions for how policy processes and actors can enhance community sustainability

Political Participation in Postindustrial America

Contemporary studies of public participation in postindustrial societies suggest that a new style of politics has emerged over the past several decades.[3] This new style of politics is characterized in major part by an expansion of what has been considered *appropriate* political action. Some scholars who carry out research in this area argue that support for new modes of participation arise out of some specific sociopolitical changes that occurred in the postwar period.[4] These widely read scholars note that historically unprecedented economic growth, a prolonged period of prosperity, and relative political stability have created an increasingly better educated public that places demands on government to address ever-changing problems arising in the management of postindustrial societies, including the challenge of sustainability. The contemporary grassroots citizen organizations and associated social movements that arise in this context are considerably more likely to engage in **protest**

Photo 4.1. Protest politics is a prominent part of contemporary U.S. society.
Source: © Elizparodi | Dreamstime.com

politics or **elite-challenging politics**, such as demonstrations and boycotts, than were previous generations of political activists.[5]

Political conflicts arising over increasingly complex issues, such as sustainable development, same-sex marriage, immigration reform, and No Child Left Behind educational reform, have generated a multitude of new interest groups, many of which draw citizens into the political process via single-issue concerns as opposed to a broad philosophical orientation to proper governance. One such policy arena with this type of political conflict is environmental policy.[6] Traditionally, in the United States environmental management was a process largely insulated from public scrutiny. By the 1970s, however, widespread concern became evident concerning the proper management of the natural environment.[7] Environmental organizations grew in size and proliferated in many economically advanced countries, and these non-governmental organizations succeeded in mobilizing citizens, in challenging traditional environmental management practices, and in presenting new environmental issues for public debate.[8]

Given the difficulty ordinary citizens have in dealing with the many scientific complexities of environmental issues, the process by which democratic societies confront complex scientific and technical issues involving the broader public interest is important to understand. The formation of NGOs and interest groups is critical in this respect. The emergence of community-based interest groups and social movements has been characterized as an "eruption from below," with demands for increased citizen input in the decision-making process lying at their base.[9] Interest groups and community-based advocacy groups have pushed for increased democratization as a fundamental component of public policy. In doing so, the activities of interest groups illustrate the inherent tensions between a politicized, issue-driven segment of the electorate and "expert" decision-makers operating in the realm of environmental, natural resource and public health policy.[10]

The prominent political scientist Ronald Inglehart argues that in contemporary society two distinct forms of political participation should be recognized.[11] The "elite-directed" mode of political action is represented by sociopolitical institutions such as political parties, bureaucratic agencies, labor unions, and industry associations that are hierarchical in nature and mobilize citizens into action in a coordinated, "top-down" fashion. In contrast to this familiar pattern of citizen mobilization is the elite-challenging mode of political action, a pattern of political activity that is generally more issue-specific, operates outside traditional political channels, and tends to make use of unconventional and sometimes disruptive tactics in an attempt to influence public policy.[12]

Elite-challenging activism is a form of political action that usually addresses specific policy goals, such as a community opposition to the location of a prison in a town or city.[13] Sometimes this type of community-based political activism has been called **NIMBY** politics (i.e., Not in My Backyard). In the area of elite-challenging environmental activism, Rothenberg has described this particular form of political action in the following terms:

Nonviolent resistance is often an important part of environmental action: lying across the road to block the onslaught of bulldozers, chaining oneself to the floor of a valley as the dammed waters start to rise. These can be powerful forms of protest. The press will take notice, and the public will follow, so the world will learn of your cause. If you are willing to lay your life on the line, they think, you must be quite convinced of the correctness of your position.[14]

According to the highly regarded political scientist David Truman, industry groups that perceive threats to existing values often are put on the defensive by such tactics.[15] One example of this is the tobacco industry after the demonstration of a link between smoking and cardiac and pulmonary disease. In response to the elite-challenging behavior of consumer, environmental, and social equity advocacy groups (e.g., National Association for the Advancement of Colored People, Sierra Club), industry groups are motivated to establish communication networks and create a common front against new policies that might hurt their ability to conduct business as usual. Instead of competing against one another as a market-based economy model would predict, industry-wide groups (e.g., cattle ranchers, wheat growers, automobile manufacturers and retailers, real estate interests) often focus on their lowest common denominator of interest and work in concert to take advantage of political opportunities to oppose these new groups. Such "coalitions of convenience" have indeed become quite common in many conflicts coming before U.S. state and local governments. The emergence of new elite-challenging forces in American society has led to the creation of a broad array of interest groups, citizen groups, political party factions, and government agencies becoming active in the state and local government policymaking process. Each of these types of key actors will be addressed briefly in the sections to follow.

Interest Groups

All postindustrial nations, including the United States, are experiencing explosive growth in the number, scope of concerns, and size of interest groups seeking to influence public policy.[16] Community-based interest groups and other grassroots organizations concerned with a variety of public policy issues are variously labeled as **public interest groups**,[17] **citizen groups**,[18] or **social movements**.[19] These particular terms are used to distinguish between citizen and community-based groups, which as a whole differ in their goals from groups representing either business or professional interests. According to the noted economist Mancur Olson's seminal work *The Logic of Collective Action*,[20] such not-for-profit groups typically experience considerable difficulty organizing and mobilizing action. Groups of this type usually seek collective benefits that are often nonmaterial, such as preserving endangered species or promoting civil rights, and are inclusive rather than exclusive in nature (i.e., the benefit sought will accrue to everyone regardless of their contribution to securing it). Despite these rather formidable obstacles, however, public interest groups have grown dramatically in number and in size in virtually all U.S.

states and in urban and rural areas alike in recent decades, and they have become important players in the American state and local government public policymaking process.

Interest groups are highly diverse in terms of their size, the resources at their command, the scope of interest and activities in which they engage, their policy preferences, and their organizational form. They can be involved in a host of state and local government policy issues, including environmental protection, poverty reduction, public safety, child health and welfare, gender equity, and transportation system reform. Such groups can be of the large-scale membership type organized nationwide, or they can be community-based and focused on local conditions. International organizations (commonly referred to as international non-governmental organizations, or INGOs), issue-focused think tanks (e.g., Heritage Foundation, Vera Institute), and activist organizations (e.g., Habitat for Humanity, Doctors without Borders, the Union of Concerned Scientists) also often engage in policymaking in U.S. state and local governments on a selective basis. According to David Korten of the People-Centered Development Forum, many community-based and grassroots public interest groups have been effective advocates for public policies that are intended to promote sustainability:

> …the environment, peace, human rights, consumer rights and women's movements provide convincing examples of the power of voluntary action to change society. This seeming paradox can be explained by the fact that the power of voluntary action arises not from the size and resources of individual voluntary organizations, but rather from the ability of the voluntary sector to coalesce the actions of hundreds, thousands, or even millions of citizens through vast and constantly evolving networks that commonly lack identifiable structures, embrace many chaotic and conflicting tendencies, and yet act as if in concert to create new political and institutional realities. These networks are able to encircle, infiltrate, and even co-opt the resources of opposing bureaucracies. They reach across sectors to intellectuals, press, and community organizations. Once organized, they can, through electronic communications, rapidly mobilize significant political forces on a global scale.[21]

Although interest groups differ quite widely in their human, financial, and organizational resources,[22] in general it can be said that community-based and grassroots groups tend to be understaffed and poorly financed in comparison with organizations that represent private sector interests such as the petrochemical industry, the pharmaceutical industry, the telecommunications industry, the insurance industry, agricultural commodity groups, and so forth.[23] Most community and grassroots nonprofit groups are managed by either an unpaid or poorly compensated staff and claim very few official members, although some have developed large memberships and/or long lists of generous financial contributors and have hired skilled researchers, lawyers, and organizational managers.[24] Moreover, interest groups can have two fundamentally different types of memberships: one composed exclusively of individual citizens, and another consisting of representatives of large institutions, business firms, or state and local governments.[25]

Some observers of interest groups also note that there is an increasing use of professional agents such as lobbyists and political consultants, professionals (often former elected public officials) who are adept at influencing policy processes and mobilizing support or posing opposition to public policy initiatives.[26] According to the research conducted by political scientist Andrew McFarland, it is as much the skill of such agents that determines a group's success as it is the size of its membership or its financial resources.[27]

Another source of influence and success in the policy process is the formation of coalitions of interests. Such alliances feature numerous smaller groups or businesses as members rather than individual citizens. These coalition-type groups can become a formidable political force due to their pooled financial resources and their freedom from dependence upon highly variable individual membership dues. Another source of group strength identified by political scientist Jack Walker is the role of powerful patrons who are located outside of the group but who provide critical financial and social networking resources.[28] The support of the many private foundations (e.g., Nature Conservancy, Russell Family Foundation, Northwest Area Foundation, John D. and Catherine T. MacArthur Foundation), of wealthy individuals (e.g., Bill Gates, Paul Allan, Norton Simon), and of government agencies (e.g., Environmental Protection Agency, Bonneville Power Authority, U.S. Department of Energy) allows some environmental and public health groups to reduce their reliance on individual membership dues.

A variety of strategies developed to influence the policy process have been identified by social scientists who study the policymaking process in state and local government. Central among these strategies are lobbying elected officials and governmental agencies, organizing grassroots activists to mobilize public opinion, building coalitions with other like-minded groups, and making strategic financial contributions to supportive politicians.[29] The specific strategy (or combination of strategies) used by a particular organization is influenced by various factors, including the types and amounts of resources available to it, the perceived effectiveness of the strategies available, and the governmental structure in place. Large memberships give interest groups an advantage in terms of writing letters, staging public demonstrations, and training volunteers to carry out grassroots activities. In contrast, organizations possessing few members but commanding large budgets generally wish to focus on influencing the election of key decision-makers or lobbying such decision-makers after they are elected. The latter has been the preferred strategy for industry and commercial interests, and as a result many industrial interests have benefited significantly from governmental programs and government subsidies.

Regardless of the size of their budgets and memberships, however, Berry observes the following about interest groups: "[they] have strong reasons to convince people at the grass roots of the righteousness of their arguments, believing that changed public opinion will eventually lead to changed elite opinion."[30] This long-term perspective is especially the case in the advocacy of sustainability, in light of the fact that issues of sustainability are becoming popular among citizens in postindustrial countries.[31]

Photo 4.2. Interest groups advertise their message. Source: Claudio Peri/epa/Corbis.

Table 4.1 provides information derived from a 2006 random sample survey of public interest groups and NGOs involved in the promotion of civil society, or civic engagement and public education on public affairs.[32] The diversity of resources used by advocacy groups working in civil society is apparent, as well as the heavy reliance on members and volunteers to raise the resources needed and carry out necessary group activities. Around two thirds of the groups taking part in the survey have some type of membership in an advocacy group, including individual and institutional members; and virtually all of the groups spend a substantial amount of their time pursuing resources rather than directly advocating on behalf of their public policy objectives.

The survey in question asked these public interest groups about the types of strategies they used and about the activities in which they engaged, including their interactions with government, the public, other groups, and the mass media. The strategies listed in Table 4.2 range from traditional forms of influence such as lobbying government officials to elite-challenging activities such as organizing and staging political demonstrations and engaging in protests. While many of these groups are active at various levels of government, most groups have more influence in state and local government rather than the national government. This observation substantiates former U.S. House of Representatives Speaker Thomas "Tip" O'Neill's often-quoted remark, "All politics is local." Another finding supportive of the discussion above is that public interest groups promoting a civil society spend a great deal of time trying to educate the public and working in concert with other groups to promote their agenda. Of course, the strategies of such public interest groups and industry-based groups are partially dependent on the structure of government and its potential points of access, as we will note later in this chapter.

Yet another interesting finding from this study is the degree of self-perceived success of these groups. The survey results presented in Table 4.3 indicate that 68% of the civil society groups believe they are either "effective" or "very effective" in working with citizens. The second highest level of self-assessed success noted is that of working with local governments, followed by working with state government and working with political parties. Working with the national government elicited the lowest level of self-assessed perceived success.

Table 4.1. NGO Resources and Capacity, 2006

Mean/median number of paid staff:	
Full time	9.3 / 5.0
Part time	4.0 / 4.0
Mean/median number of volunteers:	11.4 / 8.0
Individual memberships:	
% Yes	84.7
% No	15.3
Mean/median number of members:	363.5 / 221.5
Individual membership trend last two years:	
% Grown	30.0
% Stayed the same	52.7
% Declined	17.3
Institutional/other types of memberships:	
% Yes	66.1
% No	33.9
Mean/median number of other memberships:	23.3 / 19.0
Types of other members (% indicating members):	
% Civic/community organizations	37.7
% Government agencies, etc.	22.7
% Research organizations	36.4
% Businesses/corporations	43.9
% Labor organizations	4.0
% Clubs	26.5
% Environmental organizations	26.5
Budget status last 2–3 years:	
% Increased above inflation	31.1
% Kept pace with inflation	46.3
% Decreased	22.6
Percent time spent finding resources:	
0% to 10%	37.3
11% to 25%	48.0
26% to 50%	12.4
51% to 75%	2.3
76% to 100%	0.0
Budget sources (% receiving from source):	
Membership dues	73.4
Fees for services	63.3
Fundraising activities	71.2
Domestic donors/grants	62.1
National government	22.6
Regional (oblast/state) government	22.6
Municipal government	15.3
Business	31.6
Individual gifts	67.8
N =	177

Source: Steel et al., 2007, see note 32.

Social Movements

As discussed previously, political scientists have identified two distinct forms of political participation intended to influence public policy: the "elite-directed" and "elite-challenging" modes of political action. Contemporary studies of the policy process in postindustrial societies indicate that the elite-challenging mode of politics has been very effective in bringing about policy change when it is associated with the development of a *social movement*. Social movements are broad-based efforts to change societal institutions and practices that emphasize a collective identity reflective of an identifiable set of shared values. Social movements encapsulate a broad range of concerns and engage a large number of organizations and individual citizens who become united for a particular cause. Such movements have included the causes of the prohibition of the manufacture and sale of alcohol, workers' rights, civil rights, environmental protection, and women's rights. All of these movements affected state and local politics and public policymaking in state and local government. Currently, the gay and lesbian rights movement is also very active at state and local levels of government. Efforts to promote the recognition of benefits associated with civil unions and the legal recognition of gay marriage are public policy changes being sought by this contemporary social movement.

Sociologists and political scientists who have studied social movements have identified the following characteristics associated with social movements that have been successful in the past:[33]

1. *Sufficient financial resources to recruit and educate new members and to promote the desired policy outcomes in the general public.* Having sufficient financial support is particularly important in areas where the proposed changes are strongly opposed by groups with substantial resources.

2. *Involving people and organizations with prior grassroots experience.* Having staff and leadership skilled and experienced in grassroots politics expedites successful organizational efforts. Experienced people are more likely to know which strategies work and which do not work under given circumstances. Experienced people are also more likely to be connected with affected communities and know the political landscape within which the recruitment of movement participants can be accomplished.

3. *Identifying emotional issues to motivate people to participate.* This process is known as "dramatic spotlighting," and it occurs when events that lead to public outrage are carefully highlighted for the media and potential participants. There are many examples of injecting emotion into natural resource and environmental policy issues, such as the filming of the clubbing of baby seals in annual hunts in Canada by Greenpeace and a 1970s EPA television commercial using a stately Native American elder with tears coming from his eyes after coming upon a polluted river. While these are particularly noteworthy examples, many others could be given.

4. *Using a "micro-mobilization" approach.* Organizing small informal and formal groups at the local level, all connected to a much larger network or coalition, has been found to be an important component of successful social movements in the past. Having people interact at the local level creates social bonds among otherwise isolated persons, and these bonds increase interest in the issue and participation in social

Table 4.2. Strategies and Activities of Interest Groups, 2006

Question: "Given your organization's goals, please indicate how often your organization engages in the following activities:" [N=177]

	Never (%)	Infrequently (%)	Somewhat Frequently (%)	Frequently (%)	Very Frequently (%)
GROUP–STATE RELATIONSHIPS					
a. Participation in the work of government commissions and advisory committees	0	9	34	34	23
b. Contacts with people in local and state government	8	14	15	46	18
c. Contacts with members of national government	14	18	28	24	16
d. Contacts with leaders of political parties	9	21	31	27	12
e. Legal recourse to the courts or judicial bodies	25	27	31	14	3
GROUP–PUBLIC/GROUP–MEDIA RELATIONSHIPS					
f. Efforts to mobilize public opinion through disseminating information	2	3	20	37	38
g. Organizing demonstrations, protests, strikes, or other direct actions	18	34	32	10	6
h. Contacts with people in the media	2	5	26	36	31
i. Contacts with other NGOs	3	15	16	25	42
j. Organizing conferences and training for other NGOs	11	19	21	22	27
k. Organizing conferences and training for interested citizens	2	1	29	39	28

Source: Steel et al., 2007, see note 32.

Table 4.3. Self-Perceived Effectiveness of NGOs, 2006

Question: In your opinion, how effective is your organization in working with the following organizations and citizens? [N=176]

	Not Effective (%)	Somewhat Effective (%)	Effective (%)	Very Effective (%)
a. Local government	19	32	30	19
b. State government	23	38	25	14
c. National government	36	36	20	8
d. Political parties	29	32	24	15
e. Citizens	8	24	38	30

Source: Steel et al., 2007, see note 32.

movement activities. At the same time as local bonds are being built there must be an ongoing connection to a larger movement; locally bonded people scattered across a myriad of communities are more likely to take part in movement activities if they believe large numbers of other people are also participating in other localities facing the same problems they are dealing with in their own community. Examples of relatively successful movements would be the women's suffrage movement (i.e., "first wave" feminism), the civil rights movement, and the early environmental movement in the 1960s and 1970s.

5. *The absence of crosscutting cleavages.* Crosscutting cleavages (such as liberal vs. conservative or rural vs. urban) within a social movement often lead to political conflict and undercut efforts at building a large, cohesive, and effective movement. Successful social movements in the past have grown more inclusive over time, but they start with a core set of fairly uniform actors who maintain a steadfast focus on their shared cause.

6. *Having a diverse and "co-optable" communications network.* Successful social movements tend to develop communication networks that connect large and diverse numbers of people to the cause: the greater the number and diversity of people actively participating in the network, the more likely the movement will be successful. The communication network needs to connect individual and group participants in the movement to one another, it needs to connect participants with the mass media, and it needs to connect the movement with potential new participants.

7. *Having capable and competent leadership.* Articulate and charismatic leaders and organizers are much more likely to inspire emotion and participation than passive followers and inarticulate leaders. If leaders are identified as being too partisan or allied too closely with a particularly divisive interest group, then their ability to lead a broad- based movement is diminished.

8. *Having an optimistic expectation.* This characteristic of successful social movements is related to sense of efficacy. People have to feel they are joining ranks with large numbers of like-minded people, and that their own participation will contribute to the success of the movement. While this is a very difficult characteristic to engender in contemporary America, with only 60% of the eligible population participating in the electoral process, it is nonetheless very important for successful social movements.

9. *Encouraging solidarity instead of free-riding.* With many state and local issues in the political sphere, there are many "free-riders"—people willing to sit back and watch others take action and then benefit from those actions without themselves having contributed their fair share. Successful movements are able to move people to take private actions that contribute to collective political action (e.g., writing letters, attending public meetings, voting for supportive candidates, joining groups, donating money) despite the temptation to free-ride on the sacrifices of others.

Citizens

As discussed previously, there are a variety of ways that citizens can influence state and local policy processes. Traditional methods would include[34] (1) voting in elections; (2) working on political campaigns for candidates or political parties, which could include convincing others how to vote, attending rallies or meetings, and raising money; and (3) communal activities such as working with groups to solve community problems or contacting governmental officials. In contrast, elite-challenging or "unconventional" political participation could include (1) signing petitions; (2) participating in lawful demonstrations; (3) participating in boycotts; (4) participating in unofficial strikes; and (5) taking part in "sit-ins" and the occupation of buildings or facilities to dramatize a claimed injustice.

While citizens can take a number of steps to participate in politics, overall participation in the United States compared to many other democracies is noticeably lower, particularly in recent years. In addition, not all segments in American society participate in elections at equal rates. The statistics displayed in Table 4.4 show voting rates for the 2004, 2006, and 2008 general elections in the United States. Voter turnout is typically higher in presidential election years (2004 and 2008) than in non-presidential election years (2006). However, the types of persons who participated in the election are similar to those participating in most other elections in the United States—namely, the higher a citizen's socioeconomic status, the more likely he or she is to be registered to vote and take part in the election.

In the 2004 general election, 64% of voting-age citizens cast ballots, which was slightly higher than in the 2000 general election. In regard to who was most likely to

Photo 4.3. "Tea Party" protestors in 2009.
Protestors can be liberal or conservative.
Source: © Imagezebra | Dreamstime.com

register to vote and then actually vote, the U.S. Census study of the 2004 general election found the following:[35]

- Women were more likely to register to vote and vote in the election than men. 74% of women and 70% of men were registered to vote; 65% of women reported voting compared to 62% of men.
- Voting rates were much higher for older voters than younger ones. 72% of citizens 55 years and older voted in the election compared to 47% for the 18-to-24 age group. Just under 80% of citizens 55 years and older were registered to vote, compared to 58% of the 18-to-24 age group.
- The higher the level of educational attainment, the more likely a citizen was to register and to vote. 77% of citizens with a bachelor's degree voted compared to 40% of those with a high school diploma.
- Citizens with higher incomes and who were fully employed were significantly more likely to register and vote than those of lower income and less than full employment. A U.S. Census Bureau report notes the following in this regard: "The voting rate among citizens living in families with annual incomes of $50,000 or more was 77 percent, compared with 48 percent for citizens living in families with incomes under $20,000."[36]
- There were differences in the likelihood of voting among various ethnic and racial groups, with non-Hispanic white citizens being significantly more likely to take part in elections than Blacks and Hispanics.
- There were also some regional differences in voter turnout, with citizens in the Midwest states being more likely to register and vote than those in other regions.

While there was much interest among many groups in the 2008 General Election with the candidacy of Barack Obama, a U.S. Census Bureau Report concluded:

Table 4.4. Political Participation by Group in 2004, 2006, and 2008

Characteristic	2008 (%)	2006 (%)	2004 (%)
Race and Hispanic Origin			
White alone	64	50	65
White alone, not Hispanic	66	52	67
Black alone	65	41	60
Asian alone	48	32	44
Hispanic (of any race)	50	32	47
Sex			
Men	61	47	62
Women	66	49	65
Age			
18 to 24 years	44	22	47
25 to 34 years	48	33	56
35 to 44 years	55	45	64
45 to 54 years	63	54	69
55 to 64 years	68	62	73
65 to 74 years	70	64	73
75 years and over	66	61	68
Educational Attainment			
Less than high school graduate	34	27	39
High school graduate or GED	48	40	56
Some college or associate degree	62	49	69
Bachelor's degree	72	61	77
Advanced degree	76	70	84
Employment Status			
In the civilian labor force	59	48	65
Unemployed	43	31	51
Not in the labor force	55	48	61
Total	**64**	**48**	**64**

Source: U.S. Census Bureau, http://www.census.gov/

...voters 18 to 24 were the only age group to show a statistically significant increase in turnout, reaching 49 percent in 2008 compared with 47 percent in 2004. Blacks had the highest turnout rate among 18- to 24-year-old voters—55 percent, an 8 percent increase from 2004. The increased turnout among certain demographic groups was offset by stagnant or decreased turnout among other groups, causing overall 2008 voter turnout to remain statistically unchanged—at 64 percent—from 2004.[37]

The 2005 U.S. Bureau of the Census report on civic participation asked citizens who reported they did not vote why they did not take part in the election, and they documented the following self-reported reasons:

- 19.9% said they were too busy with conflicting schedules.
- 15.4% reported they were ill or disabled.
- 10.7% indicated they were not interested.
- 9.9% did not like any candidates or issues.
- 9.0% were out of town.
- 6.8% experienced registration problems.

- 3.4% said they forgot to vote.
- 3.0% found the polling places inconvenient.
- 2.1% had transportation problems.
- 0.5 percent reported bad weather.

Because a high level of citizen engagement in governance is an important component of civil society and sustainable communities alike, some state and local governments pursuing sustainability have tried to address some of these reasons for not participating with specific public policies. Increasing citizen participation is important to state and local government because (1) voting and attentiveness to public affairs lies at the heart of the democratic principles upon which the United States was built; (2) citizen participation provides legitimacy to state and local policy decisions to the extent that people recognize that their concerns were incorporated into the laws under which we all must live; (3) citizen engagement can increase citizens' sense of attachment to the community and engender the "co-production" of public goods—that is, citizens promote the public welfare by voluntary actions motivated by a sense of civic duty (e.g., recycle to reduce solid waste, maintain safe lighting on private property, make donations to the Red Cross, United Way, community food banks and the like to provide for those in need); (4) it helps to maintain and reinforce community networks and social connections, thus increasing the ability of communities and states to respond to natural and economic disasters; and (5) heightened public participation also can lead to enhanced momentum to implement new policies and energize the community-based initiatives needed to promote sustainability.

Some examples of state and local efforts to increase citizen participation—not only in elections, but also for service on citizen review boards, planning commissions, and other venues—include the use of e-government techniques (i.e., providing useful policy-relevant information on the Internet and allowing online voter registration), allowing voting before election day, allowing more flexible voter registration opportunities at numerous venues such as on election day, at schools, in hospitals, and in vote-by-mail systems (present in Oregon for all elections and other states for many state and local elections). Concerning this latter approach of making voting easier, many states that have traditional polling station elections are also allowing a very flexible system for absentee voting by mail.

One argument that some observers have made concerning the lower rates of election participation in the United States when compared to other postindustrial countries is that we have a large number of offices subject to election due to our federal system: it is estimated that 521,000 governmental positions are subject to election nationally when national, state, and local offices are combined. The sheer number of positions and candidates that the typical U.S. voter must consider on the ballot is overwhelming. In stark contrast, in many other democratic countries where parliamentary systems are in place (see below), citizens have only one or two offices to fill per election, making the electoral process far less burdensome on the voter.

Initiatives and Referenda

One way that citizens can affect public policy and even amend state constitutions or county and city charters directly is through the initiative process. In over a third of the states and in many local governments, the **initiative** provides citizens with a process to vote on proposed constitutional amendments, **statutes**, or **ordinances**. The initiative process starts when a certain number of registered voters (the number depends on the state and the nature of the proposal) sign a petition to place an issue on the ballot. With a sufficient number of validated voter signatures, either an indirect or direct initiative process ensues. Under the indirect form an issue is first referred to state legislature for consideration, and then if the legislature does not enact the measure, it is placed before the electorate to decide. In the direct form of the initiative, a measure is directly forwarded to voters for their consideration without passing through the state legislature.

In many states the legislatures can also refer a specific measure to the voters for approval or disapproval. This process is called a **referendum**, and it differs from the initiative process because the measure originates with the legislature. All of these types of votes collectively are referred to as "ballot measures," "propositions," or simply "initiatives," depending on the state.

The initiative and referendum process is thought to have originated in the Greek city-states studied by Aristotle, and both methods of direct legislation by the people have been used at various times throughout the centuries in countries such as Switzerland, France, Australia, Ireland, the United Kingdom, and the United States.[38] In the United

Photo 4.4. Initiative voting has serious implications for people and communities.
Source: © Svenblar | Dreamstime.com

States, the initiative and referendum processes were used by many states to both adopt and later revise their original constitutions. South Dakota was the first state to adopt the initiative process in 1898, followed by Utah in 1900, and then Oregon in 1902.

Twenty-four states now use some form of the initiative process. The impetus for the adoption of the initiative process in most states was a growing sentiment among the public that due to widespread corruption in legislative politics, the interests of citizens were too often ignored and those of "moneyed interests" were protected by nefarious lobbyists. The presence of patronage-ridden "political machines" in major cities and many state legislatures, whose exploits were covered in muckraking newspapers by investigative reporters, added to the public distrust of state legislatures at the turn of the century. Within this historical context the initiative process was adopted as a means to circumvent state legislatures by allowing voters to enact laws directly. It was expected at the time that the initiative process would serve as a check on the state legislature—a warning signal from the people that, if too long ignored, they could take matters into their own hands to pass laws they wanted even if their elected representatives were not prepared to do so.

Arguments commonly made in favor of direct democracy by its advocates include the following:[39]

- It makes legislatures more responsive to public opinion.
- It allows citizens to take their policy preferences directly to the public for action.
- It stimulates public debate over important policy issues.
- It increases citizen interest and, thus, participation in elections.
- It contributes to higher levels of trust in government.

Critics of the initiative process offer the following counter-arguments:[40]

- It often leads to the adoption of poor public policies because the public generally lacks the skills, knowledge, and/or desire to cast informed votes during elections.[41]
- It promotes the "tyranny of the majority" (majority riding roughshod over the rights of minorities) and is potentially dangerous for disadvantaged minority interests.[42]
- It often does not reflect the will of the people because those who vote on initiatives often are not representative of the population at large.[43]
- It is controlled by the very interests (i.e., special interests) that it originally sought to circumvent.[44]
- It does not contribute to more responsive and accountable legislatures.

Yet another way in which citizens can directly, or in some cases indirectly, influence the governmental process is through recall provisions. This citizen empowerment process allows registered voters to petition to recall elected (and in some cases appointed) officials through popular elections. Most states allow recall elections for local government officials, but at the state level only 18 American states permit recall elections to remove elected or appointed officials. A famous example of the use of the recall occurred in 2003 when Governor Gray Davis of California was recalled in connection with the mismanagement of the state's electric energy management policy in a way that made the state's citizens vulnerable to extremely high charges occasioned by the nefarious dealings of the Enron Corporation (some of whose officials are in federal prison today for their role in those dealings). The recall of Governor Davis gave rise to the election of the former movie actor and political novice Arnold Schwarzenegger.

Media

The mass media play an important role in state and local government policy processes. In the United States "children spend more time in front of television sets than in school," and more than two thirds of the people in the country "report they receive all or most of their news from television." Given these facts and given the growth of the electronic mass media, it is clear that the media are enormously important as a factor in state and local politics.[45] With the advent of worldwide television coverage due to the extensive proliferation of satellite transmitters and receivers, as well as the rapid expansion of the World Wide Web and the Internet, the transmission of information globally is virtually instantaneous, and the impact of this information

Photo 4.5. Former California Governor Gray Davis (left) was defeated in a recall election by Arnold Schwarzenegger. Source: Kenneth James/Corbis.

is much greater than it was in the past. The strategic use of visual images and the near-real-time dissemination of graphic scenes is a powerful means to create and maintain concern for a specific issue. For example, a picture of a dying bird mired in oil is a great deal more moving than is a short oral "talking head" report that a tanker is leaking crude oil off a coastline somewhere.[46] This type of strategic media messaging by interest groups and political parties is especially important in an era of globalization, where a wider audience has access to new sources of public affairs-relevant information, and this audience is being exposed to more diverse messages concerning state and local governance issues than ever in the past.

In addition to these aspects of the new potency of the mass media, the mass media traditionally perform certain functions that are essential to state and local government and politics, including the following:

- Formation of public opinion: The mass media provide information and diverse viewpoints that help citizens form their own views of public policy issues.
- The mass media help to prioritize public policy issues that come to the attention of state and local government. In one sense, the mass media can serve as a "marketplace" of ideas; in another sense they help determine what issues come to the attention of policymakers based on their independent assessment of the "newsworthiness" of particular stories and issues.
- The news media, particularly the print media, serve as an important "watchdog" over state and local governments and officials, providing a check on corruption, inadequate attention to matters of public concern, unethical conduct, and bureaucratic malfeasance.
- The media collectively provide an essential link between citizens and their government in a democracy by helping communicate public policy-relevant information, policy preferences, and societal values back and forth between citizens and their governmental leaders and civil servants.

According to a 2007 study conducted by the Pew Research Center, the main source of political and campaign news for most Americans is television (60%), followed by the Internet (15%), newspapers (12%), radio (8%), and magazines (2%).[47] When people were asked to list specific television sources relied upon, local television news channels were ranked the highest (40%), followed by cable news networks (38%) and nightly network news (32%). While most Americans continue to get their political information from traditional news sources such as local and national television networks, this study found that Americans age 18 to 29 are now most likely to get their information primarily from the Internet: "42 percent of those ages 18 to 29 say they regularly learn about political campaigns from the Internet."[48] It follows, then, that efforts to increase civic literacy concerning state and local government may increasingly rely on the Internet and e-government technologies, especially with regard to matters affecting young and middle-aged persons.

Citizenship: What Can I do?

In Professor Russell Dalton's book, *The Good Citizen: How a Younger Generation is Reshaping American Politics* (2008), he identifies two distinct types of citizenship by which people can get involved in their communities. The first type of citizenship is "duty-based" and the second he calls "engaged." Below are some ways people can participate in both of these types of citizenship.

Duty-based citizenship reflects traditional forms of political participation:

1. Register to vote. You can register to vote where you get a driver's license (e.g., Department of Motor Vehicles), your county courthouse, and so forth.
2. Vote in an election. Consult your Secretary of State's Web site to learn about the election schedule in your jurisdiction.
3. Join a political party. Search the Web for local meetings of political parties and attend to see if your views are in line with those of the party.

4. Contact your elected representatives by e-mail or letter and let them know how you feel about the issues.

Engaged citizenship reflects a new and broader range of activities that includes social concerns and the welfare of others.

1. Help provide housing for low-income families through programs such as Habitat for Humanity.
2. Volunteer for local Earth Day activities (April 22) such as beach and park cleanups or an environmental "teach-in."
3. Join a watershed group or council to help protect and improve streams and rivers in your area.
4. Many cities have neighborhood associations where community members design programs to enhance community livability.
5. Help your local food bank collect food for needy families.

For more information on how you can register to vote, get involved, and find information about candidates for office or initiatives and referenda, go to Project Vote Smart's Web site: http://www.votesmart.org/

For more information on volunteering and the opportunities in your community, go to the Youth Volunteer Corps of America Web site (http://www.yvca.org/) or the AmeriCorps Web site (http://www.americorps.gov/).

An additional interesting finding of a related Pew Research Center study, however, found that the highest levels of political knowledge observed were among regular viewers of the comedy programs termed "fake news"—that is, shows such as *The Colbert Report* and *The Daily Show with John Stewart*![49]

Corporations and Economic Interests

Businesses and multinational corporations are another set of actors that are extremely important in the political life of state and local government. The noted scholar Charles Lindblom argued convincingly that business enjoys a "privileged position" in American politics generally, and in state and local government in particular. In capitalist or market-based economies such as ours, private corporations rather than government run crucial sectors of the society.[50] In many democratic countries significant portions of what are private sector businesses in the United States, such as energy production, airlines, railroads, medical care, and health insurance, are "nationalized" and are operated by the government. This fact means that private interests in the United States command far more wealth, power, and influence vis-à-vis governmental authorities than is the case in virtually any other contemporary democratic nation.

Some critics of American society argue that the power possessed by private corporations has increased markedly in recent decades as a direct consequence of the globalization of local economies and the explosive growth of multinational corporations. They argue strongly that the combination of these two factors has led to the exercise of undue corporate influence on state and local governments, which are required to regulate and/or levy taxes on some of the activities of these powerful interests. The implications of this increasing role for global corporations in local communities replacing locally owned, locally financed, and locally operated small businesses are rather ominous for state and local government in the United States. This is the case in part because interests far removed from the community could decide the ultimate fate of that community rather than the community itself, and also because, generally speaking, business interests oppose public policies "that they believe would impose significant new costs on them or otherwise reduce expected profits" regardless of their potential benefit to the broader community.[51]

While virtually all political scientists agree that business interests command a great deal of influence in state and local government, there is disagreement among social scientists on just how much influence business interests actually exercise in the policy process. As the discussion of public policy models found at the end of this chapter will illustrate, some scholars argue that corporations dominate the policy process, both nationally and internationally,[52] while others argue that business is just one of the many powerful interests involved in the policy process.[53] The highly regarded American political scientist Robert Dahl persuasively argues, however, that those who own and control corporate and personal wealth pose special problems for democratic systems and public policy:

> ...ownership and control contribute to the creation of great differences among citizens in wealth, income, status, skills, information, control over information and propaganda, access to political leaders... [and] differences like these help in turn to generate significant inequalities among citizens in their capacities and opportunities for participating as political equals in governing the state.[54]

This observation suggests that in the United States and other market-based economies, business interests represent not merely one of many contending interests in state and local governments, but one of the most important actors involved in public policymaking in those governments.

Political Parties and Elections

Political parties are important actors in state and local public policy processes throughout the country. Typically, political parties "reflect a political culture with distinct world views" that are organized to "seek power in government."[55] While the Founding Fathers tried very hard to insulate the new nation from the development of factions and parties through the constitutional arrangements of federalism, separation of powers, and checks and balances, they obviously were not entirely successful in that effort. By 1800 the United States was one of the first countries in the world to have nationally organized political parties. With continental expansion and population growth through mass immigration and the resulting expansion of the electorate, in addition to historical reforms enfranchising African-Americans and women, political parties provided the principal means to mobilize voters through what we called "elite-directed" politics in our preceding discussion.

Political parties provide a means for the organization and direction of competition for political power. They prioritize issues to be addressed by government and recruit candidates to stand in elections at the national, state, and local levels of government. After elections are held, the winning party takes control of the government and the minority party calls into question the majority party's actions in areas where they believe it is subject to criticism that will resonate with citizens in the next election. This constant give-and-take, action-and-reaction between the political parties serves to keep the public informed about the actions of their government and aware of alternatives to existing policies and practices.

Political parties can also facilitate the work of state government if the same party controls both the legislature and governor's office, thus minimizing the often-divisive effect of separation of powers and checks and balances. Divided control of state government by different parties makes governance more difficult, requiring skillful negotiation to bring differing policy preferences into some degree of accord to permit effective action to address the problems requiring government attention. Typically, the presence of a divided government at the state level restrains the scope of government initiatives to address public problems and leads the respective parties to request a "mandate to govern" in the next election.

The principal function of political parties in democratic countries is "the development of a solid and durable linkage between the party's electorate and the policymakers…parties are expected to represent the social composition of those who mandate them and to respond politically to the demands of their electorate."[56] Some additional functions carried out by political parties in the United States include:

- They represent groups of interests in U.S. states and communities. Once elected, however, elected officials not only represent their own party supporters but also must govern in the interest of all of the constituents in their respective jurisdictions.
- They help to simplify choices for voters by organizing and articulating alternative positions on the issues facing state and local governments. Parties also help to recruit and educate candidates for public office so that citizens can make judgments as to whom to trust with the grant of public authority in pending elections.
- They can help to stimulate interest in public affairs, in elections, and in democratic governance in general. By explaining their positions on the issues, political parties can help to inform and shape public opinion.

There are different types of political parties in democratic countries, with **missionary parties** and **broker parties** being two of the major subdivisions. Missionary parties tend to be rather ideological in orientation, in a sense of proclaiming a "mission" to fulfill if elected to office in terms of specific public policies and programs. Missionary parties often enter elections with a "manifesto" or "platform" of specific and detailed policy actions to be undertaken if successful in the election. These parties are able to maintain a focused agenda because they tend to exercise a high degree of control over membership and carefully monitor who is allowed to make use of the party label as a candidate. The political party leadership itself selects who will be the candidates standing in local elections and who will serve as leaders of the party. Missionary parties are most often found in parliamentary-style governments and are seldom seen in state and local politics in the United States.

In our country the political parties are far less ideologically oriented and seek to "broker" a multitude of interests in order to appeal to the widest segment of the electorate. Broker parties have weak control over their membership since it is typically self-selected, and those interested in elective office generally nominate themselves in American politics. Candidates for office in our country are selected through the use of **primary elections** and **caucuses**, two candidate recruitment processes that allow interested voters within each party to select their party's candidates instead of the party leadership. The use of primaries to select candidates is a unique feature of American politics and is not found in other postindustrial democracies. This practice ensures that political parties in the United States are less ideologically cohesive than their counterparts in other countries, and the decentralized power structures of the political parties, reflecting American federalism, also ensure that regional and sectional differences will permeate the national Democratic and Republican parties alike.

American political parties can be generally characterized as centrist in terms of policy preferences when compared to parties in other postindustrial nations. Republicans and Democrats draw support from almost every major socioeconomic group, with a few noteworthy exceptions. For example, African-Americans vote overwhelmingly Democratic (90% voted for Al Gore in the 2000 presidential election). Survey data from the Pew Research Center gathered in 2004 indicate that the Republican Party tends to receive disproportionate support from middle- and upper-income groups, whites, and conservatives, while the Democratic Party tends to receive disproportionate support from African-Americans, Hispanics, liberals, women of lower income, and groups with less education (Table 4.5).[57] That said, neither party has a monopoly of support from any of these groups. Given the socially broad-based support for each party, they are first and foremost interested in winning elections and less interested in remaining ideologically "pure" in all of their actions and public positions. This desire for electoral success generally leads the Republicans and Democrats alike to try to appear ideologically moderate in general elections and to label their opponents as being "extreme" in their views.

This "playing toward the middle" approach is reinforced by the fact that many voters characterize themselves as neither Republican nor Democratic in basic leaning, but rather see themselves as independents who can vote for either party's candidates, depending on whose message is more appealing. These fundamental conditions motivate each major political party to tolerate a diversity of opinions and accommodate a wide range of policy preferences within their ranks. The American broker style of political parties has allowed both the Democratic Party and the Republican Party to absorb third parties and even broad social movements over the years. This is not to say there are no differences in policy preferences between the parties and their supporters, just that the gap between the parties is relatively narrow in comparison to parties operating in other democratic countries.

A recent example of partisan differences between Republican and Democrats can be found in a Pew Research Center public opinion poll concerning the needs of the poor conducted in 2009. That survey found that 46% of the Republicans surveyed believe government should "guarantee food and shelter for all" compared to 79% of Democrats (Table 4.6).[58]

Another important feature of the U.S. political party scene at both national and state levels is the existence of the **two-party system**. Since the 1860s the same two political parties have dominated the American political system—Democrats and Republicans. Approximately 60 percent of Americans today consider themselves to be either Republicans or Democrats, and while an increasing number of Americans are identifying themselves as independents, they still vote for the two main parties at the ballot box. For example, in the 2000 presidential election 72% of independents who indicate that they "lean Democratic" voted for Al Gore, and 70% of independents who "lean Republican" voted for George W. Bush.

Third parties have had a tough time establishing themselves in the United States because of our **single-member district** form of electoral representation: the candidate with the plurality of the vote, not necessarily the majority, wins the election. Many other postindustrial democracies have **proportional representation** systems with **multi-member districts**; such a form of electoral representation tends to encourage multiparty systems because multiple seats are proportionally distributed based on what proportion of the vote a particular party wins.

Table 4.5. Party Identification by Demographic Groups, 2004

	Republican (%)	Democrat (%)	Independent (%)
Total	30	33	37
Gender			
Women	28	37	35
Men	31	29	40
Race/Ethnicity			
African-American	6	63	31
Hispanic	20	40	40
White	34	29	37
Ideology			
Conservative	51	22	33
Moderate	22	36	42
Liberal	8	51	41
Age			
18 to 29	25	29	46
30 to 49	31	32	37
50 to 64	29	35	36
65+	32	40	28
Education			
Less than high school graduate	21	40	39
High school graduate	28	33	39
Some college	32	31	37
College graduate and more	33	32	35
Income			
Less than $20,000	19	42	39
$20,000 to $30,000	24	37	39
$30,000 to $50,000	30	34	36
$50,000 to $75,000	36	29	35
$75,000+	38	29	33

Source: Pew Research Center, 2005 (see note 57).

Two other unique features found in some state and local government elections are the **open primary** and **nonpartisan offices**. Open primaries are primary elections where voters do not need to be members of a specific political party in order to vote for that party's candidates. Voters still have to be registered to vote, but can decide to vote for their favorite candidate regardless of which party registration they hold. Most states have **closed primary** systems, which are preferred by the parties, in which only registered members of a political party can vote using the ballot of that political party.

In nonpartisan elections, candidates run for office without listing a political affiliation. Typically, the winning candidate is chosen in a runoff election from the top two vote recipients in the primary election. The candidates in nonpartisan elections are most likely aligned with one of the political parties, but they do not identify themselves as party members. Nonpartisan elections are generally held for local government offices in some counties, in many cities, and especially in the case of school districts and other local special districts and boards and commissions. Nonpartisan judicial elections are also very common at the state and local levels.

Table 4.6. Partisan Differences Concerning Needs of the Poor, 2009

	Republican (%)	Democrat (%)	Independent (%)
Government should...			
Guarantee food and shelter for all	46	79	58
Take care of people who can't care for themselves	46	77	59
Help more needy people even if debt increases	29	65	43

Source: Pew Research Center, 2009 (see note 58).

Many members of the public, journalists, and even elected officials themselves decry "partisan politics." The common argument heard is that partisan politics too often leads to stalemate in government and the election of nonresponsive public officials. Because of this supposed tendency, some argue for open primaries in state and local elections to remove the influence of parties. On the other hand, many political scientists and political parties believe that partisanship is generally a good thing in electoral processes because it offers voters cues about the choices facing them. In a sense, you know something about where candidates (or current elected officials) stand on the issues if they identify themselves as Republicans or Democrats.

Governmental Structures and the Policy Process

Parliamentary and separation of powers governments—the former exemplified by most European countries, and the latter by the United States—are the two principal forms of democratic governance in the postindustrial countries. In the United States we directly elect state governors and members of our state legislatures. Governors typically have the ability to veto acts of their respective legislatures, but legislatures can override that veto by a supermajority (varies between three fifths and two thirds) of both houses in bicameral state legislatures. The governor and one or both of the legislative chambers can be from different political parties, and they can and often do disagree over policy issues. As discussed in other chapters, this political structure is termed a "separation of powers" system and can lead to policy "gridlock" where it is very difficult (if not impossible) to pass legislation. In a sense, "there are many cooks in the kitchen and they all have their own recipe." Passing legislation in state governments, and the national government, at times can be a very unpredictable and difficult process. A member of the majority party can vote against the wishes of her or his own party and not fear having to run for reelection because the government has fallen; in a **parliamentary system**, in contrast, the consequence of such a dissenting vote could well be the failure of a sitting government and the need for calling an election. Because of our decentralized political system and weak, broker-type parties, this "gridlock" situation where legislation is very difficult to enact occurs quite often in American state government.

In parliamentary systems such as that of Great Britain, citizens vote for only their own member of the House of Commons. The political party that obtains a majority in the House of Commons then forms the government and it is responsible for policy without the undue influence of opposition parties, unless the government is part of a ruling coalition of political parties. The leader of the majority party, or head of the coalition, becomes Prime Minister (head of the government). Unlike in the United States, where we have a separation of powers, the Prime Minister selects other leading party members to become government ministers, blurring the line between executive and legislative branches of government. The Prime Minister and the other ministers must all be members of Parliament. This political system is typically referred to as featuring **integration of powers**.

This characteristic of blurring across executive and legislative branches in parliamentary systems clearly differs from the American state constitutions that established three separate, distinct, and co-equal branches of government. One effect of this clear separation of powers is that the legislative process is much more predictable in the parliamentary system since it is based primarily on the "majority rule" principle as opposed to the checks-and-balances logic of American constitutional law. In addition to these structural arrangements, there is also a tradition-based system of "collective responsibility" whereby members of Parliament nearly always vote along party lines. You don't see anywhere near the level of vote-swapping or shifting coalitions in parliamentary systems that we find in American state governments.

In terms of elections, parliamentary systems make voting decisions relatively simple. Parties run on a set of promises, sometimes referred to as a manifesto or a mandate, which will become the official set of policies for the new government if elected. Party manifestos or mandates are typically quite specific in terms of public policy positions, and parties are expected to implement the mandate if elected. In short, you know where the party stands on a specific issue—say, environmental policy or a social safety net program. If a voter doesn't like the current conditions or direction of government policies, she or he knows whom to hold accountable for policy choices.

Separation of power systems, in contrast, can be quite complicated and confusing for voters since there are multiple officials to select (e.g., governors, upper and lower legislative house members, other state-level offices, judicial offices, and ballot initiatives). In addition, candidates for partisan offices often run personalized campaigns in broker-type parties and are not necessarily representative of established party platforms. Once elected, the voting behavior of such candidates can be rather unpredictable as well. Because such candidates are not beholden to their parties so much as to their own campaign organizations in the American setting as opposed to the parliamentary setting, American legislators are particularly open to the exercise of influence by groups and interests that can promise and deliver various forms of campaign support in the next election.

A Review of Policy Models

As noted at the outset of this chapter, public policy has been defined by Thomas Dye as "whatever governments choose to do or not to do."[59] While there is general agreement among social scientists that this is a suitable working definition of public policy, there is considerable controversy regarding just how the policy process works in different political jurisdictions. Here we will introduce the two most prominent rival theories in political science and sociology that claim to explain the policy process: pluralist theory and elite theory.

Pluralist theory is an ideal-type democratic theory that holds that the American democratic political process is genuinely open to the involvement of any group that wishes to participate. Pluralist theory has many adherents among American political scientists and has deep roots in American political thought. Some of the fundamental constitutional principles embedded in the U.S. Constitution (freedom of speech, freedom of assembly, and freedom to petition government for the redress of grievances) constitute core elements of pluralist theory.

According to Thomas Dye, pluralism or "group theory" works along the following lines:[60]

> Group theory purports to describe all meaningful political activity in terms of the group struggle. Policymakers are viewed as constantly responding to group pressures—bargaining, negotiating, and compromising among competing demands of influential groups. Politicians attempt to form a majority of groups. In so doing, they have some latitude in determining what groups are to be included in the majority coalition.

From this description of the American political system as seen from a group theory or pluralist perspective, a pluralistic state and local policy process could feature such groups as business interests, teacher's unions, agricultural interests, environmental groups, gay and lesbian rights advocacy groups, and so forth. All of these groups and interests would be trying to influence the policy process governed by duly elected officials, and no single group or subset of groups would be able to dominate public policy outcomes.

A more critical perspective on the functioning of the political process is offered by the advocates of **elite theory**. Elite theory proponents describe the policy process as one that is dominated by an elite few whose powerful interests influence policy largely behind the scenes. These elites and their influence over policy are largely removed from the view and awareness of ordinary citizens within society. C. Wright Mills described this perspective exceedingly well in the following passage from his classic book *The Power Elite*:[61]

> The power elite is composed of men whose positions enable them to transcend the ordinary environments of ordinary men and women; they are in positions to make decisions having major consequences. Whether they do or do not make such decisions is less important than the fact that they do occupy such pivotal positions...they rule the big corporations. They run the machinery of the

state and claim its prerogatives. They direct the military. They occupy the social structure....

These elites are said to possess the highest forms of education, to command personal and corporate wealth, to secure the services of the best legal and medical services to protect their wealth and health, to be in a position to dictate the values of those in their employ, and to hold disproportionate political power in their hands as a consequence. Moreover, they are described as being generally unresponsive to the needs of the common citizen in society. The masses are periodically appeased with symbolic or minor concessions to their needs, but they are kept largely in the dark about public affairs by a subservient press and a trivialized and entertainment-oriented broadcast media (see a portrayal of this view of American politics in Murray Edelman's classic *Politics as Symbolic Action: Mass Arousal and Quiescence*[62]). All of this adds up to the inescapable conclusion that public policy, seen through this model, would be the direct result of economic and political elite preferences, with little impact being exercised by average citizens acting in their roles of voters and proponents of particular public policy preferences.

Because of the great disparities in wealth in the United States resulting from the operation of a market-based economy in which so much of the economic activity is in private as opposed to public hands, the danger of elite rule is a constant threat to our democratic institutions. Sociologist Ralph Miliband, in *Divided Societies: Class Struggle in Contemporary Capitalism*, describes elite theory as seen from an economic class perspective in the following terms:[63]

> ...class analysis is largely *class struggle analysis*. It is a mode of analysis, which proceeds from the belief that class struggle has constituted the central fact of social life from the remote past to the present day. The subject-matter of class analysis is the nature of this struggle, the identity of the protagonists, the forms which the struggle assumes from one period to another and from one country to another... This mode of analysis clearly has a very strong 'economic' theme; but it also has strong political and ideological themes, which are intertwined with the economic one...

It is likely that neither the idealized pluralist model nor the hypercritical elitist model captures the full picture of how state and local governments operate in the United States today. It is clear that evidence for the operation of both models can be cited, and that some state and local governments are more pluralistic than others and some are more elite-dominated than others. In the state and local governments where pluralism is present it will be possible for the advocates of sustainability—that is, the simultaneous pursuit of economic vitality, environmental protection, and social equity—to mobilize their forces within the broker parties and candidate-centered electoral processes to gain a strong position for their views. In state and local government settings where elite-dominated politics prevails, however, the forces of sustainability promotion will likely find it exceedingly difficult to make headway toward their goals.

Conclusion

This chapter has shed light on the various actors involved in state and local government and the public policy decision-making processes in which they tend to operate. Citizens, interest groups, the mass media, political parties, and social movements were all discussed in this regard. As a general backdrop to that discussion we have described the changing nature of politics in postindustrial societies and what that historical transition to a period of sustained peace and prosperity has meant for the political processes of advanced democracies, including the United States. The changing nature of state and local politics from decidedly elite-directed to elite-challenging modes of political participation has increased the complexity of policy processes, leading to multiple and competing perspectives on who has power and influence and how public policy decisions are actually made in state and local government.

The challenge of moving toward more sustainable forms of economic activity, land use patterns, energy use and production processes, transportation services, public health and social services, and food production and transport will face virtually all state and local governments in the United States in the coming decade. Global climate change may well displace globalization of the marketplace as a principal concern of state and local government officials and the citizens living in communities throughout the country. Community-based citizen groups, the mass media, private corporations, philanthropic foundations, industry-wide associations, public interest groups, and political parties are all going to have to figure out how to work in concert, state by state and local community by local community, to achieve the level of adaptation to change that sustainability will require.

We must hope that the promise of pluralism held out by its defenders, as it relates to state and local governments in the United States, is more a reality than a myth. If entrenched interests and concentrated wealth based on the status quo prevent or delay sustainability-promoting adaptations, we may all be dooming our children to a future less inviting than the one we inherited from our own parents.

Key Terms

Broker parties

Caucus

Citizen groups

Closed primary

Elite-challenging politics

Elite theory

Initiative

Institutional actors

Integration of powers

Missionary party

Multi-member district

NIMBY

Non-institutional actors

Nonpartisan offices

Open primary

Ordinances

Parliamentary system

Pluralist theory

Primary election

Proportional representation

Protest politics

Public interest groups

Referendum

Single-member district

Social movements

Statutes

Two-party system

Discussion Questions

1. What are five of the key actors in state and local government in the United States?
2. What role do the political parties play in state and local government as compared to the U.S. Congress? As comparable to their counterparts in other countries?
3. Based on the chapter reading, which theory—pluralist theory or elitist theory—do you think better fits the reality of your own state? Your own city or hometown?

CHAPTER 5

State Constitutions

Introduction

On Nov. 2, 2004, voters in Arkansas, Georgia, Kentucky, Michigan, Mississippi, Montana, North Dakota, Ohio, Oklahoma, Oregon, and Utah voted to change their respective state constitutions to make same-sex marriage illegal. In recent years voters in some of these same states, and others, have decided to attach additional amendments to their state constitutions to legalize marijuana for medical purposes, to allow physician-assisted suicide, to ban the use of dogs in the hunting of bear and mountain lions, to protect the privilege of gathering some types of edible seaweed, to increase the share of state budgets allocated to education, to ban abortion, to increase cigarette taxes, to increase the minimum wage, and to either limit or increase the scope of taxes and tax rates, among other things.

State constitutions may seem like an unusual place to pursue one's favored public policies, instead of the normal legislative process, but this way of starting off our discussion of state constitutions indicates how important foundational documents are in the daily lives of American citizens. Given that citizen familiarity (especially among younger citizens) with the U.S. Constitution and the major institutions of the national government generally is typically quite low (Table 5.1), popular familiarity with and knowledge of state constitutions is most likely even lower in most areas of the country.[1] Even among the academic community, there has been limited research regarding state constitutions, in contrast to the virtual mountain of literature devoted to the decisions and operations of the U.S. Supreme Court regarding the interpretation of the U.S. Constitution and to the selection of members of the federal bench, whose terms of office are "for life" (the sole exception from fixed terms of office in the American governmental system).

While state constitutions don't receive much attention from academic researchers and are accorded only scant public attention, their importance does indeed merit our close attention. We decided to include an entire chapter on state constitutions, given their direct connection to the question of the active pursuit of sustainability in

Table 5.1. U.S. Youth Civic Knowledge

Question: "Here are a few questions about the national government. Many people do not know the answers to these questions, so if there are some you don't know just tell me and we'll go on."

	Percent correct answer
a. Whose responsibility is it to determine if a law is constitutional or not … is it the president, the Congress, or the Supreme Court?	35% [Supreme Court]
b. How much of a majority is required for the U.S. Senate and House to override a presidential veto?	28% [Two-thirds Majority]
c. Do you happen to know which party had the most members in the House of Representatives in Washington D.C. before the election this last month?	40% [Republicans at the time of the survey]
d. What are the first three words of the Constitution?	33% ["We the People"]
e. What are the first ten amendments to the Constitution known as?	41% [Bill of Rights]

Source: 2006 Project Vote Smart Survey of Youth (18–29 years old; www.vote-smart.org).

state and local government. The mere mention of the topic usually tends to arouse fears of boredom born of painful attention to legalistic hair-splitting among students of state and local government. In reality, state constitutions represent a topic of great importance, interesting historical developments, and clear contemporary relevance. As G. Alan Tarr has reminded us:

> …the disdain for state constitutions is unfortunate; for one cannot make sense of American state government or state politics without understanding state constitutions. After all, it is the state constitution—and not the federal constitution—that creates the state government, largely determines the scope of its powers, and distributes those powers among the branches of the state government and between state and locality.[2]

State constitutions are also important to examine because they often mirror important political, economic, and social changes occurring over time. As states have moved from reflecting rural economies characterized principally by natural resource extraction in the 17th and 18th centuries (mining, timber, fisheries, and agriculture), to governing urbanizing industrial economies in the 19th and 20th centuries (manufacturing), to providing guidance to postindustrial and knowledge-based economies in the late 20th and early 21st centuries, citizens and their political representatives have made many revisions to their respective state constitutions— and even replaced them in their entirety when deemed necessary on rare occasion. Such adaptation to change is a key element in the promotion of sustainability.

While there is somewhat of a debate taking place regarding just how adaptive state constitutions have been to changing times and situations, there is little disagreement that constitutions are important documents that set the context and specify the procedures for political processes by which governors, legislatures, courts, interest groups, local governments, citizens, and others seek to influence the course of public policy. Because of the clear importance of state constitutions to American state and local politics and to prospects for sustainable governance, this chapter will:

- Review the purpose of constitutionalism and constitutions in the states
- Analyze key differences and similarities between state constitutions
- Discuss the various processes available for changing constitutions in the states
- Examine the role of state constitutions as both barriers to and promoters of sustainability

Purpose of State Constitutions

According to Francis Wormuth's classic work *The Origins of Modern Constitutionalism*, "A constitution is often defined as the whole body of rules, written and unwritten, legal and extralegal, which describe a government and its operation."[3] The use of constitutions in states mirrors the development of what we call **constitutional democracy** at our national level of government. At its most basic level the concept reflects the belief that government can and should be legally limited in its powers, and that its rightful exercise of authority depends on observing these limitations. Government in a democratic country must be accountable to its citizens and operate within the limits placed on how and when governmental power is to be exercised with respect to the rights and privileges of citizens. While most constitutions in the world, including that of the United States, are codified as single written documents, the notion of *constitutionalism* can also include multiple written documents and even some unwritten rules and procedures. In the case of Great Britain, for example, there are various written components of the constitution, such as the *Magna Carta* (1215 AD) and numerous statutes enacted by Parliament, but there are also some unwritten components, including principles derived from Common Law and Royal Prerogative.

We can trace the development of constitutionalism back to 500 to 600 BC in ancient Greece, where some city-states had partially written or customary constitutions that were organized, according to the Greek philosopher Aristotle (384–322 BC), into either good or bad forms of the *rule of one* (kingship versus tyranny), the *rule of few* (aristocracy versus oligarchy), and the *rule of many* (polity versus mob rule). Constitutionalism in the United States was influenced by various sources, including developments in Common Law in Great Britain and the well-known writings of enlightenment thinkers such as Jean Jacques Rousseau (1712–1778 AD) and John Locke (1632–1704 AD).[4]

While the U.S. Constitution is often considered the oldest written constitutional document still in use in the world, several American state constitutions

Photo 5.1. England's Magna Carta exemplifies many of the ideals of a constitution. Source: Justin Lane/epa/Corbis.

are even older than the venerated U.S. Constitution, stemming from the original charters of the 13 colonies. The constitution of the Commonwealth of Massachusetts is quite likely the oldest written constitutional document still in use; it dates back to 1780. The Fundamental Orders of Connecticut was considered the first written quasi-constitutional document of its kind in the world, dating from 1638.[5] Eleven other American states' first constitutions precede the U.S. Constitution of 1787 by at least a decade, illustrating that the concept of constitutionalism was well instilled at the state level well before the creation of our current national government.[6] In point of fact, many of the framers of the U.S. Constitution meeting in Philadelphia in the late 1780s were quite heavily influenced by their knowledge of and experience with their respective colonial constitutional documents and established governmental practices.

In general, it can be said that state constitutions establish the overall framework of state government, specifying the forms of local governments to be permitted, including all cities, counties, townships, and special purpose districts created within its territory. The state constitutions provide for all forms of state and local government finances, establish the state and local tax systems in force, and designate the range of civil liberties to be protected under state law. In a sense, state constitutions represent a form of societal contract between those in elected or appointed office and the rest of society. All disputes concerning the meaning of that contract are settled in state supreme courts. Specifically, the main purposes of state constitutions are (within the limitations placed on states by the U.S. Constitution):

- To define the general purposes and ideals of the state, including the determination of the common good of citizens
- To establish republican and accountable forms of government, with legal limits on the powers of government entities and their agencies
- To provide a framework for governmental structures, including the scope of authority, mechanisms for exercising authority, and procedures for the passage and modification of state laws, local ordinances, and administrative rules and regulations. This framework includes the executive, legislative, and judicial branches of state and local government.
- To provide for an independent judiciary that allows citizens to seek court-ordered remedies for illegal actions of government as well as a process to challenge laws they believe to be unconstitutional
- To provide legal definitions of key concepts (e.g., citizenship, property rights, parental rights) and prescribe a process for establishing basic political rights such as standing for public office and voting
- To establish and define the powers of local governments, including counties, cities, townships, and special purpose districts
- To establish the requirements for holding elective and appointed office, as well as setting the terms of office for elected officials
- To provide for a process of removal of incompetent and corrupt elected or appointed officials, which can include recall and impeachment
- To define responsibilities for major government departments and agencies, and the principal duties of the individuals heading up those state and local governmental entities
- To establish a system of taxation and budgetary processes
- To provide for the public safety of the citizenry, including regulatory authority for civil and criminal actions to be exercised to promote public health and safety and to operate effective civil and criminal justice systems
- To provide for a process of replacing or revising the state constitution (depending on the state, these processes can include initiatives, referenda, constitutional conventions, and legislative action)
- To establish the rights of citizens, including both "negative" and "positive" rights and freedoms. Negative freedoms are often called "civil liberties," which include freedom of speech and assembly, among other rights. Civil liberties are individual or group protections from a potential oppressive government. Positive rights, on the other hand, are things government can do for citizens, including the provision of education, economic assistance in times of need, timely assistance in times of natural disasters, and the preservation of cultural assets with public libraries and museums.

While these are the major purposes of state constitutions generally speaking, enormous diversity exists between the states on many of these principles, and this diversity will be discussed in the next section of this chapter. Before we begin this particular discussion we would be wise to heed Robert Maddex's cautionary advice concerning the complexity and dynamic nature of constitutionalism in a federal system:

> Unlike national constitutions, state constitutions do not simply stand alone at the apex of a system of laws but are part of an interactive organization of federal and state governments. Federalism, which is an attempt to solve the problems that arise from this interaction between national and state laws, has continued to evolve since the nation was founded.[7]

Content of State Constitutions: Diversity and Similarities

In broad terms, state constitutions and governmental structures greatly resemble the U.S. Constitution and the national governmental structure because those pre-existing features of government were used as a guide by the framers of the U.S. Constitution. State constitutions differ substantially from state to state, but they are similar in that they are not permitted to contradict the **supremacy clause** of the U.S. Constitution. Where the U.S. Constitution prescribes a legal standard of democratic governmental form or practice, all state constitutions must be consistent with that standard. In the case of **civil liberties**, for example, the several states may exceed but may not set lower standards for the protection of the rights of citizens than those set by the U.S. Supreme Court in its interpretation of the Bill of Rights of the U.S. Constitution.

The limits as to what states can do with respect to the supremacy clause are clear (Fig. 5.1). The U.S. Constitution sets specific limits on state powers in Article I, Section 10; that section restricts states from printing their own money, entering into international treaties, imposing duties on international trade, and engaging in various other official activities reserved for federal government actions. Article IV, in Sections 1 through 4, specifies other provisions pertaining to the states, including extradition of individuals accused of a crime in another state, the requirement for a republican form of government, and the process by which new states can be admitted to the Union. As noted in the chapter on intergovernmental relations in our federal system of government, the Tenth Amendment specifies that any powers not specifically granted to the federal government in the U.S. Constitution are reserved to the responsibility of the states and the people (this is known as the **reserved powers** clause).

According to research by Christopher Hammons, there have been 145 constitutions in the 50 U.S. states since 1776, with the average constitution remaining in effect for approximately 70 years. On average, American state constitutions are "almost

Article I
Section 10 - Powers Prohibited of States

No State shall enter into any Treaty, Alliance, or Confederation; grant Letters of Marque and Reprisal; coin Money; emit Bills of Credit; make any Thing but gold and silver Coin as Tender in Payment of Debts; pass any Bill of Attainder, ex post facto Law, or Law impairing the Obligation of Contracts, or grant any Title of Nobility.

No State shall, without the Consent of the Congress, lay any Imposts or Duties on Imports or Exports, except what may be absolutely necessary for executing it's [*sic*] inspection Laws: and the net Produce of all Duties and Imposts, laid by any State on Imports or Exports, shall be for the Use of the Treasury of the United States; and all such Laws shall be subject to the Revision and Controul [*sic*] of the Congress.

No State shall, without the Consent of Congress, lay any duty of Tonnage, keep Troops, or Ships of War in time of Peace, enter into any Agreement or Compact with another State, or with a foreign Power, or engage in War, unless actually invaded, or in such imminent Danger as will not admit of delay.

Article IV
Section 1 - Each State to Honor all others

Full Faith and Credit shall be given in each State to the public Acts, Records, and judicial Proceedings of every other State. And the Congress may by general Laws prescribe the Manner in which such Acts, Records and Proceedings shall be proved, and the Effect thereof.

Section 2 - State citizens, Extradition

The Citizens of each State shall be entitled to all Privileges and Immunities of Citizens in the several States.

A Person charged in any State with Treason, Felony, or other Crime, who shall flee from Justice, and be found in another State, shall on demand of the executive Authority of the State from which he fled, be delivered up, to be removed to the State having Jurisdiction of the Crime.

(No Person held to Service or Labour in one State, under the Laws thereof, escaping into another, shall, in Consequence of any Law or Regulation therein, be discharged from such Service or Labour, But shall be delivered up on Claim of the Party to whom such Service or Labour may be due.) (This clause in parentheses is superseded by the 13th Amendment.)

Section 3 - New States

New States may be admitted by the Congress into this Union; but no new States shall be formed or erected within the Jurisdiction of any other State; nor any State be formed by the Junction of two or more States, or parts of States, without the Consent of the Legislatures of the States concerned as well as of the Congress.

The Congress shall have Power to dispose of and make all needful Rules and Regulations respecting the Territory or other Property belonging to the United States; and nothing in this Constitution shall be so construed as to Prejudice any Claims of the United States, or of any particular State.

Section 4 - Republican government

The United States shall guarantee to every State in this Union a Republican Form of Government, and shall protect each of them against Invasion; and on Application of the Legislature, or of the Executive (when the Legislature cannot be convened) against domestic Violence.

Tenth Amendment

The powers not delegated to the United States by the Constitution, nor prohibited by it to the States, are reserved to the States respectively, or to the people.

Figure 5.1. Key U.S. Constitution Provisions Concerning States

Table 5.2. State Constitution Characteristics

State	Capitol	Number of Constitutions	Year Present Constitution Implemented	Length in Words	Amendments Adopted
Alabama	Montgomery	6	1901	340,136	766
Alaska	Juneau	1	1959	15,988	29
Arizona	Phoenix	1	1912	28,876	136
Arkansas	Little Rock	5	1874	59,500	91
California	Sacramento	2	1879	54,645	513
Colorado	Denver	1	1876	74,522	145
Connecticut	Hartford	4	1965	17,256	29
Delaware	Dover	4	1897	19,000	138
Florida	Tallahassee	6	1969	51,456	104
Georgia	Atlanta	10	1983	39,526	63
Hawaii	Honolulu	1	1959	20,774	104
Idaho	Boise	1	1890	24,232	117
Illinois	Springfield	4	1971	16,510	11
Indiana	Indianapolis	2	1851	10,379	46
Iowa	Des Moines	2	1857	12,616	52
Kansas	Topeka	1	1861	12,296	93
Kentucky	Frankfort	4	1891	23,911	41
Louisiana	Baton Rouge	11	1975	54,112	129
Maine	Augusta	1	1820	16,276	170
Maryland	Annapolis	4	1867	46,600	218
Massachusetts	Boston	1	1780	36,700	120
Michigan	Lansing	4	1964	34,659	25
Minnesota	Saint Paul	1	1858	11,547	118
Mississippi	Jackson	4	1890	24,323	123
Missouri	Jefferson City	4	1945	42,600	105
Montana	Helena	2	1973	13,145	30
Nebraska	Lincoln	2	1875	20,048	222
Nevada	Carson City	1	1864	31,377	132
New Hampshire	Concord	2	1784	9,200	143
New Jersey	Trenton	3	1948	22,956	38
New Mexico	Santa Fe	1	1912	27,200	151
New York	Albany	4	1895	51,700	216
North Carolina	Raleigh	3	1971	16,532	34
North Dakota	Bismarck	1	1889	19,130	145
Ohio	Columbus	2	1851	48,521	162
Oklahoma	Oklahoma City	1	1907	74,075	171
Oregon	Salem	1	1859	54,083	238
Pennsylvania	Harrisburg	5	1968	27,711	30
Rhode Island	Providence	3	1986	10,908	8
South Carolina	Columbia	7	1896	22,300	485
South Dakota	Pierre	1	1889	27,675	212
Tennessee	Nashville	3	1870	13,300	36
Texas	Austin	5	1876	90,000	439
Utah	Salt Lake City	1	1896	11,000	106
Vermont	Montpelier	3	1793	10,286	53
Virginia	Richmond	6	1971	21,319	40
Washington	Olympia	1	1889	33,564	96
West Virginia	Charleston	2	1872	26,000	71
Wisconsin	Madison	1	1848	14,392	134
Wyoming	Cheyenne	1	1890	31,800	94

Source: *The Book of the States—2006* (Lexington, KY: Council of State Governments) (see note 6).

four times longer than the 7,400-word U.S. Constitution. Most state constitutions contain around 26,000 words."[8] Currently, the shortest state constitution is found in New Hampshire, a document of only 9,200 words; in stark contrast, the longest state constitution, Alabama's, contains 340,136 words (Table 5.2). All of the state constitutions are longer than the U.S. Constitution. The reason that state constitutions are longer than the U.S. Constitution is "because they encompass such a wide range of institutions and powers" due to the dictate of the Tenth Amendment where "powers not delegated to the United States by the Constitution…are reserved to the States, respectively."[9] In addition, Hammons argues that the number of "statutory-type provisions" found in state constitutions—that is, specific mandates for specific public policies—are numerous, with the average state having 824 separate provisions, of which "324 are devoted to particularistic or statutory issues" such as the provision of hail insurance in South Dakota, citizen access to physician-assisted suicide in Oregon, the width of ski runs in New York, and the active promotion of the catfish farming industry in Alabama.[10]

Many observers argue that longer constitutions featuring many specific mandates make state constitutions overly cumbersome and time-bound, and consequently less likely to last over time. They believe that more streamlined constitutions focusing mostly on institutional issues (e.g., governmental structures and functions) with fewer specific mandates make them more durable and adaptable over time.[11] However, contrary to this conventional argument Hammons' research into state constitutions found "that longer and more detailed design of state constitutions actually enhances rather than reduces their longevity."[12] While Hammons does not know for sure why more detailed and longer constitutions can be shown to be more durable, he conjectures that this may occur because such documents provide better mechanisms for conflict resolution by more carefully identifying the rules of the game to be followed by parties in dispute. He also notes that the longer "particularistic" constitutions may have proven to be more durable because they provide competing groups a common interest to protect the important foundational document in which "their programs are institutionalized."[13]

While the length of state constitutions varies widely, there are many common themes found in their provisions, including the establishment of government institutions, the specification of powers of these institutions, the procedures to be followed by public institutions in carrying out their work, and the principles of governance to be observed. Regarding the establishment of governmental institutions, the U.S. Constitution allows a wide variety of institutions as long as they represent a **republican** form of government. Typically, when we talk about institutions in this context of republican government there are two primary issues to consider. First, there is *separation of powers* versus integration of powers, which concerns how many branches of government will be established. Branches can be divided up by executive, legislative, and judicial powers, or integrated into one body, as in a European-style parliament. The second issue involves *centralization versus decentralization*, which concerns how many layers of government will be used and how much power and responsibility each layer will have. Government responsibilities can be centralized at one level of government, or they may be broadly dispersed and decentralized among multiple layers.

For both the separation of powers and centralization versus decentralization issues, state constitutions closely resemble the U.S. Constitution in that power is separated into three branches—executive, legislative, and judicial—and government is decentralized; the governmental powers within the states are typically distributed across five possible layers, including counties, cities, townships, school districts, and special purpose districts. For the branches of government found in states, the executive branch is headed by a governor instead of a president, each state has two legislative chambers (with the exception of Nebraska, which has just a single chamber), and each state has a court of last resort (typically referred to as the state's Supreme Court). As for layers of government, each state has its own procedures for the establishment of local governments, and states differ in how much power and what range of responsibilities those local governments exercise. Forty-eight states have operational county governments (called "boroughs" and "parishes" in Alaska and Louisiana, respectively). While the states of Connecticut and Rhode Island provide for counties as geographic subdivisions of the state, these regional subdivisions do not have functioning governments in those two states.

All fifty states allow for **general purpose** municipal forms of government, and all states have school and **special purpose** (e.g., sewer, mosquito control, rural fire, soil conservation) districts. Twenty states also allow for township governments, which historically have been rural subdivisions of counties, but not always; in fact, today many metropolitan-area suburbs with growing populations have spread into previously rural locations.

Other governmental institutions typically seen in state constitutions include the establishment of state offices and officials, including executive agencies and departments such as education, transportation, agriculture, fish and game, natural resources and the environment, attorney

Photo 5.2. Separation of powers illustrated: Illinois Governor Rod Blagojevich (bottom center) at his January 2009 impeachment trial in the Illinois Senate Chamber, with the State Chief Justice presiding (top center). Blagojevich was removed from office.
Source: Jonathan Kirshner/epa/Corbis.

general, secretary of state, treasury, revenue, welfare (social services), health, **civil service**, various advisory boards, commissions, and governing boards for public colleges and universities. Typically, state constitutions also establish institutions such as state prisons, state mental health hospitals, state libraries, and state parks, and states provide for local school districts and other forms of local government-oriented entities to deal with such infrastructure matters as public utilities, irrigation, county roads and bridges, park and recreation facilities, local libraries, and health clinics and hospitals.

The powers residing in each institution and the state in general are also included in state constitutions, such as the legislative power for both upper and lower chambers; executive powers held by the governor and other executive offices, such as secretaries of state and attorneys general; judicial powers held by state supreme courts, state appellate courts, and lower courts; powers of taxation and expenditure; powers of local governments; regulatory powers over various areas, including commerce, transportation, environment, business and corporations, and criminal justice; powers to claim land or property for public use—and many more. Most state constitutions provide for a plural executive branch, with separate elections for such offices as secretary of state, state treasurer, attorney general, state auditor, and lieutenant governor. A typical U.S. state governmental structure outlined in a state

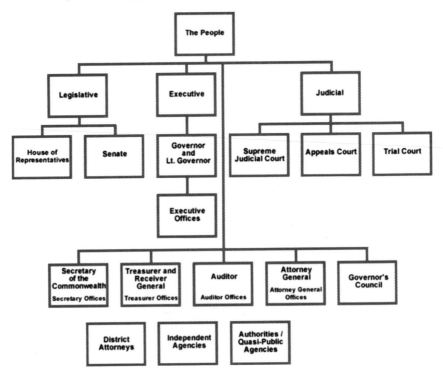

Figure 5.2. Structure of the Commonwealth of Massachusetts.

Source: http://www.mass.gov/mass_gov/includes/mgorgchart.html.

constitution looks very much like that of one of our oldest state constitutions—that of Massachusetts (Fig. 5.2).

State constitutions also outline the process and procedures of government. These can include how laws are made, including executive veto and override processes; qualifications for election and office-holding; terms of office; ballot rules; voter registration and election process rules; size of public institutions; rules for the maintenance of official records; impeachment processes; when and where elections will be held, and who is eligible to vote; processes for initiative, referendum, and referral; and many other procedures. Forty-four U.S. states allow governors to veto individual items in appropriation bills, and all but 15 U.S. states mandate the adoption into law of "balanced budgets" (that is, expenditures provided for must match anticipated revenue for the period in question) through their state constitutions. Most state constitutions feature term limits for governors (38 states), and 16 states have set term limits for state legislators in their constitutions as well.

Finally, state constitutions also provide the "guiding principles" of governance. These principles often follow the U.S. Constitution and typically include many items found in the Bill of Rights, including freedom of speech, freedom of religion, governmental accountability, the sovereignty of the people, and the purpose of democratic government being the protection of life, liberty, happiness, and property. Forty-six states also have provisions similar the U.S. Constitution's Second Amendment concerning the right to bear arms (California, Iowa, Minnesota, and New Jersey are silent on the subject). Only 10 states guarantee the right to privacy in various specific areas, including financial and medical records, but in other states these rights have been established by state Supreme Court decisions. While these fundamental rights are found in the U.S. Constitution and provide citizens with a "minimal floor of government protection for the individual, the enumerated rights in state constitutions can represent another layer" of protection of individual rights.[14]

Some controversial areas concerning the guiding principles found in some state constitutions include attempts to ban or limit abortion rights and feature provisions making English the "official language" of the state in question. For example, many states have changed their constitutions to require parental notification for an abortion, and some states (Colorado, Georgia, and Mississippi) ban abortion, even though a complete ban is now unconstitutional given the U.S. Supreme Court's *Roe v. Wade* decision.

Eight states have recognized English as their official language through a provision in their state constitution, and 21 states have statutory provisions either passed by ballot initiative or legislatively providing for English as the official language for their particular state (Table 5.3). Most constitutional provisions in this area are similar to that found in California, which reads: "English is the common language of the people of the United States of America and the State of California. This section is intended to preserve, protect and strengthen the English language, and not to supersede any of the rights guaranteed to the people of this Constitution" (Article III, Section 1).

Changing Constitutions

There are three major methods available to change or amend U.S. state constitutions: a legislative proposal, a popular initiative, and a constitutional convention. A fourth method, available only in Florida, involves a constitutional commission submitting a proposal directly to the state's voters for their consideration. Each state also has the potential for a "virtual" constitutional amendment through judicial reinterpretation of constitutional provisions. Of the four methods listed, only the constitutional convention provides elected officials with an opportunity to collaborate in a deliberative setting on the entire constitution.

Legislative Proposal

The legislative proposal method is the main avenue used in all the U.S. states to amend their respective constitutions. To demonstrate how heavily this method is used, in the 5-year period between 2002 and 2006, the legislative proposal constituted 68% of all the amendment proposals, with the initiative process representing the remaining 32%. This legislative process is ordinarily used for making limited

Table 5.3. English as an Official Language

Alabama: Constitutional amendment (1990) passed by ballot
Alaska: Statutory voter initiative, (1998), suspended by state courts pending appeal
Arizona: Constitutional amendment (2006)
Arkansas: Statute (1987)
California: Constitutional amendment (1986)
Colorado: Constitutional amendment (1988)
Florida: Constitutional amendment (1988). Petition initiative.
Georgia: Legislative statute (1986, 1996)
Hawaii: Constitutional amendment (1978) by the legislature
Idaho: Legislative statute (2007)
Illinois: Statute (1969)
Indiana: Statute (1984)
Iowa: Legislative statute (2002)
Kansas: Legislative statute (2007)
Kentucky: Statute (1984)
Louisiana: The original constitution was interpreted as having established
   an official language (1975).
Mississippi: Legislative statute (1987)
Missouri: Legislative statute (1988)
Montana: Legislative statute (1995)
Nebraska: Constitutional amendment (1920), by popular vote
New Hampshire: Legislative statute (1995)
North Carolina: Legislative statute (1987)
North Dakota: Legislative statute (1987)
South Carolina: Legislative statute (1987)
South Dakota: Legislative statute (1987)
Tennessee: Legislative statute (1984)
Utah: Statute (2000) passed by petition initiative
Virginia: Legislative statutes (1996)
Wyoming: Statute (1996)

Source: http://www.proenglish.org/issues/offeng/states.html

changes, but on rare occasions the process has been used in some states to propose rather comprehensive revisions of their constitutions.

What makes the legislative constitutional amendment proposal different than simple legislation is the requirement of a large "super-majority" consensus in both houses, with the minimum being two thirds. Fifteen states have an even more arduous hurdle called "Double Passage." This is an amendment procedure that requires majority consensus by both houses from two separate legislative sessions. Lastly, all states except Delaware require that legislative amendment proposals be submitted to the state's voters for their ultimate approval by a majority vote. With all these requirements, it seems rather a miracle that so many amendments have made it though the approval gauntlet. Contrary to popular belief, the majority of state amendments don't garner the general public's attention or cause controversy at the polls; in fact, about two thirds of all state amendments deal with rather mundane issues such as state and local governmental structure and debt management, state agency functions, and relatively minor taxation and finance issues.[15]

Constitutional Initiatives

The constitutional initiative, also know as the popular initiative, citizen initiative, minority initiative, and the "Oregon System," empowers a state's citizens to propose constitutional amendments directly to voters for their ultimate consideration. Available in 18 states, the process is broken down into either direct or indirect initiatives. The direct initiative process allows for a constitutional amendment proposed by the people to be placed directly on the ballot for voter approval or rejection, while the indirect initiative must first be submitted to the state legislature for consideration before being placed on the popular ballot. Only the states of Mississippi and Massachusetts, among the 18 states featuring the initiative process, use the indirect initiative process.

Each state has its own requirements for placement on the ballot, but typically an initiative proposal requires a certain percentage of registered voters' signatures before it can be placed on the ballot for consideration. In those states where the initiative is in place, it is particularly important that citizens keep informed about state and local government issues; these issues are very likely to come before them as voters on a regular basis.

The origins of the initiative process go back to 1902, when the Oregon legislature adopted a constitutional amendment to allow residents of Oregon to propose new laws or change the state constitution through a general election ballot measure.[16] This is why the initiative process is known nationally as the **Oregon System** of direct democracy. Its initial purpose was to provide a means to bypass the political status quo and corruption of the late 19th and early 20th centuries. It was felt, and rightly so, that many politicians of the day were "in the pockets" of the large private corporate interests of the day—the railroads and timber companies. In response to the positive public opinion developed toward the Oregon System, the initiative process was adopted by 17 additional states and became one of the signature reforms of the Progressive Era.

As in the past, those who distrust government still use the initiative today, but there is considerable concern that the process might be somewhat at risk because it tends to empower well-funded special interests that exercise disproportionate access to the ballot box through this process.[17]

Constitutional Convention

A **constitutional convention** is the oldest and most traditional method to propose a new state constitution or extensively revise an existing one. The process of initiating a convention begins with a formal call from the legislature, an action that all 50 state legislatures and the District of Columbia have the ability to undertake. Fourteen states also require submitting the question of calling a constitutional convention to their voters,[18] thereby requiring the legislature to hold such a conclave. While each state has its own requirements in this regard, most states require majority approval by voters (termed "ratification") before a new constitution can be adopted in place of an existing foundational legal framework.

Throughout the history of the United States, there have been relatively few constitutional conventions. As of the end of 2009, there have been only 234 constitutional conventions held in the United States, with Rhode Island holding the last

Photo 5.3. Contentious issues such as immigration can give rise to calls for changes to state constitutions. Source: © Shootalot | Dreamstime.com

one in 1992 in an effort to address its dire fiscal challenges; the revision proposed was soundly defeated by 62% of the state's voters.[19] The trend of decline in the rate of use of constitutional conventions has been consistent; in the 20th century only 62 conventions were held, compared to 144 in 19th century. There are a number of reasons for this sharp decline, but the most likely is the concern that holding a convention will open up "Pandora's Box" (i.e., unleash a torrent of issues on which no course of action can be agreed, and ultimate resolution of the issue is not possible). Those on both sides of an issue often fear that a convention is an invitation to provide a forum for either reactionary populism or the devotion of disproportionate attention to matters of temporary importance, thereby allowing the electorate an opportunity to insert provisions on controversial issues such as abortion, balanced budgets, and the death penalty, or address issues unrelated to the purpose giving rise to the convention.[20]

For example, in 1997 a coalition of environmental interest groups and teachers' unions in New York mobilized against a convention call. The environmentalists feared the 1894 "Forever Wild" provision that protects the Catskill and Adirondack Preserves would be altered or removed by pro-development interests. Teachers, on the other hand, were concerned about losing the constitutional guarantee of public employee pensions.[21]

The trend of declining use of constitutional conventions is unlikely to change due to the political atmosphere of partisan politics, apathy from the general public, and an overall fear of opening Pandora's box on the part of many organized interests. Framing a new constitution requires both consensus from political parties and widespread and durable support from the general public. These conditions are seldom met in most states.

Constitutional Commission

The constitutional commission is an entity that all states have the ability to use, but few in the general public have ever heard of the process. This is likely due to the fact that, with the exception of Florida, commissions have no direct contact with the public or voters. Each state commission's role and membership vary from that of other states, but traditionally the commissions represent a group of experts who are appointed, usually by the legislature and/or governor, to review the constitution and submit proposed amendments to the legislature or prepare for a constitutional convention. If members are deemed to be impartial, the commission can be successful; legislatures typically consider commission recommendations carefully if the commission is deemed to be unbiased, nonpartisan, and expert in constitutional law.

With the decline of constitutional conventions, some states are turning to constitutional commissions to make their constitutions more workable in a time of need for periodic piecemeal amendments. Utah, for example, in 1969 adopted a law to establish the Constitutional Revision Study Commission to study the state's constitution and make periodic revision or amendment recommendations to the governor and state legislature.[22] The commission was made permanent in 1997 and given the official title of Constitutional Revision Commission. This entity represents the nation's only permanent constitutional commission; all the other states with such commissions feature bodies which are the temporary creations of specific, time-bound legislation.

Florida's Taxation and Budget Reform Commission is the only state-level commission that maintains direct contact with the state's voters. Florida's commission has the authority to submit recommended budgetary and tax-related constitutional changes directly to the voters, without prior approval from the legislature. In fact, in 1992 Florida made history when its voters approved amendments submitted by the commission without legislative action.

Role of the Courts

The state courts have a major role in amending state constitutions via their exercise of the power of judicial review. Unlike the U.S. Supreme Court, which under most circumstances won't address "political questions" (legally classified as "nonjusticiable" issues), state appellate courts often rule on a wide range of both procedural and political issues. In the past, state courts of last resort have ruled on issues such as whether a particular state can call a constitutional convention, the validity of procedural mechanisms used in carrying out eminent domain powers, and whether some amendments developed by legislative and popular initiative are consistent with constitutional principles. Because state appellate court judges are elected in most states, unlike their lifetime appointment judicial counterparts in the federal courts, state court judges generally have a stronger sense of connection to "the people" than do members of the federal judiciary. As such, state courts are much more likely than federal courts to issue rulings and hear cases that federal courts would not consider.

Opponents of particular constitutional amendments enacted through the initiative process frequently have used the state courts to question the legality of such amendments in order to prevent them from being placed into effect. For example, opponents of Oregon's ballot initiative 36, which amended the Oregon constitution to say that "only a marriage between one man and one woman shall be valid or legally recognized as a marriage,"[23] unsuccessfully used the state courts to challenge the initiative, arguing in their brief that this statement represented such a radical change to the constitution that only the legislature or constitutional convention should have the ability to make such changes in the foundational framework of Oregon's legal system. State supreme courts can deny a constitutional initiative a place on the ballot on the grounds that the content of the initiative is inconsistent with provisions of the U.S. Constitution. Such was the case in Colorado when a state district court held invalid an initiative intended to restrict the legal status of gays, lesbians, and bisexuals under Colorado law. That ruling was subsequently allowed to stand as precedent in the state.

The role of the state courts known as the exercise of **judicial federalism** is a fairly recent phenomenon, emerging in the 1970s when Warren Burger succeeded Earl Warren as Chief Justice of the U.S. Supreme Court. As the U.S. Supreme

Court lost its liberal majority with the appointment of Burger and began to take a far less progressive stance on civil liberties and social equity cases, the high courts in the states began interpreting their own constitutions to establish citizen rights in their states beyond those present in the U.S. Constitution.[24] Judicial federalism is said to occur when state courts address their own state's constitutional claims first in a case, and consider federal constitutional claims only when cases cannot be resolved on state grounds. This phenomenon ties directly into the enhancement of state civil liberties in many states during the 1970s, as state supreme courts worked to secure civil rights and liberties unavailable to their citizens under the U.S. Constitution as that document was being read by the members of the conservative Burger Court.[25] This activism on the part of state supreme courts adds an important dimension to the adaptive capacity of state government in the area of the promotion of an essential element of sustainability—the promotion of social equity. Having established this capacity for court-initiated adaptation to change, this same capacity for adaptive action could be demonstrated in the area of citizen positive rights relating to governmental actions taken to address global climate change or energy shortages or access to information technology, for example; the social equity dimensions of those policies would have to pass muster with state courts even if Congress remained silent on these matters.

Constitutional Amendment Trends

Over the past two centuries U.S. states have amended and revised their constitutions for a wide variety of reasons, whether to change their fiscal structure, to modernize their practices, or to implement requirements for consistency in law coming from the federal courts. Often, though, many of these changes featured in amendments to state constitutions have been in reaction to a larger issue or policy matter arising in the nation's political discourse. We can anticipate such revisions to arise in connection with the promotion of sustainability in the years ahead as American state and local governments endeavor to adapt to the challenges of global climate change, ongoing environmental degradation, and the growing competition for and scarcity of critical natural resources.

　　The most prominent trend in state constitutional revision during the 19th century was the creation or complete revision of state constitutions through the constitutional convention process. In all, 41 states completely revised their respective constitutions a total of 94 times. Thirty of those constitutional conventions were held to create entirely new constitutions for former territories that obtained statehood, but the majority of the 94 constitutional conventions were tied to the national turmoil that came before, during, and after the American Civil War (1861–1865). Most of the states that left the Union adopted a new constitution just before or during the Civil War. During the Reconstruction Era, 10 of the Southern states used the convention process to adopt a new constitution, and other unionist states changed their state constitutions to address the change in status of African-Americans.[26] As a whole, the American states' respective constitutional agendas tended to reflect the political movements of the time, including **Jacksonian democracy** before the Civil War and the **Progressive Era** toward the end of the 19th century.[27] The aims of the Progressive reformers were reflected in the drive on the part of state legislatures and state courts alike to regulate more effectively the growing power and influence of private corporations, and to expand the suffrage beyond that of propertied white males.[28]

If the 19th century's theme with regard to constitutionalism featured the accomplishment of wholesale constitutional reform by holding many constitution conventions, then it can be said that the 20th century was a time of piecemeal reform attained through many amendments. Two possible reasons for this change are the introduction of the initiative process (the Oregon System) and the shift in the general public's perception of patriotism and sense of place. Through much of the 19th century, political activity and patriotism was centered within one's home state, but the Civil War, in the end, preserved the Union and marked a period of ascendance of national over state identity.[29] This Civil War-related outcome, combined with dramatic population growth, massive immigration from European countries, and cross-continental settlement occurring during the early 20th century made state constitutions less of a revered and out-of-reach grand symbol and more of a working document to be amended as necessary in order to govern effectively in rapidly changing times. As noted earlier in this chapter, the adoption of the constitutional initiative was part of a broad process of placing democracy more fully within the reach of the general public. This point is a key one with respect to the need for such modifications of state constitutions to promote the goals of sustainability in the 21st century.

Photo 5.4. Appomattox Courthouse. Since the Civil War, the United States has witnessed an ascendance of national over state identity.
Source: Lee Snider/Photo Images/Corbis.

The 20th century also represents a time when American states diverged widely on their approach to civil rights, with some states amending their constitutions to expand rights while others moved in the opposite direction to limit existing rights. Many Southern states took the opportunity to amend their constitutions to re-establish dimensions of white supremacy in the aftermath of Reconstruction,[30] such as North Carolina's amendments instituting a literary test and a poll tax. In stark contrast, states in the West, including Wyoming and Colorado, amended their state constitutions to establish women's suffrage well before the 19th amendment to the U.S. Constitution gave women the right to vote as a feature of American citizenship. In the latter part of the century there were numerous amendments on civil rights, and some expanding of rights that coincided with judicial federalism. Criminally accused persons were a frequent target of substantial rights restriction; of the 40 rights-restrictive amendments enacted between 1970 and 1986, 30 significantly reduced the rights of those facing criminal charges.[31]

Over time, American states have amended their constitutions to enable them to address various types of economic concerns, as well as to modify the civil liberty provisions of their foundational documents. States that came to view the power of corporate monopolies and centers of wealth as a threat to the public interest, such as the railroads and the banking and insurance industries, continued the Progressive Era efforts of the late 19th century to curb corporate influence with various constitutional amendments. These amendments permitted robust governmental regulation and shifted greater tax burdens onto these interests.[32] Just before and during the **New Deal Era**, many state constitutions were amended to facilitate various social reforms, particularly in the area of workers' rights. Some of these efforts included constitutional amendments to permit workers to unionize, to permit states to establish workers' compensation funds and minimum wage levels, and to permit states to create public agencies to promote public health and safety by allowing the inspection of private property. These amendments also gave states active oversight of child labor.[33]

While it is too early to document definitive trends in state constitutional amendments in the current century, the early years of the 21st century are somewhat reminiscent of those in the past century. Media coverage of state politics may make it appear that most constitutional amendments enacted concern very public and controversial moral issues (e.g., gay rights), but contrary to appearances the majority of state amendments enacted have not attracted the general public's attention. In fact, according to evidence systematically compiled by Albert Strum, about two thirds of all state amendments enacted in recent years deal with issues such as state and local governmental structure and debt, state agency functions, and rather arcane taxation and public finance policy.[34]

A fairly new pattern coming into play relates to a correlation between the number of constitutional amendment proposals under consideration and their occurrence in even-numbered election years. This pattern is particularly in evidence in states with the initiative process. This is no accident, of course, because thoughtful political strategists will propose a particular type of amendment as a tool to draw their respective reliable voter pool to the polls. For example, Ohio's Secretary of

State Kenneth Blackwell, who sought the Republican gubernatorial nomination in 2006, opted to delay a tax and expenditure limitation measure from 2005 to 2006 in the hopes that he would benefit from the higher turnout among conservative voters often associated with such measures.[35] In fact, there is speculation that the popularity of the 11 constitutional amendments prohibiting same-sex marriages on the 2004 presidential election ballot, particularly in the "battleground state" (i.e., highly contested state with many electoral college votes) of Ohio, may have helped George W. Bush win the closely contested presidential election over the Democratic candidate John Kerry.[36]

In the past, some state constitutional amendments were enacted to protect a state and its residents in areas in which the federal government did not extend desired protection. State environmental regulations (e.g., California's auto emission standards) and "enhanced" bills of rights are examples of this state self-protective amendment phenomenon. In 2004 California's voters approved Proposition 71, known as the California Stem Cell Research and Cures Initiative; this represents a case in which a state amended its constitution to gain relief from a restrictive federal policy (President George W. Bush's Executive Order of Aug. 9, 2001, which severely limited the number of stem cell lines eligible for federal government funding). Not only did Proposition 71, codified as California Constitutional Article 35, make stem cell research a right legally protected under the California state constitution, but it also established the California Institute for Regenerative Medicine and provided $3 billion in research funding to be allocated over a 10-year period.[37]

One interesting aspect of Proposition 71 is the impact it is having worldwide. What is considered an economic and research boon for California is giving rise to a "brain drain" for the rest of the world; premier scientists in the field of stem cell research are following the research funding and seeking out the scientific freedom to pursue their work in California research laboratories and in the state's universities.[38] Not only have several states considered legislation to compete with California, but Proposition 71 has shifted the research focus from the National Institutes of Health, the primary federal agency responsible for conducting and supporting medical research, to the U.S. states. According to Daniel Perry of the Coalition for the Advancement of Medical Research, "it's almost like the breakup of the Roman Empire."[39]

State Constitutions and Sustainability

As we indicated in the preface, a central theme of this book is the pursuit of sustainability by America's state and local governments. What role do state constitutions play in state and community sustainability? Are state constitutions to be seen as barriers to necessary societal adaptation, or as active channels for change in the promotion of sustainability and institutional resilience? Some critical observers of state government argue that state constitutions are deeply flawed, and that they have become rigid, time-bound documents reflecting only piecemeal changes with no appropriate plan for societal adaptation to change. Given their alleged hidebound nature, these governing documents require ever more amendments so that the states can govern somewhat effectively under their ponderous provisions. In adding amendment after amendment, the problem of new barriers to change is made worse yet. It follows from this reasoning that there is considerable potential for a state's constitution to become a barrier to state and local government sustainability. If this is a fair characterization, then it follows that state constitutions have grown into unmanageable documents that inhibit the flexibility required for state and local governments to adapt to major events such as global climate change. Considering that there have been over 7,000 amendments to state constitutions, some of these amendments may well become barriers to effective adaptation.

In reviewing the history of state constitutional amendments and revisions with an objective frame of mind, however, it would seem that the many changes introduced by constitutional amendments were very often a reasonable response to the politics and major issues of concern of the time. The constitutional amendments adopted in the late 19th and early 20th centuries by and large represented alterations that were in keeping with Progressive Era politics, where reformers moved toward the timely professionalization of state and local government and the introduction

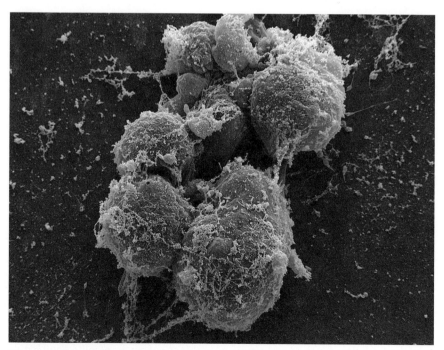

Photo 5.5. Embryonic stem cells: a constitutional issue.
Source: David Scharf/Science Faction/Corbis.

Constitutionalism: What Can I Do?

Toward the beginning of this chapter we reported some survey data showing very low levels of knowledge among youth concerning the constitution, rights, and civic knowledge in general (see Table 5.1). According to the authors of the classic study *What Americans Know About Politics and Why it Matters*, political scientists Michael Delli Carpini and Scott Keeter convincingly argue that "democracy functions best when its citizens are politically informed" (1996: 1)[39]. Here are two ways you can test your level of awareness:

1. Take the Intercollegiate Studies Institute "Civic Quiz" online and see how you fare: http://www.americancivicliteracy.org/resources/quiz.aspx
2. See how well you would do with the "100 Typical Questions Asked By Immigration and Naturalization Service Examiners" for U.S. citizenship: http://portal.cuny.edu/cms/id/cuny/documents/informationpage/002887.htm

of means to promote direct democracy through the initiative process. Later in the 20th century, the New Deal Era moved state constitutions towards social reform in the same way, often employing the means allowed by the constitutional amendment process.[40]

Thus, one could argue the state constitutional amendment processes themselves neither promote nor bar progress toward community sustainability or resilience, but that history teaches that the political will of the states at any particular time has been incorporated effectively into state constitutions through the amendment process. In the past, American states have amended their constitutions frequently in response to political and social movements of the time. As society's attention moves more fully to meeting the challenge of global climate change and sustainable development, it seems clear from our assessment of the states' track record of historical adaptation that state constitutions will be able to incorporate appropriate provisions into state constitutions. As demonstrated with California's Proposition 71, if one state can adopt an amendment that has a positive impact on the state, a number of other states will likely follow suit.

Of the three basic methods of constitutional amendment available to the states, which is best suited to promote sustainability? While the constitutional convention would be the most efficient method, allowing a thorough revision of the constitution, the potential of such a tool being used in this age of partisan politics and highly organized special interests is quite remote. The legislative amendment method has potential in some states; however, the requirement for a super-majority of both legislative houses may pose a difficult barrier in many states. The popular initiative, which is available in only 18 states, is the most likely method to be used to promote sustainability in American state and local government. A powerful tool for change, the popular initiative could be used by state-based grassroots groups to place a single amendment at a time on the ballot. Sufficient voter signatures must be garnered, and the amendment would need to win the popular vote in statewide balloting. With the impacts of global climate change becoming more apparent—for example, rising sea levels, more frequent and more violent storms, earlier snow-melt, extended droughts, raging wildfires and fires in heavily forested areas—some states with the initiative process are likely to see ballot initiatives directed toward the promotion of sustainable development and local community resilience into their constitutional fabric.[41] The non-initiative states will be witness to these developments in other states and are likely to take up their own versions of these initiatives through legislative action. It is a safe bet that American states will be at the forefront of "thinking globally and acting locally" to confront the challenges of sustainable development, and that a likely goal of the advocates of sustainability will be achieving timely amendments to state constitutions.[42]

The New "Constitutions" of Sustainable Governance

While state constitutions are important vehicles for promoting the value and institutional shifts associated with sustainable governance, the formal constitution may not move quickly enough in response to changing needs or conditions. Traditional governance viewed many aspects of the constitution and institutional arrangements as steady and continuous. Sustainable governance requires that the constitution be viewed as a general governing structure; however, it is clear that the actual day-to-day process of governance operates as a form of organized chaos, responding to changing conditions, meeting ever-changing demands, and responding to rapid technological change and scientific discovery.

The new "constitutions" of sustainable governance have actually been around for quite a while, but they are playing an increasingly prominent role in sustainability. The **intergovernmental agreement** (IGA) and the **memorandum of understanding** (MOU) are two such important legal/institutional tools available to promote sustainability in the coming years. Intergovernmental agreements are directly related to federalism and multistate arrangements within the American federal system. Intergovernmentalism might involve national–state or national–local agreements or interstate and interlocal agreements of various kinds. IGAs often recognize the interjurisdictional nature of many problems (e.g., the drug trade, human trafficking, rapid diffusion of communicable diseases, acid rain), with sustainability being one very important current dilemma. In terms of sustainability, the basic question faced by any level of government is: "Can we maintain the existing conditions or achieve an even higher quality of life and provide basic services to future generations of citizens?" Achieving a positive outcome may involve governments working together in a manner in which all achieve positive results and no party loses. IGAs are an attempt to achieve this positive "win/win" outcome for a reasonable cost, while retaining the benefits of responsiveness and the unique nature of each participating governing body.

MOUs are legal documents comparable to contracts that define the responsibilities and constraints faced by each governmental party engaged in a mutual effort to achieve a shared policy goal. MOUs define the goals and responsibilities of each participating government, often focusing on particular agencies within these governments. In an era of rapid response to emerging problems of sustainability, the service legal agreement (SLA), a specific form of MOU, defines the nature of response by each participating government and each government agency to include agreed-upon forms of intergovernmental and interagency planning and communication.

The proliferation of IGAs, MOUs, and SLAs in recent years is in part an appropriate recognition of the need for sustainable governance networks that respond to change rapidly, effectively, and efficiently while maintaining the higher-order values of the formal constitutional arrangements of participating jurisdictions. This capacity to invent new forms of interagency relationships among the states and their local governments is very important, not only because coordinated action is facilitated, but also because this process allows citizens to take an active part in their own state and local governments. Sound research instructs us that there is a strong association between the level of citizen engagement and the scale of government;[43] if communities were to pass all problems on to the national government for resolution, they would likely risk an even greater disengagement of citizens than the one now present in state and local governments.

Conclusion

State constitutions are a very important aspect of American state and local government because they set forth the supreme law of the state, subservient to the U.S. Constitution only where there is direct federal authority to act. Among other things, state constitutions establish procedures for policymaking, define the structure of state and local government, set the conditions for interstate and multistate compacts, set forth requirements for public office, specify state obligations to citizens, enshrine principles of governance, determine the responsibilities of local governments, establish voting rights and determine how elections are to be conducted, and specify processes for constitutional change. These are all important functions at any time, but they are of great importance in a time when the challenges of sustainability will confront the leaders of our state and local governments.

The most important function of state constitutions, however, is to establish the rule of law and enforce the principle of limited government. All 50 state constitutions provide protections for individual liberty, and freedom of speech and association. Most state constitutions recognize a right to privacy. While these rights mostly reiterate protections provided in the U.S. Constitution, many state constitutions extend right-based protections for their citizens beyond what is found in the national constitution as it is read by the U.S. Supreme Court. State constitutions may offer this same extension for the protection of citizens and their property in the area of sustainable development and local community resilience. Scholars who have studied the capacity for Americans to gain an understanding of difficult public policy issues and in time develop attitudes and policy preferences in line with needed change provide reason for optimism in this regard.[44] There are early signs of change in the public's understanding of sustainability noted in this chapter, and it is likely that much more change will be handled by government at the state level as spelled out in amendments to state constitutions.

Key Terms

Civil liberties	Memorandum of understanding
Civil service	New Deal Era
Constitutional convention	Oregon System
Constitutional democracy	Progressive Era
General purpose government	Republican government
Intergovernmental agreement	Reserved powers
Jacksonian democracy	Special purpose districts
Judicial federalism	Supremacy clause

Discussion Questions

1. What are the primary purposes of state constitutions? How are they both similar to and different from the U.S. Constitution?
2. What are some of the guiding principles found in state governments? From your own point of view, what types of guiding principles belong and do not belong in state constitutions?
3. What are the various procedures available to change constitutions? What methods are available in your state to change the constitution? What is your assessment of the degree to which the states have established an historical track record of adaptability to change in their pattern of constitutional amendments?
4. How do you feel about the "Oregon System" in terms of state constitutional amendments? What are some of the positive and negative aspects of allowing citizens to directly amend state constitutions through general election ballot measures?

CHAPTER 6

Legislatures

Introduction

A *legislature* is an officially elected assembly formed to make laws for a political unit such as a nation, a state, or a local government. Legislatures can be traced back to the medieval period, when "Althing" (a Nordic word for "general assembly") was established in Iceland and a uniform code of laws was proclaimed. In more modern historical times, there are various types of legislative forms, including the two most common categories of legislatures—**presidential style** systems featuring separation of powers and **parliamentary style** systems featuring integration of powers.[1] As discussed in the previous chapter, in political systems reflecting a separation of powers philosophy of governance, a dichotomy between policy adoption versus policy administration and implementation exists, separating the legislative branch and the executive branch; in line with this demarcation of responsibilities, governmental powers are fairly clearly separated in law and in practice.[2] In contrast, in political systems reflecting an integration of powers philosophy of governance, members of the executive branch are selected from and are held directly accountable to the legislative branch.[3] In the United States, state legislatures are presidential style bodies that are primarily in charge of making laws of general purpose and universal application for the respective states, with governors being responsible for the "faithful execution" of state laws. At the local level both **general-purpose governments** and **single-purpose governments** are present. The former provide a wide range of services and serve a diversity of functions, while the latter carry out a specific function such as education, the operation of utilities, the irrigation of farmlands, or transportation services, for example. There are a variety of legislative structures used in local governments, including boards of county commissioners, city councils, school district boards, and a wide variety of more specialized elective boards and commissions that will be discussed in this chapter.

The topics covered in this chapter include:

- The functions of legislatures
- Noteworthy variation in the ways state legislatures operate
- Legislatures in general-purpose local governments
- Legislatures in single-purpose local governments
- The critical legislative role in promoting sustainability

State Legislatures

All U.S. states have a popularly elected legislative branch, and each state constitution specifies the composition and method of organization of state legislative bodies. State legislatures are the primary lawmaking bodies of American government, and they are, generally speaking, quite similar in structure to the U.S. Congress. The legislature in all cases is a multimember body of popularly elected representatives. In 49 states the legislature is divided into two houses, generally a Senate and a House of Representatives, just like the U.S. Congress. Only Nebraska features a unicameral (one chamber) legislature. The "upper house" (Senate) is usually significantly smaller than the lower house, which in most states is called the "House of Representatives." Senators are most often elected for 4-year terms, but some states elect their senators every 2 years. State representatives usually are elected for 2-year terms. In many states constitutional **term limits** control the number of terms, consecutive or otherwise, a legislator is allowed to serve. Most states dictate that each legislative electoral district will elect only one representative and only one senator. However, eight states do allow multimember districts in which voters elect more than one representative for the lower house of the state legislature.

Nearly all of the American states adopted the bicameral legislature in major part because they wished to allow landowners a major voice in government disproportionate to their number in the electorate. Senators were once elected by county or groups of counties as opposed to population, in a manner similar to the U.S. Senate's apportionment of two senators per state regardless of the size of its population. This apportionment of seats in the upper chamber allowed residents in rural and sparsely populated areas of a state to exercise significantly more influence than urban residents within American state legislatures. In 1962 (*Baker v. Carr*) and again in 1964 (*Reynolds v. Sims*), however, the U.S. Supreme Court agreed to hear cases in which it was argued that the equal protection clause of the 14th Amendment to the U.S. Constitution required that the principle of "one person, one vote" should apply to **both** houses of American state legislatures. Lawyers arguing for a fundamental change in the organization of state legislatures reasoned that the U.S. Congress organized membership around a principle of representation by geography because it is a federal system in which the individual states preexisted the establishment of the United States of America. In the case of the U.S. states, however, they are each unitary governments in which all citizens, regardless of where they reside (city, suburb, or

Photo 6.1. Nebraska State Capitol. Nebraska is the only state with a unicameral legislature.
Source: © Darksidephotos | Dreamstime.com

rural area), are entitled to equal representation.

The U.S. Supreme Court determined in these landmark cases that both chambers of American state legislatures must be based upon population alone. The initial result of these decisions was that state legislatures redrew their upper chamber legislative district lines to reflect population, causing many more legislators to be representing urban areas in upper chambers of American state governments. These legislative districts must be redistricted every 10 years when the U.S. Census is taken to ensure that they conform to the equal representation ("one person, one vote") standard as closely as possible.

While the manifest intent of redistricting is to ensure equal representation in government, the process of drawing legislative district lines is the responsibility of state legislatures, and it tends to become highly politicized and partisan in states that do not establish an independent, bipartisan body to carry out redistricting. In fact, in a number of states, district lines are commonly redrawn to maximize the strength of the majority party and weaken the minority party in a process known as **gerrymandering**. This process entails concentrating the minority party's voters in as few districts as possible, and distributing the majority party's voters in such a way that they are likely to prevail in as many legislative districts as possible.

As the process of gerrymandering indicates, political parties play a very important role in state legislatures. The majority party typically organizes the election of the leader of the lower house (the House Speaker in most cases), and in most states the leader of the upper house (typically the Senate Majority Leader) is put into office on the basis of a partisan vote. The party leadership in both chambers generally appoints legislators to their committee assignments, designates committee chairs in the case of the majority party, and typically controls floor activity fairly tightly. As a result of these decisions influenced greatly by the majority political party, a relatively small number of key legislators in control of a legislative house typically dominate the agenda and content of bills heard during a legislative session.

The powers of state legislatures universally include modifying existing laws and making new statutes, developing the state government's budget,[4] confirming the executive appointments brought before the legislature,[5] and impeaching governors and removing from office other members of the executive branch.[6] All these powers and associated activities can be assigned into one of the three major functions performed by state legislators singularly and state legislatures collectively: *representation, lawmaking,* and *balancing the power of the executive (or oversight).*

Representation

A major role of a state legislator is to represent the needs and concerns of the people residing in her or his legislative district. Since legislators are responsible to a relatively small number of constituents coming from a specific geographical area, they are able to address concerns that are not as apparent to statewide officials such as the governor or state attorney general. This attention to localized needs can lead to intense debate over conflicting values when, for example, representatives of rural, conservative communities are forced to compromise with the interests of urban legislators representing liberal constituents.

Legislators also represent the interests of their constituents beyond the formal lawmaking process. Legislators are often enlisted to make a phone call or write a letter on behalf of a citizen who needs help getting a personal issue addressed or expedited by the state bureaucracy. Research conducted by political scientists has shown that such **constituency service** pays significant dividends at re-election time, with voters looking favorably on helpful legislators by either volunteering for campaign work or contributing money to re-election campaigns. Key components of sustainability as addressed in the literature include the development of civil society, active representation by elected officials, and the maintenance of continuous interaction between citizens and representatives. In this regard, how legislators interact with their constituents is an important part of the promotion of sustainability in communities where efforts to promote sustainability require some level of state approval or financial support.

The process of representation works at two distinct levels. First, at an individual representative's level there is a connection between the legislator and her or his district. And secondly, as a unit the legislature pursues policies that reflect the statewide interests and preferences of citizens.[7] The process of representation, from the perspective of political scientists, consists of four principal components: maintaining communications with constituents; demonstrating policy responsiveness by reflecting the needs of one's constituency in one's votes on bills and budgets; affecting the allocation of resources across elective districts; and providing individualized service to constituents.[8]

Another way to think about representation is in terms of the sociodemographic and gender composition of state and local legislative bodies. Many observers argue that legislative bodies should, to some significant extent, mirror the public they represent, in terms of race, ethnicity, gender, and such, to adequately represent the public at large. In this regard, "in the past, political scientists have convincingly demonstrated that race and gender matter in political representation."[9] Research has consistently shown that in state legislatures "Black legislators sponsor a higher number of Black interest measures and female legislators sponsor a higher number of women's interest measures" when compared to white men.[10]

In general, "female state legislators are reported to be more liberal than men, even when controlling for party membership, and female state legislators are more concerned with feminist issues than their male counterparts."[11] Research has also found that black women legislators are similar to white women legislators in terms of their support for "women's issues" (e.g., affirmative action, comparable worth, public support for day care). As with black male legislators, black female legislators tend to be strong supporters of minority-targeted policies such as education, healthcare, and job creation-oriented economic development.[12] However, research has also found that female legislators are generally as likely as their male counterparts to achieve passage of the legislation they introduce, whereas black legislators are significantly less likely than their white counterparts to get legislation they introduce enacted into law.[13]

In terms of the actual representation of women and minorities in state and local legislatures, there has been a noteworthy increase in numbers over the past several decades.[14] The Center for American Women and Politics, an organization that tracks the number of women in elected office, reports the following in terms of white women and women of color serving in state legislatures across the country (Table 6.1):[15]

- In 2008, 1,741 (23.6%) of the 7,382 state legislators in the United States were women. Women held 423 (21.5%) of the 1,971 state senate seats and 1,318 (24.4%) of the 5,411 state house seats. Since 1971, the number of women serving in state legislatures has more than quintupled.
- Of the 1,741 women state legislators serving nationwide, 354 (20.3%) were women of color. They included 96 senators and 258 representatives; 329 were Democrats and 25 were Republicans. Women of color constituted 4.8% of the total 7,382 state legislators.

Male minorities were similarly underrepresented in state and local legislatures. For example, "there are 27 states and the District of Columbia that have African American mayors. The cities' populations range from less than 300 to over 2 million people."[16] Some of the explanations given for the lower levels of women and minorities in state and local legislative bodies include cultural, institutional, and situational explanations.[17] Cultural explanations would include state political culture, which would affect the attitudes toward women and minorities in politics held by citizens and elites.[18] Some argue that states with more traditional political cultures deeply entrenched in history (e.g., the Southern states) may view politics as a man's world or the domain of white Americans, in comparison to states with more progressive political cultures (e.g., the Northeastern or Western states) (Table 6.2).[19] For women, this political culture aspect of the political environment can have three specific adverse consequences:[20]

First, women may not run for office because they do not believe it to be appropriate. Second, women may not be highly recruited to run for political office because party officials and other political elites are biased against female candidates. Or third, even women who are not socialized into passive gender roles and who do run despite unsupportive elites face unsympathetic voters at the polls…

A second explanation for the low levels of women and minorities in state and local legislatures concerns the institutional arrangements determining electoral success. For example, states with high levels of incumbents re-elected to office would allow for fewer seats being open to competition.[21] In addition, states with multimember districts versus states with single-member districts tend to have racially, ethnically, and gender-wise more diverse legislatures.[22] It has been argued that voters are more willing to support women and minorities when there are multiple choices to make in an electoral setting. A third explanation for the lower levels of women and minorities in state and local legislative bodies concerns situational factors such as financial resources, educational levels, and occupation, which all affect the ability to run for office and to establish important political networks to support successful campaigns. In addition, "women tend to start much later in politics than men, are less likely to be recruited than men, and have more political opportunities closed to them than men."[23]

Those who favor legislative diversity have proposed a variety of electoral mechanisms to increase the number of women and racial minorities serving in state and local legislative bodies. Some have suggested the broadened adoption of term limits because the current re-election rate of incumbents is very high, while others have suggested the creation of majority black or Latino districts by carefully drawing election district lines to favor minority districts.[24] This latter approach to the promotion of diversity in legislative bodies was struck down by the U.S. Supreme Court in *Miller v. Johnson 515 U.S. 900* (1995) and *Shaw v. Hunt 517 U.S. 899* (1996).

Table 6.1. Women in State Legislatures

Year	Women Legislators	% of Total	Year	Women Legislators	% of Total	Year	Women Legislators	% of Total
1971	344	4.5	1987	1,170	15.7	2000	1,670	22.5
1973	424	5.6	1989	1,270	17.0	2001	1,666	22.4
1975	604	8.0	1991	1,368	18.3	2002	1,682	22.7
1977	688	9.1	1993	1,524	20.5	2003	1,654	22.4
1979	770	10.3	1995	1,532	20.6	2004	1,659	22.5
1981	908	12.1	1997	1,605	21.6	2005	1,674	22.7
1983	991	13.3	1998	1,617	21.8	2006	1,681	22.8
1985	1,103	14.8	1999	1,664	22.4	2007	1,732	23.5
						2008	1,741	23.6

Source: Center for Women and Politics, Eagleton Institute of Politics, Rutgers, The State University of New Jersey. URL: www.cawp.rutgers.edu (see note 15).

Table 6.2. States with Highest and Lowest Percentage of Female Legislators, 2008

Highest		Lowest	
State	**% Women**	**State**	**% Women**
Vermont	37.8	South Carolina	8.8
New Hampshire	35.6	Oklahoma	12.8
Washington	35.4	Alabama	12.9
Colorado	35.0	Kentucky	13.0
Minnesota	34.8	West Virginia	14.2

Source: Center for Women and Politics, Eagleton Institute of Politics, Rutgers, The State University of New Jersey. URL: www.cawp.rutgers.edu (see note 15).

Lawmaking

Policymaking is accomplished through the introduction and passage of bills that eventually become law. The process usually begins with the introduction of bills in either house of the legislature. While bills must be introduced by a legislator, they usually have been crafted by a governor, an attorney general, a public agency, or an interest group. Once a legislator chooses to introduce a piece of legislation, other representatives and senators can sign on as co-sponsors, increasing the chance that the bill will survive scrutiny in legislative committees. New bills are referred to policy committees in their chamber of origin. The committee chair decides whether to hold a hearing on the bill, and whether to hold a committee vote on it. Bills are frequently amended in committee before they are voted out. If the vote in committee is favorable, the bill is forwarded to a rules committee, which decides which bills are placed on the calendar of the chamber to be heard. Bills can be amended once more on the floor, and if passed they are sent to the other chamber for its consideration. If the second chamber amends the bill and passes it, then the bill must return to its chamber of origin for reconsideration as amended. In some cases the two chambers will designate a conference committee and seek a compromise measure. If a compromise is achieved, the new bill is sent back to the floor of the Senate and House for a final vote. If the conference committee bill is approved in both houses of the legislature it is then sent to the governor, where it will be signed into law, will be vetoed, or will remain unsigned. If a bill is vetoed by the governor, it can return to the legislature for a possible veto override by a "super-majority" (usually two-thirds vote) in both chambers. If a governor neither signs nor vetoes a bill, it will become law in two thirds of the states; in the remaining third of the states inaction by the governor is referred to as a "pocket veto" and the bill dies (Fig. 6.1). Another way for a bill to become law in some states is a **legislative referral**, an action by the legislature and the governor that places the legislation on the ballot for voters to approve or disapprove.

Balancing the Power of the Executive

In a separation of powers governmental system, the three branches of government are expected to share power rather than allowing one branch to have disproportionate power over the others. This arrangement of governmental powers has been commonly known as the **checks and balances** system, a particular vision of governmental design enshrined in the U.S. Constitution by the Founding Fathers. The third principal role a legislature plays, therefore, is balancing the power of executive. This balancing role can be achieved by performing **legislative oversight**, which involves the legislature's review and evaluation of selected activities of the executive branch and exercising the "power of the purse"—that is, carrying out the responsibility of developing the state budget. In American government no funds can be spent by an executive agency unless an express allocation is made by a legislative enactment (the budget is set in a bill enacted into law just as any other statute). A main reason for state legislatures to conduct oversight is that "it has a duty to ensure existing programs are implemented and administered efficiently, effectively, and

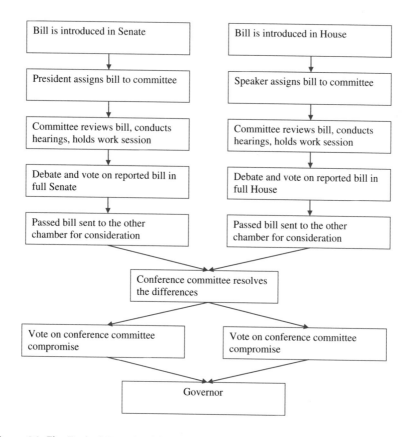

Figure 6.1. The Typical State Legislative Process

in a manner consistent with legislative intent."[25] The job of exercising legislative oversight is carried out by a combination of **standing committees**, **select committees**, and **task forces**.[26] In Ohio, for example, three such important oversight committees are the Joint Legislative Committee on Health Care Oversight, the Joint Legislative Committee on Medicaid Technology and Reform, and the Turnpike Legislative Review Committee, composed of members of both chambers of the state legislature.[27] Common forms of oversight activities include periodically reviewing **administrative rules**, enacting **sunset provisions** in legislation, passing legislation calling for studies into particular problems or existing programs, engaging in active fiscal oversight and providing advice to executive agencies, and granting consent to gubernatorial appointments.

State legislatures assume the role of oversight to ensure that laws are being implemented efficiently and effectively in the manner originally intended by the legislature. The legislature often evaluates the executive branch's policy and programs by employing policy analysts and auditors working for legislative committees. These analysts and auditors attempt to assess progress toward the objectives and goals of policies and agencies reflecting the original intent of the legislation. The use of legislative policy analyses and audits has been credited with increasing efficiency and effectiveness in state government, thereby saving taxpayers money and improving program performance.

Legislatures periodically review the rules and regulations used by the executive branch to determine whether the intent of the law is being realized. This review process often accompanies budget hearings and ultimate budget approval for state agencies. If the legislature determines that an agency's rules and regulations are unsatisfactory, they can insist that the rules be modified or suspended; in some cases the legislature retains the right to discontinue support for a program if, in its judgment, the agency in question is not following legislative intent or is determined to have failed to meet the goals set for it. Some states have determined that the "legislative veto" (an action of constraint upon a public agency by a legislature after legislation has been placed into law) is an unlawful violation of the separation of powers. Even without explicitly revoking a rule or regulation by direct action of the legislature after a law has been duly enacted, the legislature can exert great influence over previously enacted statutes by reducing the agency's budgetary allotment in order to encourage more faithful compliance with legislative wishes.

Sunset laws are pieces of legislation featuring a built-in expiration date for a statute. Legislation of this nature allows the legislature to review, implement changes in, or terminate a program simply by not renewing an existing law. While sunset laws ensure the bureaucracy will be subjected to periodic review, the process of review is often time-consuming and can be quite costly; it only rarely results in the termination of a program. According to Bowman and Kearney, "sunset reviews are said to increase agency compliance with legislative intent . . . [but] only 13 percent of the agencies reviewed are eventually terminated, thus making termination more of a threat than an objective reality."[28]

The review and control of state (and federal "pass-through") funds is one of the most significant powers exercised by state legislatures. By holding the purse strings at both the state and federal level, the independence of the legislative branch ensures that the bureaucracy and executive branch agency leadership remains quite dependent upon legislative support. Thus, oversight is permitted and the executive branch is prevented from becoming unresponsive to lawmakers and their constituency. Furthermore, by reviewing and controlling federal funds given to the state through intergovernmental programs such as interstate transportation, environmental regulation, Medicaid, and so forth, legislators are aware of how that federal government transfer money is being spent by the executive branch. Citizens who wish to know how federal funds are being spent in their state and localities can contact their legislator and request an accounting. This type of constituent service is an important part of legislative representation. In the area of the promotion of sustainability, your state legislator should be able to provide you with specific, timely information concerning what federal and state programs are in place to address sustainability concerns.

Variation Among State Legislatures

State legislatures vary across the country in terms of their official names, the length of time they stay in session, the number of legislative districts they use, their party affiliations, and the way they operate. For example, state legislatures in most states are called "Legislatures" (e.g., the Alabama Legislature, the Oklahoma Legislature, the Nevada Legislature, and the Montana State Legislature). In some states, however, the state legislature is referred to as the "General Assembly" (e.g., the Virginia General Assembly and the Pennsylvania General Assembly). In Massachusetts and New Hampshire the term "General Court" is used to designate the state legislative branch. For bicameral state legislative bodies, the upper house is most typically called the "Senate," but the terms used for the lower house vary widely (Table 6.3). Historically, most of the original American colonies were governed by unicameral legislative systems until a gradual process of adoption of bicameralism started and picked up momentum.[29] The bicameralism movement was based on respect for the British model of bicameralism of the House of Lords and the House of Commons.[30] Today, as noted previously, all but one state legislatures in the United States are bicameral; only Nebraska has maintained a unicameral legislature (Table 6.4).

Another difference between state legislatures concerns time status—some states have full-time legislatures meeting frequently on an annual basis, while other states have part-time legislatures that meet biannually and infrequently. Many rural states tend to have a part-time legislature, while the states with larger populations are likely to have full-time legislatures. Texas is an exception in this regard, with the second-largest population and a part-time legislature.[31] The National Council of State Legislatures has categorized the 50 state legislatures into three basic groups:

Table 6.3. State Legislative Houses

State	Both Bodies	Upper House	Lower House
Alabama	Legislature	Senate	House of Representatives
Alaska	Legislature	Senate	House of Representatives
Arizona	Legislature	Senate	House of Representatives
Arkansas	General Assembly	Senate	House of Representatives
California	Legislature	Senate	Assembly
Colorado	General Assembly	Senate	House of Representatives
Connecticut	General Assembly	Senate	House of Representatives
Delaware	General Assembly	Senate	House of Representatives
Florida	Legislature	Senate	House of Representatives
Georgia	General Assembly	Senate	House of Representatives
Hawaii	Legislature	Senate	House of Representatives
Idaho	Legislature	Senate	House of Representatives
Illinois	General Assembly	Senate	House of Representatives
Indiana	General Assembly	Senate	House of Representatives
Iowa	General Assembly	Senate	House of Representatives
Kansas	Legislature	Senate	House of Representatives
Kentucky	General Assembly	Senate	House of Representatives
Louisiana	Legislature	Senate	House of Representatives
Maine	Legislature	Senate	House of Representatives
Maryland	General Assembly	Senate	House of Delegates
Massachusetts	General Court	Senate	House of Representatives
Michigan	Legislature	Senate	House of Representatives
Minnesota	Legislature	Senate	House of Representatives
Mississippi	Legislature	Senate	House of Representatives
Missouri	General Assembly	Senate	House of Representatives
Montana	Legislature	Senate	House of Representatives
Nebraska	Legislature	—	—
Nevada	Legislature	Senate	Assembly
New Hampshire	General Court	Senate	House of Representatives
New Jersey	Legislature	Senate	General Assembly
New Mexico	Legislature	Senate	House of Representatives
New York	Legislature	Senate	Assembly
North Carolina	General Assembly	Senate	House of Representatives
North Dakota	Legislative Assembly	Senate	House of Representatives
Ohio	General Assembly	Senate	House of Representatives
Oklahoma	Legislature	Senate	House of Representatives
Oregon	Legislative Assembly	Senate	House of Representatives
Pennsylvania	General Assembly	Senate	House of Representatives
Rhode Island	General Assembly	Senate	House of Representatives
South Carolina	General Assembly	Senate	House of Representatives
South Dakota	Legislature	Senate	House of Representatives
Tennessee	General Assembly	Senate	House of Representatives
Texas	Legislature	Senate	House of Representatives
Utah	Legislature	Senate	House of Representatives
Vermont	General Assembly	Senate	House of Representatives
Virginia	General Assembly	Senate	House of Delegates
Washington	Legislature	Senate	House of Representatives
West Virginia	Legislature	Senate	House of Delegates
Wisconsin	Legislature	Senate	Assembly
Wyoming	Legislature	Senate	House of Representatives

Adapted from: Council of State Governments, *The Book of the States, 2007* (see note 36).

Table 6.4. Unicameral Legislature and Bicameral Legislature

Indicators	Unicameral Legislature	Bicameral Legislature
Representation	A citizen has one representative.	A citizen has two representatives.
Responsiveness to the Majority	Favors rule by the majority	Bicameral deliberation
Responsiveness to Diverse and Minority Interests	Deeper understanding of all various interests	Gives voice to disparate points of views
Responsiveness to Powerful Interests	"Almost heaven" for the special lobbyists	Hard for lobbyists to affect legislative activities
Legislative Stability	Not necessarily volatile	May be more stable
Procedural Simplicity	More	Less
Authority of Legislators	Authority of a legislator is not shared.	Authority of a legislator is shared
Concentration of Power Within the Legislature	Concentrates power in one house	Concentrates power in a few members
Quality of Decision-Making	Promotes quality by deliberate, careful decision-making	Promotes quality by slowing decision-making, by having a second thought, and by requiring approval by two chambers
Efficiency and Economy	May be more efficient in conducting its business and less costly to operate	May be more costly but also may generate more benefits

Source: G. Tsebelis and J. Money, *Bicameralism* (Cambridge, UK: Cambridge University Press, 1997).

full-time legislatures, hybrid legislatures, and part-time legislatures. Full-time legislatures "require the most time of legislators, usually 80 percent or more of a full-time job."[32] These legislatures typically feature large staffs and their members are usually paid salaries sufficient to make a decent living. Full-time legislatures are typically found in states with highly urbanized populations (Tables 6.5 and 6.6).

Legislators elected to hybrid legislatures "typically say that they spend more than two-thirds of a full time job being legislators" and their salaries are noticeably higher than part-time legislatures but somewhat lower than those of members of full-time legislatures.[33] Salaries are typically not sufficient to make a living on legislative pay alone, so additional outside employment is common among these state lawmakers. Hybrid legislatures tend to have intermediate-sized staffs, and they are typically found in states with moderate-sized populations.

Lawmakers in part-time legislatures generally spend "the equivalent of half of a full-time job doing legislative work. The compensation they receive for this work is quite low and requires them to have other sources of income in order to make a living."[34] Part-time legislatures are often called "citizen legislatures" and are most often found in rural states with relatively small populations. Fewer legislative staff

Photo 6.2. California has a full-time legislature.
Source: © Cosenco | Dreamstime.com

members are available to law-makers in these states.

State legislatures are also diverse in terms of their size and their party composition. Legislators prefer policies that favor the preferences of voters in individual districts, and thus the size of a district matters when considering the implications of certain policies. Table 6.7 shows the number of seats in state upper and lower houses. While some economists have argued that larger legislatures are less efficient and prone to conflict because "cooperation cannot be sustained in large legislatures," there has been little empirical research on this topic.[35]

In terms of partisan alignment, in 2006 Democrats gained a sizable majority of all legislative seats and won their biggest legislative victory in more than a decade. In 2007, Democratic majorities took control of both houses in 22 state legislatures, and Republican majorities control both houses in 15 states. In the other 12 states the two parties split control of the state legislature, with one party having supremacy in one house and the other party controling of the other chamber (Table 6.8).[36]

The number of bills introduced into legislatures and enacted into law also varies greatly across the states. For example, 17,000 bills were introduced and 750 bills were enacted into law in New York in 2006. In stark contrast, there were only 213 bills introduced and 121 bills enacted into law in Wyoming in the same year. Table 6.9 compares the number of bills introduced and enacted in 2006 regular sessions of the state legislatures.

Legislatures in General-Purpose Local Government

General-purpose local governments, which include county governments, municipal governments, and town and township governments, provide a wide range of services that affect the day-to-day lives of citizens. Services such as police protection; road, street, and bridge infrastructure; parks and recreation; and land use (zoning) are typical duties of general-purpose governments in the United States. These governments feature both an executive and legislative function, and the executive function is discussed elsewhere. This section focuses on the legislative role

Table 6.5 State Legislature Types

Full-Time	Hybrid	Part-Time
California	Alabama	Georgia
Florida	Alaska	Idaho
Illinois	Arizona	Indiana
Massachusetts	Arkansas	Kansas
New Jersey	Colorado	Maine
Michigan	Connecticut	Mississippi
New York	Delaware	Montana
Ohio	Hawaii	Nevada
Pennsylvania	Iowa	New Hampshire
Wisconsin	Kentucky	New Mexico
	Louisiana	North Dakota
	Maryland	Rhode Island
	Minnesota	South Dakota
	Missouri	Utah
	Nebraska	Vermont
	North Carolina	West Virginia
	Oklahoma	Wyoming
	Oregon	
	South Carolina	
	Tennessee	
	Texas	
	Virginia	
	Washington	

Adapted from: National Conference of State Legislatures, 2008. *Full- and Part-Time Legislatures.* URL: http://www.ncsl.org/programs/press/2004/backgrounder_fullandpart.htm

Table 6.6. **Legislative Job Time, Salary, and Staff Size**

Legislature Type	Average Time on Job[1]	Average Compensation[2]	Average Staff per Member[3]
Full-time	80%	$68,599	8.9
Hybrid	70%	$35,326	3.1
Part-time	54%	$15,984	1.2

1. Estimated proportion of a full-time job spent on legislative work
2. Estimated annual salary of an average legislator, including per diem
3. Ratio of total legislative staff to number of legislators

Adapted from: National Conference of State Legislatures, 2008. *Full- and Part-Time Legislatures.* URL: http://www.ncsl.org/programs/press/2004/backgrounder_fullandpart.htm

of general-purpose local governments, whose legislative bodies are county boards of commissioners, city councils, and town boards of aldermen or selectmen.

County Commissions

Counties function primarily as the administrative appendages of a state, and thus they implement many state laws and policies (such as carrying out elections) at the local level. The central legislative body in a county government is commonly a board of "commissioners" or "supervisors." Typically, a county commission meets in regular session monthly or bimonthly, and its legislative responsibilities encompass

Table 6.7. Seats in State Senates and Houses

State	Seats in Senate	Seats in House
Alabama	35	105
Alaska	20	40
Arizona	30	60
Arkansas	35	100
California	40	80
Colorado	35	65
Connecticut	36	151
Delaware	21	41
Florida	40	120
Georgia	56	180
Hawaii	25	51
Idaho	35	70
Illinois	59	118
Indiana	50	100
Iowa	50	100
Kansas	40	125
Kentucky	38	100
Louisiana	39	105
Maine	35	151
Maryland	47	141
Massachusetts	40	160
Michigan	38	110
Minnesota	67	134
Mississippi	52	122
Missouri	34	163
Montana	50	100
Nebraska	49	Unicameral
Nevada	21	42
New Hampshire	24	400
New Jersey	40	80
New Mexico	42	70
New York	62	150
North Carolina	50	120
North Dakota	47	94
Ohio	33	99
Oklahoma	48	101
Oregon	30	60
Pennsylvania	50	203
Rhode Island	38	75
South Carolina	46	124
South Dakota	35	70
Tennessee	33	99
Texas	31	150
Utah	29	75
Vermont	30	150
Virginia	40	100
Washington	49	98
West Virginia	34	100
Wisconsin	33	99
Wyoming	30	60

the enactment of county ordinances, the development and approval of the county budget, and, in some states, the setting of certain tax rates.[37]

City Councils

Municipal government in America originates from the English parish and borough system. The English parish was involved in both church service and road maintenance, while the English borough engaged in commercial and governmental affairs. These traditional aspects of civic society in England were gradually merged into a single entity and developed into the concept of municipality in the United States.[38] In contrast to a county, which is an administrative appendage of a state, a city is considered a municipal "corporation" that can produce and implement its own local laws and public policy. For example, the City of New York creates its own sales tax, apart from the New York State sales tax created by the state government.[39] The executive branch of city governments is generally organized into one of three basic forms: a mayor-council form, a city commission form, and a council-manager form. These executive structures are discussed in detail elsewhere. However the executive authority of the municipality is organized, the legislative body in each of these three basic forms is typically called a *city council*, and that legislative body exercises the power to make public policy.

Traditionally, members of most city councils were elected through at-large election, a practice that often resulted in their becoming somewhat unresponsive to some groups in their jurisdiction. In recent decades city councils have tended to emphasize district elections, and as a consequence city councils have become considerably more diverse in terms of gender, race, and ethnicity than they were in the past. Today city legislative bodies are less white, less male, and less business-dominated than they were in the past and feature many more African-Americans, Hispanics, and women.

Photo 6.3. Eighteen-year-old mayor Michael Sessions presides over a City Council meeting in Hillsdale, Michigan. Source: Rebecca Cook/Reuters/Corbis.

Table 6.8. Party Affiliation in Legislatures Across the States, 2007

State	Senate Seats			House/Assembly Seats		
	Democrats	Republicans	Independents	Democrats	Republicans	Independents
Alabama	23	12	–	62	43	–
Alaska	9	11	–	17	23	–
Arizona	13	17	–	27	33	–
Arkansas	27	8	–	75	25	–
California	25	15	–	48	32	–
Colorado	20	15	–	39	26	–
Connecticut	24	12	–	107	44	–
Delaware	13	8	–	18	23	–
Florida	14	26	–	41	79	–
Georgia	22	34	–	74	106	–
Hawaii	20	5	–	43	8	–
Idaho	7	28	–	19	51	–
Illinois	37	22	–	66	52	–
Indiana	17	33	–	51	49	–
Iowa	30	20	–	54	46	–
Kansas	10	30	–	47	78	–
Kentucky	16	21	1	61	39	–
Louisiana	24	15	–	59	43	1
Maine	18	17	–	89	60	–
Maryland	33	14	–	104	37	–
Massachusetts	35	5	–	141	19	–
Michigan	17	21	–	58	52	–
Minnesota	44	23	–	85	49	–
Mississippi	25	27	–	74	47	–
Missouri	13	21	–	71	92	–
Montana	26	24	–	49	50	–
Nebraska	Nonpartisan election			Unicameral		
Nevada	10	11	–	27	15	–
New Hampshire	14	10	–	239	161	–
New Jersey	22	18	–	49	31	–
New Mexico	24	18	–	42	28	–
New York	29	33	–	105	45	–
North Carolina	31	19	–	68	52	–
North Dakota	21	26	–	33	61	–
Ohio	12	21	–	46	53	–
Oklahoma	24	42	–	44	57	–
Oregon	17	11	2	31	29	–
Pennsylvania	21	29	–	102	101	–
Rhode Island	33	5	–	62	13	–
South Carolina	20	26	–	51	73	–
South Dakota	15	20	–	20	50	–
Tennessee	16	17	–	53	46	–
Texas	11	20	–	69	81	–
Utah	8	21	–	20	55	–
Vermont	23	7	–	93	49	2
Virginia	17	23	–	40	57	3

Table 6.8. Continued

State	Senate Seats			House/Assembly Seats		
	Democrats	Republicans	Independents	Democrats	Republicans	Independents
Washington	32	17	–	62	36	–
West Virginia	23	11	–	72	28	–
Wisconsin	18	15	–	47	52	–
Wyoming	7	23	–	17	43	–

Adapted from: Council of State Governments, *The Book of the States, 2007* (see note 36).

Town Boards

Today, official town and township governments continue to operate in 20 states in three major regions (Table 6.10).[40] In terms of legislative process, many of these towns have a tradition of direct democracy through a "town meeting" in which residents elect town officials, enact ordinances, and adopt a budget. Typically, all available voters are invited to provide input, offer amendments, and vote on township business. These types of local government legislatures are often found in smaller jurisdictions.

The Adapted City

Research by Frederickson and Johnson has found that while almost all U.S. cities were initially established as either a council-manager or mayor-council form of government, they typically adapt to incorporate the best features of both systems. They found that over time, cities with council-manager systems tend to adopt features of mayor-council systems "to increase their political responsiveness," and that cities with mayor-council systems tend to adopt features of council-manager systems "to improve their management and productivity capabilities."[41] Frederickson and Johnson argue that these developments have led to a third form of municipal governance they call the "adapted city." As emphasized in the introductory chapter regarding adaptation to change, this is a characteristic of institutional sustainability—the ability of cities to reform their governmental structures to promote economic and administrative efficiency, and to increase political responsiveness and civil society.

Legislatures in Single-Purpose Local Government

As their name implies, typical single-purpose local governments only have one principal function. These local government entities usually provide services that general-purpose local governments are either unwilling to perform or are incapable of performing.[42] Special district boards and commissions and school district boards constitute the legislative bodies in single-purpose local governments.

Special District Boards

A special district usually has a population of residents occupying a specific geographic area, features a legal governing authority, maintains a legal identity separate

Table 6.9. Bills Introduced and Enacted in 2006 Regular Sessions

State	Bills Introduced	Bills Enacted
Alabama	1,432	365
Alaska	308	113
Arizona	1,453	395
Arkansas	–	–
California	1,853	632
Colorado	651	440
Connecticut	1,550	206
Delaware	392	214
Florida	2,096	440
Georgia	1,937	509
Hawaii	2,758	354
Idaho	737	459
Illinois	2,547	346
Indiana	834	193
Iowa	1,211	191
Kansas	774	219
Kentucky	1,012	223
Louisiana	2,149	873
Maine	658	351
Maryland	2,856	636
Massachusetts	–	448
Michigan	1,752	682
Minnesota	3,139	113
Mississippi	2,819	435
Missouri	1,879	165
Montana	–	–
Nebraska	500	135
Nevada	–	–
New Hampshire	1029	328
New Jersey	6,430	237
New Mexico	1,623	112
New York	17,700	750
North Carolina	1,905	264
North Dakota	–	–
Ohio	403	134
Oklahoma	2,133	327
Oregon	–	–
Pennsylvania	4,450	365
Rhode Island	2,812	704
South Carolina	721	203
South Dakota	458	270
Tennessee	3,330	514
Texas	–	–
Utah	663	367
Vermont	485	157
Virginia	2,346	958
Washington	929	155
West Virginia	2,105	370
Wisconsin	1,967	491
Wyoming	213	121

Adapted from: Council of State Governments, *The Book of the States, 2007* (see note 36).

Table 6.10. Regions and States with Official Towns and Townships

Regions	States
New England	Maine, Vermont, New Hampshire, Massachusetts, Connecticut, Rhode Island
Mid-Atlantic	New York, New Jersey, Pennsylvania
Midwest	Michigan, Ohio, Indiana, Illinois, Wisconsin, Minnesota, North Dakota, South Dakota, Kansas, Nebraska, Missouri

Source: A. Sokolow, 1996 (see note 40).

from any other governmental authority, possesses the power to assess a tax for the purpose of supplying certain public services, and exercises a considerable extent of autonomy.[43] Special districts have been created for a variety of purposes; for instance, a watershed district aims at promoting the beneficial use of water, and a rural hospital district works to provide healthcare services in a sparsely populated area.[44] In many areas of the country a sanitary district strives to improve sewerage services,[45] and a rural fire protection district focuses on providing fire protection through a combination of professional and volunteer firefighters.[46]

While the vast majority of the special districts in the United States perform a single function, a few provide two or more services. Local government units known as **county service areas** in California, for example, provide police protection, library facilities, and television translator services in some areas of the state.

The category of special district governments includes both **independent districts** and **dependent districts**. For independent districts, the board members are generally elected by the public, but in some cases members are appointed by public officials of the state, counties, municipalities, and towns or townships that have joined to form special districts.[47] Dependent districts are governed by other existing legislatures such as a city council or a county board. For instance, the county service areas noted above are dependent districts that are governed by their county boards of supervisors.[48] The Oceanside Small Craft Harbor District in California is a subsidiary organ of the City of Oceanside, and the members of the Oceanside City Council also serve on the District's board.[49] To sum up, special districts are independent if the members of boards are independently elected or appointed for a fixed term of office; special districts are dependent if they depend on another local government to govern them.[50] However they are governed, in their financial and administrative aspects special districts are all considered fiscally independent because they exist as separate legal entities and exercise a high degree of fiscal and administrative independence from the general-purpose governments around them.[51]

School District Boards

As a type of single-purpose local government, a school district serves primarily to operate public primary and secondary schools or to contract for public school services. Its legislative body is typically called a "school board"[52] or a "board of trustees,"[53] and the members of these boards can be either elected or appointed for fixed terms of office.[54] Typically, the school board has five to seven members whose job it is to make policy (e.g., adopting special programs, approving grant applications, setting disciplinary rules, going to the public to request passage of school levies) for the school district. One major issue in policy decisions is the development and enactment of a school district budget.

School districts also consist of both independent and dependent units. Independent school districts are defined as local governments that are fiscally and administratively independent of other government entities, such as townships, municipalities, and counties. They can provide for and promote public education, but they are not allowed to use their revenues on public goods other than education. Dependent school districts, in contrast, are not counted as separate governments because they are dependent on a "parent" government that is capable of shifting public expenditure among various public goods.[55] As of 2002, there were 15,029 public school systems in the United States, and of these 13,522 were independent school districts and the other 1,507 were classified as dependent districts.[56]

Legislatures and Sustainability

The United Nations Department of Economic and Social Affairs has highlighted the importance of local governments, and hence local government legislative bodies responsible for making laws and ordinances, in the development of sus-

Photo 6.4. A mother and child at the library. Special districts often serve the needs of eager readers. Source: © Flashon | Dreamstime.com

tainable local governments. The authors of the department's 2004 report observed the following:

> Because so many of the problems and solutions being addressed by Agenda 21 have their roots in local activities, the participation and cooperation of local authorities will be a determining factor in fulfilling its objectives. Local authorities construct, operate and maintain economic, social and environmental infrastructure, oversee planning processes, establish local environmental policies and regulations, and assist in implementing national and subnational environmental policies. As the level of governance closest to the people, they play a vital role in educating, mobilizing and responding to the public to promote sustainable development.[57]

In *Governing Sustainable Cities*, Evans and colleagues present a working framework for the factors that contribute to community sustainability.[58] These scholars suggest that sustainability is in major part a function of two community-based components: *institutional capacity* and *social capacity*. Institutional capacity is defined in terms of levels of commitment from government officials, the demonstration of political will, investment in staff training, technological mainstreaming, engagement in knowledge-based networks, and provision of legislative support for maintaining network connections. Similarly, social capacity is defined by the degree of inclusion in collective civic efforts of local citizen volunteers, news media, business establishments, representatives of industry, local universities, and local nongovernmental organizations.[59] Based on the possible combinations of institutional and social capacities, Evans and colleagues identify four potential governance outcomes:[60]

Photo 6.5. Graduation: Students and districts striving for successful outcomes.
Source: © Joeygil | Dreamstime.com

- *Dynamic governing*: Communities with higher levels of social and institutional capacity have a high possibility of accomplishing sustainability-promoting policy outcomes.

Legislatures: What Can I Do?

Find out more about state legislatures by visiting the National Council of State Legislators (NCSL) Web site at: http://www.ncsl.org/ and its public involvement Web site at: http://www.ncsl.org/public/ncsl/nav_about_involved.htm. The NCSL also has many educational materials located at its "Trust for Representative Democracy" project: http://www.ncsl.org/trust/index.htm.

Visit the International City Managers Association's (ICMA) Web site to find out about current issues confronting municipalities at http://icma.org/main/sc.asp and then use ICMA's Web site to locate your own county or city government Web sites at http://icma.org/resources/govsites/. Go to your own local government's Web site, see when city council or country commissioner public meetings are held, and attend one. Former U.S. Speaker of the House Tip O'Neill once said "all politics is local"; go see for yourself what issues are confronting your own local governments.

- *Active government*: Communities with lower levels of social capacity but higher levels of institutional capacity have a medium or fairly high possibility of accomplishing sustainability-promoting policy outcomes.
- *Voluntary governing*: Communities with higher levels of social capacity but low institutional capacity have a low possibility of accomplishing sustainability-promoting policy outcomes.
- *Passive government*: Communities with low levels of both institutional and social capacity have little possibility of achieving a sustainable future.

These findings are similar to the argument of Costantinos that the active support of the state and local government legislative bodies is a critical predictor of sustainable states and communities. This support is accomplished by:

> ...developing systems whereby public opinion can be made known to members of the legislature, including (the level of) support to develop their constituency, developing the capacity of the legislature to draft and introduce legislation or amendments to existing legislation on specific subjects.[61]

Conclusion

Legislative forums in American state and local government represent a vast terrain of widely differing scales and scope of responsibility, traditions of operation, and extent of access to professional staff support. Whatever their current arrangements, traditions, and resources, however, it is beyond argument that the observations of the United Nations Department of Economic and Social Affairs are absolutely on target in terms of the importance of the "governments closest to the people" in meeting the challenges of sustainability in our collective lifetimes.[62] The evidence of global climate change, the accumulation of greenhouse gases, the extinction of species, the scarcity of natural resources, the decimation of forests, and the pollution of air and surface waters is no longer a matter of unsettled controversy, and the short timeframe for effectively coping with an endangered global ecological system requires all levels of government to become engaged in "dynamic governing" in service to sustainability.

In each of the chapters to follow we will see how the multiple actors, including state legislatures and local boards, commissions, and councils, are striving to perform their traditional duties while taking on new responsibilities for passing on a sustainable form of economic and social life to the next generation of Americans. The institutional and social capacities of our state and local communities will be tested in the coming decades, and there are signs that the identification of and dissemination of "best practices" in many sectors for a sustainable future will require the dedicated effort of legislators, public servants, civic groups, and ordinary citizens accepting their civic duty. The challenging work that lies ahead requires informed and active participants in the government processes most directly related to daily life. Some state legislatures, such as those in California, Oregon, and Washington, are taking the lead in promoting standards for automobile emissions, energy use, and carbon sequestration that go beyond federal standards required by the Environmental Protection Agency, thereby challenging the authority of the federal government, while others are watching to see the results of those challenges. Many local government mayors (over 1,000 at this writing) are following the lead of Seattle's former Mayor Nichols and the U.S. Conference of Mayors in committing to the Climate Protection Agreement, which sets out ambitious goals for reducing greenhouse gases and conserving energy consistent with the Kyoto Accords even though the United States is not a signatory to those international accords. These developments represent a hopeful beginning for the governments closest to the people rising to the challenges of sustainability facing each state government and each local community in the coming years.

Key Terms

Administrative rules	Gerrymandering
Checks and balances	Independent (special) districts
Constituency service	Legislative oversight
County service area	Legislative referral
Dependent (special) districts	Parliamentary style systems
General-purpose governments	Presidential style systems

Select committees   Sunset provisions
Single-purpose governments   Task force
Standing committee   Term limits

Discussion Questions

1. According to this chapter, what are the major functions that legislatures play in state and local government?
2. What are some of the similarities and differences in how state legislatures operate?
3. Compare and contrast the roles and functions of general-purpose and single-purpose governments.
4. How can legislatures promote economic, social, and ecological sustainability?
5. Would you characterize your hometown as featuring passive government, voluntary governing, active government, or dynamic governing?

CHAPTER 7

Executives

Introduction

The title of this chapter draws an important distinction in our discussion of executive leadership in state and local government; unfortunately, it is a distinction that provides less clarity than one would expect. In 18th- and 19th-century state and local government, the "executive" branch was generally thought of in terms of elected leadership; a governor, a state attorney general, a mayor, or perhaps even a sheriff came readily to mind. The executive, therefore, was tied directly to elective office and was often directly accountable to the people via the voting mechanism.

In the mid- to late 19th and early 20th centuries, however, a major change began to take place in this area. The rise of what is called Progressivism led to a concerted nationwide effort to clean up politics, particularly at the municipal level and over time at the state level as well. The national government was also affected by Progressive reforms, although perhaps not in the same way or to the same degree this social movement transformed state and local government.

The chapter discusses the unique qualities of the political and career administrative executive aspects of state and local government. Understanding the offices, both their similarities and their differences, will help you gain a better understanding of how state and local executives operate across the country and in your own state and local community.

This chapter will discuss:

- The power and role of the governor
- State executive branch leaders
- The roles of county and city elected leaders
- Special districts as quasi-executive/legislative institutions
- The role of administrative executives
- The role of executives in sustainability

Governor

The term *governor* has many meanings. On a mechanical device, a governor is something that regulates the speed of a machine, often a complex process. The British for some period used the word when addressing someone worthy of respect. The word also refers to a military commander. More commonly, a governor is a head of state, a key actor in a governmental body. So, do all of these definitions apply to our current topic: state governors? Unexpectedly, the answer is yes! A governor shapes the speed and direction of political debate. The governor is, in fact, a military commander—he or she does have the power to "call up" or activate the state National Guard in U.S. states. The office of governor is a position of respect and is the ceremonial head of state as well as being a key actor in a larger governing process.

Before the American Revolution, colonial governors served as executive leaders of a Crown Colony. In early colonial days, the powerful landowners chose governors, usually white men of wealth and social stature. The governor, along with a quasi-legislative council, led the colony in countless ways—managing resources; developing plans for sustainability and growth; maintaining civic virtue through the enforcement of laws; and making treaties or agreements with indigenous peoples and with other colonies. Governors also appointed individuals to help accomplish key tasks. As the British colonies became more developed, the Crown government played a much larger role in appointing governors and various administrative executives to serve as representatives of the home nation to collect taxes and assess fees, and generally to enforce the will of the British Monarch and his government on colonists.

In the colonial period, just as today, the governor is a key figure for innovative leadership, critical to establishing sustainable states and communities. The often-tragic imperialistic interactions between indigenous peoples and colonists represent a sad chapter in the development of democratic government in our county. It is useful at the outset of this chapter to imagine the circumstances faced by early colonists, moving from the familiarities of the continent of Europe to a place far less familiar and comprehensible to them. An inability on the part of the nation's early colonial governors to be successful innovators could have resulted in widespread disease and death among colonists and native tribes alike.

Leadership, then, as is the case today, is only as good as the ability of the leader to persuade others to follow him or her, and this ability is importantly shaped by a leader's personality. Popularity is one measure of the ability of a leader to persuade others to follow,[1] to gain followers, and to gain their support for innovative ideas.[2] Support can be particularly difficult to gain and maintain when promoting a vision of the future, a time and space unknown and often disturbing in consideration. Innovation requires, along with uncommon insight, boldness of action in the face of the unknown.

The dire consequences of failed innovative executive leadership still exist, but new consequences have emerged. Mass starvation is perhaps less likely, but Homeland Security issues place the governor and his or her staff on the front line as the likely first responders to a crisis, manmade or brought on by the force of Nature. For example, while failed river levies in New Orleans were ultimately a national government failure, the impact of Hurricane Katrina (2005) was immediate and devastating. Louisiana Governor Kathleen Blanco and New Orleans Mayor Ray Nagin were called upon to exercise innovative executive leadership and—in this case as perhaps in no other hurricane-related tragedy of recent memory—the consequences of failed leadership were as bad, if not worse, than issues faced by now long-forgotten colonial governors of centuries past.

In times of relative tranquility, a governor must do two principal things. First, a governor must serve as a chief administrator, managing the steady course of government towards various goals. Second, a governor must consider the future and identify areas where sustainability must be actively pursued. A governor will likely use his or her chief executive role—the role of head of state—to promote policy innovations that will better serve state and local sustainability efforts. The development of sound state and local energy policies is certainly a timely example of gubernatorial leadership; reduced reliance on imported fossil energy and increased development of state and local renewable energy sources are timely goals in this respect. Governors' efforts to promote literacy and improved educational attainment, combined with sustainable economic development providing good jobs and a quality lifestyle, are part of efforts to retain young people in states and local communities.[3] And for those individuals least benefited in society, governors have played a critical role in promoting welfare-to-work programs.

Photo 7.1. New Orleans Mayor Ray Nagin, President George W. Bush, and Louisiana Governor Kathleen Blanco surveying Katrina disaster. Source: Brooks Kraft/Corbis.

Terms of Office and Eligibility

In the United States, governors hold 4-year terms of office. The exception to this occurs when governors are elected via special election to fill a governorship when the current governor has vacated the seat before completing his or her term of office. One of the reasons that a sitting governor would not complete his or her term is related to election or appointment to another political office. President George W. Bush was the incumbent governor of Texas when he was elected 43rd U.S. President in 2000. A second reason that a sitting governor vacates the governorship before completing a term of office is due to losing a recall election. Governor Gray Davis of California was recalled as governor in October 2003. Following a successful election, the former film celebrity and now politician Arnold Schwarzenegger assumed the governorship.

A third reason why a governor might not complete a 4-year term of office is due to death, incapacity, or violation of residency requirements. While death is determinable, incapacity is not entirely clear and is defined in part by the legislative branch. At times, governors will declare themselves as being incapable of finishing their proscribed term of office.

Finally, a governor might not complete his or her term of office due to resignation for reasons other that those mentioned previously. Public corruption or other felony indictments or convictions may lead a sitting governor to resign from office. In 2003, Illinois Republican Governor George Ryan was indicted on federal charges of political corruption, ultimately resulting in conviction on over a dozen counts of public corruption and a six-and-a-half-year prison sentence (he is appealing the conviction). In 2008, New York Governor Eliot Spitzer resigned

Photo 7.2. Governor Arnold Schwarzenegger. Source: AP Photo/Steve Yeater.

from office because of his involvement with a prostitute. Most recently, in 2009 Illinois Governor Rod Blagojevich was impeached and removed from office for corruption charges, including allegedly trying to "sell" President Barack Obama's U.S. Senate seat.

In most states, when a sitting governor vacates the office before completing his or her term, the lieutenant governor becomes either the new sitting governor or the acting governor of a state. The lieutenant governor is not unlike the vice president, serving as the chief officer of the state senate and occasionally casting tie-breaking votes. Unlike the vice president, the lieutenant governor can be elected as a separate constitutional office and frequently represents a different political party than that of the governor; however, in over a dozen states, the lieutenant governor is jointly elected with a governor. Essentially, vacating the office of governor and the elevation of a lieutenant governor to the governorship would lead to significant changes in policy direction and prioritization.

In many states, the eligibility requirements for governor specify a minimum age of 30 years at the time of election to office, but there are noteworthy exceptions. Wisconsin's constitution specifically states that individuals elected to the governorship must simply be qualified electors (18 years old). Other states, such as Arizona, Montana, and Nevada, require that an elected governor be at least 25 years of age. Residency requirements prior to election are typically between 5 and 7 years. Missouri and Oklahoma constitutions require prior state residency of at least 10 years. Mississippi and New Jersey require at least 20 years of U.S. citizenship. Currently, only about half of the state governors are natives of their respective states. Of the non-native governors, 34.1% were born in the Northeast; 6% were born in the state of New York. As of 2009, two governors were born outside of the United States. It is fairly well known that Governor Arnold Schwarzenegger of California was born in Austria; it is less commonly known that Jennifer Granholm, former Governor of Michigan and current cabinet officer in the Obama administration, was born in Canada.

Term Limits

In the past few decades, term limits have gained heightened interest among voters. The executive branch of the national government saw term limitations come into effect in response to President Roosevelt's unprecedented four consecutive presidential election victories in the 1930s and 1940s. In the 1994 general election, the Republican candidates for the U.S. Congress made a major push for term limits, promising to serve only two terms of office if elected. Incumbency often appeared to be an advantage that was not easily overcome by a challenger[4]; term limits were seen as a way to offer fresh alternatives a voice in the electoral process. For good or for ill, the message of term limits resonated with voters. State governors have by no means been immune to voter scrutiny and to term limitation measures.

As of 2007, 37 states have enacted term limits on their governorship. In some states, terms limits mean that after a governor has served two full terms, he or she must wait 4 years before being eligible to run again for the governorship. In Wyoming, an individual can serve only 8 years as governor in any 16-year period. In

Table 7.1. Qualifications for Governors

	U.S. Citizen (years)	State Resident (years)	Qualified Voter (years)	Minimum Age
Alabama	10	7	✓	30
Alaska	7	7	✓	30
Arizona	10			25
Arkansas	✓	7	✓	30
California	5	5	✓	18
Colorado	✓	2		30
Connecticut	✓	✓		30
Delaware	12	6		30
Florida		7	7	30
Georgia	15	6		30
Hawaii	5	5	✓	30
Idaho	✓	2		30
Illinois	✓	3	✓	25
Indiana	5	5	✓	30
Iowa	2	2	✓	30
Kansas	✓			
Kentucky	✓	6		30
Louisiana	5	5	✓	25
Maine	15	5		30
Maryland		5	5	30
Massachusetts		7		
Michigan	✓	✓	4	30
Minnesota	✓	1	✓	25
Mississippi	20	5	✓	30
Missouri	15	10		30
Montana	✓	2	✓	25
Nebraska	5	5		30
Nevada	2	2	✓	25
New Hampshire		7		30
New Jersey	20	7		30
New Mexico	✓	5	✓	30
New York	✓	1		25
North Carolina	5	2	✓	30
North Dakota	✓	5	✓	30
Ohio	✓	✓	✓	18
Oklahoma	10	10	10	31
Oregon	✓	3		30
Pennsylvania	✓	7	✓	30
Rhode Island	30 days	30 days	30 days	18
South Carolina	5	5		30
South Dakota	✓	✓	✓	18
Tennessee	✓			30
Texas	✓	5		30
Utah	✓	5	✓	30
Vermont		4	✓	18
Virginia	✓	✓	5	30
Washington	✓	✓	✓	18
West Virginia	✓	1	✓	30
Wisconsin	✓	✓	✓	18
Wyoming	✓	5	✓	30

Source: Council of State Governments, The Book of the States, 2008 (Lexington, KY: Council of State Governments, 2008).

Table 7.2. Governors in the Territorial Possessions

Territory	Governor?
American Samoa	Yes
Baker, Howland, and Jarvis Islands	No
Guam	Yes
Johnson Atoll	No
Kingman Reef	No
Midway Islands	No
Navassa Island	No
Northern Marianna Islands	Yes
Puerto Rico	Yes
Palmyra Atoll	No
U.S. Virgin Islands	Yes
Wake Island	No

Virginia, the constitution allows the governor to serve only one 4-year term; the individual then has to wait 4 years before being eligible to run for a second term. In six states, lieutenant governors are not subject to the same term limitations as governors, perhaps in recognition of the lesser importance of the lieutenant governorship in the policymaking process. However, the lieutenant governor does serve as the president of the state senate and over a long tenure may gain significant influence over closely contested policy measures.

Governor's Office

Not unlike the president, the governor's office is shaped by the incumbent's personal style and tastes in management. Personality plays a large role in shaping gubernatorial tastes in the governance process. Governors have a personal staff appointed by him or her and organized under the managerial control of a chief of staff. The organization and access of staff to the governor are largely functions of personal management philosophy. Some governors are very hierarchical in their management style, often using the chief of staff position to limit access of personnel. In a hierarchical approach, the governor's interaction with staff is usually formal and quite structured. Other governors tend to adopt a collegial approach to management. The role of a chief of staff is more limited. Collegial governors regularly attend informal policy group meetings where discussion is freer-flowing and innovations are discussed in an open forum.

While several other elected positions exist within the executive branch—e.g., secretary of state, attorney general, treasurer, and comptroller (or controller or auditor)—the sub-governor executive offices are not beholden to the governor. While office holders might meet regularly with the governor, they do not take their direction from him or her.

In addition, an agency's staff exists below the governor's political appointees and/or below that of other elected state executives. In theory, bureaucracy is politically neutral, but organizational and individual values and priorities may subconsciously shape judgment. The ability of a governor and other political executives may be constrained by bureaucracy. Administrative reform[5] efforts are, in some instances, an attempt to break down the bureaucratic network and reduce red tape.

As with the president, state governors are generally required to organize and submit an annual or bi-annual budget to the state legislature for consideration. One of the most recognizable and important staff offices, therefore, is the budget office, headed by a governor-appointed budget director. The budget office interacts regularly with the governor and other members of his or her personal staff along with other elected executive branch officials, such as the treasurer, secretary of state, and comptroller (auditor). The budget office is particularly important when the opposition party controls the state legislature.[6] The office serves an important liaison function in promoting the governor's agenda.

Governors often establish policy advisory groups. Policy groups are often formed around related policy issues, such as crime, education, welfare, transportation, and many others. A governor's chief of staff helps the governor to coordinate the activities of the policy groups and to ensure that the governor's general and specific priorities form the nexus of policy goals. Governors will meet regularly with their policy advisors and discuss legislative priorities and budgeting.

In addition to personal staff, governors rely heavily on appointed boards and commissions. Commissions are often closely tied to specific policy issues in a state and are very important in promoting policy innovations. In relation to issues of sustainability, state energy commissions, for instance, spend considerable time studying the feasibility of alternative energy development in states. Education policy functions often have associated boards or commissions with either appointed or elected officials.

Photo 7.3. West Virginia Governor Joe Manchin, First Lady Gayle Manchin and Governor's Office staff outside the West Virginia Governor's Mansion, December 2009. Source: Photo by Eric Steele, West Virginia Department of Transportation.

Not unlike the presidency, governors also appoint a cabinet to manage related state administrative departments. In some states, certain policy areas have elected leadership. The State of Washington, for instance, has an elected Superintendent of Public Instruction. California has an elected Labor Commissioner. The presence of other elected executives in specific policy areas serves to limit gubernatorial influence and power.

Despite a large staff and executive office organization, governors are highly dependent on personal characteristics to shape policy and outcomes. In essence, the power to persuade the voters and legislators of the importance and necessity of certain policy priorities cannot be underestimated. Public opinion is a strong influence in shaping a governor's ability to promote a policy agenda. Legislative–gubernatorial relations are often shaped by party control factors: in divided government, the governor may face greater challenges in promoting a policy agenda than in times of unified party control. With the exception of Nebraska (a unicameral legislature) there is evidence that when the governor's political party controls the state senate (but not the legislative chamber), then he or she is less limited by the impacts of divided government.

Public opinion research indicates that the public expects governors to pay close attention to state economic trends.[7] When state unemployment rates rise, the governor's public opinion ratings tend to decline. Conversely, the public is generally supportive of governors who "chase smoke stacks"—that is, successfully pursue economic development in their state—although public opinion is shaped by the specific type of industrial development pursued. Increasingly, voters insist on clean industries that will not pollute the environment.

All of the actions of the governor are ultimately shaped by his or her partisan leanings and the partisan climate in which he or she operates at the state level. Beyond the state itself, the governor as a partisan actor must also work with the state's elected congressional delegation, which may or may not share the governor's policy priorities or visions for innovation.[8]

Secretary of State

In the national government, the secretary of state is an appointed cabinet-level position largely associated with diplomatic affairs, but there are many other functions of secretary of state that involve economic development and partnerships. At the state level, the functions are similar in many respects. International or interstate "diplomacy" is often seen as limited to officially welcoming heads of state or domestic state dignitaries, but secretaries of state also play an important role in informing these visitors about the business climate in a state and the benefits of locating particular industries there. In essence, secretaries of state are key economic development coordinators. The secretary of state's office in most states is also responsible for managing business licenses and business development in a state. Given the office's responsibilities in business licensing, it is a natural fit for the secretary of state's office to manage state archives and other official records. In some instances, the department of motor vehicles or its equivalent reports to the secretary of state.

Perhaps one of the most recognizable functions of the secretary of state, however, is that of managing elections. The office is responsible for officially posting the names of candidates for public office and closely managing the printing and distribution of ballots. After the ballots are cast, the secretary of state is responsible for certifying that the election has been conducted honestly and accurately. Many readers will recall Florida Secretary of State Katherine Harris's controversial decision to certify the 2000 presidential election votes despite widespread concern about the accuracy and completeness in counting punch card ballots in several Florida counties.

Every 10 years the U.S. Census Bureau requires the redistricting of national, state, and local legislative electoral districts to ensure that U.S. citizens enjoy equal political representation. Secretaries of state, the governor, and the state legislatures all play key roles in deciding on the shape of the districts resulting from this process of realignment of district lines each decade. Partisan and racial **gerrymandering** (the intentional creation of districts that will likely ensure a particular political party's victory or the victory of particular candidates who are persons of a particular race or ethnicity) historically has been and remains a highly controversial issue in many parts of the country. Secretaries of state play a key role in trying to prevent gerrymandering in most states, but become involved in perpetuating the practice in a few states.

Photo 7.4. Secretary of State Katherine Harris (R-FL) certifies the 2000 Florida vote for George W. Bush. Source: Reuters/Corbis.

Attorney General

State attorneys general serve as the chief judicial advocate for their respective states, representing state interests in all trials, investigations, and appeals involving the state as a legal party. The offices of the attorneys general also have the responsibility of organizing the state's legal profession to provide legal counsel for individuals who cannot afford to pay for their own legal representation in criminal cases. The office of the state attorney general is usually divided into separate divisions for criminal and civil matters. Consumer protection is one of the fastest-growing areas of concern among attorneys general working on the civil side, and violence against women, violence against the elderly, and cybercrime (i.e., computer-based victimization through identity theft or stalking) are the most common areas of growing attention on the criminal side. The protection of children is another prominent issue facing attorneys general, on both the civil and criminal side. The Amber Alert system, designed to disseminate information rapidly about abducted children, is typically put into place by attorneys general working in concert with local law enforcement in their states.

Attorneys general in some areas have formed close interstate relationships, at times effectively nationalizing legal policy goals. In the 1990s, state attorneys general pooled their resources and talent and pursued litigation against large tobacco companies. Ultimately, the "tobacco settlement" resulting from a federal lawsuit brought by a group of state attorneys general led to the periodic payment of literally billions of dollars in revenue to the states as just compensation for the costs to the states for the treatment of illnesses caused by smoking. In this instance and in others, state attorneys general have demonstrated that their executive powers and abilities extend far beyond state borders, in some respects outpacing the powers of state governors in terms of impact on public policy.

State Treasurer

State treasurers administer or supervise the financial transactions taking place in state government. The collection of tax, investment, and transactional revenue is the major feature of the treasurer's job. Tax revenue does not arrive all at once. State sales taxes, for instance, typically arrive in state coffers monthly from retail merchants who sell taxed goods or services. Gasoline taxes, for example, are levied on individual purchases and tallied by the familiar gas pumps found in every service station. A monthly tally is read on each pump and each station operator remits taxes due to the state and federal governments. State treasurers are responsible for managing such financial resources as they are collected, and they are in charge of distributing those resources to state agencies appropriately—that is, according to statutory formulas set forth in the state budget document. While the resources are sitting in state coffers, usually state bank accounts in private banks and investment institutions, the treasurer is responsible for the careful investing of these monies to earn interest, or in the case of longer-term investments to earn dividends and/or gain in market value.

In many instances state resources are insufficient to complete budget goals. State legislatures, with the governor's approval, will direct the state treasurer to issue bonds. Bonds are promissory notes, essentially IOUs issued in the name of the state. Investors purchase a bond for a certain amount when such bond issuances are announced. On a predetermined due date (or "call" date), the principal investment and interest earned are returned to the investor. External parties with expertise in finance rate bonds in terms of the likelihood of repayment. The best bond rating from Standard & Poor's, a major private bond-rating corporation, is AAA. Bonds receiving a lower rating entail a greater degree of financial risk but pay a higher rate of interest. State treasurers actively manage state bond issuances and seek to develop and maintain financial management plans that result in high bond ratings, which save state taxpayers money in interest payments avoided. State treasurers keep a careful eye on their state bond ratings and play a key role in maintaining financial management practices in state government.

In recent years state treasurers have begun to play an ever-larger role in the development of innovative funding programs for state investments in higher education. As any reader would likely know, the cost of a college education has been rising more quickly than the general cost of living. Fortunately, the U.S. Internal Revenue Service allows in its Code 529 provision for the development of individually funded tax-exempt college savings accounts. To encourage the continued development of a highly educated labor force, states have joined the federal effort to encourage investment in higher education by also making these plans exempt from state taxation. The monies invested by individuals in 529 plans are administered by the state in conjunction with a predetermined private investment firm, such as Fidelity Investments. State treasurers are responsible for collecting revenues, investing them, and eventually disbursing these funds to the parents and children for whom these funds have been saved.

In some states the state treasurer also plays an important role in state policy innovation by managing grant monies intended to fund novel policy initiatives. In some cases state treasurers have solicited proposals for local renewable energy projects, workplace health promotion incentives, and sustainable community development. The treasurer reviews the proposals and plays a key role in determining which grant proposals will be funded. The goal of these grant programs is to provide seed funding for ideas that promote the economic viability of the state economy that can be adopted by other localities once the ideas are shown to be worthy of investment.

Superintendent of Public Instruction

The famed educator Horace Mann in Massachusetts established the first state-level education office in the 1830s. In the 17th and 18th centuries, elementary and secondary education was either privately administered or seen as entirely a local government function. While public K–12 education remains largely locally administered, Mann's **Common School Movement** instituted a major state-level role in educational curriculum and organization. Superintendents of public instruction are elected positions, generally with a 4-year term of office. The superintendent's office has a multitude of functions, with curriculum management being a very important aspect of the superintendent's job. While individual school districts have some influence over curriculum issues, the state office plays a key role in determining the curriculum of basic educational requirements—the basic knowledge, skills, and abilities to which all students should have equal access. The superintendent's office maintains accountability through student testing. Since the No Child Left Behind (NCLB) Act was signed into law in 2001, the state office is also responsible for school performance and teacher quality management issues. Other important functions are managing state finances directed towards basic education and managing grant programs originating at the state level or filtered through the state office by the federal government. The superintendent of education and the department offices at the state level play a critical role in managing K–12 education and ensuring the equality of educational opportunity for all students, including supervising GED (graduation equivalent degree) programs for students who are not able to complete the traditional high school process and supervisors home-schooling parents.

Local Government Executives

County Commissions

Counties are among the oldest jurisdictions of government. In Western Europe, counties were units of aristocratic government, the jurisdiction of a count or an earl. In our country the role of county governments has varied considerably over time, and their relative importance has been a function of the social and economic climate of a region. Until relatively recently county governments had remained largely unchanged in their structure and method of operation,[9] often being viewed as institutional anachronisms.

Before the nation's large-scale urbanization, the county was the predominant unit of local government. County government served the blocks of farms and ranches that constituted a region's economic base. The industrialization and subsequent urbanization of many areas in the 19th and 20th centuries reduced the power of county commissions considerably. Communities that remain rural and agricultural continue to employ county commissions who carry out their work in rather traditional ways.

Typical county functions focused on public health and welfare, education, criminal justice, roads, and property rights issues. County government often maintained a public hospital and a public health department. Schools were centrally located in small rural areas, often found in the county seat of government. The county sheriff's department and county court system (and jail) were generally highly recognizable features of county government. Finally, county government focused considerable attention on the issue of water rights and land use, two issues particularly important in the arid Southwest.

The primary elected executive leadership in a county is typically the county commission. In many respects the commission serves a dual role as a legislative body, employing a majority-voting rule to determine county policy priorities. In fact, county commissions and other political executives at the county level (e.g., sheriff) are critical actors in terms of directly managing and delegating key functions of local government. Increasingly, county commissions have appointed county managers, an administrative executive position, to manage the day-to-day operations of counties. In several counties across the country, generally in large counties with significant urban populations, the office of an elected county supervisor has been created by county charter amendment to fill similar functions.

County commissions regularly create "special districts" (units with their own limited taxing authority) and elected or administrative executive positions to deal with specific issues. For instance, the cemetery board in many counties is a creation of the county commission, and the cemetery board executives may be either elected or appointed administrators. Other commonly recognized special districts created by the county commissions and associated elected or appointed executive positions involve county parks, housing authorities, and water boards.

The authority of county government is limited by **Dillon's Rule**, which is named after John Dillon, an Iowa Supreme Court jurist in the mid-19th century. In his book *The Law of Municipal Corporations* (originally published in 1872) Dillon argued that state–national government power relations were embedded in the U.S. Constitution, which grants the states almost unlimited authority aside from limitations imposed by the Constitution and resulting federal statute.[10] In terms of state–local power relations, Dillon argued that states create local government and hold supreme power over local governments. The noted exception to this is the creation of **home rule** relationships, in which states effectively grant limited and reversible power to local government to independently create governmental forms and manage policy formation at the local level.

In recent years, county government across the country has been rejuvenated through a large measure of institutional reform.[11] Counties play a very important role in coordinating sub-government activities, many of which overlap in jurisdiction. County government has played a particularly important role in law enforcement, dealing with public health and safety and terrorism-related policies and coordinating multijurisdictional efforts to react to changing conditions such as domestic violence and drug-related youth gang violence. The management of weather-related catastrophes has also benefited from county government leadership in major ways.

In terms of innovation, many county governments have taken advantage of the opportunity to bring disparate groups together to provide multiple viewpoints and to share common goals. County land management is one important method of providing an equitable future for all citizens, particularly as county demographics change and as the values of citizens evolve. In this regard, county governments have spearheaded some of the most innovative programs in the areas of renewable energy development and broadband access for households. The National Association of Counties (NACO) is an effective voice for innovation and adaptation to changing societal conditions and offers technical advice and services to counties seeking to implement "best practices" in the major areas of sustainability promotion—energy conservation, renewable energy development, alternatives to single-occupancy automobile travel to the workplace, greenhouse gas emission reduction, and so forth.

In recognition of the rejuvenation of county government, in 1991 the ICMA changed its official name from the International City Management Association to the International City/County Management Association. The ICMA conventions and technical assistance programs now feature a rich blend of city and county administrators for virtually all types of jurisdictions, large and small, urban, suburban, and rural. In this type of setting innovative local government practices that promote sustainability can be disseminated throughout the country.

Special Districts

Technically, special districts are units of local government that are *not* a county, township, or city. The general scope of power and responsibilities of a special district are governed by state laws and county ordinances, which provide legal guidelines for the governance and administration of special districts. Special districts often emerge due to the demands of citizens for certain services in their community, and citizens may petition county governments to create special districts as a way to deal with their concerns. Special districts are wide-ranging, offering services such as fire protection in rural areas and water, sewer, and other benefits to individuals within a special district's taxing jurisdiction. When creating a special district, county and state governments structure a system for the collection of additional revenue to be assigned to a dedicated fund to pay for the services demanded.

Special districts perform the executive role of governing the process of service delivery, but also through governing boards they perform the legislative function of creating policies and regulations related to district and service administration. Special districts employ their own administrators to execute district policies.

Creating sustainable communities will require the active participation of the many special districts that have proliferated at the local level, each one meeting particular needs and overcoming barriers to effective service delivery. Special districts are closer to the citizenry than state or national government and may be assumed to be more responsive to local needs. As such, the people active in the establishment, management, and operation of special districts are frequent participants in local meetings relating to sustainability. These people have demonstrated particular skill at local-level adaptation to change in the past, and they will likely be among the leading voices heard regarding policies needed to address the challenges of global climate change and related problems facing our state and local governments in the years ahead.

Municipal Governments

In municipal government, the most commonly recognized executive position is that of mayor. In most municipal government structures, the mayor is the elected executive in a city. The power of a mayor as an executive, however, is often limited in many of the same ways as other state and local executives—namely, he or she is heavily dependent on a well-defined organizational structure in which other actors exercise significant influence. Mayors typically operate within one of three different organizational conditions: **strong mayor-council**, **weak mayor-council**, or the **commission** form of municipal government, in which the role of the mayor is primarily that of coordinator.

Strong Mayor-Council

One of the most significant powers afforded the mayor is that of budget maker. The mayor's office prepares a budget document that is submitted to the council for review and eventual approval. While the details of the budget are negotiated in the council's deliberative process, the mayor's power and staff support for preparing the budget document provides him or her with significant influence over the budgeting process. In a strong mayor-council system, the mayor administers the budget after council approval, which is another source of mayoral power; the mayor is typically afforded considerable discretion over when budget expenditures will be deferred or possibly even sequestered or rescinded.

In strong mayor-council systems, mayors have significant appointment power as well. The mayor can appoint and dismiss numerous administrative municipal agency heads. With the legal power to hire or fire, the mayor does not have to negotiate or compromise with agency heads. As the chief executive in the municipality, in strong mayor-council systems the mayor's overall agenda is likely to carry the day in most important matters of municipal policy and programs.

While the executive powers of mayors in a strong mayor-council system are considerable, there are clear limitations on those powers. Mayors can be limited by the council, and most certainly the voters hold ultimate control over the mayor's continuance in office. Administrative leaders have their own power base as well in the client groups they serve; if the mayor operates with too heavy a hand, then he or she might find himself or herself politically isolated and unable to produce desired outcomes.

Over the course of the nation's history, even the strongest mayors have had to employ positive inducements to achieve their goals. The former Chicago mayor the late Richard Daley Sr., who headed a Democratic municipal political machine, found that offering inducements—often, city jobs for friends or family members of his supporters—was an effective way to build support and to get things accomplished.

As with other executives, strong mayors are only as strong as their level of public support. New York City mayor John V. Lindsay (1966–1973) is a good example of how power is relative to political support. Lindsay came from one of New York City's oldest patrician families, tracing family connections to the city back to Dutch rule in the 1660s. A handsome and articulate man, Mayor Lindsay graduated from Yale University and served in Congress during the 1960s. A moderate Republican, Lindsay was a strong supporter of civil rights. New York City elected him mayor in 1965 (he entered office in 1966) with the idea that he was a young progressive leader who would do an excellent job in bringing the city into the post-civil rights era, continuing to promote the message of social and political equality. Instead, Lindsay's mayoralty was plagued with repeated bouts of civil unrest. Harlem, a predominantly African-American neighborhood on the northern end of Manhattan, witnessed the murder of a police officer responding to a call for service at a local mosque. The neighborhood almost erupted into a riot when police officers descended on the scene. Mayor Lindsay was roundly criticized for displaying ineffective leadership.

In addition to civil unrest, Lindsay called for higher taxes, the highest per capita municipal taxes in the nation; this was a needed but highly unpopular move on his part. Despite higher taxes to support the mayor's public works agenda, the transit, sanitation, and other municipal workers went on strike. Without regularly operating municipal agencies, New York City was often a difficult place to navigate for residents and visitors alike. The worse problems became, the more difficult it was for Lindsay to lead the city. He ultimately left office in 1973, almost universally disliked by both political liberals and conservatives.

One of the most recent examples of how political support can catapult a mayor's popularity also comes from New York City. On September 11, 2001, Mayor Rudolph Giuliani was only weeks away from retiring from a successful two terms in office, having brought down crime levels in the city to record lows. On that fateful September morning, however, his leadership was challenged by the worst terrorist act on U.S. soil in history when two commercial airplanes were intentionally crashed into the World Trade Center towers in Lower Manhattan. While the details of that day are well known, Mayor Giuliani's leadership during the crisis was a sterling example of how a strong mayor system can lead to highly successful outcomes when timely and dramatic action is required. In the weeks and months following the terrorist attack, New Yorkers and the U.S. public at large nearly universally supported his leadership—he was often referred to as "America's Mayor" as a consequence of his accomplishments.

Weak Mayor-Council

In a general sense, the concept of weak mayor-council government is nearly self-explanatory. In the weak mayor-council form of government, the mayoralty is largely a ceremonial position. Unlike the strong mayor-council system, executive leadership entails a cooperative effort on the part of the entire city council. The council collectively decides on and approves appointments. The budget is a collegial endeavor and the mayor is just one of the council members involved in the budgeting process.

A weakened mayoral position is often associated with reducing the potential for political corruption and misuse of power. By dividing power and responsibility among all council members, it is believed that corruption and misuse of power will be limited. A weak mayor-council arrangement melds legislative and executive authority. All council members play both legislative and executive roles. Collectively, their leadership traits might produce better outcomes. In the modern city, it may be almost too much to ask one individual to handle all major events. Therefore, a cooperative council arrangement could reduce the stress that is placed on a single individual in a strong mayor-council system. Conversely, a weak mayor-council government might reduce the ability to assign responsibility. As small sign on President Harry S Truman's Oval Office desk stated, "The Buck Stops Here." In the case of a divided executive, it is unclear where the buck stops, as no particular individual is solely responsible for decisions or outcomes.

Municipal Commission Government

Progressive Era reformers heavily promoted the commission form of municipal government. The first use of this form of government occurred in Galveston, Texas, in 1900. A city approximately 360 miles west of New Orleans along the Texas coast, Galveston had been hit by a severe hurricane that killed over 6,000 residents and caused more than $17 million (nearly $400 million in current dollars) in property damage. Many of the storm's survivors left the city and moved elsewhere.

The city government divided the responsibilities of the municipality among council members. Each commissioner held executive power over a major public works department (e.g., water, sanitation, and roads). By dividing up the executive responsibilities, the city's commissioners were able to accomplish herculean tasks in their own areas of responsibility. Collectively, commissioners served in a legislative role, determining budgets, voting on policy directions, and approving appointments or dismissals. The mayor, a highly ceremonial figure, was selected either through a vote of the commission as a whole or by general election.

While municipal commissions are discussed elsewhere in the text, the executive power elements of commission government are highly illuminating. By dividing the executive power of commissioners along the lines of public works functions, budget debates were more likely to stake one public works interest against others. With a largely ceremonial mayoral function and at-large nonpartisan commissioner selection processes, the commission form of government selected individuals based on experience within a public works area with a sense of its relative importance in relation to other public works functions.

Outside of emergency situations, the commission form of government can be highly contentious despite its nonpartisan membership. The commission model of municipal governance may reduce the capacity of government to promote cooperative decision-making, which may be more common in the council-manager forms of government.

City Managers

During the Progressive Era, municipal government moved away from strong mayoral control over the executive aspects of governance. City managers, who are appointed executives, became a more common feature in municipal executive leadership. As with county manager developments, Progressive Era reforms leading to the creation of city managers were driven by the desire to professionalize the executive aspects of governance as well as to address substantiated and unsubstantiated concerns about political corruption in local government. It was quite commonly thought that an appointed manager, serving in an executive/administrative role, would be less likely to engage in corrupt or dishonest dealings than would persons beholden to partisan political interests.

The city manager as a municipal executive position has proven to be a popular form of municipal government, although it is a challenging governmental structure. As a non-elected position, the city manager often possesses administrative values that undergird his or her approach to executive leadership. Many city managers hold advanced university degrees or have rich experience in urban planning, public administration, and public policy. First and foremost, they are policy and adminis-tration experts. Elected council members and the mayor, however, are motivated to a major extent by the electoral process and are quite properly sensitive to changes in the city's political climate. While city managers may arrive at effective and efficient solutions to a municipality's problems, voters may not find those solutions palat-able. The result is that council members often dismiss city managers as a politically expedient solution to voter disapproval. The city manager's executive power is only as strong as his or her level of support from council. As an executive role, therefore, the city manager concept may be highly effective in the complex world of municipal governance, but the position is often constrained by the shifting fortunes of council members responding to their respective political environments.

Some research has shown that policy and budgeting processes can differ greatly depending on the type of municipal executive system in place. For example, one study found that strong mayor systems have more informal and flexible decision-making processes for capital expenditures (e.g., roads, sewers, water) based on a case-by-case approach, compared to a more formal process with many specifica-tions characterizing city-manager systems.[12]

Executives and Sustainability

State and local government executives play an important role in promoting the core dimensions of sustainability. Investment in human capital is important to all political executives discussed in the chapter. Governors are often key proponents of high-quality K–12 and higher education, as are state superintendents of pub-lic instruction. State treasurers have an important role as well, managing burgeon-ing 529 (or prepaid college tuition) plans intended to broaden admission to higher education and make it a long-term affordable goal for young people. Labor com-missioners, secretaries of state, city council members, and city managers have a vested interest in building human and social capital. Investments in the building of human capital often reinforce efforts to promote social capital—a societal resource that promotes the co-production of public goods through the coordinated efforts of individuals.

Sustained state- and local-level investment in human capital will directly affect efforts to promote the development of a sustainable economic base featuring an educated and adaptive workforce capable of adapting to an ever-changing global marketplace. Political executives at the state and local level invest significant portions of their time in creating public laws that will encourage certain types of low-environmental-impact economic growth, particularly growth that advances the goals of ecological sustainability and that will attract and retain a highly trained workforce. Secretaries of state and labor commissioners, for instance, spend considerable time crafting policies designed to attract sustainable business ventures while simultaneously ensuring that workers operate in productive and safe work environments. Governors often use their visibility to travel to other regions of the country or even to other nations to discuss the benefits of business location in their state and local areas. Businesses are often reticent to relocate to a place that cannot offer long-term opportunity, however, and as a consequence the issue of sustainability often becomes an important drawing card. At the same time, states and local areas that demonstrate a strong desire to pursue clean industries that do not damage local resources may put potential new industries on notice—namely, we care deeply about how we live. Local government executives, those most familiar with the needs of local communities and the special resources of an area, are often in the best position to balance the needs of economic development with the long-term goals of communities in preserving that which makes their place in the world so very special.

Those distinctive qualities of a state or a local area often connect strongly with environmental quality issues. While federal environmental laws have held significant sway in protecting endangered species and ameliorating the effects of environment damage of the past, state and local executives play a prominent role in upholding federal standards. Local land use policies, for instance, can have a tremendous impact on native fish and wildlife species, and on land and water resources. City councils and county commissioners, as well as a host of public agencies, are virtually always the "first line of defense" in protecting and maintaining the environmental goals of sustainable governance.

Local executives serve the institutional goals of sustainability through emphasis on equitable development plans that reduce resource impacts through reduced urban sprawl. In the past, planning and zoning has been used for the nefarious purpose of *de facto* discrimination, excluding certain races and ethnicities from living in certain areas. While federal, state, and local laws long ago moved away from these earlier and dismal times, the core principles of sustainability offer a further reminder that state and local executives must be ever-vigilant to policies that have the effect of excluding individuals from equal and broad participation in social, economic, and political life.

State and local executives can play an important role in promoting sustainability in their jurisdictions. For example, they can suggest and support legislation, issue executive orders, use their powers of persuasion as leaders, and establish various advisory boards, commissions, task forces, and working groups intended to promote sustainability. Some recent examples of executive efforts at the state and local levels of government include the following.

Executives: What Can I Do?

Find out more about state governors by visiting the National Governors' Association (NGA) Web site at: http://www.nga.org/ and its "Inside the Governor's Office" Web site to learn about how governors operate on a daily basis.

The National Association of Secretaries of State (NASS) Web site has a lot of information concerning voting and elections, including a "Can I Vote" link that provides information concerning each state's voter rules and procedures: http://nass.org/. Visit the site and see what rules there are for your state concerning absentee ballots, early voting, and where ballot boxes are located.

Visit the City Mayor's Web site to learn how mayors across the world serve as executives: http://www.citymayors.com/. If you live in a city, visit your own city's Web site to see what type of city executive you have (use ICMA's local government finder at: http://icma.org/resources/govsites/).

The National Association of Counties is an excellent source of information for county government. Visit their Web site at: http://www.naco.org/. Link to the "Learn About Counties" page and take one of their "Test Your Knowledge" quizzes about county government.

In 2000 then-Governor Gray Davis issued Executive Order D-16-00 that established a sustainable building policy to:[13]

> Site, design, deconstruct, construct, renovate, operate, and maintain State buildings that are models of energy, water, and materials efficiency; while providing healthy, productive, and comfortable indoor environments and long-term benefits to Californians.

Similarly, in 2001 Oregon's Governor John Kitzhaber supported and signed into law the Oregon Sustainability Act, a statewide comprehensive plan to pursue sustainability in all facets of government, including the following goals:[14]

> In supporting sustainable communities, state agencies shall seek to enable and encourage local communities to achieve the following objectives:
>
> • Resilient local economies that provide a diversity of economic opportunities for all citizens.
> • Workers supported by lifelong education to ensure a globally competitive workforce.
> • An independent and productive citizenry.
> • Youth supported by strong families and communities.
> • Downtowns and main street communities that are active and vital.

Photo 7.5. Former Governor John Kitzhaber (D-OR) and family. Source: Oregon State Archives, Governor John A. Kitzhaber Records, Photographs and Negatives.

- Development that wisely and efficiently uses infrastructure investments and natural resources.
- Affordable housing available for citizens in community centers.
- Healthy urban and rural watersheds, including habitats for fish and wildlife.
- Clean and sufficient water for all uses.
- Efficient use and reuse of resources and minimization of harmful emissions to the environment.

At the municipal level, perhaps one of the best-known efforts to promote environmental sustainability concerning climate change and the emissions of greenhouse gasses is Seattle Mayor Greg Nickels' effort to establish the Seattle Climate Action Plan.[15] The goal of this initiative is "not only to inform, but also to inspire individuals and organizations—both within and outside City government—to take actions that help make Seattle a model of healthy, ecologically sustainable urban living."[16] Mayor Nickels has broadened this effort into a national movement called the U.S. Mayors Climate Protection Agreement.[17] The goal of the agreement was to get 141 cities to attempt to "meet or beat" the international Kyoto Protocol that set limits on greenhouse emissions. While the U.S. Government has not ratified the protocol, as of November 2009 over 1,000 mayors have signed the agreement. The U.S. Mayors' agreement calls for participating cities to:[18]

- Strive to meet or beat the Kyoto Protocol targets in their own communities, through actions ranging from anti-sprawl land-use policies to urban forest restoration projects to public information campaigns;

- Urge their state governments, and the federal government, to enact policies and programs to meet or beat the greenhouse gas emission reduction target suggested for the United States in the Kyoto Protocol—7% reduction from 1990 levels by 2012; and
- Urge the U.S. Congress to pass the bipartisan greenhouse gas reduction legislation, which would establish a national emission trading system.

Conclusion

Executive leadership serves a very important function in U.S. state and local government. Governors, executive staff and boards, county commissions, mayors, and many other executives can be sources of leadership and policy innovation. Executive functions are either appointed or elected, and are either collegial or hierarchical. In all executive positions, there are at least two dilemmas to be considered. First, executives generally require a well-developed staff and a strong network of relationships with other executives at the national, state, and local level. In other words, executive leadership is highly dependent on support systems to accomplish innovative goals. Second, successful executive leadership depends on the ability of leaders to gain the support of others. Elected executives find that they must gain public support to accomplish their most important goals, including the promotion of sustainability. Executives must lead others, convincing both everyday citizens and other elected and appointed officials that a particular direction in governing will lead to sustainable and desirable outcomes. Finally, executives must have a clear sense of the power they exercise over the institutions they represent, and the influence that comes from developing strong connections between national, state, and local governments. When these assets of executive leadership, organizational power, and network-based influence are directed toward the promotion of sustainability in a state, county, or city government, remarkable outcomes can be the result. The 1,000-plus mayors and county commissioners who have signed on to the Climate Protection Agreement initiative exemplify this potential for positive change.

Key Terms

Commission government	Home rule
Common School Movement	Strong mayor-council
Dillon's Rule	Weak mayor-council
Gerrymandering	

Discussion Questions

1. As Table 7.1 illustrates, there is much variation between states in terms of qualifications to be governor. While some states allow 18-year-olds to run for office (e.g., California), many other states set the minimum age at 30 years (e.g., Florida).

Similarly, there are many differences in terms of residency and citizenship requirements. What do you think should be minimal qualifications for governor, and why?

2. Consider the structure of municipal executives: what are the benefits and costs of weak versus strong mayor systems? How about the city manager form of government: what benefits and costs does this form of executive have in comparison to mayoral systems?

3. Who are the various prominent state executive branch leaders, and what function do they serve in state governments?

CHAPTER 8

Courts

Introduction

When thinking about courts, many of us think about the statute of "Blind Justice," also known as Lady Justice, that adorns the front of many courthouses around the country. Often portrayed blindfolded and holding balance scales and a sword, the figure represented is *Themis*, the Greek goddess of justice and law. The blindfold she wears represents the impartiality with which justice is served, the scales represent the weighing of evidence on either side of a dispute brought to the court, and the sword signifies the power that is held by those making the ultimate decision arrived at after an impartial and fair hearing of evidence. In ancient Greece judges were considered servants of *Themis*, and they were referred to as *themistopolois*.

Whether or not state and local court systems in these modern times are providing blind justice as represented by the statute of *Themis* could be debated. While residents in communities around the country hope their own court system is impartial and immune to outside influences, few who work in or participate in American state court systems believe this is fully true; in fact, there is evidence that suggests that protection from outside influences upon the courts is becoming less and less a sure thing. Judges today are increasingly called upon to make tough public policy decisions, with the outcomes, some of which entail promoting sustainability, often being unpopular with the parties engaged in a particular policy issue. Very often such decisions affect tradeoffs of economic, social, and environmental goals, leaving some parties pleased and others anxious to "redress the balance" either in new statutory language or through further litigation in the courts. This continuation of the dispute through legal action often involves seeking "friendlier" courts with more sympathetic judges in which to file their actions.

At the beginning of the American republic the Founding Fathers clearly believed that the judicial branch would be weak, far weaker than either the executive or the legislative branches. In this regard, according to Alexander Hamilton (1788), in the *Federalist Papers* (number 78):

The Executive not only dispenses the honors, but holds the sword of the community. The legislature not only commands the purse, but prescribes the rules by which the duties and rights of every citizen are to be regulated. The judiciary, on the contrary, has no influence over either the sword or the purse; no direction either of the strength or of the wealth of the society; and can take no active resolution whatever.[1]

Simply speaking, Hamilton thought the judicial branch, with its lack of command of either physical or financial resources, could never overpower the two other branches of government.

Contemporary state, county, and municipal courts face many challenges, with some of these challenges affecting the "Blind Justice" that society expects of its courts. Despite the critical role that courts play in state and local government, many citizens are unaware of the importance of their state and local court systems. In a July 2005 survey about civic education carried out by the American Bar Association, only 55% of the participants were able to name the three branches of government.[2] In point of fact, state and local courts have 100-plus times the number of trials and handle five times as many appeals as the federal courts.[3]

This chapter will:

- Explore the major aspects of state and local courts
- Discuss how these court systems operate
- Outline selection processes for the judiciary
- Explain judicial federalism, including the challenges courts will face in the future
- Discuss the impacts courts have had and will have in the future with respect to the promotion of sustainability

State Court Systems

Unlike other countries with a single, centralized judicial system, the United States operates under a **dual system of judicial power**: one system of courts operates within each state's constitution, and the other system of courts derives from the provisions of Article III of the U.S. Constitution. Thus, each state as well as the federal government is responsible for enforcing the laws, and state and local courts and federal courts adjudicate both civil and criminal case matters. It follows that Americans are dual citizens: not only are they citizens of the United States of America, but they are citizens of the state where they live as well.

With the exception of the appellate process, and possibly in the procedural realm of injunctive relief, the national and state courts are virtually separate and distinct legal entities. For example, since the U.S. Constitution gives the U.S. Congress authority to make uniform laws concerning bankruptcies, state courts largely lack jurisdiction in the matter. On the other hand, the U.S. Constitution does not give the federal government authority over the regulation of family life; in matters of family law (e.g., divorce, child custody, probate, division of property) a state court would have

Photo 8.1. "Blind Justice" with her scales and sword.
Source: © Oleggolovnev | Dreamstime.com

jurisdiction and a federal court would likely not hear cases.[4] While operating largely separately, the two systems can come together in the U.S. appellate courts (including the U.S. Supreme Court). The U.S. Supreme Court has final interpretative authority in the country with respect to disputes regarding the meaning of the U.S. Constitution and interpretation of its provisions by all "inferior" (i.e., subordinate) courts in the country. This situation where the state and federal courts come together happens only when there is a substantial federal question of law and all remedies at the state level are fully exhausted. Even then, it is entirely left up to the U.S. Supreme Court to decide if it wishes to hear the case.[5]

State courts were in place after the American Revolution, but with fresh memories of the Colonial Courts controlled as an extension of English rule, Americans generally distrusted them.[6] Since most states were predominantly rural, conflicts between people tended to be relatively simple and were typically settled informally without the need for court intervention. It wasn't until the mid-19th century that modern unified state court systems emerged. Many of these "upgrades" in the procedures and practices of minor courts came in response to the many new legal challenges arising from the industrial revolution. With industrialization, American society was changing so rapidly in so many areas that state legislatures, most of which met for only brief periods of time, had neither the time nor the resources to develop statutes to cope with the rising problems. For example, with the advent of labor unions, patent rights and royalties associated with new technology and complaints over growing corporate monopolies such as utilities and the railroads brought many disputes to the courts for resolution in the absence of governing statutes.[7] This set of circumstances resulted in many conflicts entering into state courts when parties asked the courts to use their **common law** "equity" powers to resolve contentious commercial, real estate, industrial insurance, and similar disputes in the rapidly industrializing nation.

While **general jurisdiction** county courts were well established in American society and enjoyed growing legitimacy as the memories of colonial rule faded over time, these courts were neither adequately staffed nor properly organized to address the increasingly complicated problems of the day. When state and local courts became overwhelmed with litigation and lost faith in the legislative process to bring timely relief, the state bar associations (the professional licensing association of lawyers in a state) began to orchestrate reform in state court systems. These reforms depended on the separation of powers argument that empowered state supreme courts to create "unified" courts by **mandate of the court** as opposed to legislative action. More specifically, state supreme courts acted on their own authority as a separate branch of government, establishing a system of courts in which the state supreme court sits atop a system of interconnected courts, all of which adhere to the same rules and procedures on how cases (criminal, civil, and equity) are processed and appeals are made. In due course state legislatures codified the key elements of unified court operations into state statutory law. In virtually all of the states, this creation of unified court systems resulted in the addition of new jurisdictions, the development of uniform procedures, the common training of court personnel, and in many cases the development of specialized courts such as small claims courts, juvenile courts, and family law courts.

Through the U.S. Constitution (Article 111, Sec. 1) the U.S. Congress has the power to establish "inferior courts" to hear cases arising from federal law. As previously noted, the interaction between the federal and state courts is relatively rare, with the most notable exception being in the area of civil rights. Federal statutes such as the Civil Rights Act and Voting Rights Act can, and have, brought federal and state court systems into close contact. As a rule, state courts cannot interpret state constitutions in a way that undermines a U.S. Supreme Court ruling by condoning a less protective standard with respect to a civil right recognized to exist in the U.S. Constitution. On the other hand, state courts are permitted to interpret their state constitutions to require greater protections than those required by the federal courts.

Though federal and state court systems happily coexist in most respects, such mutual coexistence is not uniformly the case. For example, during the 1960s there was so much conflict between federal and state courts that a U.S. constitutional revision was proposed calling for the creation of the "Court of the Union," a judicial tribunal that would have addressed the alleged encroachments upon state judicial power by the federal system.[8] Even though the "Court of the Union" idea ultimately failed to gain traction with either the public or the legal community, the conflict between the two systems that gave rise to the idea has not fully abated. An example of this conflict is the deep disagreement over capital punishment arising in late 2007.

While waiting for a U.S. Supreme Court decision as to whether the current method of lethal injection represents "cruel and unusual punishment," a violation of the Eighth Amendment of the U.S. Constitution, many of the 36 states using lethal injection as a method of execution placed a *de facto* moratorium on executions. Other states boldly rebuked the U.S. Supreme Court and moved ahead with planned executions, despite the Supreme Court's plea to await the outcome of its hearing of a key case. On Nov. 2, 2007, barely a month after the U.S. Supreme Court agreed to hear the case (granted *certiori*) on lethal injection, the Florida Supreme Court unanimously ruled that the state's new method for carrying out lethal injections, after changes in the procedure were made that were prompted by a botched execution in December, did not violate the U.S. Constitution's prohibition against cruel and unusual punishment.

How State Courts Work

Comparing one state court to another is like comparing apples to oranges in some respects. Some state court systems are extremely complex, while others are rather simple in their structure. For example, the state of New York, with a population of 19 million in the year 2000, is served by approximately 3,500 full-time judges working within 13 different layers of courts. In contrast, California, with almost double the population of New York, has only three layers of courts and employs only 1,600 judges. Even though both California and New York, and their respective local court systems, operate under the same general principles and under the structure of a unified court system, they do not operate in the same way. For attorneys to practice law in state courts, they must be able to demonstrate knowledge of that particular state's legal system by either passing the state bar examination or otherwise demonstrating sufficient command of the particular state's system of courts.

The caseloads for state courts vary widely, and these workloads seem to have little to do with the size of the state's population. Generally speaking, Western states' courts, which were formed later in the nation's history, tend to be more modern and simplified compared to those of the Eastern states.

The organization of state and local courts tends to reflect two major influences: the organizational model set by the federal courts and each state's judicial preferences as manifested in state constitutions and judiciary statutes.[9] The increased influence of the state's constitution within the state judicial system, particularly in regards to civil rights, is known as **judicial federalism**. As Chapter 5 on state constitutions noted, judicial federalism is at play when state courts address the state's constitutional claims first and consider federal constitutional claims only when extant cases cannot be resolved solely upon state grounds.

The legal terminology and structure of each state's court are quite diverse, but they all follow a generic three-tiered structure. At the base is a system of general and limited jurisdiction trial courts of original jurisdiction, with an intermediate set of appellate courts in the middle, and, at the top, the Court of Last Resort (also an appellate court). In addition, many states are increasingly using specialized, sometimes known as problem-solving, courts as needed. The fundamental distinction between trial courts and appellate courts is that trial courts are those of first instance that decide a dispute by examining the facts. Appellate courts review the trial court's application of the law with respect to the facts as recorded in the official proceedings

State Court Structure

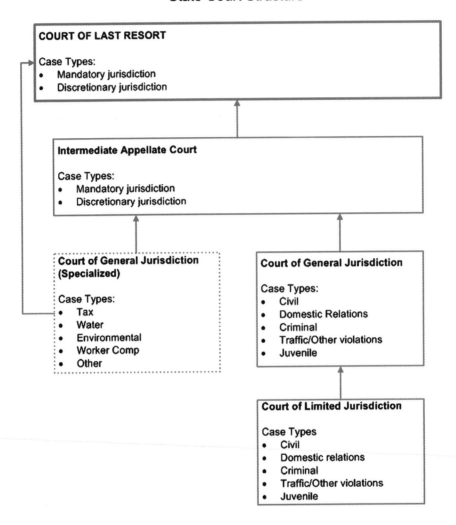

Figure 8.1. State Court Structures.
Source: Adapted from Rottman and Strickland, 2006 (see note 10).

of the case in question.[10] Figure 8.1 reflects how a generic three-tiered court system with a specialized court may operate. The court structure of some states, usually those with small populations, may be more simplified than the generic system, while in other cases the structure is more complex than the diagram implies.

Trial Courts

Trial courts often don't garner the attention of either states' higher courts or the federal courts, but they represent the veritable workhorses of the court system. Typically, each state has two types of trial courts of original jurisdiction, one of limited jurisdiction and one of general jurisdiction. Funding for trial courts of general jurisdiction generally comes from a combination of state and local sources. In most states, courts of limited jurisdiction are principally funded by local governments.

Trial courts of limited jurisdiction, as the name suggests, deal with specific types of cases and are often presided over by a single judge operating without a jury. Found in all but six states, courts of this type typically hold preliminary hearings in felony cases and exercise exclusive jurisdiction over misdemeanor and ordinance violation cases.[11] Geographically, the jurisdiction of these courts varies across the states, but by and large they possess either a countywide jurisdiction or serve a specific local government such as a city or town. If there were an entity we could call a "community court," it would be these courts. They are located within or near a community and handle cases arising from misdemeanor offenses and ordinance violations. The courts of this type include but are not limited to the following:

- *Probate Court*: Handles matters concerning administering the estate of a person who has died
- *Family Court*: Handles matters concerning adoption, annulments, divorce, alimony, custody, child support, and other family matters
- *Traffic Court*: Handles cases involving minor traffic violations
- *Juvenile Court*: Handles cases involving delinquent children under a certain age
- *Municipal Court*: Handles cases involving offenses against city ordinances

General jurisdiction trial courts are the main trial courts in the state system and in most cases are the highest trial court. These courts are generally divided into circuits or districts. In some cases the county serves as the judicial district, but in most states a judicial district embraces a number of counties, which is why they are often referred to as county courts. General jurisdiction trial courts hear cases outside the jurisdiction of the limited jurisdiction trial courts, such as felony criminal cases and high-stakes civil suits. In most states cases are heard in front of a single judge, often with a jury.

Intermediate Appellate Courts

Intermediate appellate courts go by many names, including superior court, appellate division, court of appeals, and even supreme court. With the exception of 11 states, which usually have small populations, states have some form of intermediate appellate courts. The main role of these courts is to hear appeals from trial courts. Any party, except in a case where a defendant in a criminal trial has been found not guilty, who is not satisfied with the outcome from the trial court may appeal to an intermediate appellate court. States' intermediate appellate courts are structured in a variety of ways, but typically they are regionally based and divided into "divisions," "courts" or "districts." For example, Florida has five district courts of appeal, while more sparsely populated Idaho has a single court of appeals. The courts are usually set up with the judges working in panels of three or more (always an odd number), and the majority of judges decides the outcome of the cases brought to the court. The appellate courts do not have juries and do not hear from witnesses or review the facts of the case, but instead read briefs and hear arguments from the parties' attorneys to decide issues of law or process raised in the cases brought up on appeal. The majority of the time its decisions are final, but it is possible to appeal to the next appellate court level, often the court of last resort.

Courts of Last Resort

All states have a court of last resort, primarily referred to as the supreme court, which acts as the state's highest appellate court. In fact, two American states—Oklahoma and Texas—have *two* courts of last resort; one represents a conventional supreme court and the second constitutes a criminal court of appeals. The most common arrangement, found in 28 states, is a seven-judge court; 16 states have five Supreme Court justices, while five states have nine judges.[12]

   With the exception of the 11 states that don't have an intermediate court of appeals, the courts of last resort have discretion as to whether they will hear a case. As an appellate court, it hears cases without a jury, focusing on major questions of law and constitutional issues. Many courts of last resort do have original jurisdiction in certain specific matters, such as the reapportioning of legislative districts. The decisions coming from these courts are final, with the extremely rare exception of when the U.S. Supreme Court decides to hear an appeal from a state.

Photo 8.2. State supreme courts are powerful bodies: the Florida Supreme Court (building pictured) played a key role in the 2000 presidential election.
Source: © Toddtaulman | Dreamstime.com

There are two ways a case regarding a state can be heard in the U.S. Supreme Court. The first, and almost nonexistent, is with the U.S. Supreme Court's original jurisdiction; these situations involve cases between the United States and a state, between two or more states, and between a state and a foreign country. These cases typically go through the federal system and therefore rarely involve a decision from a state court. The second path for a state-based case is through the U.S. Supreme Court's appellate jurisdiction. In these instances, the U.S. Supreme Court can choose to hear a case appealed from a state's court of last resort. For this to occur there must be a substantial federal question involved and the case must be viewed as "ripe," meaning the petitioner has exhausted all potential remedies in the state court system and the resolution of the case can set a useful precedent for the future resolution of similar cases.

The Fifth Amendment case of *Dolan v. City of Tigard* serves as a good example of such a case. This case centered on zoning regulations and property rights. Dolan, an owner of a plumbing supplies store, appealed her claim though the Oregon court system. The Oregon Supreme Court found for the city and rejected the argument that an **unconstitutional taking** of private property by government without just compensation occurred as a result of a zoning decision made by the city. As the case involved Fifth Amendment constitutional rights, the federal courts determined that this case raised a question of federal law. Given that essential determination, Dolan was able to appeal her case to the federal courts, and ultimately all the way to the U.S. Supreme Court. The U.S. Supreme Court found in her favor, causing local governments across the country to take notice of new requirements for determining just compensation in similar cases.

Problem-Solving Courts

Problem-solving courts, commonly referred to as "specialized courts" dispensing "therapeutic jurisprudence," have emerged in most American states over the past decade. Problem-solving courts relieve overwhelmed legal systems dealing with persons and families whose actions stem from problems better dealt with by "supervised treatment" rather than incarceration or similar forms of punitive governmental sanctions. These courts represent an attempt to craft new, adaptive responses to chronic social, human, and legal problems that are resistant to conventional solutions associated with the adversarial process.[13]

Though lacking a precise definition or legal philosophy, problem-solving courts share a basic theme: a desire to improve the results that courts achieve for victims, litigants, defendants, and communities through a collaborative process rather than the conventional adversarial process.[14] Traditional courts tend to focus on the finding of guilt or innocence, entail looking backward in time, and are conducted in an adversarial way. In comparison, specialized courts focus on the identification of therapeutic interventions, seek to affect future outcomes, make use of a collaborative process, and involve a wide range of court-based and community-based services and stakeholders.[15]

A number of factors have led to the rise of special courts, including prison (state facilities) and jail (county and city facilities) overcrowding, highly stressed social and community institutions, and increased awareness of social issues such as domestic violence. While increased social awareness has indeed played some role in the development of these specialized courts, the lack of resources available to state and local court systems has been the major driver behind the broadening use of such courts; the caseloads of the courts have increased substantially in recent decades while the resources available to the courts have not increased proportionately. For example, from 1984 to 1997 the number of domestic violence cases in state courts increased by 77%.[16] Commenting on rising caseloads, Minnesota Chief Justice Kathleen Blaze stated, "You just move 'em, move 'em, move 'em. One of my colleagues on the bench said, 'you know, I feel like I work for McJustice: We sure aren't good for you, but we are fast.'"[17]

Problem-solving courts got their start in 1989 when Dade County, Florida, experimented with a drug court. The drug court, in an attempt to address the problem of criminal recidivism (re-offense) among illegal drug use offenders, sentenced such repeat offenders to a long-term, judicially supervised drug treatment instead of incarceration. Reflecting Dade County's success with this alternative to incarceration, drug courts taking a similar approach to drug use offenders began to crop up all over the United States. As of April 2007, the U.S. Department of Justice reported that there were 1,699 fully operational drug courts in the United States, and another 62 tribal drug courts.[18]

Since this development in 1989, a variety of specialized courts have emerged, primarily designed to tackle difficult social issues. For example, New York City opened its Midtown Community Court in 1993 to target misdemeanor "quality-of-life" crimes, such as prostitution and shoplifting. Instead of relying upon traditional sentencing involving incarceration, offenders were required to pay back the community for the harm they caused by community service work such as cleaning local parks, sweeping streets, and painting over graffiti. In addition, to address the underlying cause of the problem behavior, the offenders were mandated to receive "therapeutic" social services, such as counseling, anger management instruction, substance abuse treatment, and job training.[19] Typically, elements of the local community are also engaged in the work of the problem-solving courts by participating on advisory panels, providing volunteer services, and taking part in town hall meetings. The City of Portland, Oregon, for example, opened a number of "Community Courts" throughout the city, in many cases holding court at existing local community centers.

Evidence collected in evaluation studies conducted on many drug courts indicates that these problem-solving courts tend to achieve favorable results in terms of keeping offenders in treatment, reducing their drug use, reducing recidivism, and reducing jail and prison costs. The rate of retention in drug abuse treatment ordered by drug courts is typically 60%, compared to only 10% to 30% for voluntary programs. Moreover, drug court participants have far lower re-arrest rates than do persons taken into the traditional court process.[20] Even after fully accounting for administrative and overhead costs, in a 2-year period the drug court in Multnomah County, Oregon, saved $2.5 million in criminal justice system costs, with an additional savings being made in costs outside the court system such as reduced theft and reduced public assistance payments. Those associated costs were estimated to come in at $10 million.[21]

The types of problem-solving courts are many, but the majority of them fall into the categories of limited or general jurisdiction **trial courts** (courts of original jurisdiction). The most common specialized courts are those that work on social issues, primarily substance abuse and family courts. Some examples of specialized courts include gun courts, gambling courts, homeless indigent courts, mental-health courts, teen courts, domestic violence courts, elder courts, and community courts involving lay citizens in the process of arranging for property crime offenders to engage in compensatory justice for those they victimized.

Some states have taken it upon themselves to establish specialized courts to protect the environment and to address the economic costs and benefits of pursuing sustainability. Such specialized courts have been created to deal with highly complex issues that require extraordinary scientific and technical knowledge on the part of the court. For example, Montana created a Water Court to expedite the statewide adjudication of state water right claims; once the adjudication process is complete the state may dissolve the court.[22]

In addition to the difficult adjudication of rival water rights claims, Colorado's version of the Water Court has jurisdiction over the use of water and all water matters within its statewide jurisdiction.[23] Vermont has established an Environmental Court to hear matters on municipal and regional planning and development, to hear disputes over state solid waste ordinances, and to handle cases arising from the enforcement actions of the Vermont Agency of Natural Resources. As matters relating to global climate change and the more rigorous regulation of greenhouse gases arise, it is likely that more specialized courts will be created in other states to deal with the disputes arising from the active pursuit of sustainability in our state and local governments.

States are also developing specialized courts to manage economic disputes that arise in the course of commercial activity (such as business formation, business transactions, and the sale or purchase of business assets). Five states have tax courts that deal exclusively with tax disputes. Montana, Nebraska, and Rhode Island developed specialized courts to deal exclusively with workers' compensation cases.

In many states that do not have such specialized courts there has been a steady trend in the growth of the number and range of activities of **administrative law judges**. These "hearings officers" work within administrative agencies that engage in regulatory actions that give rise to many disputes (e.g., environmental regulations, labor/management actions under collective bargaining agreements, compensation for damages incurred from state government action on one's property). These administrative law judges hold quasi-judicial hearings, carefully weigh the arguments of the agency and aggrieved citizens, and have the authority to mediate, arbitrate, and ultimately decide upon an outcome that is binding on all parties. While such decisions made by administrative law judges can be appealed to the courts, state court judges seldom overturn their rulings.

Judicial Selection

The manifest aim of the judicial selection process in the American states is to select a judiciary that is as impartial as the Greek goddess *Themis*, but one that is at the same time accountable to the will of the people of the state. Unlike the federal judiciary, where lifetime appointments are made to the federal district, circuit, and supreme courts, in the states nearly all judges serve for fixed terms of office and most are subject to some method of retention in office based upon a vote of the people. Each state uses a system of selecting judges it feels is best suited to accomplish the dual goals of impartiality and accountability to the people. In most cases, a state's judicial selection process does not catch the public's attention, given the limited knowledge citizens typically command regarding the courts and the actions of their judges; some particularly cynical observers have characterized judicial selection processes as being "about as exciting as a game of checkers . . . played by the mail."[24]

There is no simple way to describe states with respect to their form of judicial selection system, because judges in different (or even the same) levels of courts within one state may be selected through different methods.[25] A system to select a judge for the intermediate appellate court, for example, may be different than the system used for the court of last resort, and different again from the system used for recruitment to the trial courts. Making things even more complex, the selection process for subsequent terms may be different than for the initial term of office.

No single selection process—such as gubernatorial appointment, merit commission screening for gubernatorial appointment, nonpartisan election, partisan election, legislative appointment, nomination to vacancies by county commissioners—currently dominates over other processes, nor do these selection processes within each state remain static over time. For example, in 1980 45% of the states used partisan elections and 29% used nonpartisan elections as their methods for selecting judges to trial courts. By 2004, however, those figures were just about reversed: 44% of the states were using nonpartisan elections and 35% were using partisan elections for selecting their trial court judges.[26]

While there are many types of selection processes, four principal processes are used in the United States for judicial selection within the states: partisan election, nonpartisan election, appointment, and the merit system (known as the Missouri plan). No one process dominates the others in terms of extent of use or the level of controversy associated with its use. There are some regional differences in evidence: for example, some of the nation's most conservative states, including Texas and Deep South states, use partisan elections principally, while many Midwest states tend to use the gubernatorial appointment process. Table 8.1 shows how each state selects its judiciary at present.

Table 8.1. Judicial Selection Method by State

	Court of Last Resort Name(s)	Method of Selection	Intermediate Appellate Court(s)	Appellate Court Justices	General Trial Court(s)	Method of Selection
Alabama	Supreme Court	Partisan election	Court of Criminal Appeals	Partisan election	Circuit Court	Partisan election
			Court of Civil Appeals	Partisan election		
Alaska***	Supreme Court	Appointment	Court of Appeals	Appointment	Superior Court	Appointment
Arizona***	Supreme Court	Appointment	Court of Appeals	Appointment	Superior Court	Appointment
Arkansas	Supreme Court	Nonpartisan election	Court of Appeals	Nonpartisan election	Chancery/ Probate Court Circuit Court	Nonpartisan election
California	Supreme Court	Appointment	Court of Appeal	Appointment	Superior Court	Nonpartisan election
Colorado***	Supreme Court	Appointment	Court of Appeals	Appointment	District Court	Appointment
Connecticut	Supreme Court	Appointment	Appellate Court	Appointment	Superior Court	Appointment
Delaware	Supreme Court	Appointment			Superior Court Court of Chancery	Appointment
Florida	Supreme Court	Appointment	District Courts of Appeals	Appointment	Circuit Court	Nonpartisan election
Georgia	Supreme Court	Nonpartisan election	Court of Appeals	Nonpartisan election	Superior Court	Nonpartisan election
Hawaii	Supreme Court	Appointment	Intermediate Court of Appeals	Appointment	Circuit Court	Appointment
Idaho	Supreme Court	Nonpartisan election	Court of Appeals	Nonpartisan election	District Court	Nonpartisan election
Illinois	Supreme Court	Partisan election	Appellate Court	Partisan election*	Circuit Court	Partisan election
Indiana***	Supreme Court	Appointment	Court of Appeals Tax Court	Appointment Appointment Appointment	Superior Court Probate Court Circuit Court	Partisan election
Iowa***	Supreme Court	Appointment	Court of Appeals	Appointment	District Court	Appointment
Kansas***	Supreme Court	Appointment	Court of Appeals	Appointment	District Court	Appointment

Table 8.1. continued

	Court of Last Resort Name(s)	Method of Selection	Intermediate Appellate Court(s)	Appellate Court Justices	General Trial Court(s)	Method of Selection
Kentucky	Supreme Court	Nonpartisan election	Court of Appeals	Nonpartisan election*	Circuit Court	Nonpartisan election
Louisiana	Supreme Court	Partisan election	Court of Appeal	Partisan election*	District Court	Partisan election
Maine	Supreme Judicial Court	Appointment			Superior Court	Appointment
Maryland	Court of Appeals	Appointment	Court of Special Appeals	Appointment*	Circuit Court	Partisan election
Massachusetts	Supreme Judicial Court	Appointment	Appeals Court	Appointment	Superior Court	Appointment
Michigan	Supreme Court	Nonpartisan election	Court of Appeals	Nonpartisan election	Circuit Court	Nonpartisan election
Minnesota	Supreme Court	Nonpartisan election	Court of Appeals	Nonpartisan election	District Court	Nonpartisan election
Mississippi	Supreme Court	Nonpartisan election	Court of Appeals	Nonpartisan election*	Circuit Court	Nonpartisan election
Missouri***	Supreme Court	Appointment	Court of Appeals	Appointment	Circuit Court	Partisan election
Montana	Supreme Court	Nonpartisan election			District Court	Nonpartisan election
Nebraska***	Supreme Court	Appointment	Court of Appeals	Appointment**	District Court	Appointment
Nevada	Supreme Court	Nonpartisan election			District Court	Nonpartisan election
New Hampshire	Supreme Court	Appointment	Appellate Division of Superior Court	Appointment	Superior Court	Appointment
New Jersey	Supreme Court	Appointment			Superior Court	Appointment
New Mexico	Supreme Court	Partisan election	Court of Appeals	Partisan election	District Court	Partisan election
New York	Supreme Court	Appointment	Appellate Division of Supreme Court; Appellate Terms of Supreme Court	Appointment	Supreme Court; County Court	Partisan election; Partisan election

State						
North Carolina	Supreme Court	Nonpartisan election	Courts of Appeals		Superior Court	Nonpartisan election
North Dakota	Supreme Court	Nonpartisan election			District Court	Nonpartisan election
Ohio	Supreme Court	Partisan election	Court of Appeals	Partisan election	Court of Common Pleas	Partisan election
Oklahoma***	Supreme Court Criminal Court of Appeals	Appointment Appointment	Court of Appeals	Appointment*	District Court	Nonpartisan election
Oregon	Supreme Court	Nonpartisan election	Court of Appeals	Nonpartisan election	Circuit Court	Nonpartisan election
Pennsylvania	Supreme Court	Partisan election	Superior Court Commonwealth Court	Partisan election Partisan election	Tax Court Court of Common Pleas	Nonpartisan election Partisan election
Rhode Island	Supreme Court	Appointment			Superior Court	Appointment
South Carolina	Supreme Court	Appointment#	Court of Appeals	Appointment#	Circuit Court	Appointment
South Dakota	Supreme Court	Appointment			Circuit Court	Nonpartisan election
Tennessee	Supreme Court	Appointment	Court of Appeals Court of Criminal Appeals	Partisan election Partisan election	Criminal Court Chancery Court Probate Court	Appointment Appointment Appointment
Texas	Supreme Court Criminal Court of Appeals	Partisan election Partisan election	Court of Appeal	Partisan election	District Court	Partisan election
Utah***	Supreme Court	Appointment	Court of Appeals	Appointment	District Court	Appointment
Vermont	Supreme Court	Appointment			District Court Superior Court	Appointment Appointment
Virginia	Supreme Court	Appointment#	Court of Appeals	Appointment#	District Court Circuit Court	Appointment Appointment

Table 8.1. continued

	Court of Last Resort Name(s)	Method of Selection	Intermediate Appellate Court(s)	Appellate Court Justices	General Trial Court(s)	Method of Selection
Washington	Supreme Court	Nonpartisan election	Court of Appeals	Nonpartisan election	Superior Court	Nonpartisan election
West Virginia	Supreme Court of Appeals	Partisan election			Circuit Court	Partisan election
Wisconsin	Supreme Court	Nonpartisan election	Court of Appeals	Nonpartisan election	Circuit Court	Nonpartisan election
Wyoming***	Supreme Court	Appointment			District Court	Appointment

*Justices chosen by district
**Chief Justice chosen statewide, associate judges chosen by district
***Uses of the merit system for judicial selection
#Legislative appointment
Source: Adapted from D. Rottman, 2006 (see note 2).

Partisan and Nonpartisan Elections

As of 2006, 39 states elect some or all of their judges; this represents nearly 90% of state judiciaries across the country. From this statistic alone it is clear that the goals of impartiality and public accountability are both important elements of state and local government judicial selection in the United States. Alexander Hamilton (1788) spoke for the Founding Fathers in *Federalist Paper* No. 78, in which he argued that if judges in federal courts were chosen by elected officials they would harbor "too great a disposition to consult popularity to justify a reliance that nothing would be consulted but the Constitution and the laws."[27] In 1939, well over a century after Hamilton's warning, President William Howard Taft described judicial elections in the United States as "disgraceful, and so shocking . . . that they ought to be condemned."[28]

Alexander Hamilton and former President Taft may well be turning in their graves, as the results of one national survey conducted in 2000 found that 78% of Americans believe their state and local judges are influenced (that is, their impartiality is compromised) by having to raise campaign funds.[29] Even so, voter turnout for judicial elections is habitually low, as many voters skip past these elections. At times the biases in the operation of courts associated with popular elections can be severe. For example, 1990 the U.S. Justice Department used federal antidiscrimination statutes to invalidate the State of Georgia's system of electing judges because it was found to discriminate against African-Americans.[30]

Photo 8.3. Judge congratulates drug court graduate. Source: Star-Ledger Photographs © The Star-Ledger, Newark, NJ.

Citizens are poorly informed about judges because, in most states the state supreme court issues limits or guidelines, derived from the American Bar Association's judicial canons, as to what a judicial candidate can say or do while campaigning for judicial office. These limitations tend to be especially strict in states with nonpartisan elections. For example, the Minnesota Code of Judicial Conduct Canon 5(A)(3)(d)(i) prohibits judicial candidates from announcing their views on disputed legal or political issues.[31] Yet there are a handful of states, such as Texas, where the judicial elections are highly partisan, extremely expensive, and vehemently contested.

According to Henry Glick and Kenneth Vines, in a great many cases judicial seats that are nominally up for election are vacated by sitting judges shortly before the end of their terms of office and filled by judges who are appointed by the sitting governor.[32] The governor's appointee then runs as an incumbent judge during the next election. The impact of such interim appointments has greatly shaped the composition of the nation's state and local judiciary: between 1964 and 2004, more than half (52%) of the judges serving in partisan election states gained their position through an interim appointment, with the state-specific percentages ranging from 18% to 92%.[33] These interim appointments more often than not become permanent due to the extremely high retention rate that judicial incumbents enjoy in their elections once they get to the bench.

Partisan elections are those in which judicial candidates, including incumbents, run in party primaries and are listed on the ballot as a candidate of a political party.[34] In contrast, nonpartisan elections are those in which the judicial candidates run on a ballot without a political party designation. There are a few cases where candidates are chosen in a party primary and backed by the party, but they appear without the label on the ballot. The party affiliations of judges aren't exactly the best-kept secrets; judicial candidates often list a party affiliation in their official biographies, and political parties will often endorse particular judicial candidates.[35]

Each elective system has its pros and cons. The proponents of partisan election tend to feel strongly that the party affiliation next to a judicial candidate's name provides important information to voters with respect to the candidate's likely political philosophy. Opponents counter that "justice is not partisan"—that is, there is no Democratic or Republican form of justice, only the impartial justice dispensed by the blindfolded *Themis*, who is unaware of whether the parties coming before her are Democrats or Republicans. The proponents of partisan election counter that in the nonpartisan judicial elections it is the voters who are blindfolded and unable to exercise popular accountability over judges as intended in the election process.

One additional drawback associated with partisan judicial elections is that they can lead to an imbalance among a state's judiciary in cases where a state features strong one-party dominance. Texas encountered this problem during the indictment of former House Majority Leader Tom Delay on corruption charges. Since Texas judges are elected on a partisan ticket, and often contribute openly to partisan causes, quite a scramble was necessary to identify an impartial trial judge who was acceptable to both the prosecution and defense in the Delay case.[36]

Judicial Appointments and the Merit System

There are two common methods of judicial appointment, "simple" gubernatorial appointment and the "merit system" of appointment. The simple gubernatorial appointment is much like that for federal judges, where the highest elected official (the president in the federal government and the governor in the states) fill vacancies on the bench. How judges are selected by state governors depends on the governor in question and traditions in the state. Generally speaking, the background of the judge (e.g., former prosecutor, defense attorney, type of *pro bono* work done, level of activity in local bar associations), the political needs of the governor (someone from a particular area of the state is needed to balance out an appellate bench), presence or absence of advocacy for particular persons by interest groups (e.g., women attorneys, minority attorneys), the views of leaders of the state Bar Association, and the preferences of the political parties are all more or less in play when state governors make their judicial appointments.[37]

The **merit system** or **Missouri plan** system for judicial appointment was designed to "take politics out of judicial selection" by combining the methods of appointment with election in a very particular way. Featuring three distinct components, it is the most complex of the judicial selection processes. Fourteen states use some version of the Missouri plan, with some additional states using a modified version of this type of selection process. Under the Missouri plan, candidates for judicial vacancies are first reviewed by an independent, bipartisan commission of both lawyers and prominent lay citizens. From a list of nominees submitted to the commission, three names are provided to the governor, and one person is selected to fill the vacancy. If the governor doesn't pick one of the three persons put forward by the commission within 60 days, the commission is empowered to make the selection.

Once the judge selected by this process has been in office for 1 year or more, he or she must stand in a "retention election" during the next scheduled general election period. In such an election there is no opponent: voters are either voting to retain the judge in office or remove him or her from the post. If there is a majority vote to remove the judge from office, the judge must step down and the process starts anew. By making the appointed judge stand for a retention election, the people over whom the judge exercises judicial authority have the ability to remove a judge they feel does not perform his or her duties well. Whether or not this was intentional on the plan of Missouri plan designers, judicial removal is exceedingly rare; in the first 179 elections held under the Missouri plan only one judge did not retain his position, and this was a case in which extraordinary circumstances were present.[38]

The term "merit" in the Missouri plan judicial selection process implies that nominating commissions are disengaged from party politics, but the extent to which this disengagement is achieved depends in large measure on who selects the commissioners and how they carry out their duties. These two factors vary considerably across the states using the Missouri plan. In a number of states the governor has a major role in picking members of the commission, and in other states interest groups play a significant role, thereby to some extent circumventing of the "de-politicization" goal of the merit selection system.

The geographic basis for the selection of trial court and appellate judges is somewhat different for each state, and for each type of court within the state's unified court system. For trial courts, a useful general rule is that judges are elected from within the jurisdiction over which they preside. For example, Montana's municipal court judges are elected in a nonpartisan election within the city where the court operates, while the judges of the Water Court, which exercises statewide jurisdiction, are elected in a nonpartisan election from throughout the state. In 30 states, levels of the state's appellate courts are either elected or appointed statewide, while 6 states select all of their appellate justices by district or region.

When it comes to discussions on judicial selection, the most contentious debates arise over how judges on the courts of last resort should be selected. Even though they are appellate courts, and often use the same process for selecting the immediate appellate court judiciary, there are nonetheless noteworthy differences. The geographic basis for selecting a judge is usually statewide, although in eight states the courts of last resort select judges via districts. This difference between district and statewide selection can be a source of considerable contention within states, particularly in states with liberal urban centers and conservative rural areas. Terms of office for a judge on the court of last resort ranges from a low of 5 years to a high of 14 years. There are three exceptions to the fixed-term system of judicial appointment: Massachusetts, New Jersey, and Rhode Island all appoint their justices until they reach the age of 70 or die in office. Judicial terms of office are 8 years or less in 29 states, and more than 8 years in 18 states.[39] Naturally, the shorter the term of service, the more often a justice has to run in a retention election and must rely upon supporters to organize and finance his or her campaign. Everyone who runs for public office, whether a governor, a legislator, or a judge, will need to raise campaign funds and ask citizens and interest groups for their endorsements and "get out the vote" efforts for their candidacy. This type of "politics" carried out by judicial candidates and their challengers raises the questions of "from whom and how much money was raised," and how much influence that citizen or group will have when the judge decides cases brought to his or her court.

An overarching question on judicial selection is whether the method of selection really matters or affects the way courts operate. Evidence suggests that different selection processes produce different results both in terms of who tends to make it to the bench and in terms of rulings made. For example, Nicholas Lovrich and Charles Sheldon found that judicial selection systems that require judicial candidates to campaign actively in competitive elections result in judicial electorates (voters who participate in elections for judges) who are better informed than in judicial selection systems that feature only retention elections.[40] Similarly, it has been reported that appointed judges are likely to respond to a wider variety of groups and interests and to support individual rights more strongly in their rulings than elected judges.[41]

Current and Future Challenges Facing State and Local Courts

State court systems are facing many challenges, both with respect to their work-load and their resource limitations. The civil and criminal caseloads of state and local courts are rising appreciably, but their resources are not growing to match the demands being placed upon a "stressed" system of justice in America. The threat to physical safety in the courts and its judiciary is a serious one in many places, and a quite justifiable concern in some urban areas in particular. Rural courts, with their broad geographic reaches, face challenges not contemplated in America's ur-ban centers. The rapidly rising costs of judicial elections in many states reflect an attempt to politicize the courts on the part of some interests, and in the minds of some observers this movement toward high-cost judicial elections represents a threat to our independent judiciary. In North Carolina the state legislature grew so concerned about this danger that they set up a system of publicly financed judicial elections as an experiment.

The demand upon state court systems is rising in all sectors, and at a more rapid rate than the increase of the general population. Between 1993 and 2002 trial courts across the country saw a 12% increase in civil case filings, a 19% increase in criminal case filings, a 14% increase in domestic relations case filings, a 16% increase in juvenile case filings, and a 2% increase in traffic cases.[42] Though traffic cases account for about 60% of all cases filed in trial courts, complicated and time-intensive cases such as civil, criminal, and domestic relations case filings place a far greater strain on the courts than the more routine traffic cases. The number of judges and courtrooms in operation has not kept pace with the growth in caseloads; in the period 1993 to 2002, state court system judiciaries increased by only 5%.[43]

Court-related violence and courtroom safety is a chronic, costly preoccupa-tion for professionals working in the criminal justice system, but it is not one that gets much public attention.[44] Although this is an ongoing issue throughout the country, a number of high-profile incidents that occurred in 2005 served to high-light the serious threats state and local courts must plan for on a regular basis. In February 2005 a federal judge arrived at her Chicago residence to find her husband and mother murdered by Bart Ross, a 57-year-old electrician whose medical mal-practice claim was dismissed in a court hearing. A mere 2 weeks later, in Atlanta, Georgia, four people, including a state judge and court reporter, were murdered when a defendant on trial for rape overpowered the sheriff's deputy escorting him to the courtroom and took the deputy's gun. In a less violent but more common case of threatening behavior toward judges, the Florida state court trial judge who ordered the feeding tube removed from Terri Schiavo, who was severely brain-damaged, was harassed and received death threats from people who disagreed with his ruling.

In reaction to such events, a study on courtroom safety in California courts found that two thirds of the state's courthouses lacked adequate security, and a companion survey found that 40% of California's state and local prosecutors felt threatened in their jobs. Areas with the poorest security provisions were rural and local courts, which usually rely on local funding for their operations. As an appellate court judge noted, "In a society as litigious as ours, the courtroom has become the theater for emotional catharsis."[45]

Heavy caseloads, the lack of resources, and inadequate courtroom security are real concerns for professionals working in the criminal justice system, but it is the increased **politicization of the courts and judiciary** that is considered the greatest long-term threat to the state and local court systems. This term applies to attempts made to give one political party or interest group an unfair advantage to promote its interests at the likely expense of the public interest. While all Americans have an interest in the existence of impartial, efficient, and legally competent court services, narrow interests sometimes seek to "plant" judges on the bench to gain an advantage in cases involving the adjudication of their affairs. The independence and impartiality of the judiciary, as well as the effective operation of the checks and balances between the three branches of government, are compromised when excessive politicization occurs. The two means used most frequently to politicize the courts are "court stripping" and judicial selection.

According to the *Oxford American Dictionary*, "Court stripping is when legislatures try to remove power from the courts, usually federal but often state, so that the courts can't rule on laws they passed."[46] The most blatant instance of this method of politicization of the judiciary occurred in 2005, when the Republican majority in the U.S. Congress attempted to strip Florida state courts of their jurisdiction over a state matter—in this case the regulation of medical practice—by imposing federal jurisdiction and ordering the federal courts to consider the claims of Terri Schiavo's parents. The Florida court ordered that Terri Schiavo's feeding tube be removed, an action that would ultimately end her life; her parents wanted the tube to remain in hopes she would one day recover from her injuries. Ultimately, the Florida state court decision stood as a consequence of the reaffirmation of state authority to regulate medical practice within state jurisdictions.

There are, and will continue to be, further attempts at court stripping. Upset with some court rulings, some Arizona legislators tried, without success, to enact legislation that would have shifted the power to write court rules from the Arizona Supreme Court, their court of last resort, to the legislature. Court stripping can sometimes happen after a court ruling; for example, although clearly an unconstitutional action in violation of the separation of powers, the Delaware legislature recently enacted legislation overturning its Supreme Court's interpretation of "life imprisonment with the possibility of parole."[47]

Often veiled as "judicial reform," political parties and interest groups in some states are trying to alter the process of how judges are selected and retained in order to change the political makeup of the judiciary. Usually the techniques used appear to be politically neutral "improvements," such as changing the geographic location of selection, the process of selection, and the term lengths. However, underlying the proposed changes are plans for "stacking the deck" with judges more friendly to their interests. For example, in 2006 Oregon Ballot Measure 40 was introduced to amend the Oregon State Constitution to require judges for the Supreme Court and the Appellate Court to be elected by district rather than statewide. The candidate would have to be a resident of the newly formed district for at least a year before the election.[48] The ballot measure failed, with 56% of the voters opposing. Had the measure passed and been enacted, the political makeup of the Oregon courts could have been altered, as the state's sparsely populated rural areas are typically conservative and the heavily populated urban centers are generally liberal.

This type of politicization of courts is nothing new, of course. In 1997 the Illinois General Assembly changed the state's Supreme Court districts to make it more difficult for Democrats to dominate the judiciary. In an attempt at politicization, a 2006 initiative in Montana was circulated permitting the recall of a judge "for any reason acknowledging electoral dissatisfaction." Due to fraud uncovered in the collection of signatures, the measure was removed from the ballot before the election.[49]

In yet another case, state legislators, unhappy with some court decisions made in Missouri, introduced legislation to reduce the initial term of service for appellate judges from 12 to 5 years, and to require a two-thirds voter majority rather than simple majority for retention. Clearly, in the balance between judicial independence and popular accountability it is likely that parties that disagree strongly with the decisions of their state courts will in some cases seek to limit the independence of the courts and create a judicial selection process more likely to put judges of their own liking onto state and local benches.

Nowhere has the politicizing of courts and the judiciary been more apparent than in judicial elections, especially in partisan elections. The 2002 U.S. Supreme Court decision in *Republican Party of Minnesota v. White* accelerated the politicizing of judicial elections. Before *White*, judicial candidates in Minnesota, which used the nonpartisan election process for judicial selection, were forbidden by Canon 5 of the Minnesota Code of Judicial Conduct from announcing their views on disputed legal or political issues, from affiliating themselves with political parties, or from personally soliciting or accepting campaign contributions.[50] In *White* the U.S. Supreme Court ruled that the three clauses of Canon 5 violated the First Amendment rights of judicial candidates, and in so ruling invalidated them and all comparable limitations in place in other states.

The decision of the U.S. Supreme Court in *White* made nonpartisan judicial election processes nonpartisan in name only. Judicial candidates in states featuring judicial elections can now personally solicit campaign funds from lawyers or litigants, they can engage in partisan political activities, and they can declare their views on virtually any matter of public concern, whether or not the matter may be the subject of current or future litigation brought to the court. While Canons of Judicial Conduct continue to exist in all states, the ability of a state Supreme Court or state bar association to sanction a judicial candidate for violating such professional and ethical standards has been undermined by the *White* decision.

Photo 8.4. Do we want judges to be elected on a partisan ballot, or do we want judges to represent impartiality? Source: © Geotrac | Dreamstime.com

Partisan elections, as noted previously, are increasingly becoming more like those of the other two branches of government: expensive, oriented to the mass media, and rancorous. Surprisingly, in recent years the most expensive elections have been "retention-only" elections, where voters only need to decide whether to keep a judge in office. In 1986 almost $12 million was spent in California to remove the state Supreme Court's Chief Justice and two of her colleagues because of their opposition to the death penalty and because of the claim that they were "soft on crime."[51] In an obvious case of conflict of interest, plaintiffs in a $25 million punitive damages suit made contributions to two of the state's Supreme Court justices who were up for re-election and scheduled to hear the case; the justices refused to recuse themselves, or refrain from participating because of a conflict in interest, and ruled in the favor of the plaintiffs.

Special interests are more visible in judicial elections today than ever before; the most visible and active are those with the financial resources to "contribute" and with the most to win or lose in decisions made by courts. For example, the Ohio Chamber of Commerce spent $3 million to defeat a judge who had overturned a tort reform law worth many times as much for business; trial lawyers and unions spent about $1 million in a counteroffensive to retain the judge in question on the Ohio court.[52] Large amounts of funding, and tides of negative advertising, can be attributed to efforts by special interest groups to pursue their policy agenda. The ongoing fight between large corporations and plaintiffs' attorneys over tort reform is a current source of politicization.

Despite strong pressures to further politicize the courts and the judiciary, the public's general perception of the courts is still generally one of presumed independence and impartiality. A national public opinion survey conducted in 2005 found that while the public's knowledge of the judiciary is rather poor, its belief in their courts' adherence to the original principles of *Themis* are strong.[53] Americans believe that their courts represent fairness, due process, and impartiality and play a key role in the preservation of citizen rights. Furthermore, 61% of the respondents to the 2005 survey be-

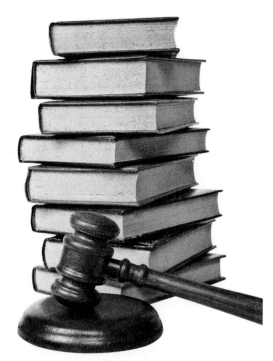

Photo 8.5. Courts uphold the rule of law.
Source: © Broker | Dreamstime.com

lieve that "politicians should not prevent the courts from hearing cases, even on controversial issues such as on gay marriage, because the purpose of the courts is to provide access to justice to everyone, even those with unpopular beliefs."[54]

State and Local Courts and Sustainability

The judicial branch may not "hold the sword" as does the executive branch nor "command the purse" as does the legislative branch, but contrary to Alexander Hamilton's view, it does have great influence over American society. In many areas of American life the courts have fostered needed change

Courts: What Can I Do?

1. Find out more about state courts by visiting the National Center for State Courts (NCSC) Web site at http://www.ncsconline.org/ and consider taking one of their free online courses on state judicial issues at http://www.ncsconline.org/D_ICM/freeresources/index.asp.

2. Visit NCSC's states homepage to learn more about your own state's court system: http://www.ncsconline.org/D_kis/info_court_web_sites.html

3. Visit your local county or city court and watch the proceedings. Many court activities and trials are open to the public. Locate your local county or city court through the National Association of Counties Web site (http://www.naco.org/), the International City Managers Association (http://icma.org/), or the U.S. Courts Web site (http://www.uscourts.gov/courtlinks/).

when the "political branches" could not do so. In the areas of freedom of speech, racial equality, business regulation, the rights of the accused, and environmental protection, the victories made along the way were often seen not in legislation, but rather in the American courts. State and local courts may be somewhat reluctant participants in the public policy process, but they do have an important role as policymakers nonetheless. Judges are called upon to exercise judicial review of both the legislative and executive branches, interpret laws and constitutions, and make judicial policy. While unified state courts ensure a high level of consistency in the operation of courts, the decentralized operations of local courts make it possible for judges to become key actors in local political life by dealing with litigation reflecting local social, economic, environmental, and political conflicts in impartial and constructive ways. Many of the decisions trial court judges make have the potential of establishing important policies affecting local practices in such important areas as zoning, public access to information, legal services for indigents, policing practices, and equal access to education.

Cases heard in a local trial court can have an important impact on sustainable development throughout the nation; the most recent such case is that of *Kelo v. City of New London, Connecticut*. The case in question, as with the *Dolan* case from Oregon discussed above, concerned Fifth Amendment rights set forth in the U.S. Constitution. The controversial issue arose when the City of New London chose to use its power of **eminent domain** to condemn some private homes so that the property on which they sat could be used as part of the city's economic development plan; the plan would have resulted in this private property being condemned for use by another private party working in concert with the City of New London. The homeowners on the property in question filed a lawsuit in which they challenged the right of the City of New London to exercise its power of eminent domain for this purpose, and their case moved all the way from Connecticut trial and appellate courts to the U.S. Supreme Court. A majority of justices on the U.S. Supreme Court found that the benefits to the community involved justified the condemnation, and that the City of New London had provided just compensation for the loss of property suffered by the affected homeowners.

In reaction to this decision, many state legislatures viewed the U.S. Supreme Court's decision as benefiting large corporations at the expense of families and neighborhoods. As a result, legislation was introduced in several states and ballot measures were placed on the ballot in other states aimed at amending state constitutions to provide greater protections of private property rights from this type of use (i.e., economic development) of the municipal power of eminent domain. That power is typically employed when there is some pressing need for public ownership of some private land to serve clearly public purposes (for example, creating a roadway for traffic control).

Some could say the City of New London's action condemning some private land for the economic benefit of the entire community represents an action in line with the philosophy of sustainability, since economic vitality is one of the pillars upon which sustainability rests. Others might argue that such actions threaten sustainability because they displace neighborhoods and promote social inequity in the form of privileged access to large, outside corporate interests. Such varied interpretations are clearly possible, and it is certain that more court cases such as this will be filed and heard as a consequence of municipal actions taken to promote economic viability coming into conflict with property owners seeking to preserve the current use of the land in question.

The *Kelo* case has caused the strengthening of private property rights in many states because this is a politically popular (and apparently cost-free) action for elected officials to take. However, by strengthening private property rights, states enacting greater protections to homeowners may make it more difficult to promote sustainable development. For example, should a municipality seek to use its power of eminent domain to locate solar collectors to provide cheaper and renewable energy to its utility subscribers, should private property owners adversely affected by the location of those collectors be allowed to prevent such a use of eminent domain? Should the pursuit of sustainability goals be one of the "reasonable grounds" justifying the use of eminent domain in the states where laws more protective of homeowners' rights were enacted in the wake of the *Kelo* case? One thing is for certain: state courts and the judges sitting on trial court and appellate court benches in our states will be hearing just such cases in the years ahead.

State and local court decisions have affected sustainability in the past, and they will most certainly do so in the future. Generally speaking, the higher the level of the court, the larger the swath of impact its actions have on sustainability. If a state's court of last resort makes a ruling that sets precedent, then the state's lower courts must follow the dictates of that ruling. This is not to say trial courts are unimportant, as they are most often the first to hear a case that could lead to a change in the law, good or bad, around the rest of the state. An example of the importance of courts in the area of sustainability promotion in state and local government is the case of a widowed grandmother in Orem, Utah. This elderly woman was arrested and taken away in handcuffs for refusing to give a policeman her name so he could issue her a ticket for failing to water her lawn on a regular basis, a violation of an Orem zoning ordinance. If the case goes to trial, it would be heard in the Orem Municipal Court. The reason the grandmother provided for not watering her lawn was that she could not afford to maintain a green lawn. However, the national attention generated from the case has led some to question why a woman should have to defend herself in court for a practice that is both uneconomical and wasteful of a precious natural resource—particularly since Utah is the second driest state in the nation.

Conclusion

There are two clear areas within the purview of state and local courts that can have a major impact on sustainability: judicial federalism and the maintenance of judicial impartiality. Judicial federalism characterizes situations in which state courts give priority to a state question addressed in state constitutional law over a federal question addressed in federal constitutional law. In the recent past, judicial federalism has focused on enhancing the civil rights of a state's vulnerable minorities (e.g., racial and ethnic minorities, the criminally accused) beyond the rights provided in the U.S. Constitution. Today, in the context of the need to address global climate change and actively pursue sustainability, judicial federalism could expand its purview to include the protection of other vulnerable environmental minority interests such as wildlife, water resources, ecosystem services, and rural communities. The well-being of these interests coincides with the economic and social vitality of local communities, and their interests could be served more flexibly in state law than in federal rules and regulations. For judicial federalism to be able to work in this area, the state legislatures must refine their constitutions and statutes to reflect the states' desire to pursue sustainable development so that judges in state and local courts can do their part to support public and private actions intended to promote sustainability.

The second area of particular concern, maintaining judicial impartiality, requires judges and their courts to be independent from outside influences, making decisions based only on legal principles, fairness, and equity rather than giving special consideration based on political party or privileged interest. As much as Americans would love to maintain their current belief in the ideal of blind justice, human fallibility will always be present. The recent trends toward a politicization of the courts and the judicial selection process in the wake of the *White* decision open the door to the possibility that private interests that benefit from unsustainable practices such as urban sprawl, sole reliance upon automobile travel for transportation, overharvesting of forests, and excessive extraction of natural resources will seek to "plant" judges friendly to their interests on state trial and appellate court benches. Efforts are needed by those who support the goals of sustainability to promote both the independence of their state and local courts and to stem the rising tide of the politicization of courts and the judiciary.

Key Terms

Administrative law judges
Certiori
Common law
Dual system (judicial power)
Eminent domain
General jurisdiction courts
Judicial federalism

Mandate of the court
Merit system of judicial appointment
Missouri plan
Politicization of courts/judiciary
Trial courts
Unconstitutional taking

Discussion Questions

1. Of the two common methods of judicial appointment—gubernatorial appointment and the merit system (Missouri plan), which do you think is the better method, and why? Is it really possible to remove "politics" from judicial appointments?

2. What are the various types of state and local courts, and what functions do they serve? Do problem-solving courts increase the institutional sustainability of communities?

3. What are some of the current and potential challenges facing state and local court systems? Do you think the politicization of judicial processes will increase or decrease in the future? Why?

CHAPTER 9

State and Local Bureaucracy and Administration

Introduction

When many Americans think about government bureaucracies, negative stereotypes immediately come to mind: "red tape-bound," "impersonal," "unresponsive,"
"lethargic," and "undemocratic." Similarly, bureaucrats themselves are often labeled
as "lazy," "incompetent," "insensitive," and "power-hungry." However, even though
many Americans carry these negative stereotypes around in their reservoir of thinking, most adults in the workforce are employed by some type of private, public,
or nonprofit bureaucracy and depend on government bureaucracies for the wide
range of services they provide, such as schools, hospitals, fire and police agencies,
the U.S. Postal Service, the Social Security Administration, and so forth. Without
bureaucracy, very little in the way of public services would be provided in modern
society. In addition, the social, economic, and ecological sustainability we need to
promote depends on the institutional sustainability of those entities of state and
local government, which endeavor to organize and implement government policies
and programs.

Despite the broadcast media's inordinate focus on the national government,
state and local governments actually create and implement the vast majority of
public policy, often serving as critical linkages between elected and administrative
personnel working at all levels of U.S. government. The number of sub-national
governmental units, particularly special districts, continues to grow vigorously in
the United States. New units of government reflect growing and changing demands
on the part of local communities. More extensive government often means a greater number of elected officials and public administrators (or bureaucrats). For the

reader interested in a career in state and local government, employment opportunities in public administration experienced tremendous growth over the past decade, and this workforce expansion involved the creation of opportunities for persons possessing a wide variety of skill sets and abilities. With this setting as a backdrop, this chapter will discuss:

- The basic tenets of bureaucracy
- Administration conceptualized as a system
- Networking
- Knowledge, skills, and abilities of the 21st-century administrator
- Women and minorities in public administration
- E-government
- Volunteers and public and nonprofit administration in local communities
- Historical trends in state and local government employment
- Salary trends in state and local government
- State and local agencies' initiatives for working towards sustainability and adaptive innovation in the promotion of resilient communities

What is Bureaucracy?

Bureaucracy is nearly as old as civilization itself. Any reader who has had an interest in archaeology, for instance, knows that some of the earliest examples of human writing are the official documents of bureaucrats or public administrators. The Sumerian clay tablets, found in present-day Iraq, were written by official government scribes, the bureaucrats of that long-lost society! Bureaucrats are the most visible aspect of government in daily life; consumers of government goods and services have regular contact with postal workers, law enforcement personnel, road repair or sewage engineers, the water department, traffic engineers, city planners, and many other administrators representing local, state, and national administrative agencies.

Formally stated, the term **bureaucracy** reflects a rationally organized hierarchical structure and administrative process composed of professionals working in and communicating from well-defined positions within a coordinated formal structure designed to achieve complex goals with maximal effectiveness and efficiency. Bureaucracy is, therefore, a specific type of formal organization. In the late 19th century, the highly regarded sociologist Max Weber (pronounced "Vey-bur") wrote a now-famous treatise on the "ideal" bureaucracy, and this treatise is considered to this day the definitive definition of bureaucracy for scholars and researchers worldwide.[1]

Weber developed his thinking on bureaucracy after close study of many large formal organizations widely regarded as successful in his day, and he identified the principal characteristics of a perfect or "ideal-type" bureaucracy—that is, an organization of large scale that could accomplish very difficult tasks such as the mass production of complex durable goods, the harnessing of the energy of a mighty river, or the gaining of victory in armed combat with a worthy adversary. Not only was it possible to accomplish these grand tasks, but also the goals could be attained with maximum effectiveness and efficiency. One of the basic assumptions of Weber's model was that the ideal bureaucracy could accomplish any goal in any nation, be it the production of goods or services for the private market or for a town, city, state, or nation.

Weber thought of bureaucracy as reflecting the application of science to the task of building organizations, with science taking the form of rationality (as opposed to tradition, family ties, religious preference, myth, sentiment, and so forth) in the design and management of a formal organization. The design of the organization reflects a scientific division of labor and a type of management characterized by the pursuit of effectiveness and efficiency without regard to personal favor or sympathy.

Bureaucracies in Weber's ideal-type sense are composed of professionals who are carrying out specialized tasks requiring specialized training and/or targeted experience. Professionalism is a very important concept in bureaucracy, and the idea is closely tied to the subject of this book—namely, the capacity to build innovative, adaptive, and sustainable communities and to promote the ability among state and local government public administrators to develop the plans, policies, and programs in their respective governments and agencies that facilitate the maintenance of sustainable communities. Professionalism first entails the idea that an individual who occupies an important position in a bureaucracy has gone through appropriate formal education and/or training that prepares him or her to carry out the duties of the position. Professionals require both appropriate prior education/training and a commitment to **lifelong learning** related to their chosen profession. With respect to sustainability, such learning is a necessity as our knowledge expands regarding global climate change and the types of state and local government problem-solving challenges that will have to be taken on in the coming decade, and beyond.

Along with professionalism, communication is another very important component in the operation of an ideal-type bureaucracy. In Weber's bureaucratic model, communication was a direct function of an individual's position within the hierarchy of a bureaucratic system. Accordingly, the boss communicates "down" to the worker in a manner that is unique to being a boss; workers may communicate to each other, but they take orders from their boss and do not communicate back to him or her unless asked to do so. Formal communication, both written and oral and that which concerns decision-making, is documented so that there is strict accountability for all outcomes (successes and failures alike) and so that the record of activities can be carefully studied to improve effectiveness and efficiency.

Finally, bureaucracy in Weber's sense was developed to accomplish complex goals, such as the mass production of consumer goods like automobiles or the establishment of rural electrification in a nation, through the scientific division of

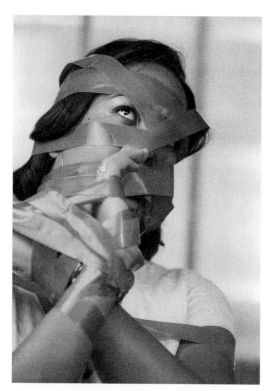

Photo 9.1. Bureaucracy and sustainability: avoiding the red tape is important. Source: © Creatista | Dreamstime.com

labor. This specially created structure called bureaucracy designates the specialization of tasks and the careful coordination of activities using a hierarchy of official positions. The bureaucratic system uses official channels of communication where activities are documented as to who decided what, to what effect, and at what cost to the organization. Complex goals virtually always entail long-term objectives, involving problems that cannot be solved easily or quickly. From your reading of earlier chapters, you realize that good governance in state and local government entails a strong dose of bureaucracy viewed in Weber's framework.

Weber's ideal-type model is an important place to start in our discussion of organizational forms present in state and local government, but it is fair to ask: Do things really work this way in practice? The simple answer is "no." While bureaucratic structure is easily discernible in state and local government, everyday work activities are a great deal more varied and complex than the ideal-type model would lead one to believe. For the most part, formal structure does not accurately describe the nature of work carried out in state and local government. This being the case, it is fair to pose another leading question: Is there a better way to inform ourselves regarding the actual role of public administration and public administrators in the governance process? Fortunately, the answer to that question is "yes!"

Moving from Bureaucracy to Administration as a System

If you were to visualize bureaucracy as an object, what would you see? While some would say a python, with all the negative connotations, a more common and realistic perspective would be that of a pyramid. Just as pyramids have a single tip at the top, so too do bureaucracies: they have one official leader. The base of a pyramid is wide, symbolizing the large number of offices or positions all reporting to the top of the bureaucracy. Similar to a pyramid, bureaucracy might be seen as largely immutable and enduring—an inelastic and highly structured process, something that endures despite changes in the world around it.

Viewing state and local government bureaucracy and bureaucrats in this Weberian light would convey the impression that they are not active participants in governance; they simply do the bidding of elected officials. With all of the training and professionalism required of bureaucrats, however, would it not be wasteful to leave such a large group of well-trained, well-informed, and experienced persons out of the state and local government governing process?

It turns out that while Weber's ideal-type model of bureaucracy would have us believe that bureaucrats in state and local government are simply passively carrying out the directives of their politically elected "bosses" in the legislative and executive offices of government. The truth is, state and local government bureaucrats play a far more active role in American government than is commonly known.

The recognition of a legitimate active engagement role for bureaucracy in governance began when public administration and political science scholars and reflective practitioners in government service began to conceptualize public administration as an organic process. What would organic administration look like? Unlike bureaucracy, an organic process would view public administration in the United States as a highly collaborative enterprise involving people (animate administrative professionals) rather than offices and official positions.[2] In an organic process, individuals within an organization are seen as possessing unique conditions and values, characteristics that cause them to shape the organizational mission and accomplishment as well as strategic planning for the future.[3]

Within the paradigm of active engagement, the act of administration is an interactive process occurring between professionals and citizens rather than involving simply a one-way bureaucratic enterprise of policy implementation strictly following the dictates of elected officials.[4] The sociopolitical environment is affected by what administrators do and how they accomplish their goals; responsiveness to changing conditions is critical for state and local government agencies.[5] In the area of parks and recreation, for instance, the changing demographics of our population and changing tastes and preferences of succeeding generations require that the locations and programs reflect changing patterns of use and demand. Organic administration entails the active interaction between legislative and executive officials and bureaucrats within a network that is adaptive and can respond to the ever-changing needs of agency clientele, all the while balancing these adjustment concerns with the need for the efficient use of public funds. Public administrators are expected to take part in this interaction as able and confident collaborators.

In the 21st century, governance at the state and local level clearly entails building and supporting sustainable communities.[6] Sustainability requires the core traits of adaptability and innovation. While these traits may create desired outcomes in the statutes and ordinances placed into law by elected officials, accomplishing these outcomes requires the active involvement of public administrators responding to changing local, state, national, and even international conditions.[7]

Around the country, in urban, suburban, and rural areas alike, public administrators, nonprofit agency managers, and private organizations are increasingly working in an environment in which they attempt to learn from each other and communicate, coordinate, and collaborate to bring solutions to the attention of the elected officials to whom they report.[8] Administrative capacity for such adaptation and innovation born of a collaborative learning process is a critical element in the promotion of sustainability in American state and local government. U.S. state and local governments must not become so much the victim of the "hollow state" phenomenon—a concept of minimalist government entities and maximal use of contracted services[9]—that collaborative learning in service of sustainability does not take place.[10]

Networks to Somewhere: The Intertwined Process of Administrative Governance

Network approaches involve a type of formal organization that is substantially different from Weber's ideal-type bureaucratic model. The network organization is touted as a genuinely modern arrangement facilitated by the revolution in intra- and inter-organizational communication permitted by computers and the Internet, but the concept itself has been quite long-established. A reading of the history of organizations that have successfully adapted to change in their environments suggests that organizations that maintain extensive "boundary-spanning" activities tend to make adaptations that make them resilient to changes in their environments, while those that stubbornly insist on maintaining long-established practices unique to the organization tend to "collapse."[11] The adoption of a network approach to bureaucratic organization is prevalent in contemporary American state and local government.[12]

What is a network organization? First off, network organizations require the regular interaction of individuals in a variety of positions and with a wide range of different organizations (e.g., other local, state, national, public, and private organizations). Thinking back to the bureaucratic model for a second, one could say that there were two dimensions to bureaucracy—the vertical (power and authority) and the horizontal (equal communication across similar positions). In network approaches to organization, there are multiple dimensions of interaction and there are few fixed bureaucratic relationships; this is because the character of the network depends on the circumstances existing at any given time. Communication organizes itself at one point in time around a hub of positions or of knowledge (i.e., the persons or organizations that possess or control relevant knowledge).

Actions taken by network organizations are based on knowledge acceptance in relation to organizational will or goals. Action is often informally initiated and is referred to as *swarming*—the near-simultaneous movement by individuals or organizations to accomplish a goal. Network organizations are so loosely and flexibly organized that the clear command and control exercised by an organizational elite, a common feature frequently criticized in the bureaucratic model, is often not tenable.

The flexibility and looseness of an organization is both its strength and weakness. Weaknesses arise with respect to holding specific subunits or persons accountable for their work. However, a network organization that has highly professional and ethical employees who reliably follow through on commitments made to other members of the network can be exceptionally effective.[13]

Network organizations are a critical component of the innovative approach emerging in 21st-century democratic governance,[14] although due caution must be observed in establishing and maintaining networks and in ensuring the quality of collaborative efforts over time.[15] Responsive public administration must be aware of private sector adaptations and must be willing to engage in public–private partnerships in an increasing number of areas such as green technologies, telework options for employees, and archival database sharing and joint or collaborative analysis.[16]

Knowledge, Skills, and Abilities of the 21st Century Administrator

Government's need for people with diverse knowledge, skills, and abilities means that no matter what your specialty, a career in state and local public administration is likely an option. Good governance at all levels of government requires the education, training, and skills of a wide array of backgrounds in areas as varied as physical science, social science, law, medicine, education, engineering, agriculture, criminology, and linguistics, to name but a few. If you are interested in public

Photo 9.2. Networks—casual, yet professional. Source: Monalyn Gracia/Corbis.

administration and state and local government service as a career, it is possible to pursue educational goals directly related to your own areas of interest and personal passion—and, most likely, state or local government public administration will have a place for you in the years ahead. The building and governing of sustainable states and local communities will require professionals with a whole host of skills and knowledge for maintaining a vibrant local economy, becoming a steward of the natural environment, and promoting social equity.

In this regard, because new forms of knowledge are emerging at a rapid pace, public service professionals must be committed to lifelong learning and networking. This adaptability will continue to be critical in the coming decade. In the past, bureaucratic organizations valued this type of professionalism, but stultifying hierarchical command and control structures had a devaluing effect. Traditional bureaucracy has a clear tendency to constrain the behavior of bureaucrats rather than fostering their growth, and inhibiting the development of personal responsibility and good judgment that comes from active networking with peers in other organizations (public and private and nonprofit alike). In the administrative governance paradigm described in this chapter, professionalism and a commitment to lifelong learning are valued and rewarded because they foster innovation and the adaptability of thought and actions needed to develop, promote, and preserve plans, public policies, and public programs that enhance the sustainability of our communities and promote the adaptability of our states.

The ability to acquire relevant new knowledge and to determine its utility in the governance process is a multifold enterprise. First, governance in our democratic setting necessitates efficacious communication between administrators, elected officials, and citizens to determine the full meaning and value of the new knowledge in question. Administrative governance as we have described it in this chapter plays a crucial role in the initiation and maintenance of this three-way dialogue. Second, the networked communication among similarly trained administrators in other jurisdictions collectively assesses the value of information, clarifying its validity and relevance to the particular state or local government in question. Finally, communication is a two-way process between a sender and a receiver of communication. An important governance role for administrators is to create dialogue with client stakeholders and elected officials in a manner that builds and empowers rather than erodes their sense of efficacy.[17] In the administrative governance process, state and local government public administrators are both "doers" and "facilitators" who help others become doers.

A clear distinction between "administrators" and "elected officials" must be made here. State and local government administrators must be proficient leaders and executives, but they are not empowered to lead in the same way as elected officials. Good governance requires that public administrators convince others, through active networking, of the virtue of their solutions to problems, even though this networking activity may not always follow the established ways of doing business. Just as elected officials sometimes seek to convince voters that change is needed, administrators use the public forums available to them (e.g., legislative testimony and public hearings, workshops and conferences) to demonstrate their own type of leadership in the governance process. Within their respective agencies, state and local government public administrators act as executives, directing their personnel towards large goals and seeking to develop interagency ties that will provide the resources needed to promote effective current and future administrative governance.

Women and Minorities in Public Administration

In the 19th century, public administrative offices were often used by elected officials to reward their political supporters. A system of **patronage** inordinately benefited the dominant political force of the time—namely, white men. Despite the development of professional public administration, the new civil service systems remained notably biased against ethnic and racial minorities, and against women. While the

Photo 9.3. Women and minorities have made great contributions to governance.
Source: TRBfoto/Blend Images/Corbis.

1950s and 1960s witnessed critical national and state legislation dealing with civil rights and equal employment opportunity, substantial barriers to equal employment and equitable promotion persist. So-called **glass ceilings**—barriers against advancement to executive positions within state and local bureaucracies[18]—remain a significant obstacle to promotion up the ranks. These barriers to advancement are often a function of managerial bias in the promotion and evaluation process, and reflect systematic biases that have become codified into the administrative structure.

Even more noxious and persistent has been the "gendering" of certain professions within public administration. The most obvious example of this process was the notion that secretarial and management assistant staff positions were viewed as "female jobs." Similarly, in law enforcement agencies women were systematically excluded from jobs in patrol divisions because such work was seen as "a man's job." The area of cultural values and beliefs has proved to be the most difficult obstacle to overcome in the advancement of women into the managerial ranks in state and local government public administration. In many jurisdictions, women have sustained claims of sexual harassment against those who perpetrated impermissible actions; however, many other legal actions taken by women seeking to redress inequitable treatment have proven extremely difficult to bring to successful conclusion.

Minorities have long faced serious challenges in gaining equal opportunities in employment. Historical discrimination against minorities in state and local administration remains a serious challenge to diversifying administrative employment. While great strides towards equal treatment have been made in the law, much work remains for people carrying out discretionary actions in hiring and promotion decisions that are based on the true merit of an individual as opposed to considerations of race, ethnicity, and gender.

Despite the obstacles facing them, women and minorities have contributed greatly to the building of the 21st-century administrative systems needed to create sustainable states and communities. Glass ceilings are beginning to shatter: women have taken many notable positions as leaders in public administration. Contrary to the uninformed concerns and blatant stereotypes of white males of an earlier generation, women and minorities have regularly proven to be among the most effective and vocal leaders in administration today and are making critical contributions to the governance process.

E-Government

Creating sustainable governance is perhaps the principal challenge of the 21st century. Sustainability does not occur in isolation, but rather in a competitive environment: while one state or community is attempting to create stable and livable conditions, other states and communities are competing for resources and for the attention of sustainable, clean industries. In this competitive environment, state and local governments frequently find themselves acting in an entrepreneurial way. A major part of being entrepreneurial in the current setting is streamlining governance,[19] and e-government plays an important role in this streamlining process.

One example of the power of e-government concerns efficiency in managing paperwork. In the past, private industries interested in locating plants and offices in a particular state or region faced a great deal of bureaucratic **red tape**—the seeming mountain of legal paperwork and permits involved in attempting to pursue economic development. The time lag between filing paperwork and winning ultimate approval is said to have driven away countless private industries and entrepreneurs that sought more lucrative business climates.

Revolutionary changes in information technology in the 1980s and 1990s led to more accessible, more affordable, and faster computing systems, forever altering the interface between state and local government public administration and their business community clientele. Increasingly, state and local government public administration has moved toward what is called an **e-government** model. Using the Internet, e-government makes use of online forms and processing, reducing unnecessary face time between administrative staff and private industry and small business representatives. This same process has also streamlined the process of requesting and issuing permits and approvals, thus reducing the costs to investors seeking to develop in a particular state or area.

E-government frees up administrators to complete other important tasks in the pursuit of sustainable development. More attention can be devoted to unique cases, in the process improving the quality of administrator–client relations. Administrators can use this additional time to conduct outreach efforts to actively promote business relocation and development in their states and communities. The improved computing network system attracts and retains Generation Y workers and citizens in urban areas. The continued improvement and development of the seamless administration–client interface of e-government is an important part of sustainability in 21st-century governance.

Volunteers, Nonprofits, and Administration

Sustainable government poses challenges to previous perspectives of administrative governance. Until quite recently, administration was thought of as an insular activity carried out by trained professionals. Administrative governance was something that government did *for* or *to* citizen clients. Administrators were experts who required little guidance beyond the strictures of statute, ordinance, or common law; citizens were largely passive players in the modern governance process.

Recent developments have led administrators to actively recruit community volunteers to work along with administrative agencies.[20] The oldest members of the Baby Boomer cohort are soon to enter their 60s, and many of these well-educated individuals were organizational leaders in the public and private sector and played critical roles in building the governance and private sectors. As these

Photo 9.4. A volunteer teacher. Source: Ariel Skelley/Corbis.

individuals retire, they are taking with them highly valuable knowledge, skills, and abilities not easily replaced. The well-educated and highly motivated Generation X-ers (the generation following the Baby Boomers) is relatively small, lacking the sheer number of people needed to fill critical administrative governance roles. Adding to the problem, administrative costs are rising significantly, and as the Boomers age, the costs of employee benefits have increased dramatically. In an atmosphere characterized by both budgetary shortfalls and mounting debt, requesting additional resources to meet administrative goals is not likely to be rewarded with new allocations of state or local government resources.

Under these circumstances, "doing more with less" is the name of the game. Considering all of these factors in combination, scholars and practitioners realize that sustainable governance is not solely an administrative enterprise—it is quite clearly a genuine community enterprise.

In recognition of these circumstances, in the early 1990s President Bill Clinton promoted community-based volunteerism through his AmeriCorps initiative, a policy designed to bring a greater number of young people into a broader spectrum of volunteer community and public service activities, with the hope that some involvement in one's youth would lead to a lifelong commitment to volunteering. Along with preexisting programs such as Volunteers in Service to America, Learn and Serve America, and the Senior Corps, AmeriCorps is part of the Corporation for National Service. The AmeriCorps program is noteworthy because volunteers work through a network of nonprofit organizations delivering public goods and services. Nonprofit organizations are playing important roles once fulfilled by administration or are supplementing insufficient administrative resources.[21]

Incorporating volunteers into administrative enterprise is both rewarding and challenging. Volunteers often bring the community closer to administration, and vice versa. Administrative governance is positively served by keeping a

Photo 9.5. AmeriCorps volunteers rebuilding after Hurricane Katrina. Source: David Rae Morris/epa/Corbis.

finger on the pulse of the community through a network of volunteers. In the case of retired volunteers, administrators often note that they are among the hardest-working individuals in their office, showing up on time and expending considerable energy performing critical tasks such as answering phones, dealing with clients, and filing paperwork. Because they are well versed in etiquette, older volunteers often put clients at ease and are very effective at obtaining needed information to best solve clients' dilemmas. Volunteers may also bring with them the tremendous enthusiasm of youth as they learn new skills and seek to help others. For example, the involvement of AmeriCorps in reading programs has demonstrated the role that volunteers' enthusiasm can play in accomplishing the goal of adult literacy. The same is also true in environment-related programs that have young volunteers planting trees, repairing stream flows, and restoring lost indigenous species habitats.

Relying on volunteers in the administrative governance process also proves challenging. Unlike paid employees, volunteers often need to be motivated in unique ways. They generally need to feel a sense of purpose while carrying out their work, and their efforts to improve governance must be recognized in ways meaningful to them. Volunteers may indeed offer administrative agencies their time and skills, but they also require time and attention as well. If they feel ignored or underappreciated, volunteers often rapidly disengage. One pitfall associated with relying on volunteers is that administrators tend to derive a false sense of their own capacity when goals are accomplished without additional full-time staff. When this occurs, agencies and political leaders may under-invest in full-time human resources, placing agencies at future peril.

All difficulties aside, however, there is no doubt that volunteerism continues to have a vital place in the functioning of state and local government administration.

Historical Trends in State and Local Employment

Over the past 25 years, the story of state and local government employment has been one of growth in scale and scope alike. While variations exist in state-by-state comparisons and across local jurisdictions, government employment at the state level grew by 39% overall and local government employment increased by over 53%. By comparison, national government civilian employment actually *decreased* by approximately 4% between 1982 and 2007.

Workplace diversity is an important issue in state and local government employment. While state variation exists, on average the proportion of women in state and local government employment has increased from 41% in 1981 to nearly 45% in 2003, roughly a 9% increase.[1] Women are still underrepresented in state and local government employment when compared to the general population demographic: as a proportion of the population, women represent over 51% of the total residents

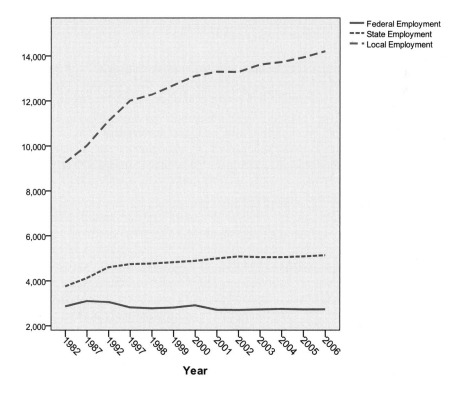

Figure 9.1. Government Employment Trends

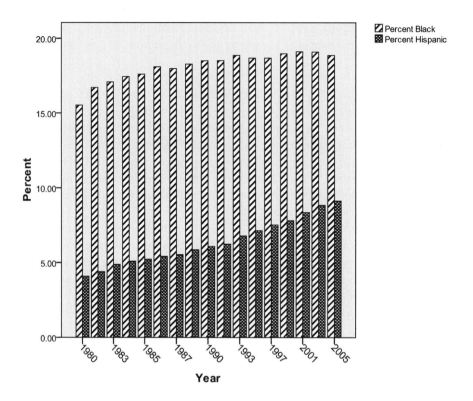

Figure 9.2. Racial and Ethnic Composition of Government Employees

in the United States. The proportion of state and local employees identifying themselves as black increased from 16.7% in 1981 to slightly more than 19% in 2003. Self-identified Hispanic employees in state and local government increased from 4.4% in 1981 to nearly 9% in 2003. The black population tends to be slightly overrepresented in state and local government employment in comparison to Hispanic population. Being aware of how well community diversity is represented in government remains an important consideration.

In terms of employment trends, client service, and salaries, the state and local government picture has looked increasingly rosy over the past quarter-century, but all of these data must be considered carefully. First, there has been an increase in the percentage of employees at the state and local level who are part-time workers. Part-time workers are often ineligible for many of the benefits associated with full-time employment. From the managerial perspective, however, the flexibility engendered through managing part-time workers, in essence, brings workers into the workplace on needs-only basis, thus increasing organizational efficiency. In addition to the growth of part-time employment at the state and local level, private sector contractors play a much larger role in state and local government work. In some cases, private contractors have taken over the functions of government previously managed by full- or part-time state and local government employees.

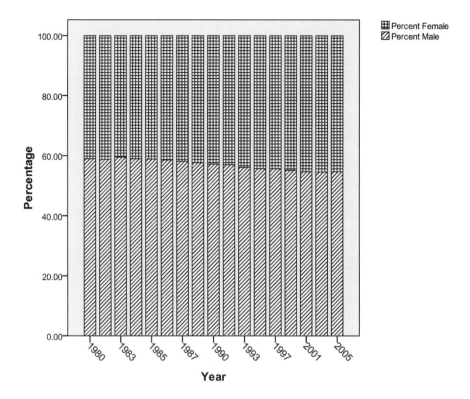

Figure 9.3. Gender Composition of Government Employees

Salaries in State and Local Government

Analyzing national, state, and local government payrolls offers insight into the general trends in employee investment at each level of government. All three levels of government witnessed a real double-digit increase in payroll on a per-employee basis, and state and local government outpaced the national government in this regard. Between 1982 and 2004, national payroll on a per-civilian-employee basis increased by approximately 14.6% in real dollar (i.e., inflation-adjusted) terms. State and local government real payroll per employee increased approximately 17.1% and 15.3%, respectively.

Salaries have risen over the past quarter-century in real dollar terms. When studying salaries from a diversity perspective, Figure 9.4 illustrates well the persistent inequities in state and local government salaries. Women are still paid substantially less than men. White employees still make noticeably more money than minority employees. In trend analysis, it is evident that the salary trends for population subgroups are paralleling one another: in studying median salaries at the state and local level of government as a whole, there does not seem to be any movement towards greater convergence or equity in pay. Pay and benefit equity vary across state and local government, serving as an incentive to attract the highly qualified and diverse workforce needed in public service. A lack of

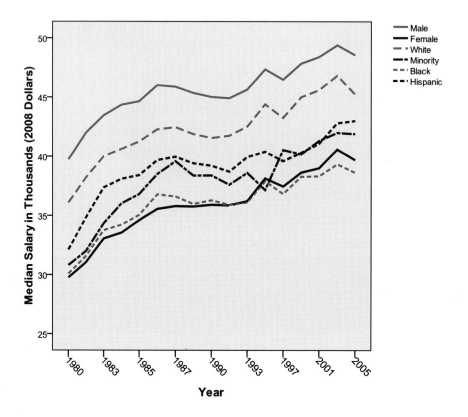

Figure 9.4. Compensation for Government Employees

diversity in public employment tends to parallel unresponsive state and local government. This is particularly problematic in a period necessitating strong links with the community that build an inclusive, innovative, and sustainability-promoting society.

State and Local Employees: Where Do They Work? What Do They Get Paid?

Bureaucracy is a tool of government. Earlier sections in the chapter illustrate the growth of state and local bureaucracy and the rise of a diverse workforce. But an important purpose of this book is to help readers figure out the current focus of state and local government and where they might become contributing players in governance. Therefore, a quick look at the top ten sectors for administrative employment in state and local government and a general look at the top ten average salaries is in order at this point.

The greatest area of employment at the state level is in higher education. Instructors and professors are only one aspect of higher education, of course. Administrators, buildings and grounds specialists, clerical staff, teaching and research assistants, student employees, and a whole host of other personnel play a significant role in higher education. After higher education, corrections—the incarceration and community supervision of convicted individuals—is the second largest state employment sector. Nearly 10% of state employees across the country work in corrections. Public health and welfare are prominent employment sectors, as is street and highway management. Financial administration deals with the proper allocation and accounting of state revenues—in essence, the maintenance of fiscal accountability. Natural resource management accounts for roughly 3% of state employment.

Average salaries are determined by studying total annual payroll in state employment sectors and dividing by the number of employees in that sector. It is admittedly a rough measure, but nonetheless provides interesting evidence. On average, the top salaries at the state level tend to be in science- and engineering-intensive professional fields. Electric power, air transportation, transit, and sewerage are employment sectors that usually entail substantial engineering and physical science education. Readers who wish to pursue a well-paying position in state government might want to consider pursuing math and science education. Training in criminal justice or law is also of great value in terms of well-compensated state employment.

Elementary and secondary education employs nearly 55% of all local government employees. Police protection is the second largest employer, but at a drastically smaller portion of the local government sector: less than 7% of local government employees work in police protection services. Other prominent employment sectors in local government are fire protection, public health, parks and recreation, and public welfare. General government administration accounts for 3% of local government positions.

As with the state-level salaries, the best-compensated positions in local government are in sectors requiring a strong science and/or engineering background. Criminal justice and legal training will also improve a graduate's chances of gaining a high-salaried local government job. Fire protection increasingly requires a solid understanding of knowledge in the areas of criminal justice, Homeland Security, emergency medical assistance, chemistry, biology, physics, health care, engineering, and material science, to name but a few. Education does not rank in the top ten highest-paying jobs in this sector at either the state or the local level.

Administration, Governance, and Innovation

When governments are first developed, leaders define institutions; later, it is institutions that define and often constrain leaders. At the state and local level, for elected leaders, age-old institutional constraints shape and limit their choices. In many ways, elected leaders' position in state and local **governance** has weakened. Governance is the regular decision-making, implementation, and evaluation of policies designed to ensure that public goods are effectively managed or delivered to citizens. The process of election and re-election also limits state and local elected leaders, often drawing them towards more partisan decision-making as they seek voter support and campaign contributions.

Administrative leaders do not face the same pressures as elected officials. First, administrative leaders are chosen based on their tenure in administrative ranks and **merit-based performance**. Merit relates to the knowledge, skills, and demonstrated abilities of an individual in relation to a job description within an administrative organization. Second, administrative leaders are hired based on demonstrated merit, which is usually evaluated in relation to objective analysis of formal training, past experience, and performance on a job-related examination. Third, administrators are generally granted **tenure**, a limited property right to employment so long as their job performance remains satisfactory. For these reasons, administrators are often less distracted in the governance process; constrained by statutory and common law, public administrators are usually guided by principles of justice in their decision-making rather than by partisanship.

Theoretically, public administrators represent the interests of no single person or group of people; instead, they pursue politically neutral goals. In the process of serving the public interest, however, administrators come into contact with individuals and groups who have unique needs. In some cases, groups may attempt to influence administrative governance through appeals to elected administrators or through other forms of political pressure. In either case, administrators are ultimately driven to pursue the public interest, guided by a solid knowledge and understanding of statutory and common law.

Statutes and common law are frequently silent on how day-to-day administrative governance should occur, and on what types of decisions should be made. In political decision-making, sources of guidance might be voter or campaign contributor preferences or even partisanship. In administrative decision-making, legal precedents, administrative capacity, and a professional code of ethics are key sources of guidance in the governance process. Administrators function closely at the client level, close to the consumer of a public service, placing them in a good position to assess the intent of elected governing institutions in relation to statutory and common law constraints. Administrators are often keenly aware of how government decisions promote or detract from judicious outcomes.

Not all administrators serve so closely to citizen consumers. Over the course of a career, administrators are promoted from positions closely tied to a customer base into senior positions of authority. The group with greater authority is generally composed of well-educated, long-serving, and tightly networked individuals. Education is a product of formal training melded with years of practical experience. Long career service can be both beneficial and distracting, however. It is beneficial to the degree that administrators have a sense of what has worked and what has not worked in past attempts at policy innovation and governance. It is potentially distracting, however, in the sense that long service is often associated with a more conservative or defensive stance, and resistance to pursue important and justifiable risks in governance—risks capable of producing positive results for communities.

Finally, long-serving administrators have had time to meet people—lots of people—and to cultivate trust and mutual respect through regular interaction. Administrators develop professional networks with elected leaders, interest and community group leaders, and other administrators. A solid network involves interactions with individuals and groups from different levels of government on an inter-jurisdictional basis. Senior-level administrators often have access to critical governing networks, greater knowledge, and more experience with day-to-day governing than do most politicians.

Bureaucracy and the Core Dimensions of Sustainability

Although often decried by critics, state and local bureaucracy is very well positioned to advance the core dimensions of sustainability. Bureaucracy has both the formal and informal structure to meet a complex set of objectives effectively and efficiently. While traditional formal bureaucratic structures can be viewed as hierarchically organized, the day-to-day operations of bureaucrats tend increasingly towards network structures. Individual state and local government administrators form around and connect with information/knowledge hubs to solve problems of the moment and to meet pressing objectives. The rise of e-government has streamlined bureaucratic processes and reduced costs at a time when costs are rising and demands on government are growing exponentially. Additionally, bureaucracy is well situated to meet the needs of sustainable governance because it is one of the few forms of government institutions that is designed to govern the commons, and whose basic premises focus on equitable distribution of public resources for the individual and collective benefit. Elected branches of state and local government are frequently heavily influenced by the demands of a winning coalition, and the individuals and groups who gain the most influence over elected leaders or candidates for public office are the leading forces within those electoral coalitions. Finally, unlike the elected branches, public administration has a long-term commitment to creating a diverse workforce, a workforce that reflects the nature of a community in the grandest sense of the word.

Looking at the four major objectives of sustainability, as outlined in the first chapter of this book, the principles of sustainable governance are already embedded in the basic principles and goals of numerous familiar bureaucratic agencies. Elected officials have, in many instances, created public institutions to meet the pressing issues of a society. Social objectives are often met through public health offices, social workers, K–12 schools and universities, corrections agencies, labor bureaus, fish and wildlife agencies, and a host of other bureaucratic offices. In the current economic crises facing state and local governments across the country, politicians may propose increased investment in human capital and the building of strong social capital, but it is often the work of bureaucrats at the street level that turns those often high-minded goals into real-world realities. If these real-world efforts to enhance human and social capital in the service of community sustainability are not being done by public servants operating by themselves, it is the work of thousands upon thousands of hard-working, highly motivated volunteers who support the efforts of bureaucrats working in a variety of human capital-related initiatives and enterprises.

Sustainable economic activity is one of the core dimensions of sustainability and sustainable governance. Sustainability demands that the marketplace of the future offers high-quality products produced with and made use of with low environmental impact and purchased at a reasonable cost. In many cases, this means that important trade-offs must be considered and managed effectively. Locally grown food and locally produced goods and services require that state and local workplace dynamics and market conditions must be understood and managed to ensure that the goals of sustainability are achieved in a way that is least intrusive on individual economic freedom and liberty, but that simultaneously protects the interests of the broader community in both the short and long term. Politicians may come and go, but it is state and local bureaucrats who will serve in regulatory agencies over the long haul, getting to know the "regulated" (i.e., the industry actors in their communities) and carefully balancing the needs of the regulated with the needs of the greater society. The networked bureaucrats in these agencies will have access to their peers in other state and local governments, and efforts to disseminate "best practices" and "evidence-based" programs that promote economic sustainability will be privately advocated first by these people. The best ideas will be endorsed and publicly advocated by elected officials in due course.

Environmental sustainability objectives are inextricably wedded to issues of economic sustainability. Again, bureaucratic agencies, often operating independently or semi-independently of the political process, who manage natural resources will be in forefront of public policy development. State departments of forestry, state offices of environmental quality and workplace safety, water quality offices, fish and wildlife agencies, and parks and recreation offices are examples of agencies seeking to meet the goals of environmental sustainability. The work of these agencies is often multi-agency in character and increasingly involves the use of multiparty collaborative processes designed to find ways in a particular state or in a specific geographic area in which productive economic activity can be sustained without undue harm to environmental assets.

Finally, institutional objectives such as facilitating higher population density and reduced urban sprawl in metropolitan areas are often dealt with through the interaction between a multitude of municipal, county, and state planning offices. Bureaucrats and the bureaucratic agencies in which they work have the know-how, skills, and time available to conduct the long-range planning processes required to anticipate changes that could call into question the sustainability of communities. Sustainability demands that state and local governments consider the needs of communities today and in the future, and keep in mind the goal that the current generation must not leave a diminished range of options to achieve prosperity, environmental health, and social equity to the next generation. The infrastructure redesign for the development of renewable energy systems, for instance, will require a commitment of a century or longer to a better way of providing energy to

Bureaucracy: What Can I Do?

When many students in political science think about post-graduate studies, they typically think about law school. However, there are many other opportunities, such as master's programs in public administration, public affairs, and public policy. Learn more about these types of programs at the National Association of Schools of Public Affairs and Administration (NASPPA) Web site: www.nasppa.org

You can also learn more about public service and public administration through NASPPA's networking sites on Facebook and Linkedin:

Facebook: http://www.facebook.com/pages/Washington-DC/Go-Public-Service-MPAMPP-Degrees/80891490654

LinkedIn: http://www.linkedin.com (MPA/MPPs)

NASPPA has also created a MPA/MPP channel on the video-sharing site YouTube where you can find interviews with prominent graduates as well as student-created videos:

YouTube: http://www.youtube/mpampp

permit our way of life to endure. The planners of state and local government will play a critical role in the education of elected officials and the general public alike as to the need for such long-range investment in a sustainable future.

Sustainable Bureaucracies

This chapter has discussed many initiatives, policies, and programs of state and local bureaucracies that contribute to sustainability. These include the use of e-government, networking, life-long learning for personnel, a workforce that represents citizen diversity, and the strategic use of volunteers. State and local administrators are also reorganizing and **reinventing government** to improve the efficiency of programs, to harness resources outside government in the service of public policy goals, and to facilitate the input of state-level interests, private sector groups, and the general public.[22] The move to share bureaucratic decision-making power with citizens and personnel in the lower reaches of organizational hierarchies, to embrace partnerships with private agencies and nongovernmental organizations, and to reform dense rules and hierarchy as necessary components of an efficient and accountable public administration is occurring across a broad range of areas, including community policing,[23] tax administration,[24] education,[25] the federal Job Opportunities in the Business Sector (JOBS) program,[26] and rural[27] and public policy areas.[28] This effort, called **collaborative governance** or **cooperative governance**, could include watershed councils, Granges in rural locations, and neighborhood councils in urban areas.

The propensity to adopt alternative institutional arrangements premised on decentralization, collaboration, and citizen participation is especially pronounced in the environmental and natural resources policy world.[29] Regulatory negotiation, which actively involves a broad range of stakeholders in specifying and implementing regulations, has become more widely used for pollution control. The federal Environmental Protection Agency has developed the Common Sense Initiative (CSI) in league with corporate America, state regulators, national environmentalists, and locally-based environmental justice groups. Their goal is to encourage innovation by providing flexibility and to rationalize existing regulatory rules for each industrial sector through the use of a place-by-place approach to achieving pollution control standards.[30] EPA's Project XL (Excellence and Leadership), announced in 1996, features an ongoing series of pilot projects that follows the lead of CSI. Project XL authorizes site-based stakeholder collaboratives "to allow industrial facilities to replace the current regulatory system with alternative strategies if the result achieve[s] greater environmental benefits."[31] While there is still much to be learned about collaborative governance in terms of where it will be most effective, it may hold much promise in solving difficult problems at state and local levels.

Conclusion

The chapter began by discussing the negative stereotypes many Americans have concerning bureaucracy and bureaucrats. While there are many reasons for these negative stereotypes, ultimately they may have much to do with what Barry Bozeman calls the "inherently controlling" nature of bureaucracy:[32]

> Unless all action is voluntary, coordination of activity requires control. Most of us do not like being controlled, even for the collective good. Even worse, bureaucracy strives (even if it does not always succeed) to deliver even-handed treatment and to administer policies in a disinterested manner, showing no favoritism.

However, as this chapter has emphasized, while state and local bureaucracy does often involve control by seemingly "disinterested" administrators, state and local bureaucrats are also key actors in the ultimate achievement of sustainable communities.

While the bureaucratic model may be a thing of the past in American politics, good governance will always be an ongoing goal. State and local government administrative models are evolving into increasingly sophisticated enterprises at a rapid pace. Community needs are changing and increasing in scope, and as a consequence administrators in state and local government need to find ways to meet these needs while keeping the costs of operation as low as possible. The use of e-government, as mentioned earlier, has greatly increased the efficiency and effectiveness of government administration. A cooperative relationship within and across organizations is making better use of human and fiscal resources. The demand for person-to-person service has forced innovation, and the strategic use of retirees and youthful volunteers has become a prominent element in modern governance as a consequence. Employment at the state and local level will continue to improve in the years ahead. Bureaucrats, in the truest sense, play an essential role in the organization and administration of our state and local governments.

Key Terms

Bureaucracy	Merit-based performance
Collaborative governance	Network approaches
Cooperative governance	Patronage
E-government	Red tape
Glass ceiling	Reinventing government
Governance	Tenure
Lifelong learning	

Discussion Questions

1. What are the historic trends in state and local government employment in terms of numbers employed and demographics (race, gender)? Do you think these trends will continue into the future?
2. What is the role of state and local bureaucracy in promoting sustainable communities? Can you think of some specific examples?
3. Is the role of "red tape" in bureaucracy always a negative phenomenon, or is it important in preventing corruption and maintaining even-handed treatment of citizens?
4. What are some of the new skills and abilities required of state and local administrators in the 21st century?

CHAPTER 10

Budgeting and Sustainability

Introduction

Attending conferences on sustainability organized for government officials is often a very uplifting experience. Keynote speakers typically come from a variety of backgrounds, including business, science, the mass media, and academia. It is clear that the sustainability tent is a large one indeed, and includes ample room for private–public sector partnerships between emerging industries and government. Eager and informed citizen stakeholders and administrators can frequently be found working in cooperative enterprises of one type or another. While nearly always concluding with warnings for the challenges to be faced along the path ahead, the keynote speakers usually offer the promise of a responsible and prosperous future if all reforms of consumption and production practices and processes are achieved as expected. One generally walks away from these gatherings better informed, more deeply concerned, somewhat optimistic, and highly motivated to contribute to achieving the goal of sustainability for our progeny.

The mood tends to change a bit, however, when one faces the realities of budgeting for sustainability; making changes from "business as usual" is generally more expensive than sticking with the status quo and nearly always requires a substantial financial commitment to be maintained over a long timeframe. All too often, that sense of cautious optimism inspired by keynote speakers at sustainability conferences dissipates when the reality of getting through the end of the fiscal period sets in. Those setting the budget have to justify monies requested for the year ahead.

A decade ago, the state and local government budget horizon looked rather bright. The technological boom associated with computers and information processing produced needed new revenue in the 1990s. In the first decade of the 21st century, however, a much darker economic scenario looms.[1] The continuing cost of wars against terrorism abroad, a seriously faltering housing market, a slowdown in economic growth, unresolved healthcare system problems, and pension system failures all translate into forecasts for weak revenue streams coming to state and local governments for an extended period. Energy markets have tightened as peak oil predictions look more convincing, and inflationary trends combined with a weakening currency have led many fiscal analysts to anticipate constrained public sector budgets at the state and local levels. The need to prepare for disasters—either manmade, of the type the Department of Homeland Security seeks to prevent, or the natural phenomena that global climate change may well occasion—is yet another significant constraint that will face budgeters in state and local government over the coming decade.

This chapter will:

- Discuss how the typical state and local budgeting process works, including the various actors and institutions involved
- Present information on sustainable budgeting practices and revenue sources
- Examine historical budgeting patterns in state and local governments
- Discuss intergovernmental sources of revenues for transportation, education, public health, and many more state and local services
- Examine historical state and local expenditure patterns
- Present various approaches for budget reform that have been advocated for state and local government

Why Do We Budget?

Simply put, we "budget" (both a noun and a verb) because we nearly always have limited financial resources and multiple demands on those resources that exceed the actual cash balances, current assets, or expected cash and financial assets available to us. Public budgeting is the process by which elected and appointed officials, acting in the interest of the governed, determine methods of collecting government resources and securing assets through forms of taxation or appropriation (e.g., the holding of public lands, forests, surface waters) and then allocating those financial and associated resources on priorities determined by the democratic political process.

The politics of budgeting means choosing among priorities, deeming some more important than others. The result might be that revenues collected are, as a result of budgeting choices, directed to certain priorities while other noteworthy issues receive less financial support or even no support at all. Human nature being what it is, hardly anyone relishes the thought of losing out in a budgetary process, and virtually nobody who thinks that a priority is worthy of public funding would be pleased to discover that the majority of individuals making budgeting decisions think otherwise. The common result of the periodic budgeting process is that it creates great angst while it is going on, and the results of the process often are that conflict is sown

Photo 10.1. Budgeting . . . if only it were that easy. Source: © Johnkwan | Dreamstime.com

for the next round of budget allocations.

Most proponents of particular state and local budget priorities believe that becoming a funded priority of government is more likely if budget decision-makers (elected and appointed officials) also value a particular priority and are acquainted with the methods for accommodating a budget request. The budgeting process is iterative, meaning existing priorities are continually "explained" and the methods for securing funding have become increasingly sophisticated over time. In the case of pursuing sustainable governance, priorities and budgeting practices have shifted somewhat. Efforts on the part of some powerful advocates to promote sustainability are adding significantly to the traditional challenges of public budgeting. Budgeting is, as a consequence, an increasingly complex process in American state and local government.[2]

In most American state and local governments, budgeting occurs either annually or biannually. Items established in previous budget cycles, if they are politically popular, are more likely to have a higher priority and gain funding than are newer items seeking a piece of the proverbial "budget pie." Unfortunately, many of the new budgetary items involving sustainable governance and the promotion of resilient communities are too new to seem a priority for seasoned budget-makers. This harsh reality means that the task facing sustainability advocates is a challenging one because new ideas must be promoted at the cost of established priorities, and they must gain broad favor to receive the lifeblood of public financial investment.

Generic Budgeting Processes

When we look at a list of the major steps taken in the process of building a state and local government budget, the universal budget process appears deceptively simple:

1. Revenues and expenditures are estimated.
2. An executive budget is compiled and submitted to a legislative body.

3. The legislative body deliberates and issues budgetary approval.
4. The executive signs the legislative enactment containing the budget into law.
5. Budget execution occurs with the allocation of resources to public agencies.
6. Systematic post-authorization audits are conducted to monitor budgetary compliance.

Preparation of Estimates

The beginning of a budget cycle generally requires the input from government agencies on the financial resources they expect to need for the next budget cycle. Similarly, a process is generally in place in which a unit of state and local government prepares revenue estimates for the coming year or biennium. The agency's expenditure estimates are shaped by many considerations, including the following:

- Existing statutes and rules: Agencies consider their statutory requirements. State and local elected officials often develop new policies or adjust older policies through new or revised legislation, then work to estimate the costs associated with them.
- Statutes and rule additions and changes: Agencies consider the costs of implementing and enforcing statutes through administrative rules and other policies. The agency's interpretations of the meaning of statutes—which are frequently subject to the accession of elected leaders and the courts—will affect the expenditure estimates associated with implementation and goal accomplishment.
- Federalism impacts: State and local government agencies often must consider the statutory and administrative rule requirements emanating from other levels of government. Local county and municipal governments are often constrained by state and national laws, rules, and resource provision; states are highly responsive to national politics and federal policy.
- Demographics: Many budgetary priorities are a function of population—the numbers and types of people who live in a jurisdiction currently and who are expected to live there in the future. As demographic changes occur (e.g., school-aged population, percentage of population requiring public health services), the public expenditures associated with accomplishing certain priorities change as a result.
- Agency-related issues: Public agencies at the state and local government level must consider the changing role and nature of their personnel and their operations (e.g., the computerization of records, the adoption of e-government links to the public). An agency's anticipated expenditures often rise or fall independently of statutory additions or changes.

After the agency's estimates have been drawn up, these are typically submitted to an elective executive leader. At the state level, the leader in question is the state governor; at the local level, it may be the county commissioners, the mayor, or the city manager.

Executive Budget Compiled and Submitted to Legislative Body

The political executive is powerful in the budgetary process, without exception. Executives in state or local government review, alter, and compile all agency budgets before submitting their own budget for legislative consideration. Frequently, the executive has offered agencies some guidance in the preparation of their estimates, indicating the executive's priorities as well as expressing expectations about resource availability for the budget derived from the revenue forecast as a whole, and often for constituent parts of the budget as well. In many cases state and local government agencies request resources that do not line up fully with executive expectations or preferences. Often adjustments are made before submitting the budget to the legislative body in question that reflect the executive's preferences and priorities.

The politically responsible, elected executive authority must take into careful consideration the priorities of different levels of government, particularly when those levels of government mandate certain expenditures. Mandates may come with funding to support a priority or may be "unfunded," meaning that the state or local government must carry the cost of complying with the mandate. For example, Congress might require all public agencies to provide easy access to the disabled in all public buildings; if funds are set aside for the reimbursement of costs incurred, this would be a funded mandate. If, on the other hand, few if any such funds are provided, this would be an unfunded mandate.

In addition to mandates, the executive budget must also consider that certain public expenditures are directly related to entitlement programs. Entitlements require that government pay for certain individual needs of a beneficiary meeting a set of prerequisites. For example, indigent people without private assets qualify for state medical benefits, usually in the form of Medicaid. The high costs incurred in meeting mandated and entitlement expenditures limit resources for the introduction of new, cutting-edge policies related to sustainable communities and citizen-engaged governance.

At the state and local level, the political executive usually enjoys the services of a staff budget officer and budget office, and this office is highly responsive to the political executive and his or her own set of priorities. This executive staff office works with agency budget personnel to make adjustments in the expenditure estimates sent from the agencies, and it ultimately submits a compiled budget request to a legislative body for its consideration. The executive budget is usually submitted as a **balanced budget**, with a discussion of expected revenues derived from the revenue forecast and a detailed accounting of expenditure priorities recommended for adoption.

Legislative Body Deliberations and Budget Approval

Both a fiscal management document and a political document, the executive's budget reflects the current administration's ideology and establishes priorities along those lines. State and local legislative (deliberative) bodies are composed of other elected representatives with a wide range of values and issue priorities. In many cases, the executive branch and the majority of legislators are from different political parties, a common situation slowing down the budget process. A governor, for instance, may create a budget built around increases in tax revenues through tax rate adjustments, while a majority of the state legislature is opposed to increasing tax rates. In such a case, the legislature would decline to support the requested level of spending.

The result of these differences is a budget "deconstruction" (significant reconfiguration), after which an entirely new budget is created through the legislative process. Legislatures usually conduct their budgetary business through an elaborate system of subcommittees, whose work is then submitted to the principal budgetary appropriations committee. Through a combination of the subcommittees and the legislative body, the process of establishing budgetary priorities takes shape. Administrative research offices associated with the legislature, as well as the personal staff of legislators, work to coordinate the process and to offer information about various preferences and priorities, and the expected relative costs. In the spirit of institutional checks and balances, revenue analyses are conducted by legislative research offices independently of executive research work.

Eventually, the appropriations committee's work on the budget is compiled into a unified budget document that is discussed, amended, and eventually passed by the legislative body. The legislative budget is then subject to approval or rejection by the political executive. The budget could continue to revert to the legislative body until it either overrides the wishes of the political executive or the political executive approves the budget. In most states and in many local government jurisdictions the executive is permitted to exercise a "line-item veto" over particular budgetary items for some period of time (30 to 60 days, generally), but this power is used sparingly where it is given to the governor, commissioner, or mayor.

Budget Execution

After budget approval, budget instructions are sent to the agencies that will execute its provisions. Budget instructions are usually rather detailed accounts of the goals and priorities of the agency, relating back both to statutory requirements and county or municipal ordinances. Budget instructions, provisos and "fiscal notes" may include expenditure rates and goals, as well as the borrowing authority permitted for agencies. Borrowing authority relates to an agency's capacity to enter into loan agreements for needed resources. Some public agencies may be permitted to issue government bonds as a method of gaining resources. Loans and bonds ultimately involve a promise of repayment of monies to a lender or bond-holder, as well some amount of interest on principal. This aspect of public budgets is particularly important where separate operations and capital budgets are prepared. Capital projects frequently entail public borrowing, while operations budgets seldom do so.

Budget execution requires that agencies submit regular and detailed financial statements and reports to political executives and to the legislature, demonstrating that expenditures comply with established policy priorities. If fiscal resources from another level of government come in the form of a grant, then budget execution may also include regular reports to granting agencies. At times, the agency's expenditures will exceed the amount budgeted to it. In the executive phase, agency budget administrators promptly alert political executives and legislators of possible shortfalls in needed resources. This relatively rare event occurs when there are either unanticipated problems (e.g., a natural disaster) or a serious breakdown of administrative processes (e.g., the Enron energy price scandal), and can result in mandated budget cuts or the identification of other sources of resources through new or increased fees, through tax rate enhancements, or through the sale of public assets.

Post-Audit

At the end of the budget cycle, public agencies are held accountable for their spending actions. The system of accountability that is used in state and local government involves either an independent or in-agency audit of the financial records of agencies. The purpose behind the audit is to ensure that public funds were spent in accordance with the goals and priorities intended, and to determine if any resources were misused or wasted in the process of carrying out the people's business. If an audit is positive, the fiscally responsible agency might benefit by finding its budget requests funded during the next budget cycle. Conversely, shoddy record-keeping and poor financial expenditure choices might hurt an agency and reduce its chances of getting additional public funds for its priorities.

Sustainable Budgeting and Sources of Revenue

State and local governments are the bedrock of the U.S. federal system. The budgetary decisions made at these levels of government have a tremendous influence on the lives of citizens, community organizations, and businesses. Some areas affected by state and local budgeting include lifestyle choices and living arrangements; spending patterns; and business development or relocation. To attract citizens and businesses, state and local governments must help to develop a welcoming, rewarding, and sustainable economic environment. New residents wishing to settle down and raise families, building their personal and professional lives in a place where they feel secure, often need the assurance of a lasting commitment on the part of government and the nonprofit and private sectors where they wish to reside. In many ways commitment is a key element in sustainability. Commitment to a secure quality of life in a specific place on the part of the public, nonprofit, and private sectors often requires dedicated and persistent revenue investment in sustainable governance and enterprise support.

In a sense, the revenue collected from taxpayers represents a commitment on the part of citizens to sustainability: commitment, after all, is a two-way street of mutual obligation. Most satisfying to community members is the view that money being paid to the government is fair or equitable. Likewise, revenue collected must be steady and predictable so that the government can build budgets that focus on meeting the commitment of sustainability. Agreement on equitability and predictability, however, is a major challenge to state and local revenue collection systems, and both equitability and predictability are frequently the source of public dissatisfaction.

Taken in combination, state governments collect approximately a half-trillion dollars per year in revenue. This revenue is collected in a variety of ways, including the following typical categories of state receipts:

- Sales and gross receipts taxes
- Personal income taxes
- License fees
- Corporate income taxes
- Property taxes
- Severance taxes
- Other taxes: death taxes, gift taxes, stock and documentary transfer taxes

Sales and Gross Receipts Taxes

In total, state governments collected over $333 billion in sales and gross receipts taxes in 2006, the last year for which such data are available. Sales taxes are those taxes paid on everything sold in retail transactions, ranging from household appliances to clothing to food. Forty-five states and the District of Columbia impose sales taxes. Each state has the authority to set its own sales tax rate. In most American states unprepared food items are not subject to a sales tax: only five states make unprepared food subject to sales tax; with Tennessee imposing the highest tax rate on unprepared food (5.5%). Taxing unprepared food is often thought to impose a higher cost on low-income individuals and families, and this type of tax is widely viewed as unfair or inequitable as a consequence.

Sales taxes fall within the general category of **excise taxes**, taxes related to consumer consumption behavior. Beyond sales taxes, three other commonly known forms of excise taxes are motor fuel taxes, cigarette taxes, and distilled spirits taxes. Motor fuel taxes generally are used to fund road construction and road and bridge maintenance. Cigarette taxes are used generally by state governments to fund public health and education programs. Tobacco product taxes are potentially inequitable, given that smokers are commonly from lower-income brackets. Nevertheless, it is thought that by increasing the cost to smokers through high excise taxes, the state can cause the demand for tobacco products to decline, likely leading to improved community health and economic sustainability. Nearly all states have cigarette and distilled spirits taxes (so-called *sin taxes*), but the rates vary significantly from state to state.

Personal Income Tax

One common method of collecting state and local revenue—state-level individual income tax—is used in 40 states and the District of Columbia. The lowest bracket

Photo 10.2. Income taxes . . . don't forget to pay! Source: © Mellimage | Dreamstime.com

income tax rate is found in Iowa (0.36%), for those making less than $1,407, and the highest bracket rate is found in Oregon and Hawaii (11.0%), for those making $250,000 and $200,000, respectively. Eight states have a flat rate for state income taxes. The highest flat-rate state income tax is in Massachusetts (5.3%). States with income taxes collected over $245 billion in revenue from personal income taxes in 2006. As a whole, state personal income taxes are the second largest source of revenue for American states and the District of Columbia.

License Fees

License fees are collected by state government for a variety of activities. States collect license fees from businesses and individuals who incorporate within their borders. Businesses usually identify states with low incorporation fees (e.g., Delaware and Nevada charge minimal fees) to reduce their costs of operation. Fees may also be collected for use permits for hunting and recreation in state parks. License fees are a significant source of revenue for the states in total, generating approximately $45 billion dollars in revenue. License fees are usually "visible" only to those individuals and corporate entities that are required to pay them. Nevertheless, the costs associated with the fees, particularly in the case of business-related license fees, generally are passed on to consumers in the form of higher prices. License fees associated with hunting and outdoor recreation may be more visible to individuals, but only to those individuals interested in hunting or recreation in particular locations.

In regards to sustainability, license fees can be used to encourage certain types of business and recreational behavior deemed beneficial to states and communities;

at other times, license fees may actually drive away business development needed for sustainable economies or encourage overuse of state recreational areas, producing environmental degradation. Fees associated with water use and recreational use of public lands are of particular importance in this regard, and many sustainability efforts are aimed at the strategic imposition of fees that promote conservation of natural resources.

Corporate Income Taxes

Corporate income taxes are another important source of state revenue. Business development and retention is a key element in developing a sustainable economic base. Businesses provide jobs to individuals, which in turn help finance other aspects of the local economy. Businesses also contribute to other forms of state revenue, such as license fees. To attract and retain businesses, state corporate income tax rates must be competitive with other states and communities. If tax rates are too high, corporations might find it more lucrative to relocate their corporate offices and manufacturing facilities elsewhere. In many cases corporations find overseas locations more economically beneficial because corporate income tax rates typically are very low. Many states in the Northeast and California in the West have relatively high corporate income tax rates—in the vicinity of 9%. The highest state corporate income tax rate in 2008 was found in Pennsylvania (9.99%). The lowest state corporate income tax rates can be found in several Midwestern and Western states. Most American states that have corporate income taxes impose **flat rates**. A flat tax is a single rate regardless of income level. Eight U.S. states have **graduated** corporate income tax rates: higher-income corporations pay a higher percentage of their income in state corporate income tax than lower-income corporations. As of 2008, Nevada, Washington, and Wyoming do not impose corporate income taxes.

Severance Taxes

Severance taxes are imposed on the extraction of natural resources. States own subsurface mineral rights, some own forestlands, and many protect fish runs through their ownership of surface waters. When natural resources are extracted through activities such as mining, timber harvesting, or fishing, the states can collect excise taxes on earnings derived from those activities. From a rights-based perspective, the state collects on resources that technically belong to all citizens. The tax money collected represents a portion of the price the state is charging extractors for the resource; viewed that way, severance tax rates illustrate the very low price private enterprise pays for rights to natural resources.

High-quality, well-protected, and readily accessible natural resources are key factors in maintaining sustainable state and local communities in many areas of the country. Unless the resources in question are renewable, the extraction of resources could represent a decline in sustainability potential. Hydrocarbon fuels are destroyed through combustive processes, making them non-renewable as energy sources. While use of these resources is not a sustainable practice, hydrocarbon fuels remain the foundation of the world's energy portfolio. Technically, fisheries and timber are renewable resources, but due to restraints on habitat (e.g., hydroelectric dams blocking salmon runs) and aggressive timber harvesting, these natural resources require the collective aid of humankind and the power of government regulation and planning in order to retain or regain levels of sustainability. The viability of plant and animal communities may be compromised during the process of resource extraction by mining, fishing, and timber harvesting.

In the now-famous case ***Northern Spotted Owl v. Hodel*** 716 F. Supp. 479 (W.D. Wash. 1988), U.S. District Court Judge Thomas Zilly decided in favor of the preservation of an endangered species over the continuation of intensive timber harvesting, particularly old-growth timber. The case represents a landmark decision that illustrates a governmental commitment to sustainability and the active pursuit of social and environmental justice through governmental action. This federal court decision has had a widespread impact on state and local governments throughout the country. The court decision made it clear that the pursuit of sustainability entails much more than the maintenance of a regional lifestyle and meeting society's demands for resources and products. Rather, human needs and wants must be understood in the context of a broader view of ecological sustainability, not solely constructed as a zero–sum game in which the natural environment loses while human society gains. The court's interpretation of the Endangered Species Act as seen in the Spotted Owl decision dictates that those extracting natural resources must consider more than profit.

Severance taxes go a small way towards the recognition of the environmental loss associated with many forms of resource extraction. The taxes levied in this area also raise the price of resources extracted, compensating for the hidden costs associated with environmental degradation and reducing the demand for nonrenewable natural resources.

Revenue: Past and Future

Spending is up in state and local government,[3] but revenue streams are tightening. How is this seeming imbalance possible? Good revenue streams exist, but balancing concerns for equity and sustainability is a key aspect of sustainable budgeting. In the past, property taxes and income taxes were highly touted methods of revenue generation.[4] In recent decades, however, the property tax has come under severe political attack. In 1978, California voters passed a property tax limitation measure known as Proposition 13 that severely constrained the property tax as a revenue stream for state and local government in that state. In the decades since the passage of Proposition 13, voters in several other states have supported **tax and expenditure limitation measures** (TELs), resulting in decreased reliance on "broad-based taxes (specifically property taxes)."[5]

State and local governments continue to rely heavily on income and sales taxes, but questions of equity remain. Elderly and low-income individuals, for instance, may be unduly burdened by income taxes.[6] Sales tax rates have risen and in many

Photo 10.3. People protesting school cuts due to Proposition 13. Source: Bettman/Corbis.

cases rate increases have been linked to specific program needs, such as building and maintaining transportation infrastructure. In their study of California taxes, Crabbe and his associates concluded that citizens may find tax rates and increases (specifically sales tax rates) acceptable if taxes can be clearly linked to specific program benefits.[7] Arguably, this finding is largely consistent with a more market-oriented society in which individuals have become accustomed to think in terms of specific expenditures for tangible products.

With respect to predictability, both sales and income taxes are closely tied to economic cycles. The rise and decline of the tech bubble left some state and many local government revenue streams in a rather precarious situation at a time of great need. State budget processes have generally adjusted to revenue instability by tightening up spending commitments[8] and through the artful display of political leadership. Government demonstration of fiscal restraint as a timely action and government accountability as a priority are examples of this political leadership. Former Arkansas Governor Mike Huckabee (a candidate for the Republican presidential nomination in 2008) argued that political leaders must make citizens aware of fiscal constraints and their impact on budget choices.[9] Making empty promises about budget inclusions only sends false signals to citizens about the government's ability to provide services in times of financial stress. Sustainable budgeting requires honest and open government and thoughtful leadership alike.[10]

Despite the recession, the longer-term future may not be unduly grim with respect to government revenues; nonetheless, state and local government budgeters will need to make tough decisions regarding the "three E's" of sustainability—a vibrant economy, a healthy environment, and the active promotion of social equity.[11]

Writing during an earlier period of fiscal constraint, the proponents of reinventing government David Osborne and Ted Gaebler called upon state and local government leaders to become more entrepreneurial in their search for revenue and the operation of their agencies, to look for bargains in their acquisitions processes, and to experiment actively with new methods and techniques of governing.[12] Budgeting in today's challenging times calls for the same level of pragmatism, being realistic about revenues, expenditures, and the needs of citizens.[13] Revenue management in state and local government also entails making good investments. Osborne and Gaebler's model for budgeting during tough economic times shows the importance of concentrating spending in areas that produce future revenue, but that type of prioritization might cause some pain and inequity in the short run.[14]

In another model of budgetary allocations in times of highly constrained budgets, Bowen and his colleagues found that budgetary expenditures ("investments") made in urban areas produced a greater return on investment than similar investments made in rural areas.

Revenue collection and management in state and local government is more than simply fine-tuning a tax system: it is also about enforcement. State and local government systems operating under fiscal stress must strive for efficient and effective tax enforcement and debt collection. Enforcement may be easier today than in the past given the advent of electronic banking and financial transactions. Former Nevada State Controller Kathy Augustine, as with her counterparts in other states, found during her term of office that the use of information technology in tax enforcement was highly effective.[15]

One major revenue stream for state government comes from the 1998 tobacco settlement. One element of the **Master Agreement** requires that "U.S. tobacco companies . . . pay approximately $229 billion between 1999 and 2025 to 46 states, the District of Columbia, and five U.S. territories."[16] Johnson found that states are using the tobacco settlement monies primarily for healthcare, education, and

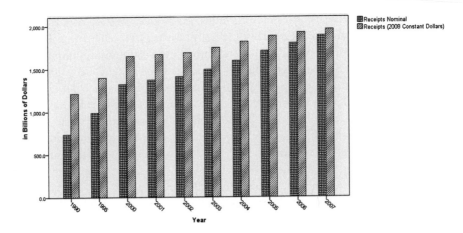

Figure 10.1. Annual Total State and Local Government Receipts (in billions)

infrastructure projects and as the basis for debt issuance. Nevertheless, state budget-makers consider this funding a short-term fix to any future revenue problems: 2025 is no longer on the dim horizon. As a *slack resource*, the tobacco settlement monies could serve as an important part of the public policy innovations necessary to build sustainable governance. Slack resources have been shown to have a positive effect on the budget process and on achieving favorable outcomes.[17]

Federal Grants-in-Aid: A Key Source of Revenue

Federal grants-in-aid are transfers of governmental revenues from the national to state and local governments. There are a variety of types of federal grants. **Categorical grants** are funds given to the state and local level for the accomplishment of specific purposes specified in federal statute and enumerated in considerable detail in administrative rules. When the federal government offers categorical grants to state and local governments, the federal government expects goals to be accomplished and attendant conditions to be maintained while the work is being done (e.g., workplace safety standards, the use of prevailing wage rates, nondiscrimination in hiring and in workplace treatment). In contrast, the amount of federal grant money available to a state or local government in a **formula grant** is not tied to goal accomplishment but rather depends on the characteristics of the citizens living in the recipient state or local government who qualify for a benefit or service to be provided by the state or local government involved. As with categorical grants, formula grants are usually given

Photo 10.4. President Ronald Reagan felt that block grants maximized state and local government freedom. Source: Galen Rowell/Corbis.

to a state or local government to accomplish a national policy goal adopted by Congress.

Categorical and formula grants are usually directed towards specific state and local units of government facing particularly difficult policy dilemmas (e.g., high incidence of domestic violence, the presence of endangered or threatened species, a high level of infectious disease) or are widely available to all state and local governments willing to make an effort to address a public problem (e.g., conduct a hazardous material in transport study for emergency management planning, promote the recycling of waste materials). Alternatively, **competitive grants** require that state and local governments to demonstrate their need for resources as well as develop innovative policy proposals for how a national public policy goal would be addressed in a favorable way if the requesting government were awarded the grant monies.

Unlike competitive grants, **block grants** do not require a state or a county or municipal government to follow strict grant guidelines in policy development or implementation. Rather, grant recipients exercise a great deal of discretion in establishing policy goals and developing innovative implementation strategies. The goal of block grants is to provide seed money for the development of local government policy innovations. While block grants have the potential to be misused and wasted, they have been used to great benefit to promote sustainable community development, globalization of economic processes, and the mediation of adverse effects of global climate change.

Federal Grants for Sustainability and Community Development

As can be seen in Figure 10.2, federal grants for community and regional economic development have increased greatly since 1990. In the 17-year period featured in Figure 10.2, community and regional development grants have increased by over 400%! Other ecological-sustainability grant categories listed did not fare nearly as well. Federal energy grants made to state and local governments and grant funds provided for rural community advancement are of only moderate scale. Environmental protection and national resource grants have experienced only modest gains, likely not even keeping pace with the rate of inflation. If these trend lines are any indication of commitment and prioritization, the community development grants do not appear to equally value all three dimensions of sustainable communities—namely, economic vitality, environmental protection, and social equity.

Federal Grants for Transportation

Beyond doubt, sustainable communities will require more energy-efficient modes of transportation. The cost of fossil energy is high and vehicle emissions are a growing concern for climate change phenomena. Renewable energy and hybrid vehicles

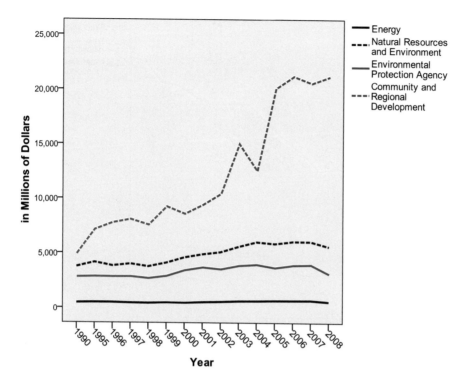

Figure 10.2. Federal Grants for Sustainability and Community Development

face escalating demand and short supply. Mass transportation systems might be one very important method of reducing demand for fossil energy. Alternative-energy mass transportation vehicles are becoming increasingly visible in society—natural gas and clean diesel-powered buses are now quite common across the nation. Similarly, cutting-edge hydrogen-powered buses are part of several mass transportation demonstration projects in the United States and in several cities abroad. Nevertheless, it is fair to say that federal transportation-related grant trends would seem to provide more support for a tenuous status quo than to promote more efficient and sustainable transportation schemes.

For leaders and administrators at the state and local level, sustainable transportation requires grassroots policy innovation and funding. Many states have instituted their own transportation and energy initiatives to counteract the rather tepid commitment of the federal government to support transportation policy renewal through grants-in-aid. Also, rebuilding city centers and developing high-concentration housing units, such as condominiums, may increase use of public transportation and bring about reductions in reliance on the personal automobile.

Federal Grants for Education
Education grants have risen steadily since 1990. Money for education workforce enhancement and training has risen most noticeably; in large part these grants have

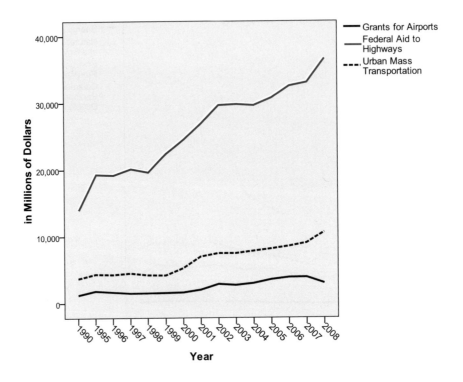

Figure 10.3. Federal Grants for Transportation

resulted from the increased emphasis on teacher quality and retention. Education and social services funding has increased in response to new awareness of the relationship between educational achievement and social conditions of students. Federal funding for special education and the education of the disadvantaged represents a significant portion of the federal funds transferred to state and local governments in the form of grants-in-aid. Noticeably, money for school building improvement has declined, despite increased awareness of classroom overcrowding and school building disrepair. School building infrastructure grants are not only an important part of current education quality, but they are also critical to the sustainability of public schools as a core element of civic infrastructure.

Federal Grants for the Least Advantaged—Public Health and Income Security

Federal grants for public health services for the least well-off in society are critical in efforts to create and maintain sustainable communities. A community's level of success or failure depends on the achievement of both individual and collective goals. While individual goals may be highly varied, collective goals are defined by

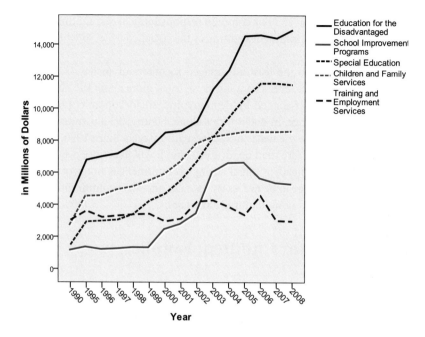

Figure 10.4. Federal Grants for Education

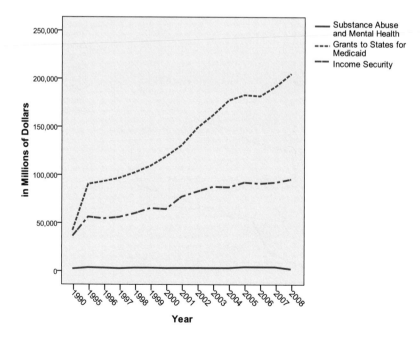

Figure 10.5. Federal Grants for the Least Advantaged—Public Health and Income Security

what we share in common and our common responsibility to one another. Recognition of our collective commitment legitimizes the social contract to which we have agreed.

Our commitment to the least advantaged members of society is and always will be a work in progress, ever-changing as we learn more about the nature of our society and the social ills shaped by demographic, socioeconomic, political, and even environmental change. In dollar terms alone, Figure 10.5 illustrates our growing commitment to serve the needs of the least advantaged. Since 1990, the federal grant commitment has more than quadrupled, and it will likely rise even more significantly in the years ahead. While a strong commitment is noteworthy, federal grants-in-aid will continue to be necessary as states and local communities struggle to establish sustainability along multiple dimensions.

Federal Grants for Children, Families, and Veterans

Figure 10.6 places a number of program areas into comparative terms for an important reason. We believe that the comparison featured is across groups of individuals in our society who are among the most vulnerable and yet are critical to our social sustainability. Commitment to caring for children, families, and veterans represents

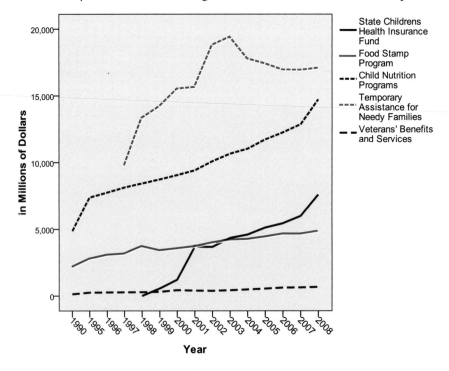

Figure 10.6. Federal Grants for Children, Families, and Veterans

a core value in American society. While all the dimensions of sustainability will ultimately require "commitment," it struck us as a unique opportunity to illustrate in one table some of the most recognizable examples of commitment!

Commitment to children and families has risen enormously since 1990. While some might applaud the growing commitment, it also signals something else: as with all the other charts discussed previously in this chapter, it signals critical disparities in our states and local communities that American society, through private actions, public policy, and budgetary choices, has determined must be overcome if sustainability is to be achieved. The decline in **Temporary Assistance to Needy Families** (TANF) in terms of grant funding might in part be explained by the success of President Clinton's collaborative efforts with a Republican congressional majority to hammer out welfare reform provisions. Those reforms resulted in moving many individuals off welfare rolls and into the workforce. Alternatively, it has been argued that TANF and welfare reform has resulted in an ebbing commitment to families[18]— the decline in grant funding started shortly after Republicans regained control of both chambers in Congress in 2003.

Federal grants for veterans' programs at the state and local level has been flat for several years, despite the rise in the number of disabled veterans resulting from warfare in Afghanistan and Iraq. Veterans of the Second World War, Korea, Vietnam, and the Persian Gulf War eras have been joined by veterans of more recent

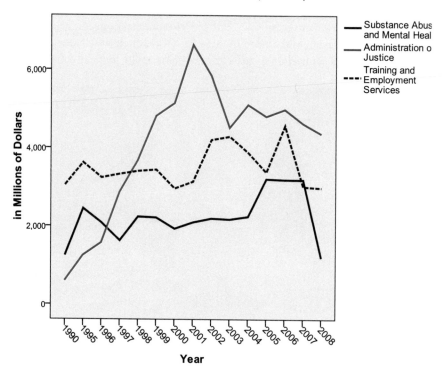

Figure 10.7. Federal Funding for Programs of Hope and Corrections

military commitments arising from the global war on terrorism. Rather incredibly, federal grant monies have remained steady in nominal terms—and if inflation were factored in, the amount of grant money being provided for veterans' programs is actually declining in real terms.

Federal Funding for Programs of Hope and Corrections

Again, in Figure 10.7 we have placed in comparison a number of federal grant areas that often affect young adults who find themselves in trouble with the law. How youths are treated is a significant factor in community resiliency; each generation in a community must achieve progress and improve its performance in order for its community to be sustained in the context of ever-changing global, regional, and local conditions.

The program funding in Figure 10.7 shows our commitment via federal grants to programs that are intended to deal with such issues. As can be seen, the commitment to most of the program areas began to decline in the early years of the 21st century. The one program area that has not declined—although it has fluctuated—pertains to funding for vocational and adult education.

Federal grants are important sources of revenue indeed, and many of these grants contribute directly to economic vitality, environmental protection, and social equity. The federal revenues provided in these grants are often attached to national policy goals, and this connection to goals gives us some ability to make comparisons

Photo 10.5. Adults in the classroom. Source: © Monkeybusinessimages | Dreamstime.com

over time between grant efforts made and goals being accomplished. Funding for many policy areas is on the rise, but in some cases funding is either stagnating or even declining. While federal grants to state and local governments are very important to our discussion of budgeting and sustainability, it is equally important to explore independently the budget expenditures of state and local governments.

State and Local Budget Expenditures

Budget expenditures are a good way of determining the priorities of state and local governments. In looking at total state budget expenditures (Fig. 10.8), it is clear that education and public welfare represent over half of state budget expenditures. The third most common expenditure is for insurance trust funds, an allocation that covers public employee retirement benefits and private sector unemployment insurance. Highways and bridges and health/hospital expenditures also constitute large portions of state government expenditures. All other functions of government—for example, law enforcement, corrections, courts, natural resource management, and utilities—are covered by roughly one quarter of the total state budget expenditures. The area of Veterans' Services garners only the tiniest of fractions of total state budget expenditures.

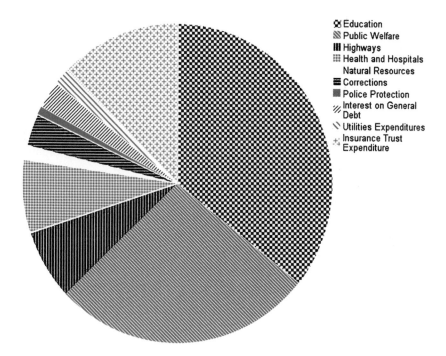

Figure 10.8. State Budget Expenditures, 2007.
Data Source: Statistical Abstract of the United States, 2009.

As with state governments, local government expenditures are predominantly focused on education expenditures. Approximately one third of total local government expenditures in the United States are spent on elementary and secondary education. Public assistance expenditures amount to roughly one quarter of local government expenditures, while allocations to insurance trust funds are between 15% and 20% of total local government expenditures. A little over a quarter of local government expenditures covers all other government services—for example, fire, parks and recreation, and criminal justice (courts, jails, and law enforcement).

In both state and local governments, public assistance and education are by far the biggest expenditure categories in public budgets. In terms of sustainability, education represents a direct investment in the future. With the proper education, tools, technology, and knowledge, a new generation could be better prepared to deal with the challenges of the future than past and current generations. For example, the adoption of renewable energy sources requires that citizens understand the bigger system of energy generation, distribution, and use. Through local communities, well-educated citizens will have to make wise choices about energy supply and demand. Education is also a key ingredient in government and private sector innovation. Future quality of life will rely heavily on new knowledge and scientific breakthroughs.

As with education, the area of social assistance consumes a significant portion of the state and local tax dollar, as well as intergovernmental transfers (frequently in the form of grants) coming from the federal government. A sustainable society promotes social justice. A tenet of social justice is that society and government must actively address socioeconomic disadvantage. A vertically divided society—a society in which a small group of individuals control a large proportion of available resources while a large number of individuals have little or no access to resources—is not a sustainable society. The vertically divided society, particularly a society facing near-term shortfalls of basic energy and natural resources, will prove to be politically and socially volatile and could even lead to disarray. Social assistance programs represent a commitment to addressing such inequities and preventing social and political conflict.

Many important categories of expenditure associated with sustainability—categories related to natural resource protection, environmental protection, and basic infrastructure maintenance—tend to be overshadowed by the education and social assistance functions. Commitment to funding those who have suffered in personal efforts to protect us—the veterans of our wars—is paltry compared to other functions of government. Is commitment to funding these items that tend to be overlooked important to sustainability? The answer is an emphatic "Yes!"

Budget Reforms

Over the years, state and local governments have tried to use various techniques to manage expenditures more effectively while accomplishing goals related to good governance. In many cases, budgetary techniques have been driven by partisan politics, and these techniques have proven to be myopic in design and self-limiting in execution.[19] At times, attention has been focused on the input side of budgeting—essentially, tightly controlling agency spending as a method of increasing efficiency in the budget process. Spending control has been attempted through state-level debt limitation measures and the use of the executive line item veto. At other times, some state and local governments have focused on the output side of budgeting, through control of public spending. Finally, the methods by which services are delivered have also been related to the budget process and the promise of more efficient and effective budgeting and related policy outcomes.

Debt limitation measures are commonly found at the state and local level. Most states[20] and virtually all local governments require that annual budgets be balanced. Revenue in balanced budgets could be in the form of tax revenue or revenue from bond issuances. Both forms of revenue are monitored and approved by state and local governments. Debt issuance limitations prove to be very important in maintaining a long-term rational budgeting process.[21]

Another method of controlling the input side of budgeting is the executive line item veto. We often hear about the **line item veto** in terms of presidential politics. Presidents have requested a long-term solution to the budgeting process that would result in line item veto authority. The line item veto is often believed to be a solution to out-of-control wasteful spending habits. In a study of Georgia's line item veto, it was found that the executive power was often not used for the purpose of removing spending categories.[22] Instead, Georgia's governors have used the power to influence the construction of budget documents. Interviews with former governors, such as President Jimmy Carter, find that the threat of line veto is more common than the actual use of the power in the budget process.

Performance-based budgeting is an important part of connecting expenditure to outcomes.[23] Performance-based budgets link requests for resources with documentation illustrating the outcomes of budget choices made in previous years. If sustainability is to be attained under budget constraints, budget writers must understand how efficient and effective expenditures are at accomplishing stated goals. Since the budget process is cyclical and iterative, good information about outcomes in the previous budget cycle can lead to informed budgetary decisions in future years. Performance-based budgeting is most commonly found in bureaucratic agencies or related to a specific program. All-encompassing performance evaluations are not as common in the U.S. states.

Performance budgets are potentially critical to long-term sustainability goals despite the significant amount of time and effort necessary for their preparation. Documentation on previous performance must be linked with previous expenditures and then tied directly to justifications for future expenditures. As with all budgeting techniques, performance-based budgeting remains a work in progress. However elegant it may be in its current form, this budgeting practice will always need to be improved because policies, circumstances, and budgets are constantly changing; this dynamism is especially true for sustainable communities.

In numerous American cities[24] and state governments performance-based budgeting is being attempted, with only mixed results being documented to date.[25] In recent years, performance-based budgeting has waxed and then waned in popularity, and it is currently witnessing renewed interest.[26]

Finally, contracting out government functions is frequently hailed as a method of reducing costs and creating better public sector budgets. Contracting out means that private sector providers are paid to accomplish certain government functions and the government discontinues its direct delivery of services. Irene Rubin concludes that contracting out cannot be equated with better budgeting because contracting authority and costs are often hidden within program or agency budgets and are largely invisible to most decision-makers.[27] She suggests that contracting should become a budget line independent of agency or program general funds; in this way contracting out would become more visible and its outcomes would be better understood.

Sustainable Budget Focus: Five Key Areas of Future State and Local Budget Needs

The traditional budget categories discussed previously will continue to consume much of state and local budget revenues, but a sustainable future will require a continued and likely stronger budget commitment to growing areas of need. Projecting need is a tricky business because so much about the future remains unknown to us. Nevertheless, it is a fairly safe bet that the following five categories will require substantial increases in state and local budget commitment soon and for the foreseeable future.

Alternative Energy Sources and Energy Conservation

It is projected that "peak oil" will occur within in the next 15 years—that is, if it has not already occurred. Towards the end of the 21st century, much of the globe's accessible petroleum will have been depleted. Reliable access to energy is a prerequisite for modern society and the key to sustainability. Alternative energy will likely be produced using a variety of methods. So-called fourth-generation nuclear energy is very likely to play a significant role in electricity generation, as is thermal energy generation. Fossil fuel-based energy sources will continue to be harnessed in the form of coal and natural gas. Renewable energy in the form of solar electric, solar thermal, wind generation, ocean thermal energy conversion, tidal generation, and geothermal will be used to provide a sizeable portion of state and local energy needs in future years, if state and local governments have access to those sources. As we near a time when greenhouse gas emission restrictions and carbon sequestration will become common terminology, the development of locally suited alternative forms of renewable energy will be priority concerns for American state and local governments. Sustainable communities will require significant participation from state and local government in the form of financial commitments to public–private partnerships and tax incentives for the development of alternative energy systems that will contribute to community sustainability.

Climate Change Impacts

Significant climate change impacts are projected to occur within the next few decades. Depending on a community's location, climate change may lead to rising ocean levels and flooding, severe heat and drought, increased extreme weather, and more frequent range and forest fires, to name but a few possible adverse climate-related phenomena. The widespread destruction witnessed along the Gulf Coast by Hurricanes Katrina and Rita, the multiyear drought in the early years of the 21st century affecting the South, and devastating wildfires in California and other Western states have all been attributed to climate change. Preparing for highly probable and disruptive climate-related events is a key part of the pursuit of sustainability and community resiliency, and such preparation will require significant budget resource commitments.

Climate change studies frequently tie back to the issue of carbon emissions from fossil energy use. The development of alternative energy, as discussed previously, is an important part of meeting future energy demands, but it is also beneficial in terms of reducing carbon emissions into the atmosphere; these emissions lead to ozone depletion and the risk of further global atmospheric warming.

Infrastructure Renewal

Infrastructure renewal is a multifaceted phenomenon. Tremendous resource commitments are required just to maintain current infrastructure, but in the long run commitment to maintaining infrastructure is less costly than neglect and subsequent failure. For example, in 2007 a major urban highway bridge collapsed in Minneapolis-St. Paul, Minnesota, killing and injuring many citizens. The bridge collapse opened a policy window[28] and brought the issue of U.S. infrastructure renewal to the national, state, and local policy agendas. It is estimated that hundreds, if not thousands, of the nation's highway and road bridges may require substantial retrofitting or replacement if we are to avoid a repeat of the Minneapolis experience.

In addition to this long-neglected problem, it is very likely that the suburban sprawl of U.S. cities, and the long commutes to and from work that are associated with this sprawl, are not sustainable. Infrastructure renewal may require a commitment to redesign as well as selective renewal. Rising energy costs may likely affect residential choice and give rise to the need for new forms of transportation infrastructure in American population centers.

Beyond roads, many government buildings such as schools, administrative offices, and corrections facilities are aging and beginning to show signs of disrepair. The technology available in these buildings is often insufficient to the needs of e-government and effective data management, analysis, and transfer. Older buildings frequently "leak" thermal energy and make poor use of natural light, requiring more electricity. Sustainability means investing in upgrades and making a sincere commitment to good ("green") design and timely maintenance.

Bio-Equity

Bio-equity calls for equal treatment for both human society and other elements of the "biosphere," and acting on a commitment to building communities that do not develop at the expense of the environment in which they exist. Understanding and mandating bio-equity through regulation may have begun with the passage of the **National Environmental Policy Act** (NEPA) and the passage of the **Clean Air Act**, the **Clean Water Act**, and the **Endangered Species Act**, but it has been interpreted and has evolved on the local level to encompass more.

Technology and Innovation

Sustainable communities will have lower demands for transportation corridors and transport infrastructure if technological development and communications innovations continue into the future. Public–private partnership commitments to the promotion of new environment-regarding technologies will make resource use more efficient, creating well-paying jobs while simultaneously reducing the relative cost of living. For example, many of the industrial manufacturing jobs of the future could be completed from home computers managing robotic systems on a distant factory floor. In fact, much of the technology needed to expand these systems is already available; a budgetary commitment on the part of government might speed the process towards more widespread use of these technologies. And, of course, what the long-term future holds in the way of related communication technology innovations will likely only bring us closer to sustainable communities.

Budgeting and the Core Dimensions of Sustainability

Budgeting establishes or formalizes communal or individual priorities. Accomplishing goals within the core dimensions of sustainability will require effective budgeting. Budgeting for sustainability is not a one-time event: within the sustainability paradigm, circumstances evolve and priorities change due to increased understanding and changing preferences. The social objectives of sustainability, for instance, will change as demographics change. As the Baby Boomer generation fades into history, a new demographic will likely emerge—a more youthful, more energetic, more mobile, and more diverse society lies ahead. Investing in human capital will become more complex as traditional transmission of human capital within traditional family units becomes less common and as the changing educational needs of a mobile workforce become increasingly evident. Traditional perspectives of social capital (e.g., lifelong commitment to civic institutions in particular communities) continues to decline and is replaced by nonprofits that draw youthful participation and that change as times and conditions change. Budgeting plays a big role in the ever-changing sustainable communities, offering tax incentives and grant resources to help support the public welfare, education, and community needs of a future society.

As with the social objectives of sustainability, economic objectives can be encouraged or discouraged through the state and local government budget process. Tax incentives to sustainable industries encourage the growth of new green economies, while restrictive tax codes might discourage polluting or non-sustainable industries. In creating equitable market conditions and reducing economic disparity, budget resources in communities built around the sustainability paradigm will likely offer a helping hand to the least benefitted members of states and the poorest local communities through redistributive policy.

Environmental objectives are advanced through budgeting for environmental regulation. The sustainability paradigm will require that state and local governments strictly regulate polluting industries and products. Regulation, however, requires a strong and well-financed bureaucracy that monitors environmental quality and ensures industry and broader community compliance.

Finally, the institutional change needed to advance the sustainability paradigm will most likely occur if clear priorities are established through the budgeting process. Agencies and policy objectives that are of higher priority can be bolstered through a strong financial commitment on the part of budgeters. Social welfare, education, and environmental policy agencies and policies, for instance, would likely receive even greater financial assistance. In the future, particularly when the health and welfare costs of the large Baby Boomer generation have faded, budget

Budgeting: What Can I Do?

As we are writing this book, state and local governments are experiencing the greatest budget shortfalls and making some of the most drastic cuts to services since the Great Depression in the 1930s and early 1940s. As we have discussed in this chapter, budgeting in good times can be a complicated process, let alone in times of severe fiscal stress. The Senate Ways and Means Committee for the State of Washington has put together a budget-balancing exercise for citizens and students called "Ax and Tax." Download the exercise, make the budget, and see how you match up with what the legislature actually did: http://www.leg.wa.gov/documents/Legislature/ScholarProgram/2009%20Ax%20and%20Tax.pdf

Learn how your state compares to other states' tax rates, tax burden, and tax sources at the Federation of Tax Administrators Web site: http://www.taxadmin.org/

Learn more about your own state's budget process through the National Association of State Budget Officers (NASBO) at: http://www.nasbo.org/

resources will likely shift in new and different directions to meet the evolving objectives of sustainability.

Conclusion

Sustainability requires commitment. Commitment, however, is only a word of promised future action; it means very little until acted upon. Analyzing public budgets is a critical method of determining what we mean by commitment, and determining how that commitment ties into the issue of sustainability at the state and local level. Through our analysis of budgeting in state and local government we found that commitment requires the expenditure of considerable resources over time. The resources in question will come from a variety of sources both internal to and external from state and local government, and sustainability requires the development of reliable and non-injurious resource bases to support the programs and policies required to meet the needs of the private sector and civil society. While the needs to be addressed are many and the challenges facing us are rather daunting, the resource base available to state and local governments is likely to be relatively constrained for quite some time into the future. The challenge for the accomplishment of sustainability in state and local government in the years ahead may have less to do with resource provision and much more to do with strategic spending choices. In terms of sustainability, the "healthy" and resilient community relies less on the size of its tax base and much more on the wise spending and budgetary vision featuring the balanced pursuit of economic vitality, environmental protection, and social equity.

Key Terms

Balanced budget	Line item veto
Bio-equity	Master Agreement ("Tobacco
Block grants	Settlement")
Categorical grants	National Environmental Policy
Clean Air Act	Act (NEPA)
Clean Water Act	*Northern Spotted Owl v. Hodel*
Competitive grant	Performance-based budgeting
Endangered Species Act	Tax and expenditure limitation
Excise tax	measures (TELs)
Flat rate tax	Temporary Assistance to Needy
Formula grant	Families (TANF)
Graduated tax	

Key Terms

1. How does the typical state budget process work, and what are the various actors involved in that process?

2. What are the various sources of intergovernmental revenues that state and local governments use to support services?
3. What have been the various approaches advocated to reform budgeting processes at the state and local levels?
4. What are the main characteristics of a sustainable budget?
5. What are the main sources of revenues for states and local governments? Is it possible to balance the demands for government services with existing revenue sources?

CHAPTER 11

Entitlements

Introduction

An *entitlement* is a governmental benefit to which a person is legally entitled if he or she meets certain eligibility criteria. For example, if an individual is accused of a serious crime and is unable to afford an attorney, he or she is entitled to legal representation at public expense. Similarly, an individual who loses his or her job may be entitled to unemployment benefits from the state in which he or she lives. A third example would be that of an elderly person living in the United States who is entitled to an old age pension and healthcare benefits from the federal government in the form of monthly Social Security payments and Medicare benefits.

Entitlements play a very important role in the promotion of sustainability in several ways. First, social and economic justice is a core element of sustainability. Sustainability entails more than just survivability—it is survivability within the context of an equitable social, political, and economic value structure. In modern democratic societies, the value structure providing for an equal voice in elections and equal protection under the law points us in the direction of fairness in the distribution of goods and services (often expressed in terms of the **social safety net** concept). The challenge of promoting sustainability into the future will bring us face to face with issues of limited resources again and again, and the difficult tradeoffs to be made between the economic vitality, environmental protection, and social equity core values of sustainability will require the utmost care and skill to manage. The nation's state and local governments, and the citizens of the communities involved, will be called upon to engage in this difficult tradeoff management process repeatedly in the coming decades. Given the importance of this area of concern to every community, this chapter is included in this book as a key element of the study of state and local government.

This chapter will discuss:

- The background of state and local government entitlement programs
- The relationship between entitlements and sustainable communities
- Types of public assistance programs

- State and local government healthcare programs and policies
- The role of state and local governments in Medicare and Medicaid programs
- The State Children's Health Insurance Program (S-CHIP)
- Public unemployment compensation programs

Background and Types of Entitlements

While virtually all observers of modern democratic countries would agree that entitlements are essential to good governance, it is also the case that the boundaries of discussions related to governmental entitlements are often unclear. In part, this is due to the ever-changing conceptualization of the nature and proper scope of entitlements. Public health protection, for instance, once meant principally that government authority was used to isolate individuals who were infected with communicable diseases via quarantine. In some cases such persons were simply left to die in isolated asylums. Similarly, assistance for the chronically unemployed often revolved around private charity, almshouses, and public begging in designated places. These examples from the past may appear quaint or laughable to many Americans today, but they were the most common forms of public health and welfare promotion practiced in this country in the not-too-distant past. As the demographics of our state and local government populations have changed, our collective understanding of entitlement has changed, either becoming broader in scope or more exclusive in terms of eligibility. This chapter will highlight a few basic entitlements associated with sustainable communities, and illuminate some of the dynamics associated with expanding and contracting conceptions of governmental entitlements. The chapter will identify some areas of likely entitlement growth and other areas where governmental entitlements might become more limited as our society seeks to promote sustainability.

Meanings of "Entitlement"

In his 2004 *Columbia Law Review* article "The Political Economy of Entitlement," legal scholar David Super outlines six principal definitions of entitlement:

1. *Subjective entitlement*: This represents a belief that an individual has certain benefits due to him or her, regardless of whether a legal foundation for that belief exists. Politicians will sometimes use phrases such as, "everyone has a right to own a home," even if there is no legal foundation to the statement.
2. *Unconditional entitlement*: According to Super,[1] this represents a "benefit that is not subject to conditions or reciprocal obligations." As Super correctly notes, most governmental entitlements are conditioned

upon some aspect of reciprocal obligation. For example, a person receiving unemployment benefits must have been previously employed and been part of a layoff and must be looking for a job actively in order to continue to receive benefits.

3. *Positive entitlement*: This represents "a legally enforceable individual right."[2] This is the most familiar definition of entitlement. Individuals have a form of property right attached to a positive entitlement, such that an illegal deprivation of such an entitlement provides ground for a lawsuit based on the suffering of a substantive harm.

4. *Budgetary entitlement*: The concept is often referred to as "mandatory spending" in the law. Social programs that are budgetary entitlements are prioritized above all other expenditures in that they are not subject to caps on spending.[3]

5. *Responsive entitlement*: These governmental expenditures are made based on a need-based formula.[4] Public education programs driven by student headcounts are an example of a responsive entitlement; government payments to the victims of natural disasters would be another example.

6. *Functional entitlement*: Some governmental programs meet "some qualitatively definable need of its beneficiaries."[5] Super argues that many food and nutrition programs assume that "healthful sustenance" will be accomplished for a person if a certain food and nutritional benefit level is established. His example in this area is food stamps: a certain benefit level is established with the idea that a recipient household's food needs will be met.

The distinctions that Super draws in his effort to define the concept of governmental entitlement are valuable, helping us to understand what it is we mean by entitlement and, thinking normatively with respect to "good" and "bad" forms of government entitlement, what entitlements *should* be maintained to promote sustainability in the communities served by American state and local governments. In many cases where the major state and local governmental entitlement programs are discussed, it will be clear that several of Super's types of entitlements might apply to any particular policy discussed.

In contrast to Super, John Skinner provides a greatly simplified approach to thinking about entitlements.[6] He distinguishes between only two forms of governmental entitlement, those being *earned* and those being *implied*. According to Skinner, Social Security is an example of an "earned" entitlement because one contributes a portion of one's earnings to Social Security and the level of contribution directly affects the level of benefit received. In contrast, Medicare is an example of an implied entitlement because it is assumed that once one reaches retirement age one is entitled to Medicare health benefits regardless of one's contribution level through payroll deductions over a career and regardless of one's extent of need.

Entitlements and Sustainability

While the social justice and equity concepts underlying governmental entitlements are central to sustainability, the cost of providing social justice oriented entitlements is tremendous. As a percentage of total costs, state and local health and public assistance programs consume a substantial portion of state and local government budgets. Critics of "social spending" argue that if existing health entitlement programs are left unchanged, they will consume an ever-growing portion of state and local budgets, thus limiting the ability of government to allocate resources to other important needs.[7] One solution proposed by critics is to thoroughly reform the current public assistance and healthcare entitlement programs, to judiciously trim costs where possible, and to adopt "best practices" and innovative programs to more effectively target health and public assistance funds. Another approach to reform in this area is to focus investments on prevention of illness and early screening and diagnosis, hence achieving cost containment via citizen wellness practices and early treatment of preventable illnesses.

In the 1990s, state and local governments across the country took the lead in reforming existing public assistance programs and placing limits on welfare eligibility and promoting active re-engagement in the workforce for many recipients.[8] The result was a precipitous decline in the number of welfare recipients in nearly all states. From the perspective of the former welfare recipients, many of them benefited from **welfare-to-work programs**; however, simply getting individuals off welfare rolls and into the workforce is not the end of the sustainability story when it comes to entitlements. In the case of welfare reform, one of the biggest issues facing former public assistance recipients beyond employment is the difficulty of maintaining and improving their existence; for example, balancing new employment with the need for quality child care.[9] The stresses and strains of life off the welfare rolls after years of dependence often prove to be too much all at once, and the ability to deal with these pressures comes at a time when the cost of services is rising and the range of family needs (e.g., access to cable TV and the Internet) is growing.

One of the areas of entitlement that was almost immediately affected by welfare entitlement reform falls into the healthcare policy arena. The meteoric rise of expenditures for healthcare entitlement programs such as Medicaid and S-CHIP, for instance, are frequently bewildering to the average citizen. Why should healthcare cost so much? What are the healthcare professionals doing with all the money? These questions may prove maddening until one understands what the term "healthcare" really means. Unfortunately, healthcare conjures up many out-of-date images. One image is the clean hospital bed with the considerate and caring nurse attending to the young patient with tonsillitis. Another image is that of the physician examining the expectant mother. Perhaps another image is the kindly country doctor listening to a man's heartbeat with a stethoscope. These are all very appealing images; however, not one of them accurately captures the direction and scope of healthcare today—and perhaps they never did capture the true meaning of healthcare. Nonetheless, the myth of healthcare derived from the long-gone past proves persistent.

In the United States, healthcare policy has been tied closely to issues of defense, economics, urban planning, immigration, age, class, race/ethnicity, and a whole host of other issues. National programs in healthcare began as early as the 18th century with the Marine Hospital Service. Community-level healthcare initiatives were primarily privately managed until the late 19th century, when large-scale immigration resulted in rapid urbanization.[10] Major epidemics such as a cholera outbreak in New York City led to the widespread creation of public programs for sanitation and healthcare in state and local governments across the entire country.[11] As our society has continued to urbanize, the need for such programs has increased tremendously. Healthcare has progressively come to be viewed as a benefit not only to the individual receiving healthcare services but also to the community as a whole. Healthy people provide a good workforce, they spend more time in productive activity than under medical care, and they have less need for collective resources to be devoted to healthcare services for the indigent.

In sustainable economies of the future, all elements of production must be able to work in unison; healthy workers are a critical part of the economic enterprise. Beyond work, there is the issue of healthy children. As a society, we commit a tremendous amount of money and time to educating and caring for young people; proper investment in the future is, after all, a critical dimension of sustainability. Children who are not healthy are unable to benefit from education and will likely develop other physical ailments that adversely affect their social and economic potential. Technology has made us more aware of new and growing issues related to prenatal and child healthcare. Problems such as birth defects and autism can be treated if diagnosed early, and those conditions can be medically managed far better today than was the case in the past.

As the **Baby Boomer** generation ages, an increasing proportion of our governmental resources will necessarily be spent on medical needs. A sustainable community, facing this known pending demand on its resources, must be both compassionate and pragmatic. The demonstration of governmental compassion for the elderly and infirm is very important to building inclusivity within society and to promoting social justice. Pragmatically, a sustainable community is aware of the great benefit of maintaining a healthy and productive population. Older, often richly experienced individuals generally bring with them economic resources (e.g., skills, social networks, accumulated wealth) that can help local economies and generate employment. Older individuals often have substantial intellectual capital gained from years of experience in the workforce; by employing these retirees in new capacities, this intellectual capital can be tapped to improve society. Disabled individuals often possess many valuable skills and knowledge that is all too frequently "lost" to society and to the individual when physical limitation separates them from the larger community.[12] While many of these individuals receive some level of federal healthcare benefits, there are a substantial number of disabled individuals who, in midlife and early older age years, would remain inaccessible if it were not for state and local government health resource entitlements. Health care for the elderly, therefore, is critical to improving community sustainability.

The very meaning of the word "healthy" has changed substantially. One could have perfect physical health (e.g., normal blood pressure, cholesterol, heart rate, and eyesight) but suffer from severe mental health maladies. Health issues related to depression, bipolar disorder, and personality disorders have long existed in society. However, in the past individuals had little or no access to healthcare for the problems of mental illness. The solutions that did exist often involved institutionalizing individuals in sanitariums rather than helping them to remain within the general community and achieve a productive and respected role in society. Addressing the problems of mental health has become an increasingly important matter for state and local governments in the United States as the size of the population affected and the problems arising from mental illness for society have become more evident.[13]

The stresses of the school setting (high-stakes testing associated with the **No Child Left Behind** [NCLB] policy discussed elsewhere), the workplace, and living in general under the conditions of the threat of terrorist attacks and prospects of global climate change have become overwhelming for many individuals and families. Work schedules have become extended with the advent of computers and advances in communication technology, changing the boundaries that once separated office and home settings. The itinerant nature of contemporary society and the high-technology world tend to separate people from one another rather than bringing them together. The aging of the U.S. population in many cases means that older individuals have either become separated from their families or have become so reliant on their relatives that social and economic strains begin to appear within caregiver families. Healthcare issues, then, clearly extend to problems previously known, such as mental health, but all too frequently ignored as a matter of governmental concern.

As a final example, the issue of substance abuse is a growing public healthcare concern. In the past, substance abuse was assumed to be the rational choice of individuals—addiction and possible death as a result was viewed as the price one paid for a bad personal choice. A sustainable community, however, cannot rationally make the choice to simply ignore problems associated with substance abuse and drug addiction. Philosophically, societies agree to care for their members. Practically speaking, it is a serious drain on society to simply let the forces of drug addiction and substance abuse sap the strength of the community. In all state and local government settings drug addiction and substance abuse prevention and treatment have become important aspects of healthcare (and the criminal justice system). Substance abuse problems cross age, gender, and ethnicity boundaries. While substance abuse among the youth remains troublesome, there is evidence to indicate that the rate of substance abuse is either leveling off or declining among this population. A rising trend, however, is the incidence of substance abuse among Baby Boomers,[14] which

Photo 11.1. President George W. Bush was a proponent of the No Child Left Behind legislation. Source: Brooks Kraft/Corbis.

will likely require local communities to refocus their substance abuse efforts on this demographic group.

Public assistance and healthcare are closely intertwined, and both areas constitute an important part of a dialogue on sustainability. Termed entitlements, policy programs falling under the auspices of public assistance and healthcare are far-reaching and have inspired a next-generational perspective on social programs designed to address public assistance and public health problems. Many of the governmental programs previously discussed in terms of entitlements—the implication being that there are narrowly defined givers and a receivers of benefit—are increasingly discussed in terms of "community" assistance and health-promotion programs. The new perspective to be discussed next recognizes that the entitlement of yesterday is more properly seen as a collective community commitment or investment made to proactively address shared needs, and that this collective response to public assistance and public health needs benefits communities as a whole.

Public Assistance

In 1996, a bipartisan coalition of senators and representatives in the U.S. Congress passed the **Welfare Reform Act** and President Clinton signed the act into law. With an eye to achieving outcomes similar to those associated with the state and local welfare reforms of the prior decade, the Republican majority in Congress hoped to eradicate one major element of the "welfare state." The state and local welfare policy reforms preceding the 1996 act generally tightened eligibility requirements for recipients and placed time limits on the length of time one could receive welfare benefits.

After over a decade of experience with the welfare reform movement, we can say with some confidence that the 1996 act represents the beginning of a change in American thinking about what public assistance as an entitlement might mean in a new millennium. The new target of public assistance is less the individual recipient of the benefit than it is the community as a whole. **Temporary Assistance for Needy Families** (TANF) is the primary federal policy on public assistance in the United States. As a result of the 1996 act, TANF replaced Aid to Families with Dependent Children (AFDC). A block grant program, TANF requires states to develop specific public assistance plans to reflect state and local values, but within the general TANF requirements.

The Office of Family Assistance (OFA), Administration on Children and Families (ACF), a unit within the U.S. Department of Health and Human Services (HHS), is the federal office that oversees TANF block grant disbursements and oversees state policy requirements to determine if they meet TANF eligibility guidelines. With the 1996 federal statute as the primary guideline, OFA outlines four major goals for the TANF program:[15]

- "Assisting needy families so that children can be cared for in their own homes"
- "Reducing the dependency of needy parents by promoting job preparation, work, and marriage"
- "Preventing out-of-wedlock pregnancies"
- "Encouraging the formation and maintenance of two-parent families"

Individuals can receive federal TANF money for 5 years, although states can impose either shorter or longer time limits—but no more than 20% of the state welfare caseload can go beyond the 5-year time limit. If a state wishes to use its own resources to extend welfare benefits, it may do so at its own discretion. Proponents of TANF argue that the time limits are flexible enough to allow states to make their own choices about public assistance, but critics argue that states with the greatest need are often incapable of self-financing extended welfare benefits and may not be able to access other federal, state, or local revenues to meet the needs of citizens and local communities requiring this form of support.

TANF requires that recipients meet work requirements unless approved waivers are granted by state and national TANF administrators. Two-parent families must work 35 to 40 hours per week, while single-parent families must work 30 hours per week. Certain exceptions are made for single parents who have children under 6 years of age who cannot find adequate child care and thus cannot balance their employment requirements with child care responsibilities. "Work" may constitute full-time employment in salaried positions or participation in employment training programs, on-the-job training, civic service activities, or even successful

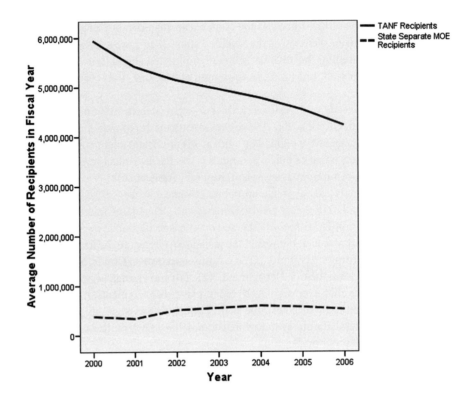

Figure 11.1. TANF Recipients, Average in Fiscal Year (2000-2006).
Source: Statistical Abstract of the United States, 2008. URL: www.census.gov/compendia/statab/

participation in formal secondary education. Proponents of TANF argue that the work requirements are broad enough to provide TANF recipients the opportunity to gain skills necessary for financial independence after receiving assistance. Critics of the work requirement generally focus on the potential for limited access to the full scope of "work" activities in states and local communities. Ultimately, assistance recipients must find jobs after their eligibility expires, but in communities lacking employment opportunities TANF recipients are faced with little hope for the future. TANF does make accommodation for states to create jobs directly or to provide job incentives for private employers so that TANF recipients will have a greater chance of obtaining jobs when their eligibility expires.

TANF monitors all U.S. state programs to determine if the federal statutory requirements associated with the program are being met. If a state fails to meet these requirements, then TANF grant amounts to the state can be reduced administratively. As a consequence of these strong sanctions, state reporting requirements are quite stringent. Proponents of TANF argue that reporting requirements keep states in line with the national goal of streamlining the program and moving welfare recipients into the workforce. Critics argue that the reporting requirements excessively limit each state's ability to be innovative and responsive with public assistance programming to meet state and local needs. Despite these complaints, however, it is indeed clear that state and local governments in the United States have a great deal of latitude in crafting public assistance programs for both individuals and communities as a consequence of the 1996 Welfare Reform Act.

TANF requires that the states spend a certain percentage of their own funds to support public assistance programming efforts. These local fund matches are calculated by TANF under their Maintenance of Effort (MOE) as a percentage of the amount of money spent by ACF-TANF in a given state. MOE monies are calculated in terms of state MOE requirements and in terms of state separate voluntary MOE commitments. As seen in Figure 11.2, general federal commitment to TANF (in constant 2006 dollars) has remained very flat—even trending down slightly in 2006 dollar terms, with a slight increase in 2005, which was the year of TANF reauthorization. The rate of annual increase in state monies allocated toward MOE requirements grew tremendously from 2000 until 2004, then declined in real dollar percentage terms in 2005 and 2006. Separate state MOE allocations tend to be the most variable in the analysis, possibly reflecting state budget commitments in other areas and state economic conditions. The steadiest resource base for TANF is the federal government, but as noted

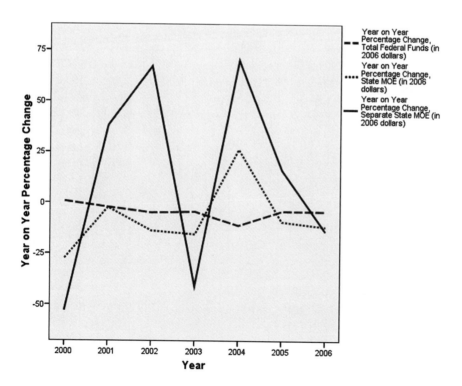

Figure 11.2. Year-on Year-Change in TANF Allocations (in 2006 dollars).
Source: *Statistical Abstract of the United States, 2008.* URL: www.census.gov/compendia/statab/

previously that commitment is clearly flattening out and even showing some diminishment in real dollar year-on-year percentage terms. In part, this decline in federal funding reflects the decline in the average number of recipients in TANF programs, which may be a sign of success for the long process of welfare reform in the United States.

As noted in Figure 11.3, a significant portion of TANF expenditures are for non-assistance purposes (i.e., administrative expenditures). Between 2000 and 2002, the trend for administrative expenditure as a proportion of TANF total expenditure was on the rise. The trend reflects the fact that many expenditures made under the TANF program are not benefits to individuals but rather reflect administrative investments in the local community for job preparation training and job creation for the clients making a transition from public assistance to employment.

Healthcare

Whereas it can be said with some confidence that welfare reform is showing some progress towards flexible adaptation and proper orientation toward sustainable

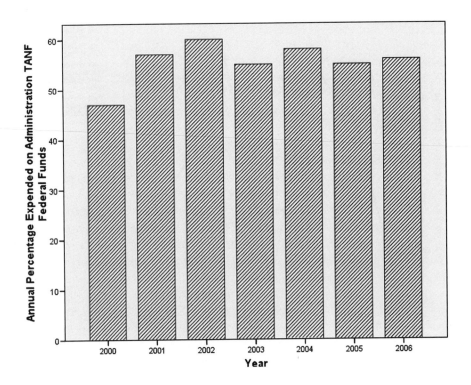

Figure 11.3. Percentage of Federal TANF Monies Spent on Non-Assistance
Source: Statistical Abstract of the United States, 2008. URL: www.census.gov/compendia/statab/

community development in state and local governments across the country, healthcare largely remains an unresolved issue in many states and local communities. Healthcare entitlement programs are the subject of a great deal of current political debate, and it became a major campaign issue in the 2008 presidential election. Healthcare reform has begun in the United States, with the passage of health insurance reforms legislation in 2010, and serious efforts must continue to be made to streamline the process of service delivery, improve the quality of care provided in many areas (especially in early diagnosis and preventive care), and temper rising costs.[16] While revolutionary changes have occurred and will continue to occur in American healthcare services available to those who can pay for them by virtue of insurance coverage,[17] a great deal of additional change is needed to extend that access to the many citizens who are not covered by insurance. Perhaps the greatest tragedy lies in the fact that a substantial portion of the nation's youth are not covered by their parents' health insurance and are at best only unevenly covered by state insurance programs (more on that subject below). Hence, the benefits of preventive medicine and early diagnosis are unavailable to this portion of our population, whose contribution to the sustainability of our local communities is essential. Given the recessionary conditions under which the Health Care Reform Bill of 2010 was enacted, many of these improvements will come into effect over the course of a decade so that the costs of implementation can be absorbed gradually.

The United States is "graying" as the Baby Boom generation moves towards retirement. Aging populations are the single greatest challenge to the nation's health entitlement programs in terms of uncontrollable costs; this is also the case in other developed nations.[18] Some additional new challenges face the U.S. healthcare system that are not related to Baby Boomers, such as the virtual epidemic of childhood obesity and diabetes and the need to address the mental health and substance abuse and addiction issues alluded to above. In addition, the character of the American family unit has changed, with single and divorced parents facing multiple health challenges for themselves and their children.[19]

At this writing, three major forms of healthcare policy entitlement exist in the United States that affect state and local governments in major ways:

• Medicare
• Medicaid
• S-CHIP

Medicare is a *federal* healthcare program for the elderly. Medicaid is a *state* program, cooperatively managed at the state and federal levels of government to meet the healthcare needs of low-income individuals and families. S-CHIP, or the State Children's Health Insurance Program, is also a state program, cooperatively managed at the state and federal level, intended to meet the healthcare needs of uninsured middle- and low-income children.

Photo 11.2. President Lyndon Johnson signed the Medicare Bill in 1965. Source: Bettman/ Corbis.

Medicare and Medicaid

Medicare

While it is a national program, **Medicare** is an important part of maintaining sustainable state and local communities. The Medicare plan provides for the healthcare needs of individuals 65 years of age or older. Recognized Medicare program healthcare providers privately supply healthcare under Medicare. There are four major components to coverage:

- *Part A—Hospital insurance.* Part A covers specified costs of hospitalization, nursing care facility stays, home healthcare, hospice care, and blood transfusions for patients staying in the hospital or during covered stays in a skilled nursing care facility. Medicare does not cover all costs of every medical procedure.
- *Part B—Medical insurance.* The Medicare program covers a percentage of Medicare-approved procedures. Costs that exceed those covered by Part B are the responsibility of the patient. The patient may choose to enroll in private health insurance plans to cover additional expenses, or choose to enroll in the government-sponsored Medigap insurance. Expenses not covered by either private insurance or Medigap are the responsibility of the patient.[20]
- *Part C—Medicare Advantage.* "Part C combines Plans A, B, and D into a larger more comprehensive plan designed to increase user flexibility

while reducing health care costs. Part C is noted as being beneficial to Medicare-qualified individuals who have chronic conditions requiring regular medical care. The plan relies heavily on health networks, such as HMOs, to provide care, but there is a preferred provider option. Additionally, Part C has a medical savings account plan, allowing consumers to establish medical savings accounts."[21]

- *Part D—Prescription drug program.* The prescription drug program covers expenses for various generic and brand-name drugs. The copayment of the patient will vary, depending on the type of drug. Medicare Part D coverage limits the amounts of drug dispensed at any given time.

The oldest members of the Baby Boom generation are now in their early 60s, close to retirement, and are becoming increasingly susceptible to the infirmities of age. By 2030, it is estimated that there will be 2.7 workers for every retiree drawing health and retirement benefits.[22] Clearly, economic sustainability is potentially challenged by a growing tax burden and budget constraints. The sustainability of the Medicare program, as it currently exists without significant change, is highly dubious. Either a reduction in benefits or changes in eligibility might be necessary to make the program viable for future generations even if an alternative healthcare financing system is created.[23]

These policy changes at the national level, however, will not reduce the expanding healthcare needs of the elderly. Preventive care, good health practices, and effective outreach to at-risk populations are all important ways of limiting healthcare needs and economizing on health care expenses. Regular exercise and balanced diets are important to maintaining good health, and avoidance of smoking (and second-hand smoke) and moderation in the use of alcohol are likewise important means of reducing healthcare costs. Public–private partnerships involving national, state, and local government are critical to making available the "wellness" information, healthful foods, and exercise facilities needed for the elderly to stay healthy and remain active contributors to their communities.

The healthcare entitlements of Medicare are critical to the health status of the nation, but they will likely fall short in providing for many of the basic everyday needs of the elderly. While the Administration on Aging in the Department of Health and Human Services provides significant guidance for eldercare and endeavors to protect the elderly from abuse, most of the resources and energy needed to sustain a quality of life for our elderly citizens will come from the hard work, personal resources, and patience of private individuals living within our local communities.

Community eldercare is an important part of developing sustainability in our nation's local communities. A growing number of middle-aged adults are seeking to balance child-raising, career, and eldercare responsibilities for relatives and friends. Many individuals already face these challenges, and more will do so in the coming

Photo 11.3. Caring for the elderly is a key aspect of health policy. Source: © Lisafx | Dreamstime.com

years. Cooperative effort will be necessary to cope with the added responsibilities, and "family-friendly" workplace policies will be needed to accommodate persons taking on these caregiver roles.

Medicare, and its related healthcare programs for the elderly, provides a solid foundation for healthcare entitlement in the United States. Sustainable eldercare, however, involves much more than healthcare dollars for hospitalization, health insurance, and prescription drug benefits. The essential margins of healthcare sustainability for the elderly will most likely be provided by **sustainable community-based eldercare.** Communities that provide for the needs of both young workers and the elderly individuals for whom they care on a daily basis will likely prosper, but those that leave their elderly to rely entirely upon the federal government's Medicare program will experience serious dislocation as the Baby Boomers move into their retirement years.

Medicaid
Medicaid is a national–state cooperative healthcare plan designed to serve the medical service needs of low-income individuals and families. Standards commonly associated with eligibility for the Medicaid entitlement benefit include the following:[24]

1. "Families who meet states' AFDC/TANF eligibility requirements in effect on July 16, 1996"
2. "Pregnant women and children under age 6 whose family income is at or below 133% of the Federal poverty level"
3. "Children ages 6 to 19 with family income up to 100% of the Federal poverty level"
4. "Caretakers (relatives or legal guardians who take care of children under age 18 [or 19 if still in high school])"
5. "Supplementary Security Income (SSI) recipients [who meet certain requirements]"
6. "Individuals and couples who are living in medical institutions and who have monthly income up to 300% of the SSI income standard"

In addition to these standards, states can establish their own eligibility requirements. Individuals who qualify for Medicaid receive hospitalization, insurance, and drug benefits similar to those received by Medicare recipients.

Medicaid is a very important program with respect to advancing sustainable states and local communities. Without the benefits provided under the Medicaid program, a great many low-income individuals would have extremely limited access to healthcare. In many cases, low-income individuals are the virtual backbone of a sustainable community, working in low-salary jobs in the agricultural, service, and production industries. Increasingly, private sector employers are eliminating employer-provided healthcare benefits for their workers, leaving low-income workers and their families in a highly vulnerable position. Without access to healthcare, worker absenteeism tends to be high and productivity low; undiagnosed illnesses that could be treated inexpensively frequently become acute and require extremely expensive emergency treatment and hospitalization. Poor access to healthcare for children, in particular, has a depressing effect on their school attendance and learning. Sustainable communities will require high levels of employee productivity and the production of high-quality goods and services, and they will require that children make adequate progress in their education. Healthcare entitlement programs such as Medicaid represent a critical societal commitment to low-income individuals and the sustainability of the local communities in which they live and work. The Medicaid program is a quintessential illustration of how the "social safety net" connects to the promotion of sustainability.

While clearly a direct benefit to the promotion of sustainable communities and to the low-income individuals with healthcare concerns, Medicaid represents a substantial and growing financial burden on state government. Beneficiary enrollments since the beginning of the millennium increased by 28%, from 42.8 million to 50.1 million individuals between 2000 and 2004. Even more dramatically, healthcare payments during that same period increased by a staggering 53%, from $168.4 billion in 2000 to $257.2 billion in 2004. Despite dramatically rising costs, Kronick and Rousseau conclude from their careful studies that with close management of costs and a modest degree of reform, the Medicaid program is sustainable for a considerable period.[25] A streamlined and more efficient process of Medicaid benefit delivery and a reformed reimbursement-for-service schedule are two methods of reforming Medicaid believed to improve program viability.[26]

Community health centers are another important tool in developing sustainable community health programs. Health centers are particularly important in rural communities, which may lack readily accessible hospital facilities. Farmers, ranchers, and farm laborers and their families are important beneficiaries of community health services. In urban settings, community health services can reduce the inflow of patients into emergency departments for medical care. Urgent care facilities set up in local communities are also designed to ease the burden on emergency departments. In terms of cost, community healthcare and urgent care facilities are often far less expensive to operate and maintain than hospital emergency departments. In smaller communities local hospitals are acquiring the role of community health centers, not only providing hospital beds and surgical services but conducting active health-promotion campaigns of many types that promote prevention and early detection of illness.

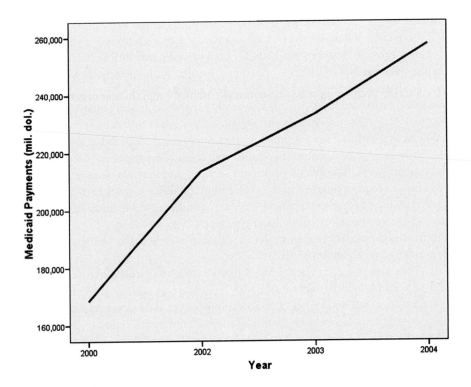

Figure 11.4. Medicaid Payments 2000–2004 (in millions of dollars).
Source: Statistical Abstract of the United States, 2008. URL: www.census.gov/compendia/statab/

Community health centers serve as important and cost-effective hubs for pro-viding preventive care services. Child immunization services and health screening can be done effectively in community health facilities. Health education classes can be taught in community health centers for both the young and the elderly. Drug and alcohol dependency programs are also important parts of community outreach ser-vices to be coordinated through community health centers. In essence, community health centers represent the widespread recognition in urban and rural areas alike that sustainable communities require high-quality healthcare provided through a variety of means. Wellness and good health practices are seen as both individual benefits and community benefits rather than as commodities to be purchased solely by those who can afford it.

Community health centers might also help to overcome current inequities in Medicaid patient care delivered by private commercial providers. Landon and his colleagues found that Medicaid patients served by commercial providers tend to receive lower-quality care than privately enrolled patients in commercially provided care programs.[27] Community health centers might also be a long-term solution to the need to combine health and public assistance benefits with day care for work-ing mothers, an unfilled need that may weaken the benefits of the aforementioned programs.[28]

State Children's Health Insurance
Program (S-CHIP)

The **S-CHIP** program, a state and nationally funded program that began in 1997, is intended to extend health insurance to children who would not meet the income requirements of Medicaid. Eligibility for S-CHIP is a function of a child's age, family size, and household income level. The S-CHIP program serves children from work-ing-class and middle-income families. This healthcare entitlement helps these fami-lies remain in the middle class and working poor categories: without this healthcare entitlement, the eligible families would likely lose their socioeconomic status if one of their children developed any type of serious medical condition. As with Medic-aid, S-CHIP offers health insurance, emergency medical care, immunization pro-grams, and health screening. S-CHIP also helps reduce the cost of adult healthcare by managing the healthcare needs of adolescents before they become chronic and expensive to treat.

Childhood obesity, for instance, has led to serious concerns about the future healthcare needs of Americans. Many children are being diagnosed with obesity-related diabetes, which can lead to other serious health issues, principally vision, renal, coronary, and circulatory disorders. Obesity itself can also lead to heart problems, stroke, and premature death. Increasing access to medical testing, preventive treatment, and information through the insurance resources of the S-CHIP program means that many chronic health issues can be either prevented or effectively treated to forestall serious health consequences.

Enrollment in S-CHIP has risen dramatically since 2000. In just 6 years, enrollment increased from 3.36 million children in 2000 to over 6.6 million children in 2006. In percentage terms, the increase has been over 97%! S-CHIP expenditures also reflect this tremendous rise in program enrollment. Expenditures increased from $1.93 billion in 2000 to a staggering $7.03 billion in 2006—a 264% increase in expenditures in just 6 years.

A state–federal entitlement, S-CHIP is a noteworthy commitment to many middle-class American families with young dependents, helping many of those families to avoid economic devastation and offering hope to millions of children. What certainly cannot be ignored, however, is the rapid growth of the program and the constraints that its success place on state budgets. State program managers must prioritize and manage a myriad of state and local community needs. However, to place matters into some perspective, it is useful to consider that as a program,

Photo 11.4. Healthcare for the future generation is a critical part of sustainability.
Source: © Iofoto | Dreamstime.com

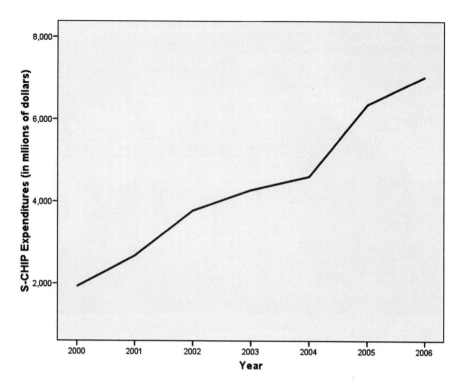

Figure 11.5. S-CHIP Expenditures (in millions of dollars) 2000–2006.
Source: Statistical Abstract of the United States, 2008. URL: www.census.gov/compendia/statab/

S-CHIP costs less than 0.5% of all state and local government receipts combined; S-CHIP costs $7.03 billion, while state and local revenues exceeded $1.7 trillion in 2006.[29]

Sustainable communities can rely on the ability of their individuals and families to respond to changing conditions and needs. S-CHIP helps working-class families, who could be financially devastated if one of their children became seriously ill.[30] This program allows these families to maintain the slack resources needed to respond to other changing needs, such as caring for an elderly relative or covering the costs of further education. Slack resources might also be used to help other community members in times of need, providing shelter and food for a neighbor whose home burned down or helping a friend with a serious illness who needs the support of his or her close friends.

Unemployment Compensation

A national government policy administered through and supplemented by the states, **unemployment compensation** represents a commitment made to address

Photo 11.5. People at an Unemployment office. Source: Peter yates/corbis.

temporary economic dislocations. The program is funded at the national, state, and local levels, using a combination of sources of funds. It is intended to provide financial assistance to unemployed individuals through direct payments to be used to purchase many of the basic necessities of life. Unemployment compensation is an example of a policy commitment type of entitlement, recognizing that there are times when members of our local and state communities are incapable of fending for themselves due to circumstances beyond their control.

The states and the federal government have different roles in managing unemployment compensation. Federal government responsibilities include the following:[31]

1. Ensure conformity and substantial compliance of state law, regulations, rules, and operations with federal law
2. Determine administrative fund requirements and provide money to states for proper and efficient administration
3. Set broad overall policy for administration of the program, monitor state performance, and provide technical assistance as necessary
4. Hold and invest all money in the unemployment trust fund until drawn down by states for the payment of compensation

State government responsibilities under this program include the following:[32]

1. Determine operation methods and directly administer the program
2. Take claims from individuals, determine eligibility, and ensure timely payment of benefits to workers
3. Determine employer liability, and assess and collect contributions

Unemployment compensation is generally fixed at 26 weeks, although some states, such as Massachusetts, offer a 30-week initial compensation period. During periods of sustained high unemployment, where it is highly unlikely that an unemployed person would be able to regain employment, extended unemployment benefits are generally paid for an additional 13 weeks. Unemployment compensation tax money is collected from employers by state governments but is then deposited with the federal government under federal statutory guidelines.

Entitlements and the Core Dimensions of Sustainability

In the broadest consideration, the sustainability construct we are using in this book can be viewed as requiring a rather inclusive discussion of the need to balance rights and responsibilities in a society that relies less on resource extraction and environmental degradation and more on the careful and wise use of the renewable resources available to all individuals. Sustainability requires due consideration of the needs of today, but keeps in mind the needs and conditions of future generations. For now, we are here—alive, thinking, speaking creatures. One of the reasons that societies first formed was because individuals and groups of individuals tried to figure out a better way to amass and distribute the resources needed to make life bearable, and to increase the likelihood that their offspring and future generations would both survive and be able to improve their respective lots in life.

Viewed in the context of sustainability, entitlements focus our attention on both short-term and long-term goals associated with community well-being. In the short term, entitlements are designed to meet the immediate objectives of providing for the educational, economic, and social welfare benefits of individuals who are often unable to provide for themselves. In doing so, entitlements provide for the long-term goal of making survival and improvement possible for the beneficiaries and for future generations of people living in that community. In this sense, the entitlement programs discussed in this chapter touch directly upon the social and economic objectives of sustainability.

Reform efforts are bringing social safety net entitlements closer into line with the environmental and economic core objectives of sustainability. The evolution of entitlements in the 20th century focused on the rights of the individual within society. Many entitlement policies focused state and local government efforts on issues of social welfare for the indigent; policies designed to help those who had or who were currently suffering from the effects of historical racial, ethnic, and gender-based discrimination; and policies promoting equality in education. The sustainability paradigm embraces these initiatives to promote social equity; however, sustainability calls for a somewhat broader view of rights and responsibilities. Increasingly, the focus of our attention is on communal rights and the rights of nature. Should community benefit and the environment, broadly defined, be

Entitlements: What Can I Do?

As we learned in this chapter, one of the nation's largest health insurance program is Medicare, which covers people 65 or older and some people under 65 who are disabled. Perhaps you have someone in your family—such as parents or grandparents—who receives Medicare benefits. Ask him or her about how the program works for him or her, including costs and benefits of coverage.

Go to your city's or county's Web site and try to identify what types of entitlement programs are offered by your local government. Try to identify if these programs contain intergovernmental revenues from the state or federal governments.

Go to Google's video search Web site and type in "entitlements." There are many videos of elected officials, commentators, and interest groups of all ideological orientations. Try to identify videos of different perspectives, watch a couple, and see what you think of the various perspectives. Many of the videos will argue that entitlements are not sustainable with the upcoming retirement of many Baby Boomers (the generation born in the middle of the 20th century).

Google video search: http://video.google.com/

considered in a discussion of entitlements? The focus on such issues is so current that it would be foolhardy to predict how it will be decided in the end; nevertheless, it is a central part of the sustainability paradigm and would significantly change the way states and local communities consider the issue of sustainability in the governance process.

A major reason for writing this book in this way at this time is that the present generation of college students will doubtless be the deciding generation for this critical question. If the core values of economic vitality, environmental protection, and social equity are to be achieved in our communities, the challenge of providing a sustainable set of entitlements as a collective benefit to all citizens will have to be met by those who manage our state and local governments and those citizens who take an active interest in the well-being of their communities, through participating in civic affairs, through volunteering in community organizations, and through doing their fair share to promote wellness and good health in their own lives and those of their family members.

The concept of individual rights and responsibilities is deeply embedded in the institutional arrangements of American state and local governance. Liberal democratic governance was built around the idea of inalienable individual rights and the promotion and protection of individual freedom and equality, carried out within the confines of orderliness in civil society. Notions of global justice and transgenerational justice, for instance, were likely not at the forefront of 17th- and 18th-century liberal democratic thinkers' minds. Nonetheless, the thoughts and words of our Founding Fathers and their predecessors continue to govern American political institutions. A major challenge facing the leaders of state and local government today is to incorporate into the American individual rights tradition thoughtful consideration of future consequences so that collective action can take place to preserve the social safety net as progress is made toward maintaining vitality in our economic activities and protecting our environmental heritage.

Conclusion

Governing for sustainability means that we are committed to one another in our individual and collective pursuit of a good society. Part of that commitment means ensuring that vulnerable individuals are offered assistance based on their needs. The elderly, children, unemployed individuals, and the poverty-stricken are four examples of groups who are vulnerable and who often require the special attention of society. In sustainable governance, commitment is not about charity; it is about maximizing the opportunity of all members of society to contribute to the common welfare. For the elderly, opportunity means the chance to live a good life and to contribute the wisdom of experience to the community—be it their shared knowledge of living through challenging times and their experience implementing tried-and-true methods of meeting those challenges, or sharing child-rearing responsibilities for young adult family or community members who work full-time. For children, among the most vulnerable of any community's residents, opportunity means the chance to grow up and mature into healthy and happy adults; reliable access to quality health-care is a critical part of achieving this goal. For the unemployed and the poverty-stricken, opportunity means the chance to regain the dignity associated with economic independence; the opportunity to experience gainful employment provides that dignity.

The concept of "entitlement program" is used here because it is a term that is most frequently associated with the aforementioned programs. It reflects a philosophically liberal tradition regarding the rights of the individual and the need for the state to promote social justice. While the rights of the individual are critical in sustainable governance, the programs detailed here are equally important for the preservation of sustainable communities. A focus on sustainability, therefore, requires policymakers and citizens to redefine entitlements, painting for themselves a broader picture of the use and value of such programs. We are increasingly aware that we are all givers and we are all recipients of the benefits offered by such programs, and there is evidence that the entitlement policies of the United States are responding to this recognition.[33]

Key Terms

Baby Boomers

Medicaid

Medicare

No Child Left Behind (NCLB)

S-CHIP

Social safety net

Sustainable community-based eldercare

Temporary Assistance
   for Needy Families (TANF)

Unemployment compensation

Welfare Reform Act of 1996

Welfare-to-work programs

Discussion Questions

1. What are the various types of state and local government entitlement programs? What are the purposes of these programs?
2. Discuss the relationship between entitlement programs and sustainable communities. Is it possible to cut entitlement programs and yet maintain sustainability?
3. What are the various types of state and local public assistance and healthcare programs?
4. Discuss the role of state and local governments in the Medicare and Medicaid programs.

CHAPTER 12

Traditional and Visible Services:

Criminal Justice, Education, Transportation, and Emergency Management

Introduction

This chapter covers four of the largest and most "visible"—in terms of budget allocations—services that are provided by state and local government: criminal justice, education, transportation, and emergency management. By "visible" we mean those public services encountered frequently, or services we are likely to be aware of on a continual basis. The criminal justice system in each state includes state and local police, prosecutors, crime laboratories, prisons and jails, various corrections programs such as work release and community service, state and local probation and parole officers, and numerous other types of uniformed and plainclothes personnel. The state, county, and municipal court systems are also a part of the criminal justice system, but given the great importance of the courts this branch of government is discussed separately in Chapter 8.

The education system, which is often the largest single expenditure at the state and local level of government, includes K–12 public schools and school districts, Head Start programs, disability and special education programs, community colleges, and public universities. In addition, each state typically has a department of education, or similar agency, that administers education policy and monitors implementation for compliance with national and state school standards. Because every state has compulsory education required to a certain level, all citizens have some exposure to the education system, whether it is through public schools or private schools and academies (private schools are regulated by state and local governments).

Another service that many citizens take largely for granted, but which is an integral part of everyday life for everyone, is the transportation system. Depending on location, this could include mass transit (e.g., buses, light rail trains, subways), airports, park-and-ride lots, streets and alleys, freeways and turnpikes, car and passenger ferries, waterways, port facilities and marinas, streetlights, bike and walking paths, and bridges and overpasses. State and local governments are also involved in the regulation of private transportation services such as bus lines, taxis, rental vehicles, trucking, and the like. As with public education, state governments typically have departments of transportation established to coordinate and monitor commercial and common transport and travel activities and services.

Finally, services and programs concerning emergency management and homeland security have become much more visible after the terrorist events of Sept. 11, 2001, in the wake of natural disasters such as Hurricanes Katrina and Rita in 2005, and with international health concerns such as mad cow disease and possible avian and swine flu (H1N1) pandemics. Often acting in cooperation with the federal government, state and local governments have been developing plans, procedures, and programs to ensure public safety and assistance the next time a major disaster takes place. State and local public health authorities, state and local firefighters and emergency medical technicians, and local law enforcement (often the county sheriff) are all involved in the identifying hazards and vulnerabilities and planning for prevention, mitigation, response, and recovery associated with either manmade or natural disasters requiring emergency services.

As discussed in Chapter 1, all four of these government services and programs are integral factors in developing and maintaining sustainable and resilient states and communities. Lack of investment or proper maintenance and management of these services threatens the social and economic basis of communities and reduces their ability to adapt to the various socioeconomic changes taking place in postindustrial America. In addition, **unfunded mandates** by the federal government, such as the recently enacted stormwater management standards of the Clean Water Act and some components of the 2002 No Child Left Behind Act requiring high-stakes testing and intensive instruction in math and science literacy (see below), have added weighty responsibilities to state and local governments without adequate resources.[1] With the rising costs of delivering these services, and the additional burdensome unfunded mandates, state and local officials must now consider new approaches to service delivery and new ways of finding adequate funding. We will discuss some of these new public policy and public finance approaches to the provision of traditional and visible services in this chapter.

More specifically this chapter will:

• Compare and contrast state criminal justice systems and policies, including a focus on new and innovative approaches to adult and juvenile crime prevention, and discuss criminal justice programs and

operations that promote community sustainability rather than expand
the reach of criminal justice
- Examine the government's role (federal, state, and local) in K–12
  and higher education systems, and how education can promote
  sustainability
- Discuss the importance of state and local governments in the
  development and management of a variety of transportation
  systems and infrastructure investments that promote sustainability
- Present information on the increasing role of state and local governments
  in planning and implementing emergency management services

Criminal Justice

In the United States, state and local (county and municipal) governments are
the most important actors in the criminal justice policy area. While federal law
enforcement agencies such as the Federal Bureau of Investigation (FBI) and the
Drug Enforcement Administration (DEA) are frequently headlined in the mass
media, the vast majority of criminal justice activity takes place at the state and local
levels of government. State and local criminal justice systems consist of agencies
and personnel which are responsible for enforcing criminal codes, state statutes, and
local ordinances. These agencies and personnel include commissioned
law enforcement officers, criminal and general jurisdiction courts, correctional facilities (e.g., jails and prisons) and community-based corrections programs, prosecutors, crime victim advocates, and legal aid (including public
defenders).

While these many agencies and legal system professional groups can be found
in any state, very different perspectives on criminal justice inform criminal justice policy at the state and local levels of governance. The debate over criminal justice policy is often fueled by a profound disagreement about the causes of crime,
and what those causes imply for the appropriate countermeasures to be adopted.
In general, policymakers hold three different views regarding the causes of crime,
the origins and characteristics of offenders, and the purposes of criminal law.
These three views can be labeled the *sociogenic*, the *psychogenic*, and the *biogenic*
perspectives.

The sociogenic school of thought focuses on the crime-causing aspects of the
environment, and its advocates place primary responsibility for the occurrence
of crime on social conditions. Poverty, poor education, unreliable employment,
unstable homes, the absence of affection, and improper socialization into social
norms are cited as common causes of crime.[2] The sociogenic approach typically
reflects a liberal political ideology.

The psychogenic school of thought reflects a psychological approach that
considers the individual's propensity and inducement to violate social norms
and commit crime.[3] That propensity is determined by the individual's ability to

conceptualize right and wrong, to manage impulses, to take reasonable risks, and to anticipate the future consequences of his or her actions. Inducement refers to situational factors, such as unguarded access and easy opportunity, which can act as incentives to crime. According to this view, the individual is responsible for his or her behavior because he or she makes a choice whether to commit a crime. This view generally underlies conservative thought, and it explains why the advocates of this understanding of criminal motivation favor severe penalties (such as capital punishment) thought to deter individuals from making the wrong choices.

A third approach to crime is the biogenic or sociobiological explanation.[4] This viewpoint is not highly common among criminologists but has been popularized by the scholar James Q. Wilson.[5] This school of thought relates criminal behavior to such fundamental biological phenomena as brain tumors, endocrine abnormalities, neurological dysfunctions from adverse prenatal and postnatal experiences, and chromosomal abnormalities.[6] Preventive crime policies would entail developing appropriate screening and other diagnostic tests for persons suspected of having such crime-inducing physical or mental disorders.

Those who subscribe to the sociogenic school of thought are less likely to be supporters of punishment as the sole solution to crime than are those who adhere to either the psychogenic or biogenic schools of thought. Proponents of the sociogenic explanation do not hold the individual as always primarily responsible for his or her criminal behavior; because of this, they do not see punishment as an effective deterrent to most types of criminal behavior. Instead, they tend to favor a **civil libertarian** approach, which emphasizes the rights of individuals accused of crimes and advocates treatment and rehabilitation-focused programs for juvenile offenders and most adult offenders alike.

In contrast, those who view criminal behavior as a matter of individual choice (the psychogenic school) are likely to see swift and certain punishment as an effective deterrent because punishments constitute a tangible consequence as individuals calculate the amount of risk involved in committing a crime in relation to the potential consequence. Adherents of this perspective will support policies that take a **law and order** approach, where emphasis is placed on protecting the public order by close monitoring of conduct and the imposition of stern punishments on those who commit offenses.

Those who adhere to the biogenic school differ slightly from the psychogenic ideology in that they may or may not view punishment as a deterrent to crime, but they most likely feel that capital punishment is the appropriate punishment for individuals who cannot be cured of their criminal predispositions. However, the primary emphasis for the advocates of the biogenic perspective would be on preventive policies to identify persons who are biologically predisposed to commit crimes, which would be measurable through reliable diagnostic tests of various kinds.

Crime in America

The two most comprehensive sources of crime data in the United States are the annual National Crime Survey (NCS) and the FBI's Uniform Crime Report (UCR).

The NCS conducts very large-scale household surveys each year to determine whether citizens have been the victims of major crimes such as rape, robbery, burglary, larceny, or other crimes. The NCS is a good measure of crime because it collects data on crimes that have occurred that have not been reported to police. The UCR, in contrast, is a measure of crimes known to police (i.e., those that are actually reported to the authorities). Typically the NCS reveals far more serious crimes being committed than the UCR registers because many crimes go unreported for a variety of reasons, such as fear of retribution, a belief that the police could do nothing about the crime, or the desire to "drop the charges" on the party responsible for the crime. For example, the NCS conducted in 2006 revealed that only "49% of all violent victimizations and 38% of all property crimes were reported to the police; 57% of robberies and 59% of aggravated assaults were reported to the police" (U.S. Department of Justice, 2007a: 1).[7]

Using data from the UCR, the FBI periodically publishes a "crime clock" for serious crimes reported from across the nation. The data in Table 12.1 for 2004 indicate that every 3.1 seconds a property crime (e.g., burglary, larceny, theft) is committed, and every 23.1 seconds a violent crime is committed. While crime rates—both reported and unreported—can vary from year to year, these are disturbing numbers and are an indication of the enormous challenge and burden facing state and local government criminal justice systems. Not only are the human costs of these crimes enormous, such as loss of life and long-term debilitating effects, but the monetary costs are great as well, not only for the victims but also for state and local government budgets. According to the U.S. Bureau of Justice, "local jails" (locally operated correctional facilities) have the following traits:[8]

- At midyear 2006, 766,010 inmates were held in the nation's local jails, up from 747,529 at midyear 2005.
- In 2006, jails reported adding 21,862 beds during the previous 12 months, bringing the total rated capacity to 810,863.
- 94% of the rated capacity was occupied at midyear 2006.
- On June 30, 2006, local jails were operating 6% below their rated capacity.
- From 1995 to 2005, the number of jail inmates per 100,000 U.S. residents rose from 193 to 256.
- Almost nine out of every ten jail inmates were men. However, the number of women in jail has increased faster than men since the mid-1980s.
- Between 1990 and 2006, the number of white and Hispanic jail inmates increased at the same average annual rate. The number of black inmates increased at a slower pace.
- Blacks were almost three times more likely than Hispanics and five times more likely than whites to be in jail.

The majority of inmates in both our prisons and local jail facilities are black or Latino, possess few educational or vocational skills for legitimate employment, are

Table 12.1. FBI Crime Clock

Every 3.1 seconds: One Property Crime
- One burglary every 14.7 seconds
- One larceny-theft every 4.5 seconds
- One motor vehicle theft every 25.5 seconds

Every 23.1 seconds: One Violent Crime
- One murder every 32.6 minutes
- One forcible rape every 5.6 minutes
- One robbery every 1.3 minutes
- One aggravated assault every 36.9 seconds

Source: FBI Crime Clock: URL: http://www.fbi.gov/ucr/cius_04/summary/crime_clock/index.html

often involved in the chronic use of drugs, and are likely to have grown up in poverty and to have received relatively little nurturance from parents or extended families. In fact, in one of the first comprehensive studies on the "prevalent handicaps" present among prison inmates, Albert Roberts identified five characteristics common to most institutional correctional facility inmates:[9]

1. "Character disorder," which means antisocial behavior due to inappropriate socialization as a child
2. "Unemployability," the lack of job-related skills and work motivation
3. "Relationship hang-ups," lack of constructive interpersonal relationships and support with family and friends
4. "Social stigma," being labeled a felon or socially undesirable
5. "Immaturity," inability to take appropriate responsibility for one's own actions and to make socially acceptable life choices

These same five characteristics are as relevant today as they were in the early 1970s, when Roberts did his pioneering research in corrections.

Remedies

As discussed previously, there are differing theories concerning the causes of crime, and as a consequence there are different remedies offered by the advocates each theory. The three main countermeasures to crime advocated are *punishment*, *rehabilitation*, and *treatment*; in many instances a combination of all three approaches is being attempted in state and local settings across the country.

Punishment has been a very popular approach to crime in the United States, as evidenced by historically popular support for the death penalty; large majorities of citizens support its use in cases of murder and other heinous crimes (Table 12.2). While only 26 countries in the world used the death penalty in 2006 (including China, Iran, Syria, and the United States), 50% of U.S. citizens in 2003 support its use for purposes of revenge ("an eye for an eye") and punishment thought to deter serious crime (Table 12.3).

Table 12.2. Public Support for the Death Penalty for a Person Convicted of Murder

Year	% Favor	% Oppose	% Depends/No opinion
2009	65	31	4
2006	65	28	7
2003	71	26	3
1995	77	13	10
1994	80	16	4
1991	76	18	6
1988	79	16	5
1985	72	20	8
1981	66	25	9
1978	62	27	11
1976	66	26	8
1972	57	32	11
1971	49	40	11
1969	51	40	9
1967	54	38	08
1965	45	43	12
1960	53	36	11
1957	47	34	18
1953	68	25	07
1936	61	39	NA

The Gallup Poll, www.gallup.com Question: "Are you in favor of the death penalty for a person convicted of murder?"

The popularity of punishment among citizens and elected officials has led to the adoption in most states of mandatory sentencing laws, including **three-strikes laws.** These state statutes are aimed at deterring potential offenders and incapacitating convicted criminals through long-term prison terms. One of the unfortunate results of mandatory sentencing and the punishment approach in general is that many new state and local correctional facilities have had to be constructed to house an increasing number of prisoners in communities that could afford that investment of public funds. Where that investment was not possible, existing correctional facilities have been filled to capacity or overfilled. In this connection, correctional facilities in 22 states were either filled or overfilled in terms of prisoner capacity in 2003. This same year there were 42 states at 90% capacity or higher.[10] A study of California's three-strikes statute, one of the earliest such laws, by the U.S. Department of Justice found that:[11]

- The prison population in California over the next quarter-century would triple.
- Costs would increase during the same period by $5.5 billion per year, on average, for a cumulative additional cost of $137.5 billion.
- Serious crimes would be reduced by 28%, at a total correctional cost saving of approximately $16,300 per crime averted.

As costs and the number and nature of participants in the overwhelmingly punishment-based criminal justice systems have dramatically increased, many scholars

Table 12.3. Reasons for Favoring the Death Penalty Among the U.S. Public, Gallup Polls 1985, 1991, and 2003

	1985	1991	2003
Revenge: "an eye for an eye"	30%	50%	37%
Acts as a deterrent	22%	13%	11%
Murderers deserve punishment	18%	NA	13%
Costly to keep murderers in prison	11%	13%	11%
Keeps murderers from killing again	9%	19%	7%
Removes potential risk to community	7%	NA	NA
Judicial system is too lenient	NA	3%	NA
All others	13%	11%	31%
No opinion	2%	2%	2%

The Gallup Poll, www.gallup.com. Question: Why do you favor the death penalty for persons convicted of murder? [Open-ended] *Note:* Totals add to more than 100% due to multiple responses.

and practitioners believe the current system is neither economically, socially, nor institutionally sustainable.[12] Alternatives to punishment and imprisonment include new community-based policing procedures, juvenile aftercare programs, community service and residential centers, fines, restitution, intensive probation, and shock incarceration/boot camps, among others.[13]

For example, due to prison overcrowding and the high costs of incarceration, many state and local governments have moved to the use of "intermediate sanctions" for nonviolent offenders. One such intermediate sanction is intensive probation supervision, a conditional release program that features strict curfews,

Photo 12.1. Overcrowding in a prison: policies such as three-strikes laws have led to larger prison populations. Source: Ted Soqui/Corbis.

routine and random (unscheduled) drug testing, community service, and restitution to victims. While this is not the approach taken for violent or habitual offenders, it is much less costly and provides an opportunity for rehabilitation for the first-time offender. In this type of program, offenders are both held accountable for their actions and are given the opportunity to act responsibly in the community to make proper amends.

Other approaches to building sustainable criminal justice systems include **community policing**. In general, community policing can involve police officers being assigned to specific neighborhoods rather than being on call for responding to 911 calls citywide; the creation and maintenance of neighborhood police stations or "storefronts" in high-crime areas; and police participation in neighborhood meetings and home visits. All of these activities are undertaken in an attempt to connect police with citizens in their respective neighborhoods and communities instead of just performing drive-by patrols in their cars. Community policing also emphasizes "problem-solving methodologies" and partnership-building policies, where police agencies work closely with community groups and local businesses to identify current and future problems and then work together collaboratively to address those problems. The federal government's U.S. Department of Justice established the Office of Community Oriented Policing Services (COPS) in the 1994 Crime Bill to provide federal resources to local communities so that they could train their officers in community policing and implement these programs, which are designed to sustain safe and crime-free communities in which the police and the citizens they serve are involved in an active partnership to preserve public order and promote public safety.

Photo 12.2. Police patrolling on bicycles in Seattle's Pike Place Market: an example of community-oriented policing strategies to bring law enforcement closer to the community. Source: Karl Weatherly/Corbis.

Many innovations in dealing with crime as well as new programs reflect the values of sustainability, and some of these successful approaches should be noted. One example includes "designing, implementing, and monitoring sentencing guidelines that balance several goals of crime response, establishing mandatory drug treatment instead of prison for first- and second-time drug possession," and providing in prison "basic schooling and drug and alcohol treatment to those offenders who can benefit from those services" to help prisoners "graduate" to freedom at the end of their term. Prison and jail programs that can provide job training and job placement at the end of confinement have also been found to reduce **recidivism**.[14] In addition, some programs that target **at-risk youth**, such as early intervention programs including counseling, organized constructive activities, and out-of-home placement for serious offenses, have been found to be effective as well.[15] While no one single approach or combination of approaches will eradicate crime completely, many states and communities have been testing out new and different approaches to criminal justice that represent alternatives to incarceration and move toward the goal of sustainability.

Education

Public education is typically one of the largest expenditures and is probably the most visible service provided by state and local governments. With over 48 million students, over 93,000 schools, more than 3 million teachers, and nearly 3 million support staff and administrators involved in K–12 education in the United States, public education has an enormous effect on state and local budgets, on local economies, and on the socioeconomic fabric of communities. Add to this set of totals the 1,720 4-year public universities, the 2,516 2-year public colleges, and their respective professors, administrators, and staff, and the effects of public education on society are even greater. The connection of public education to the promotion of sustainability is clear and direct, as schools, colleges, and universities are a key part of the visible services experienced by virtually all citizens. How the education system teaches about and models behavior regarding sustainability is a matter of great importance to contemporary professional educators and education policymakers.

The history of education policy in the United States reflects the nation's steady transformation from a rural natural resource-based and agricultural economy in the 1700s and 1800s to a postindustrial society in the late 20th and early 21st centuries (Table 12.4). The first public school in the United States was established in Boston in 1635 to educate the sons of the city's wealthy elites. Elite access to education was primarily the norm until the period of industrialization in the mid-1800s. At this time there was an expansion of educational opportunities, especially in the growing cities, for students of middle- and working-class families. This is when mandatory attendance laws began to be enacted by state legislatures in recognition

Table 12.4. Key Dates in U.S. Education Policy History

Year	Event
1635	First Latin Grammar School established in Boston to educate sons of wealthy families for leadership positions
1635	First "free school" established in Virginia
1636	Harvard College becomes the first higher education institution.
1647	Massachusetts Law of 1647 decrees that every town with at least 50 families hire a schoolmaster to teach reading and writing.
1821	First public high school opens in Boston.
1827	Massachusetts passes a law requiring public high schools in towns of 500 families or more.
1829	New England Asylum for the Blind is the first school in the U.S. for children with disabilities.
1837	Mount Holyoke becomes the first college for women.
1852	First mandatory attendance law in passed in Massachusetts; all states will have mandatory attendance laws by 1918.
1856	First kindergarten is started, in Wisconsin.
1862	Land Grant Act ("First Morrill Act") donates public lands to states to establish colleges and universities.
1890	Second Morrill Act provides more public lands for colleges, including the creation of 16 Black land grant colleges.
1896	Supreme Court rules "separate but equal" schools are constitutional in *Plessy v. Ferguson*; the decision affirms racially segregated schools.
1916	American Federation of Teachers is founded.
1926	Scholastic Aptitude Test (SAT) is developed and used.
1944	Servicemen's Readjustment Act ("GI Bill") is passed, providing education for returning WWII veterans.
1952	Veteran's Readjustment Act is passed for veterans of the Korean War.
1954	U.S. Supreme Court decision *Brown v. Board of Education* overturns 1896 case *Plessy v. Ferguson* by ruling that separate educational facilities are inherently unequal.
1957	President Eisenhower sends federal troops to enforce integration in Little Rock, Arkansas, public schools.
1958	As a result of the Soviet Union's launch of Sputnik, the National Defense Education Act is passed, increasing funding for science education.
1964	Civil Rights Act is passed. It prohibits discrimination based on race, sex, color, religion, or national origin.
1965	Elementary and Secondary Act (ESEA) is passed, which provides funds to help low-income students.
1965	Project Head Start provides preschool education for low-income children.
1966	The Equality of Educational Opportunity Study (the "Coleman Report") concludes that African-American children benefit from attending integrated schools. Study serves as the basis for busing to integrate schools.
1972	Title IX of the Education Amendments of 1972 prohibits sex discrimination in education.
1975	The Education of All Handicapped Children Act is passed, requiring free, appropriate public education for all handicapped children.
2001	No Child Left Behind Act (NCLB) becomes law, holding schools accountable for student achievement.

of the fact that an industrial workforce and economy require adequate levels of literacy. In the 20th century, as the United States was developing into a postindustrial economy, many efforts were made by the federal and state governments alike to ensure better educational opportunities for all races and for disadvantaged students as well.

State governments are primarily responsible for providing educational services in our country, although the federal government has passed many laws concerning the access to and quality of state school systems (i.e., the **No Child Left Behind Act**). Every state has established a department of education of some type and has enacted laws regulating curriculum, teacher qualifications, school finance, student attendance, and the like.

The almost 15,000 local school districts in the United States today oversee the day-to-day administration of schools. Many school districts are heavily supported by local taxes, a fact that ties schools closely to their communities and can influence the types of programs and curriculum offered as well as the quality and quantity of educational infrastructure and school personnel. However, there are many differences among states in how school funding is provided and who provides it. For example, schools in Illinois receive 62% of their funding from local sources, while schools in Hawaii receive over 87% from the state government. There is quite a wide variation in average state and local spending per pupil as well, with New Jersey spending on average $13,781 per student in 2005-06 compared to Utah at $5,347 (Table 12.5). This wide variation can also be found in higher education spending, with Hawaii spending $9,733 per student compared to Colorado spending only $2,361 per student.[16]

Importance of Education

Education is one of the most important factors underlying the promotion of sustainable communities. Higher levels of education have been associated with a wide range of individual, social, and economic lifelong benefits; similarly, communities and taxpayers derive a multitude of benefits when citizens have access to education. In fact, most research concerning resilience and sustainable communities identifies education as a **pivotal variable** for the simultaneous achievement of economic vitality, a civil society, healthy families, low rates of crime, and environmentally sensitive practices. The following facts about education translate into individual and societal benefits:[17]

- There is a correlation between levels of education and higher earnings for all racial/ethnic groups, and for both men and women.
- Higher levels of education correspond to lower levels of unemployment and poverty, so in addition to contributing more to tax revenues than others do, adults with higher levels of education are less likely to depend on social safety net programs, decreasing their demand on public budgets.

Table 12.5. State Education Statistics, 2006

State	Per-Pupil State and Local Support for Public K–12 ($)	Pupils per Teacher in Public K–12	Per-Pupil State Support for Public Higher Education ($)	Average Resident Public University Tuition ($)
Alabama	7,303	15.7	6,124	4,773
Alaska	10,171	16.8	8,354	3,808
Arizona	5,585	21.5	3,039	4,429
Arkansas	6,309	13.8	5,876	4,888
California	8,205	19.9	4,818	4,543
Colorado	8,277	17.0	2,361	4,200
Connecticut	12,436	13.3	7,423	6,573
Delaware	11,423	14.9	5,659	7,050
Florida	7,650	16.6	4,865	3,213
Georgia	9,147	14.8	6,187	3,760
Hawaii	8,745	16.1	9,733	3,697
Idaho	6,966	17.6	5,519	3,922
Illinois	10,271	15.9	4,639	7,214
Indiana	8,978	16.9	5,356	6,170
Iowa	7,807	13.8	5,207	5,619
Kansas	8,178	14.3	4,375	4,826
Kentucky	8,195	15.9	6,098	5,124
Louisiana	8,812	14.8	6,259	3,734
Maine	11,285	11.9	5,244	6,000
Maryland	9,622	15.4	4,802	6,767
Massachusetts	12,276	14.6	4,877	7,403
Michigan	10,069	17.8	4,026	7,031
Minnesota	9,675	16.0	5,656	6,981
Mississippi	6,763	15.8	5,689	4,232
Missouri	7,680	13.3	3,960	6,361
Montana	8,361	14.3	4,085	5,088
Nebraska	7,980	13.8	5,820	5,455
Nevada	7,085	19.4	5,783	3,060
New Hampshire	10,206	13.5	2,883	8,656
New Jersey	13,781	12.7	6,610	8,601
New Mexico	8,629	15.0	5,917	2,854
New York	13,551	12.7	6,901	5,031
North Carolina	7,465	14.8	7,514	3,674
North Dakota	7,760	12.9	4,975	5,074
Ohio	10,034	16.2	4,556	9,047
Oklahoma	6,745	15.6	4,385	3,924
Oregon	8,141	19.8	3,706	5,430
Pennsylvania	10,052	15.0	5,288	8,700
Rhode Island	11,089	11.3	4,568	6,439
South Carolina	8,531	14.6	4,450	7,416
South Dakota	7,911	13.6	4,399	4,911
Tennessee	7,079	15.6	5,376	4,773
Texas	7,397	14.9	4,889	5,414
Utah	5,347	22.6	4,586	3,583
Vermont	12,326	10.9	3,567	9,494
Virginia	9,275	11.8	4,633	6,034
Washington	81,66	19.3	5,220	5,252
West Virginia	9,790	14.1	3,732	3,860
Wisconsin	10,072	14.7	4,240	5,656
Wyoming	11,971	12.6	6,994	3,429

Source: The Council of State Legislators, *Book of the States*, 2006 (see note 10).

Photo 12.3. Academic achievement is an important part of building a sustainable community. Source: © Alkir | Dreamstime.com

- Higher levels of education are associated with lower smoking rates, more positive perceptions of personal health, and lower incarceration rates.
- Higher levels of education are correlated with higher levels of civic participation, including volunteer work, voting, and blood donation.

Politics and Education

While the benefits of education are recognized among most segments of society, education policy, like criminal justice policy, has historically been a battleground for different value systems and ideologies. For example, supporters of the religious right and many conservatives have objected to the content taught in public schools, from Darwin's theory of evolution in biology to the contemporary emphasis on contributions by minority groups to American history and the writing of women in literature. In response, many highly religious conservatives have withdrawn their children from public schools and engage in home schooling. In some states these people use a **voucher system** to enroll their children in religious schools. Supporters of a voucher system argue that such educational systems provide parents more freedom in deciding what schools their child may attend. This choice to parents comes in the form of a voucher, which has, depending on the state, a predetermined amount of money to cover student tuition.

However, while many conservatives strongly support such systems, liberal and pro-public education groups, such as the National Education Association (NEA), strongly oppose voucher systems for the following reasons:

> Teachers, parents, and the general public have long opposed private school tuition vouchers—especially when funds for vouchers compete with funds for overall improvements in America's public schools. The NEA and its affiliates have been leaders in the fight to improve public schools—and oppose alternatives that divert attention, energy, and resources from efforts to reduce class size, enhance teacher quality, and provide every student with books, computers, and safe and orderly schools.[18]

The next step for those opposed to public schools, for a variety of reasons, has been the establishment of a large number of **charter schools** as alternatives to traditional public schools in 40 states (10 states have no charter school legislation). Charter schools are public schools that can operate with fewer regulations than apply to traditional public schools. The "charter" that establishes such schools is a contract detailing the desired curriculum, mission, goals, and methods used to assess achievement of educational outcomes and student performance. Each state has different legislation concerning the length of time charters are granted, but most are issued for 3 to 5 years with the possibility of renewal. Charter schools are accountable to either a local school district or a state agency. Charter schools are granted increased autonomy in return for enhanced accountability. The main reasons often given for charter schools are that they can serve a special population, they allow for more innovative teaching methods, and they can specialize in certain areas of academic study.[19]

Similar to the use of voucher systems, pro-public school organizations and advocates such as the NEA have opposed the creation of charter schools for a variety of reasons, including concerns about the quality of instructional facilities, the content of the curriculum, and the credentials of teachers. The NEA proposes the following alternative to the use of charter schools:

> NEA believes that what's really needed to improve student achievement are programs and resources—smaller class sizes, quality pre-K and after-school programs, expanded professional development for educators, safe and modern schools—that will result in great public schools for all children.[20]

Another area where there has been much political conflict in public education concerns the issue of busing children to achieve racially and ethnically integrated schools. The desegregation of public facilities preceded the desegregation of public schools. In 1896, the U.S. Supreme Court ruled in ***Plessy v. Ferguson*** that "separate but equal" public facilities provided for in public policy were consistent with the equal protection clause of the 14th Amendment to the U.S. Constitution. The Supreme Court's ruling meant that racial segregation was acceptable so long as the services provided by government for different races were basically comparable.

In this case Homer Plessy, who was 7/8 white and 1/8 African American, lost his lawsuit to be treated equally based on his attempt to sit in a "whites-only" railroad passenger car instead of a racially segregated car provided for blacks.

This decision wasn't overturned until nearly 60 years later, in 1954, when the U.S. Supreme Court, in the landmark case *Brown v. Board of Education*, ruled that separate schools for blacks and whites were unconstitutional. In upholding the decision in 1955 in *Brown v. Board of Education II*, the Court held that:

> . . . the problems identified in Brown required varied local solutions. Chief Justice Warren conferred much responsibility on local school authorities and the courts, which originally heard school segregation cases. They were to implement the principles which the Supreme Court embraced in its first Brown decision. Warren urged localities to act on the new principles promptly and to move toward full compliance with them "with all deliberate speed."[21]

Since this time, many school districts and subsequent state and local government court decisions supported the busing of racial and ethnic minorities to schools that were predominantly white. In 1971, the U.S. Supreme Court ruled in *Swann v. Charlotte-Mecklenberg Board of Education* that local education districts across the nation should use mandatory busing as a policy to achieve racial integration in their schools. This decision led to the development of court-supervised desegregation busing plans in cities during the 1970s and 1980s. Much turmoil and conflict ensued in many U.S. communities. Conflict was intense in many locations in the South and North alike, including Boston, Massachusetts, where police had to escort African-American schoolchildren bused into white neighborhoods in 1974.

There are still those who ardently support or strongly oppose busing for racial integration in many communities today, and some observers continue to note the extreme inequality that persists among school districts. For example, Jonathan Kozol, author of many books detailing inequality in America's schools (including *Savage Inequalities*), has argued:

> Many Americans who live far from our major cities and who have no firsthand knowledge of the realities to be found in urban public schools seem to have the rather vague and general impression that the great extremes of racial isolation that were matters of grave national significance some thirty-five or forty years ago have gradually but steadily diminished in more recent years. The truth, unhappily, is that the trend, for well over a decade now, has been precisely the reverse. Schools that were already deeply segregated twenty-five or thirty years ago are no less segregated now, while thousands of other schools around the country that had been integrated either voluntarily or by the force of law have since been rapidly re-segregating.[22]

President Johnson's 1965 **Elementary and Secondary Education Act** (ESEA) represents the first major effort made by the federal government to provide aid to low-income and disadvantaged children by distributing federal funds to state and local educational systems. The assumption underlying ESEA was that children from low-income homes required more educational resources and services than children from higher-income households. As part of the ESEA, Title I allocated billions of federal dollars every year to schools with high concentrations of low-income children. Several programs emerged from ESEA over time, including **Head Start**. This is a preschool program for young disadvantaged children with the stated purpose of getting these children ready for the rigors of the first grade. However, as Hess notes: "Over time, critics of both the left and right expressed concerns about the failure of Title I to improve achievement visibly among low-income students."[23] The slowly emerging consensus among liberals and conservatives, Democrats and Republicans alike, was that ESEA, as well as state and local education efforts of similar design and purpose, were not working for all children. This consensus led in time to the passage of the No Child Left Behind (NCLB) Act in 2002.

No Child Left Behind Act

NCLB is "arguably the nation's most significant piece of federal legislation on K-12 schooling adopted since the ESEA, and it is undoubtedly the most ambitious federal intervention into a public policy domain long regarded as the preserve of state and local government."[24] NCLB requires the following:

1. States must meet deadlines to implement the scope and frequency of student testing, or federal funds will be lost.
2. Schools must sign a formal written guarantee that teachers are highly qualified in their subject areas.
3. Schools must demonstrate annual progress in increasing the percentage of students shown to be proficient in math and reading.
4. Schools must narrow the gap in test scores between disadvantaged and advantaged students.

To help achieve these objectives, NCLB provides some federal funding in targeted areas such as K–3 reading programs and before- and after-school programs. Students attending schools that perform poorly and that have not shown annual progress for 2 consecutive years have the ability to transfer to better-performing schools. States and school districts are also mandated to provide technical assistance for poorly performing schools.

While the intent of the NCLB is to provide all children with a good-quality education, or as Abernathy argues, "it makes the kinds of promises to our most disadvantaged citizens and their children worthy of a great liberal democracy," the act has many vocal critics.[25] Most of the criticism of NCLB concerns the use of tests for assessment as well as funding issues. NEA has called for reforms in three specific areas of NCLB:

1. The use of alternative methods of assessment besides tests scores to measure student learning and school performance, including multiple measures of student learning and school effectiveness rather than a "one-day snapshot based solely on standardized tests"

2. A reduction in class sizes to provide students more teacher contact and individual instruction

3. Increasing the number of highly qualified teachers in schools by providing financial incentives and more flexibility in areas of expertise[26]

The National Council of State Legislatures (NCSL), an organization that represents lawmakers in state governments, would also like to see many reforms to NCLB. The NCSL believes that the NCLB represents a federal infringement on states' rights; that it is "an unfunded mandate in the way it requires states to spend their own money, or change their accountability systems to comply with the law;" and that "states should be granted the ability to use value-added or student-growth approaches" to conduct student learning assessment in their accountability plans.[27]

Not surprisingly, the Bush Administration had a different position and viewed the act as a great success, with much progress made, and as worthy of reauthorization in the coming years:

> This progress has occurred as the academic bar has been raised and our schools have become more diverse. In fact, some of the largest gains are being made by children once left behind, including many in big-city public schools. Under *NCLB*, fourth-graders in a majority of sampled urban school districts made greater gains in reading and math than students nationwide on average, according to the NAEP Trial Urban District Assessments. The Council of the Great City Schools also reported double-digit gains in large urban districts for fourth-graders in both subjects between 2002 and 2005.[28]

Some states have considered opting out or not fully participating in NCLB and risk losing federal funding for education in the process. For example, the 2004 Republican-controlled legislature in Utah introduced and passed legislation that would allow school districts to eliminate federal education programs when the federal government does not provide adequate funding to support the programs in question (an unfunded mandate). Many other school districts and some states have also considered such legislation. Vermont also passed a similar law that prohibits expenditure of state funds to comply with NCLB.[29] As NCLB entered into the reauthorization process in 2008 and 2009, both political parties came to the defense of the act and it remains an important part of our nation's commitment to K–12 education.

Higher Education

So far we have discussed the role of the states and their local governments in K–12 education, but states are also heavily involved in providing higher education opportunities to their citizens, such as community colleges, trade schools, 4-year colleges, and research universities. There are 4,236 higher education institutions in the United States, with 1,720 public 4-year schools, 1,086 2-year public schools, 1,896 private 4-year schools, and 620 private 2-year schools.[30] Many states have coordinating boards that set out broad policy for public universities. For example, Washington has the Washington Higher Education Coordinating Board, a state agency governed by a 10-member citizen board. The charge of the board is to represent the "broad public interest" in higher education and to review and approve all degree programs at the state's public 4-year universities and colleges. Washington, like many states, also has a Board for Community and Technical Colleges that plays a similar role with respect to the state's 30+ public 2-year community and technical colleges.

Some states also have a chief executive officer for the entire state public university system who serves as the leader of the higher education board. For example, the Ohio University System and the Oregon University System both have chancellors whose job it is to oversee the entire system and to provide liaison between elected officials and the state's higher education institutions.

In most states there have been three major issues facing public higher education in recent years: access, affordability, and accountability. As Heller has argued, "With more than 80 percent of all undergraduates in the United States attending public colleges and universities, very few discussions on higher education take place without one or more of these issues being central to the debate."[31] As Chapter 10 on state and local budgeting described, state budgets have been severely strained by the increasing costs of providing services while revenue sources have not kept up with the pace of inflation and growing demand. Often public higher education budgets suffer from constrained revenues as other essential services, such as K–12 education, criminal justice, and healthcare, are given higher priority.

Higher Education Access

As discussed previously, education is one of the most important factors for the creation of sustainable communities. However, there are grave concerns in most states about who has access to public higher education. More highly educated people are more likely to earn higher incomes, to participate in their communities, to vote in elections, to have a higher level of knowledge about policies and their communities, and to be more satisfied with life (Table 12.6).[32] As a 2003 report by State Higher Education Executive Officers concludes:

> No state can prosper with a poorly educated workforce, nor can it continue to prosper if its workforce fails to learn continuously. Most of the workers of the next two

Table 12.6. Educational Attainment Related to Poverty and Income

Educational Attainment	Poverty Rate for Population 25 Years and Over	Median Earnings for Population 25 Years and Over
Less than high school graduate	23.7%	$18,641
High school graduate or equivalent	11.5%	$26,123
Some college or associate's degree	7.8%	$31,936
Bachelor's degree	4.1%	$45,221
Graduate or professional degree	3.1%	$59,804

Source: U.S. Census Bureau, 2006 American Community Survey.

decades are already over twenty-five years old. These simple truths require states to assess the knowledge and skills of their adult population and to develop and implement policies that enable current workers, as well as the next generation, to compete more effectively in the global economy.[33]

A comprehensive study conducted by the College Board concerning access to and participation in higher education found the following:[34]

- Among students with the top 10% SAT scores, virtually all in the top half of the household income level enroll in some form of higher education, yet only 80% of those in the lowest fifth of household income pursue higher education.
- Participation rates in higher education vary by race and ethnicity, with whites and Asians more likely than African-Americans and Hispanics to enroll in higher education.
- After high school graduation, students of parents who attended college are significantly more likely to attend college than those with similar incomes whose parents do not have a college education.

One approach that many states have pursued to increase diversity and enhance the number of underrepresented racial and ethnic minorities in public higher education has been through the use of affirmative action, specifically with respect to admission policies. The idea of affirmative action was first promoted by President Kennedy in 1961 as a policy for redressing historical discrimination in both education and employment. Affirmative action policies have typically required active measures to ensure that African-Americans, Hispanics, and other racial and ethnic minorities receive the same educational opportunities as whites for admissions, scholarships, and financial aid.

While affirmative action was originally justified as a temporary remedy until equal opportunities for minorities and non-minorities could be secured, it has been a highly controversial policy from the outset, leading to ongoing complaints of "reverse discrimination" among some disadvantaged whites and conservatives in general. In 1978, Allan Bakke, a white man, had been rejected 2 years in a row by the University of California-Davis medical school. The medical school in both years had admitted less-qualified minority applicants through its affirmative action program (16 out of 100 places were reserved for minority applicants). Bakke sued the medical school on the grounds of reverse discrimination (**Regents of the University of California v. Bakke**). The U.S. Supreme Court ruled by a 5-4 vote that inflexible quota systems in affirmative action were not permissible under the equal protection clause of the 14th Amendment of the constitution. However, in the same decision the court also upheld the legality of affirmative action in general so long as the remedies applied were carefully tailored to the situation at hand, contributed to the quality of education for all students, and were temporary in nature. A citizen's initiative—Proposition 209—passed in 1996 which banned all forms of affirmative action in California, illustrating the continuing controversial nature of the concept.

The most recent and important case following the Bakke decision was **Grutter v. Bollinger**, heard in 2003. In this case, the U.S. Supreme Court upheld the University of Michigan Law School's affirmative action policy, deciding as it did in the Bakke case that race can be one of several factors considered when making admission decisions because it furthers "the educational benefits that flow from a diverse student body." However, the court also ruled that the university's undergraduate admission program, which used a formula that awarded extra points to minority students, was not constitutional and ordered the original trial court to work on appropriate modification to pass muster on equal treatment. As a consequence of this decision, state public colleges and universities that wish to enhance diversity can consider race and ethnicity in their admissions, but they cannot use strict formulas or quotas to make such decisions on who is admitted to study.

Higher Education Affordability

Closely related to the issue of access to higher education is the question of affordability. Higher levels of tuition obviously limit access for lower-income students. The National Center for Public Policy and Higher Education's biennial study entitled *Measuring Up 2006: The National Report Card on Higher Education* (2007) documents the increasing problem of the rising cost of higher education at public colleges and universities.[35] The report gave 43 states an "F" for affordability, an increase from the report issued 2 years earlier. Most other states received "Ds," except for California and Utah, which both received "C" grades. According to Patrick Callan, a contributor to the report:

> College affordability continues to decline in the United States. Of all the performance categories in the *Measuring Up* report cards, the state results for affordability are the most dismal. Since our previous edition of *Measuring Up*, the number of states receiving "F" grades increased from 36 to 43. Even after all financial aid is taken into account, students and their families must devote an increasing share of their income and borrow more to pay for a year of college education at almost all public and private two- and four-year campuses. Only the wealthiest of American families are exempted from declining college affordability.[36]

The study also reports that since the 1980s, the annual rate of increase "in the price of college has far outstripped price increases in other sectors of the economy, even health care. Over these years, median family income increased by 127%; college tuition and fees by 375%."[37]

While higher education costs have increased everywhere, the data displayed in Table 12.5 indicate that there is disparity between the states in terms of both per-pupil state support for public higher education and average resident tuition. While several factors are involved in state support of higher education, such as regional and state differences in the cost of doing business (e.g., Alaska and Hawaii) as well as the health and size of the state budget, there are still enormous differences between the states in this area. For example, Alaska, Connecticut,

Hawaii, and North Carolina all spend more than $7,000 per pupil in public higher education; Colorado and New Hampshire spend less than $3,000 per pupil. Average resident tuition also varies widely, with New Hampshire, New Jersey, Ohio, Pennsylvania, and Vermont charging each student over $8,000 compared to 13 states that charge less than $4,000 per student; Nevada has the lowest average tuition, $2,854 in 2006.

Besides having states increase higher education budgets to keep tuition costs down and therefore provide more student access, several reforms have been suggested to enhance the capacity of higher education. Some of these reforms are:

1. Improving the quality of K–12 education, thereby eliminating the need for remedial courses (e.g., writing, foreign language) offered at the university for unprepared students
2. Allowing high school students to take more advanced placement (AP) courses to earn college credit
3. Encouraging more collaboration between community colleges and universities so that the transition from 2-year to 4-year institutions is more efficient
4. Encouraging more students to attend lower-cost community colleges, thereby creating greater efficiencies in the state higher education systems
5. Improving retention and graduation rates at universities to ensure greater efficiency and student success

Higher Education Accountability

In the past decade there has been a call for increased accountability in higher education by policymakers, business leaders, college administrators, and some voices among the public at large. There is a sense that higher education in the United States has lost its competitive edge internationally, and the higher education community needs to assess what is working well and what things don't deserve to be continued. For example, the State Higher Education Executive Officers (SHEEO) established the National Commission on Accountability in Higher Education, which issued a 2005 report arguing the following:

> The United States system of higher education led the world in the 20th century by creating wide access to opportunity and a network of exceptional colleges and universities. But these achievements are no longer good enough. The *status quo* in higher education is unacceptable because: 1) a high school diploma is no longer adequate for work in a competitive economy, supporting a family, or meeting the full responsibilities of citizenship; 2) other countries are beginning to attain and surpass our educational achievements; and 3) the fastest growing segments of our population—minorities and low-income students—have been the least successful in our educational system. We must improve performance.[38]

Following the momentum of accountability measures and policies in K–12 and state higher education systems, institutions are adopting accountability standards that set minimum learning outcomes for students and require the use of an appropriate assessment process for measuring those outcomes. It is common now for universities and colleges to have specified learning outcomes for the institution at large, for individual colleges within the institution, for individual departments within the colleges, and for specific courses. While most states are just beginning to adopt such accountability programs, some states, such as Arizona, Florida, and North Carolina, and the University of Wisconsin system already have well-established accountability reporting procedures in place.[39]

The National Governors Association (NGA) has also weighed in on enhanced accountability systems for higher education. In a report issued in 2002, the NGA stated that effective accountability systems should include five goals that are very closely attuned to increasing affordability:[40]

1. Increasing the number of high school graduates who go on to college
2. Reducing the number of high school students needing remedial courses in college
3. Increasing retention and 5-year graduation rates
4. Increasing the number of community college transfers to 4-year schools
5. Increasing the amount of resources spent on instruction as opposed to other uses (e.g., administration, research, and faculty salaries)

Given the importance of higher education to state economic and social development in a postindustrial, knowledge-based society, it is likely that the issue of higher education accountability will remain an important issue for U.S. state governments for years to come.

Higher Education Technology and Sustainability

Advances in technology over the past decade and a half have created new ways of teaching that have potentially enormous benefits for higher education's role in the states and their respective communities. Virtual education, distance education, and asynchronous learning offer new forms of course and program delivery and may well enhance the sustainability of higher education systems. As Heller has argued, "The impact of Technology cannot be overstated. It is becoming ubiquitous in all aspects of university life: teaching, learning, research, administration, service."[41] He identifies as potential benefits of the enhanced use of information and communication technology:

1. They can overcome geographical boundaries and offer courses and programs to place-bound students, such as those living in an isolated rural community.
2. They can overcome "temporal boundaries," allowing students to take classes when the time is convenient for them, such as after work in the evening.
3. Depending on the college or university, distance education courses can reduce the cost of delivering education (e.g., not needing a

physical classroom space reduces infrastructure and energy costs, and the use of computer simulations can reduce the cost of using expensive experiments).

4. Library costs are reduced by using electronic versions of materials.
5. More effective, interesting, stimulating, and visually appealing materials, exercises, and simulations are available through technology.

Transportation

One very visible service that some citizens take for granted, until a disaster such as the I-35 bridge collapse in Minnesota in 2007 strikes, is the transportation system, which involves a complicated and extensive system of public and private roads, bridges, tunnels, highways, railroads, subways, light rail, ferries, airports, bicycle and pedestrian lanes, and waterways and ports. The transportation system is used by millions of individuals, by thousands of businesses, and by hundreds of government agencies every day and affects the delivery of numerous services, such as healthcare, education, business transactions, jobs, housing, and so forth. All levels of government, including the federal, state, county, municipal, and even special districts, are involved in the building and maintenance of the transportation infrastructure. For roads and streets alone, Table 12.7 details who manages the nearly 4 million miles in the United States.

The transportation system is not the same in each state.[42] For example, in many states in the East, such as Connecticut, Massachusetts, and Vermont, county governments are not involved in road building and maintenance; these are the prerogative of state and municipal governments. In stark contrast, in the West, Midwest, and South, county governments are likely to build and maintain more roads than state governments.

All 50 states have a department of transportation, roads, or highways that is responsible for designing, planning, and operating the streets, highways, transit systems, ports, airports, and railroads under state control to provide for the safe movement of people, goods, and services. These state-level departments also work

Table 12.7. Total Road and Street Mileage in the United States

	Rural Mileage	Urban Mileage
Under state control	652,522	120,033
Under county control	1,623,786	156,598
Municipal, town, township control	580,825	647,448
Other jurisdictions (e.g., parks, toll roads)	55,792	13,331
Under federal control	120,208	3,560
Total miles	3,033,133	940,970

Source: The Council of State Legislators, *Book of the States*, 2006 (see note 10).

with and oversee local county government road departments, often sharing financial and regulatory responsibilities with local government. In comparison to the
U.S. federal government, state and local governments play the largest role in terms
of financing and managing the nation's transportation systems. Of the approximately $177 billion in public funds spent on transportation in 2004 at all levels of gov-
ernment, state funds represented 52% of the total expenditures, while federal funds
accounted for 28% and local governments and special districts accounted for 15%.
Toll roads, turnpikes, and toll bridges (some of which are state-owned) accounted
for 5% of public funds for transportation.[43]

Most federal transportation aid to states is financed through collections
made on the federal gasoline tax, which currently is 18.4 cents per gallon. In 2005,
Congress authorized over $284 billion for federal transportation grant assistance
to states (i.e., the Highway Trust Fund), which was a 30% increase over previous
allocations. However, the U.S. Office of Management and Budget announced in its
2008 mid-session budget projections that the Highway Trust Fund is expected to
face a $4 billion deficit by 2009 and a $15 billion deficit by 2011.[44] As a result, states
will likely be responsible for an ever-increasing share of transportation funding in
future years.

Like the federal government, the states also levy gas taxes to fund their transportation services. State gas taxes are levied in various ways, including a flat rate per
gallon, a tax similar to a sales tax in that it applies to the cost of the gasoline sold. In
some states local governments are allowed to levy gasoline taxes in addition to state
taxes (e.g., Florida). As federal grant funding for the transportation system declines,
states will face many challenges to find additional revenues.

In a report for the U.S. Chamber of Commerce, the National Chamber Foundation estimates that the following fiscal resources will be needed in the future
to sustain the nation's transportation infrastructure by all levels of American
government:[45]

- To maintain the current condition of the nation's pavements, bridges, and
  transit infrastructure, an expenditure by all levels of government of $222
  billion was needed in 2005, and $295 billion more will be needed by 2015.
- To improve highways and transit systems, in 2005 an expenditure of
  $271 billion was necessary, and $356 billion will be necessary by 2015.
- Revenues from all sources were estimated at $180 billion for 2005, $42
  billion short of the $222 billion needed to maintain and $91 billion short
  of the $271 billion to improve.
- Total national needs for the period from 2005 to 2015 will be $3.4
  trillion to improve the system, but total revenue will be only $2.4
  trillion, leaving a gap of approximately $1.0 trillion.

This situation has led the NGA to state:

The present transportation finance structure does not appear sustainable. Although
the public was willing to be taxed to build the national transportation system over
the last 50 years, there seems to be less support for the more diffuse benefits of

system reconstruction, maintenance, operation, and integration—the financing needs of the future. State and regional proposals to increase gas, sales, and property or other taxes to fund transportation needs may draw less public support as well.[46]

Although increased state and local financing of the transportation system will be needed in the future, there will be competition for resources from such services as education, criminal justice, healthcare, and a host of other services provided by state and local governments. This situation has led some groups, such as the NGA, the U.S. Chamber of Commerce, and the Government Accountability Office (GAO), to advocate some new approaches, including the use of toll roads and bridges, road-pricing strategies such as paying a premium to drive in less congested lanes or locations, the increased use of debt financing, and new strategies to reduce the growth of travel demand or increase the use of mass transit systems, especially in metropolitan areas. These last two strategies—reducing travel demand and increasing use of mass transit—have been advocated by organizations and policymakers interested in smart growth and sustainable transportation systems.

Sustainable Transportation Systems

The GAO recently convened a group of transportation experts to provide policy guidance on how to build a more sustainable transportation system.[47] Their report concluded that the present system of transportation finance would be adequate to maintain present conditions and to fund some growth over the next 15 years, but that traffic congestion levels could not be reduced with the current transportation finance system. In addition, the report raised other concerns about the current transportation system, which is heavily reliant on the use of cars and trucks, including environmental degradation (e.g., loss of habitat and wetlands, water and air pollution, energy use), social equity (transportation access, especially for the growing retiree population), and quality-of-life issues such as sense of community and the development of cohesive, inclusive, diverse, and resilient local communities.

The GAO study, as well as the NGA, recommended a host of funding mechanisms and a rethinking of how taxes are collected for the support of transportation services.[48] For example, one problem with the current system is that "taxing fuel consumption, rather than street and highway use, disconnects the price travelers pay for using the transportation system from the actual cost of providing the capacity they use…As a result, efficient use of the system is not rewarded, and inefficient use is not penalized, precipitating a variety of adverse productivity, environmental, and community impacts."[49] It follows that a tax on road use rather than a tax on fuel consumption would constitute a more equitable system that properly rewards conservation and preservation of the environment.

Other sustainability-oriented reforms could include *congestion pricing*, a practice used in cities abroad that tries to influence drivers' behavior by charging them higher fees to use public roads during peak congestion hours. An example of this approach can be found in London, where drivers of private vehicles must pay £5 (about $10) to drive in London's central city between 7 a.m. and 6.30 p.m., Monday through Friday, excluding holidays. This sanction has been successful in discouraging private car traffic and congestion in the inner city by taxing drivers. The GAO and NGA also suggest the increased use of tolls to finance road and bridge maintenance and improvements, as well as other types of **user fees**. They also call for more public–private partnerships in transportation to reduce costs and leverage resources.[50]

Many advocates of sustainable transportation system suggest a comprehensive paradigm shift in how local communities think about transportation. For example, these advocates suggest that walking and using bicycles, where feasible, will greatly reduce costs, pollution, and congestion while promoting public health and wellness among citizens. It follows that planning for bike lanes and paths is important, along with the development of urban "hubs" that have commercial space for jobs and stores and restaurants located near high-density residential areas to encourage walking and biking. One community that has encouraged this approach to urban planning is Davis, California, where residents voted to eliminate school bus transportation to encourage children to walk or bike to school. The community explicitly included bike and walking plans into the development of new neighborhoods.

Davis is relatively small in terms of population, at approximately 64,000 people, but Portland, Oregon, is an example of a larger city, with over a half-million people, that is committed to providing for pedestrians and bikers. Portland has a bicycle network that connects most parts of the city. Sixty percent of Portland's downtown police officers ride bikes as their principal means of transportation.

Photo 12.4. Couple standing on a Metro platform in Washington, DC: an example of sustainable transportation. Source: John and Lisa Merrill/Corbis.

Other modes of urban transportation considered sustainable in terms of producing less pollution and less congestion—and perhaps more feasible for people with longer commutes—are light rail and/or elevated rail and subway systems. The Metrorail and Metrobus transit services in Washington, DC, Maryland, and Virginia; the Bay Area Rapid Transit District (BART) in the San Francisco–Oakland metropolitan area; the New York subway system; and Chicago's Metra railroad and integrated bus system all provide relatively inexpensive, rapid, and reliable service for millions of citizens every day. In addition, some cities—most notably Portland, Oregon; Salt Lake City, Utah; and Seattle, Washington—have been building light-rail systems similar to those found in many European cities. Metropolitan Area Express (MAX) is integrated with Trimet public bus services that provide mass transit to most of the three-country Portland metropolitan area.

While there are some opponents of adopting such systems due to initial construction and operating costs, as well as the urban neighborhoods that might be affected or displaced due to the location of lines, light-rail and other urban rail systems offer a sustainable alternative to congestion and the automobile-based urban society.

Emergency Management

Emergency management is the process of how governments prepare to protect citizens from perceived threats, and how they seek to prevent, respond to, and recover from natural and manmade disasters. These threats to public health and safety can include natural disasters, terrorist actions, political crises, and public health emergencies. Preparedness planning focuses on events beyond a minimum calculated probability that could have catastrophic results for a community.[51] Government preparedness efforts embody collective security ideals achieved by unifying local governments and relevant state and federal agencies to prepare thoughtfully for potential emergencies.

Because different emergencies require different responses, decisions must be made about which risks to prioritize. State and local agencies often prepare for the catastrophes that are most feared rather than those that are more probable.[52] Often the potential depth of a catastrophe guides collective preemptive actions, regardless of how remote the likelihood of occurrence. Government emergency planners from federal, state, and local governments work to determine which disasters could be lessened by institutional response, and they make subjective consensus judgments based on a combination of experience, specialized training, and political agenda-setting influences. Emergency management is a way of anticipating surprises, coordinating plans for collective action, and educating the public on steps they can take to promote preparedness and resilience while calming public fears.

Planning for emergency management collectivizes individual risk instead of securing the population at large.[53] Emergency management typically involves the protection of individuals and groups as well as the preservation of critical infrastructures. Government institutions help vulnerable communities during a crisis because of a collective dependence on infrastructure, such as healthcare, communication, and transportation systems. In large part, emergency management is the process of formalizing an institutional response to a wide array of political crises.

Emergency Management Strategies

Emergency management prepares communities to maintain order during a catastrophe, regardless of how likely that crisis is to happen. Emergency preparedness differs from risk avoidance because it is a strategy of how to respond after a major event rather than how to avoid contingent harm.[54] External, largely unpredicted danger is then the basic premise of emergency management.[55] Because major emergencies affecting large numbers of people can range widely from political to environmental events, diverse strategies are required to deal with potential crises. Establishing an emergency plan serves to coordinate response efforts and assists with procuring relief resources from outside the area immediately affected by the disaster in question.

Emergency management systems are carried out by local, state, and federal government agencies. Professional emergency responders include over 30,000 local fire departments and 18,000 local police departments that act in conjunction with 30,000 local government agencies and 3,400 county governments.[56] To help coordinate the efforts of all of these actors, the United States employs two major institutional response strategies: the National Response Plan (NPR) and the National Incident Management System (NIMS). These federally instigated management systems rely heavily on state and local response during an emergency.[56] These complex intergovernmental relationships are established and maintained to collect, evaluate, and disseminate emergency management information and coordinate relief efforts in the case of mobilization during a disaster (Table 12.8).

Emergency simulation training is used extensively by all levels of government to simultaneously expose institutional vulnerabilities and strengthen response capabilities. By engaging in a staged crisis, first responder and emergency management administrative personnel learn to execute efficient decision-making strategies and prioritize multiple sub-crises. Government agencies simulate different scenarios periodically to improve their communication, increase their speed of response, and enhance their ability to limit the scope of various threats.

Immediately after an emergency has occurred, government agencies use community networks to foster efficient response efforts. Strategies to maximize social capital (mutual sentiments of concern and capacity for effective collection action) within communities and fortify regional networks of information sharing and trust increase the sense of collective efficacy among community residents.[57] To reinforce this social capital, technology is needed to connect professional emergency responders to civilians. Strategies to unite these often-disparate groups

Table 12.8. State Emergency Management and Homeland Security

State	Emergency Management Organization	Number of Employees	Homeland Security Organization	Number of Employees
Alabama	Dept. of Emergency Management	89	Homeland Security Dept.	12
Alaska	Adjutant General/ Military Affairs	44	Adjutant General/ Military Affairs	13
Arizona	Governor's Office	61	Governor's Office	13
Arkansas	Dept. of Emergency Management	78	Emergency Management	8
California	Governor's Office	473	Governor's Office	53
Colorado	Dept. of Local Affairs	27	Public Safety	15
Connecticut	Emergency Management/ Homeland Security	75	Emergency Management/ Homeland Security	35
Delaware	Dept. of Safety & Homeland Security	35	Dept. of Safety & Homeland Security	35
Florida	Dept. of Community Affairs	132	Law Enforcement Dept. Comm.	NA
Georgia	Governor's Office	101	Governor's Office	101
Hawaii	Dept. of Defense	40	Department of Defense	5
Idaho	Adjutant General/ Military Affairs	48	Adjutant General/ Military Affairs	48
Illinois	Governor's Office	267	Emergency Management	8
Indiana	Dept. of Homeland Security	261	Homeland Security Dept.	279
Iowa	Dept. of Public Defense	42	Dept. of Public Defense	25
Kansas	Adjutant General/ Military Dept.	37	Emergency Management	37
Kentucky	Adjutant General/ Military Dept.	81	Governor's Office	20
Louisiana	Governor's Office	64	Governor's Office	10
Maine	Adjutant General/ Military Dept.	22	Adjutant General/ Military Affairs	4
Maryland	Adjutant General/ Military Dept.	67	Governor's Office	4
Massachusetts	Public Safety	75	Public Safety	9
Michigan	State Police	77	Emergency Management	10
Minnesota	Public Safety	53	Public Safety	53
Mississippi	Governor's Office	64	Public Safety	12
Missouri	Adjutant General/ Military Dept.	58	Public Safety	13
Montana	Adjutant General/ Military Dept.	21	Emergency Management	4
Nebraska	Adjutant General/ Military Dept.	32	Emergency Management	6
Nevada	Public Safety	24	Public Safety	5
New Hampshire	Public Safety	46	Public Safety	1
New Jersey	State Police	366	Attorney General	1,160
New Mexico	Public Safety	39	Governor's Office	2
New York	Public Safety	123	Governor's Office	86

Table 12.8. Continued

State	Emergency Management Organization	Number of Employees	Homeland Security Organization	Number of Employees
North Carolina	Public Safety	175	Emergency Management	15
North Dakota	Adjutant General/ Military Dept.	54	Adjutant General/ Military Affairs	7
Ohio	Public Safety	101	Public Safety	23
Oklahoma	Governor's Office	32	Public Safety	12
Oregon	Governor's Office	34	Homeland Security Dept.	2
Pennsylvania	Governor's Office	162	Governor's Office	3
Rhode Island	Adjutant General/ Military Dept.	26	Emergency Management	6
South Carolina	Adjutant General/ Military Dept.	50	State Police	10
South Dakota	Public Safety	16	Public Safety	3
Tennessee	Adjutant General/ Military Dept.	108	Governor's Office	28
Texas	Governor's Office	65	Governor's Office	6
Utah	Public Safety	65	Homeland Security Dept.	100
Vermont	Public Safety	20	Public Safety	5
Virginia	Public Safety	108	Governor's Office	3
Washington	Adjutant General/ Military Dept.	105	Adjutant General/ Military Affairs	25
West Virginia	Military Affairs & Public Safety	43	Governor's Office	4
Wisconsin	Adjutant General/ Military Dept.	49	Adjutant General/ Military Affairs	NA
Wyoming	Dept. of Homeland Security	NA	Dept. of Homeland Security	NA

Source: The Council of State Legislators, *Book of the States*, 2006 (see note 10).

include the Internet and mobile communication devices such as cell phones and PDAs. Reverse 911 texts and calls from emergency managers to residents help disseminate information needed by citizens so they can help in disaster recovery. Cellular telephones and other portable wireless devices need to be integrated so they can serve as an uninterrupted channel of communication during a crisis. Access, affordability, and training for various Web-based interfaces are key elements of effective use of response technology. Improved communication networks allow civilians to help each other and aid in a more effective emergency response.[58]

Using technological innovations and community response networks also connects government efforts with many non-governmental, community-based organizations such as the American Red Cross, Doctors without Borders, and the Voluntary Organizations Active in Disasters. These organizations serve a critical role in disseminating services and resources to citizens in times of dire need because the public sometimes trusts non-governmental organizations more than government agencies in disaster situations. The perceived objectivity and noble motivations of these groups allow them to gain greater penetration within some local social networks than is possible for many public agencies.

Political Crisis Preparedness

An important facet of emergency management is civil defense, which involves the use of military mobilization (the National Guard) to maintain peace and public order and to protect human life.[59] To prepare for wide-scale attacks involving either conventional or nuclear or biological weapons, state and local governments depend on the ability of government acting collectively to deploy appropriate military forces immediately. Civil defense aims to protect the civilian population against war and terrorism and to minimize the devastating impacts of either form of manmade disaster.

As a result of the September 11, 2001, attacks on the power centers of U.S. government, the Department of Homeland Security (DHS) was created to bolster the nation's domestic security efforts. DHS uses an "all-hazards" approach to enhance emergency management capabilities across the country. Preparedness in this context is the "measurable relation of capabilities to vulnerabilities, given a selected range of threats."[60] DHS examines the relative likelihood for crisis, as compared to other government efforts, which are guided by the greatest fear and not the greatest probability.

Agencies such as DHS have changed the expectations of Americans regarding the government's response to a political crisis. By centralizing emergency management planning efforts, first-responder agencies and major political leaders can strengthen their efforts at timely cooperation and collaboration.

Natural Disaster Preparedness

Natural disasters are unplanned geographical and environmental events affecting human populations; they include earthquakes, floods, hurricanes, tornadoes, fires and wildfires, volcanic eruptions, tidal waves (tsunami), and droughts. Natural disasters are managed both through preventive measures and planned recovery efforts. The effect of floods can be mitigated through levees, fires may be prevented through forest management, and earthquake damage can be reduced by enforcing building codes. However, not all emergencies can be prevented or fully anticipated in terms of scope and scale of damage and harm to humans, and as a result proper reactive actions need to be planned.

Due to the growing interface between human populations and vulnerable landscapes, there is a greater probability that extreme natural events will affect life and property. For example, as the U.S. population grows and moves outside of its urban boundaries, more people are living within floodplains, in the midst of dense forests, and out in high desert areas prone to seasonal fires. As communities expand into these more volatile areas, extreme natural events will have a greater impact.

Preparation for natural disasters in many ways mimics strategies of civil defense. While both efforts rely on the tactic of anticipatory mobilization in the event of a catastrophe, the governing structures for the two types of emergency management situations have traditionally differed: civil defense relies on a hierarchical command structure, but natural disaster management uses a decentralized system within many levels of the government.[61] Federal Emergency Management Agency (FEMA), created in 1979, was a result of combining these previously disparate management strategies. FEMA consolidated "federal emergency management and civil defense functions under the rubric of 'all-hazards planning.' "[62] Combining federal strategies and local efforts to manage natural disasters led to new collaborations and funding opportunities for emergency management personnel at all levels of government. Despite the efforts of FEMA officials, however, tensions exist between civil defense and natural disaster planning largely because of the disparity in the scale of government response that is required.

Health Emergency Preparedness

Public health preparedness is a wide-ranging process intended to mitigate the effects of bioterrorism and infectious disease outbreaks upon citizens. Public health crises may also entail shortages in food, water, medicine, and medical staff. Health preparedness involves many federal, state, and local agencies dedicated to protecting human health in both normal times and times of crisis.

Healthcare providers and hospitals can be particularly challenged during an emergency because of limited resources to expand their capacity. Healthcare

Photo 12.5. Emergency management and sustainability: a FEMA inspector tries to locate a missing home in Grand Forks, North Dakota, after a flood. Source: Bob Sacha/Corbis.

Traditional and Visible Services: What Can I Do?

Is your college or university a participant in Association for the Advancement of Sustainability for Higher Education (AASHE)? If not, take steps to organize your campus for participation. If yes, then play a leadership role in sustainability on your campus and apply for a Student Leadership Award with the association. For more information go to: http://www.aashe.org/

As mentioned in the text, some states have "three-strikes laws" or other legislation that increase the number of individuals in state and local jails and prisons. The movement to be "tough on crime" with more frequent and longer jail sentences for repeat offenders appeals to many Americans. However, these laws sometimes include nonviolent crimes as the third strike (e.g., shoplifting and drug possession), leading to increased costs of incarceration at the expense of other state programs and services (e.g., education, social services). What do you think about this issue? Contact your state or local law enforcement officials and ask them what they think about this issue at: http://www.officer.com/links/Agency_Search/

- How close to capacity are the facilities?
- What offenses receive jail time?
- Has there been recent legislation that is increasing the number of individuals incarcerated? If so, how much will it cost?
- What do local officials suggest as effective ways to maintain the sustainability of the system? Education programs? Tougher laws?

systems may be limited in space and staffing and may face competing priorities within each regional system. Innovative solutions are based on collaborations between public health systems and emergency management response teams, such as local police and fire departments.[63]

Threats to the nation's biosecurity are a major concern within the public health professions. Biosecurity efforts aim to prevent the development and deployment of biological weapons and germ warfare using pathogens such as bacteria or a virus to attack human populations. After the Cold War, access to biological agents increased greatly due to reduced safeguards and changes in the geopolitical balance of power. Genetic technology has also improved, creating greater access to some of the most virulent weapons. To ensure biosecurity, U.S. public health professionals need strong communication systems with emergency management responders, immunized and trained staff, and the ability to interrupt likely patterns of attacks.[64] After the events of September 11, 2001, the Council of State and Territorial Epidemiologists

(CSTE) was created to bolster state preparedness programs. The budgets of state governments have been adjusted to reflect greater preparedness efforts, in compliance with DHS guidelines. While greater investment in this area is clearly in evidence, there is no way of knowing with certainty whether current preparations for emergency management are adequate.[65]

Sustainability in Preparedness Efforts

Fostering sustainability in emergency management involves supporting the governments' ability to respond to a variety of crises. To maintain effective response, organizational and communication infrastructure needs to be supported through adequate funding, targeted training, and ongoing agency collaborations. Coordination between locally-based public health, law enforcement, and emergency response teams can also foster a strong response to crisis.[66] Planned preparedness activities and periodic "table-top exercises" simulating extreme events increase response capacity through the interagency collaboration they generate.

 Mobilizing communities during a crisis involves weaving together the social fabric to create an "emergency community." Reinforcing existing infrastructures within communities, such as schools, churches, and community centers, establishes a base for disseminating information and distributing aid. Emergency management involves preparing for a variety of threats, including the devastation resulting from natural disasters, environmental crises, and the many weapons that might be used in political warfare carried out through terrorist attacks. This relatively new field of government is based on the fear of a catastrophic event. Because the nature of such emergencies is that they are unpredictable, perfect knowledge to guide government intervention does not exist.[67] The one finding from research that stands out in this area is that those communities which possess social capital of the bridging type – with strong connections across social, racial and professional/occupational groups—are the most likely to develop sustainable preparedness plans and processes.

Conclusion

This chapter has reviewed some of the most visible services provided by state and local government and some of the largest items found in state, county, and city budgets. For example, 21.4% of the average state operating budget in 2006 went to K–12 education, followed by 10.4% for higher education, 8.1% for transportation, and 3.4% for corrections. All of the services discussed are central to the building and maintenance of sustainable states and sustainable local communities. Lower crime rates and less recidivism; higher levels of education; reliable, safe, and energy-efficient transportation systems; and efficacious and responsive emergency services are pivotal for resilient states and communities as they adapt to the many changes coming their way in modern America. As we noted throughout this chapter, many of these vital services currently are not adequately funded or managed properly, limiting the ability of public officials to adapt to changes and possibly jeopardizing the long-term viability of each and every state and local government. Given these circumstances, the "laboratories of democracy" provided by the American federal system will have to provide the framework for the creation of best practices and innovations in funding schemes that will give rise to the essential services to be disseminated across state and local governments. Just as biodiversity is an asset to ecosystem sustainability and resilience, so should the diversity of approaches taken to solve common problems prove to be of lasting value in the pursuit of sustainability in American state and local government.

Key Terms

At-risk youth
Brown v. Board of Education
*Brown v. Board of
    Education II*
Charter schools
Civil libertarian approach
    (criminal justice)
Community policing
Elementary and Secondary
    Education Act (ESEA)
Grutter v. Bollinger
Head Start program

Law and order approach
    (criminal justice)
No Child Left Behind Act (NCLB)
Pivotal variable
Plessy v. Ferguson
Recidivism
*Regents of the University of California
    v. Bakke*
*Swann v. Charlotte-Mecklenberg Board
    of Education*
Three-strikes laws
Unfunded mandates
User fees
Voucher system

Discussion Questions

1. How do state and local criminal justice policies affect community sustainability? What types of programs have been suggested for enhancing sustainability?
2. What responsibilities do federal, state, and local governments have in K–12 and higher education? How can education promote sustainable communities?
3. Discuss the importance of state and local governments in the transportation sector. How can transportation policy affect community sustainability?
4. What is the role of state and local governments in providing emergency management services? How do these services affect sustainability?

Glossary

Prepared by Kirsten Winters

adaptive capacity: the ability of institutions, systems, and individuals to adjust to potential damage, to take advantage of opportunities, or to cope with the consequences

administrative law judges: "hearings officers" who work within administrative agencies, engaging in regulatory actions that give rise to many disputes (e.g., environmental regulations, labor/management actions under collective bargaining agreements, compensation for damages incurred from state government action on one's property)

administrative rules: rules and regulations issued by state executive branch agencies arising from the implementation of laws enacted by the legislative branch

amenities: things that bring about comfort and convenience; luxuries

anthropocentric concerns: a philosophical perspective that views human needs and interests as of the highest value and importance—contrasting with various *biocentric* (life-centered) perspectives, which assume that nonhuman species also have inherent value

at-risk youth: children and teenagers who are considered especially vulnerable because they live in circumstances and engage in activities that might expose them to far-reaching negative consequences in their life course

Baby Boomers: the generation of individuals born following the Second World War, between roughly 1946 and 1964

balanced budget: a situation in which forecasts of budget revenue (tax revenue plus monies raised through bond issuances) match budget expenditures for a given period (usually one year)

biocentered: an approach which elevates the requirements and value of all natural organisms, species, and ecosystems to center stage and, in some versions, makes the earth or nature as a whole the focus of "moral considerability"

bio-equity: advocates for equal treatment of individuals in human society and the other elements of the "biosphere"

block grants: broad grants to states for certain activities—including child care, education, social services, preventive healthcare, and elder health services

broker parties: political parties trying to appeal to the largest number of people, more concerned with gaining votes than with maintaining rigid ideologies, and willing to alter their policies in order to gain electoral support

Brown v. Board of Education: a landmark 1954 case in which the court ruled that separate schools for black and white children were an unconstitutional denial of the 14th amendment's "equal protection" clause

Brown v. Board of Education II: a court decision in 1955 holding local school authorities and the courts responsible for integrating public schools, as stated in *Brown v. Board of Education*

Brundtland Report: The common name for the *Our Common Future* report created by the United Nations World Commission on Environment and Development (WCED) and published in 1987. The report is deemed the origin of sustainability and sustainable development and laid the groundwork for the 1992 Earth Summit

bureaucracy: a rationally organized hierarchical structure and administrative process composed of professionals working in and communicating from well-defined positions within a coordinated formal structure designed to achieve complex goals with maximal effectiveness and efficiency

bureaucratic capacity: the ability of government agencies to attract and retain professionals to bureaucratic positions. To do so public agencies must be relatively well-funded, professional in operation, and effectively organized

categorical grants: funds appropriated by the U.S. Congress for a specific purpose, such as providing school lunches or building airports and highways; subject to detailed federal conditions; often made on a matching basis (i.e., the local jurisdiction provides a portion of the funding needed to undertake the purposes of the grant)

caucus: a meeting, in particular a meeting of people whose goal is political or organizational change

certiori: a writ of a superior court to call up the records of an inferior court or a body acting in a quasi-judicial capacity for purposes of appellate review

charter schools: public schools that can operate with fewer regulations than traditional public schools

checks and balances: when the three branches of government share power rather than allowing one branch to have substantial power over the others

citizen groups: organized aggregations of citizens advocating for specific public policy

civil libertarian approach (criminal justice): ideology emphasizing the rights of individuals accused of crimes and advocating treatment and rehabilitation programs

civil liberties: also referred to as "negative freedoms," civil liberties are individual or group protections from a potentially oppressive government

civil service: refers to government or federal employment gained through competitive consideration rather than partisan political appointment

classical liberalism: a political philosophy placing high value on individual freedom based on a belief in natural rights that exist independent of government

Clean Air Act: the law defining U.S. Environmental Protection Agency (EPA)'s responsibilities for protecting and improving the nation's air quality and the stratospheric ozone layer; this legislation authorized the development of comprehensive federal and state regulations to limit emissions from both stationary (industrial) sources and mobile sources; this very important legislation was adopted at approximately the same time as the National Environmental Policy Act, which established the Environmental Protection Agency (EPA)

Clean Water Act: Based on the Federal Water Pollution Control Act from 1972, the Clean Water Act (CWA)—renamed in 1977—establishes the basic structure for regulating discharges of pollutants into the waters of the United States and regulating quality standards for surface waters. The CWA made it unlawful to discharge any pollutant from a point source into navigable waters, unless a permit was obtained.

closed primary: a primary in which only persons who are registered members of a political party can vote using the ballot of that political party

collaborative governance: the move to share bureaucratic decision-making power with citizens and personnel in the lower reaches of organizational hierarchies, to embrace public–private collaborative partnerships, and to reform structures and hierarchies for efficiency

commission government: city government that divides the responsibilities of the municipality among council members; each commissioner holds executive power over a major public works department (e.g., water, sanitation, roads)

common law: a system of legal principles established on judicial precedents rather than statutory laws; may be codified into a statute or overruled by a statute enacted by the government

Common School Movement: a policy innovation started by Horace Mann in the 1830s to create state-level coordination of public instruction in the promotion of universal elementary education for all of the nation's children

communitarianism: a political philosophy emphasizing the need to balance individual rights and interests with those of the community, positing that individuals are shaped by the culture and values of their communities

community policing: movement to connect police with citizens, emphasizing problem-solving methodologies and partnerships, and building policies to identify current and future problems

competitive grant: grant proposal in which the applicant designs a project and a funding agency ranks rival proposals to provide grant awards through a competitive process

confederal system: system of government where the states operate as a sovereign government and the legislature of any one state can set its own laws independently of any other state

constituency service: assistance given to constituents by members of Congress in non-legislative areas; generally involves interceding on behalf of constituents with a federal agency

constitutional convention: the most traditional method to propose a new state constitution or revise an existing constitution; requires a formal call from the legislature, which all 50 state legislatures and the District of Columbia have the ability to do

constitutional democracy: a system of government based on the belief that government can and should be legally limited in its powers, and that its rightful exercise of authority depends on observing these limitations

cooperative federalism: concept of federalism where federal, state, and local governments are integrated to act cooperatively, solving common problems, rather than making policies separately but more or less equally, or clashing over a policy in a system dominated by the national government

cooperative governance (see **collaborative governance**)

county service area: local government unit that provides public services within a county; services such as police protection, libraries, and television translator services are examples

democracy versus technocracy quandary: problem arising due to rapid technological innovation in the United States, where many policy problems are highly technical in nature and require scientific knowledge to manage effectively; this "quandary" questions whether the authority of those with specialized technical knowledge will supplant the democratic process of decision-making

dependent (special) districts: a type of special district based on a specific geographic area; features a legal governing authority and maintains a legal identity separate from any other governmental authority; can assess a tax for supplying public services; exercises considerable autonomy

developed community: a community planned with specific goals for function in mind; developed communities can be freestanding homes, condominiums, or apartment complexes

Dillon's rule: state–national government power relations are embedded in the U.S. Constitution, granting the states almost unlimited authority aside from limitations imposed by the Constitution and resulting federal statutes; in terms of state–local power relations, Dillon argued that states create local government and hold supreme power over local governments

dual federalism: concept of federalism positing that the U.S. Constitution gives a limited list of powers to the national government, leaving the rest to the sovereign states; each level of government is dominant within its own sphere; the Supreme Court serves as the mediator between the national government and the states

dual system (judicial power): the system of separate state and federal courts that make up the judicial system

e-democracy: technological innovation where government uses the Internet to engage citizens in the policymaking process through electronic voting, electronic information exchange, on-line transactions with public agencies and conducting on-line forums

e-government: the use of information technology to provide and improve government services and interactions with citizens and businesses and between branches of the government; this technological development has also been referred to as "online government" and "transformational government"

Elementary and Secondary Education Act (ESEA): a law passed by Congress in 1965 that aids low-income and disadvantaged children through the distribution of federal funds to state and local educational systems

elite-challenging politics: dramatic political action aimed at creating change by challenging the powerful elite through direct action such as demonstrations, petitions, and boycotts intended to attract mass media attention to a cause

elite theory: the theory that political power is held by a small and wealthy group of people sharing similar values and interests and mostly coming from relatively similar privileged backgrounds; it is argued that the power elite can dictate the main goals for policymaking because they control the economic resources of the major business and financial organizations in the country

eminent domain: a principle of law by which the government can appropriate private property for purposes of promoting the public welfare

Endangered Species Act: enacted in 1973, this law provides for the conservation of ecosystems upon which threatened and endangered species of fish, wildlife, and plants depend

engaged citizenship: a type of citizenship whereby members of a community take an active role in matters of the promotion of the public welfare

excise tax: taxes related to consumer consumption behavior, such as sales taxes, motor fuel taxes, cigarette taxes, and distilled spirits taxes

fiscal federalism: in public economics, refers to how the central government applies grants and payments to lower levels of government

flat-rate tax: a term applying to a form of tax on personal income whereby a single tax rate is applied to all persons regardless of income level

formula grant: grant given to a state or local government to accomplish a national policy goal adopted by Congress

gated community: a developed community with physical barriers to entry and movement, the privatization and communal control of public spaces, and privatization of public services such as trash removal and police forces

general jurisdiction courts: courts that deal with both civil and criminal cases, and whose jurisdiction is based on a specific geographical area

general-purpose government: responsible for a wide range of public services, including counties, parishes, and municipalities (cities, towns, villages, townships); can be contrasted with special purpose governments (or special districts), such as school districts, water districts, and transit districts

gentrification: transformation of a neighborhood that includes the renewal and rebuilding of deteriorating areas and the displacement of low-income residents living in inexpensive housing with high-income residents living in high-cost housing

gerrymandering: the process by which district lines are redrawn to maximize the strength of the majority party and weaken the minority party

glass ceiling: barriers against advancement of women to executive positions within state and local bureaucracies

globalization: the current worldwide expansion of economic markets through trade and financial flows, and the transfer of culture and technology

governance (see **collaborative governance**)

graduated tax: a term applying to a form of tax on personal income whereby the tax rate is based on income level; those with higher incomes pay a higher rate

green tags: also known as renewable energy certificates, green tags are a form of certification confirming that energy has been generated using legally recognized forms of renewable energy generation

Grutter v. Bollinger: U.S. Supreme Court case upholding the University of Michigan Law School's affirmative action policy, deciding that race can be one of several factors considered when making admission decisions because it furthers "the educational benefits that flow from a diverse student body"

Head Start program: a preschool program for young disadvantaged children with the stated purpose of getting these children ready for the rigors of the first grade

higher-order needs: theory developed by Abraham Maslow related to motivation: when lower needs such as physiological, safety, and love/belonging needs are met, higher needs such as esteem and, finally, self-actualization become attainable

home rule: the power of a local city or county to make independent decisions on governmental form and functions that is granted by some states

independent (special) districts: a type of special district that includes more than one county

individualistic political culture: societal problems are seen in terms of individual solutions and communal solutions are not highly valued; this school of thought emphasizes the concept of the democratic order as a marketplace in which government is instituted for strictly utilitarian reasons to handle functions demanded by the people it is created to serve

initiative: a form of direct democracy in which a petition signed by a minimum number of registered voters can force a public vote on a proposed statute, constitutional amendment, charter amendment, or ordinance

institutional actors: subjects, including legislative bodies, executive departments, and the judicial branch, that are involved in the public policy process and deal with public affairs

institutional resiliency: the ability of institutions to withstand or react to major stressors without crossing a threshold to a situation featuring different structures or significantly altered outputs

integration of powers: a political system, such as a parliamentary system, where the executive and legislative branches are integrated rather than reflecting a separation of powers

intergovernmental agreement (IGA): directly related to federalism and multi-state arrangements within the American federal system, this term refers to national–state or national–local agreements or interstate and interlocal agreements of various kinds

Jacksonian democracy: a political philosophy promoting the strength of the executive branch of government over the legislative branch, while also seeking to broaden the public's participation in government

judicial federalism: refers to the allocation of power between federal courts and state courts: state courts address their own state's constitutional claims first in a case consider federal constitutional claims only when cases cannot be resolved on state grounds (an example of the increased influence of a state's constitution in its judicial system, particularly in regards to civil rights)

law and order approach (criminal justice): ideology emphasizing the protection of public order through close monitoring of conduct and severe punishment for criminals

LEED®: Leadership in Environment and Energy Design is an ecology-oriented building certification program run by the U.S. Green Building Council (USGBC); focuses on five key areas of environmental and human health: energy efficiency, indoor environmental quality, materials selection, sustainable site development, and water conservation

legislative oversight: the legislature is responsible for reviewing selected activities of the executive branch and developing the state budget

legislative referral: action by the legislature and the governor that places legislation on the ballot for voters to approve or disapprove

lifelong learning: continual acquisition of knowledge and skills

line item veto: power of an executive to strike or cancel specific provisions of a bill, usually budget appropriations, without vetoing the entire legislative package. This action is subject to legislative override

linkage mechanisms: processes by which governmental institutions and the associated governmental policies and actions affect the lives of citizens; for example, the amount and method of distribution of social security benefits constitute key linkage mechanisms in the United States

mandate: an authorization to act given to a representative

mandate of the court: a legal document stating the opinion of a court

Master Agreement (tobacco settlement agreement): federal court settlement agreement from 1998; tobacco companies agreed to compensate states for some medical costs associated with the effects of smoking-related illnesses as well as to curtail the promotion of tobacco products among youth

McDonaldization effect: international homogenization in culture, lifestyles, and technology that accompanies globalization; coined by George Ritzer, whose own ideas of McDonaldization and hyperrationality derive from the theories of Max Weber

Medicaid: a national–state cooperative healthcare plan designed to serve the medical needs of low-income individuals and families who have no access to health insurance

Medicare: national plan providing for the healthcare needs of individuals 65 years of age or older; the three major components are hospital insurance, medical insurance, and prescription drug assistance

memorandum of understanding: an agreement between two parties in the form of a legal document; often used to define partnerships between departments or public agencies

merit-based performance (civil service): system of pay where compensation depends on the performance of employees

merit system of judicial appointment (see **Missouri plan**)

missionary party: these parties are ideological in orientation and enter elections with a "manifesto" or "platform" to be undertaken; they tend to maintain a high degree of control over their members and carefully monitor who is allowed to make use of the party label as a candidate

Missouri plan: complex system for judicial appointment that was designed to combine methods of appointment with election; under the Missouri plan, candidates for judicial vacancies are reviewed by independent, bipartisan commissions of lawyers and prominent lay citizens before selection by a governor. An election for retention of the judge is held after 1 year of the judge's service

moralistic political culture: societal problems are seen in terms of community dilemmas that must be identified through interchange and community choice; this school of thought emphasizes the commonwealth concept as the basis for democratic government, whose responsibility it is to promote the general welfare

multi-member district: an electoral district returning more than one member to a representative assembly

National Environmental Policy Act (NEPA): one of the first environmental laws ever written, NEPA (1969) requires federal agencies to consider the environmental impacts of proposed federal projects

neo-liberalism: political view promoting the importance of economic growth, free markets and free trade, and reduced government regulation of the economy; it asserts that social justice occurs most fully in conditions featuring minimum interference in the marketplace by the government and maximum reliance on the forces of the free market

network approach: a system of organizing where there are multiple dimensions of interaction and few fixed bureaucratic relationships; communication organizes itself at one point in time around a hub of positions or of knowledge (i.e., the persons or organizations that possess or control relevant knowledge)

New Deal Era: economic reform package initiated by Franklin D. Roosevelt in the 1930s that sought to relieve the effects of the Great Depression by reforming financial and business practices and offering aid to the unemployed and retirement benefits to the aged

No Child Left Behind (NCLB): federal educational act of 2001 created to improve the performance of schools using standards-based reform to measure goal attainment in primary and secondary public schools

non-institutional actors: individuals or groups independent of the government that are involved in the policy process, including political parties, interest groups, social movements, non-governmental organizations (NGOs), the mass media, and individual citizen activists

nonpartisan offices: candidates run for office without listing a political affiliation; generally held for local government offices such as school districts, local special districts, judicial and boards and commissions

Northern Spotted Owl v. Hodel: a major environmental case decided in 1988 in which the judge ruled in favor of preserving an endangered species over the continuation of timber harvesting; considered a landmark decision in social and environmental justice through governmental action

open primary: primary elections where voters may cast a vote on a ballot of any party and do not need to be members of a specific political party in order to vote for that party's candidates

ordinance: an authoritative decree or law set forth by governmental authority

Oregon system: system of government where voters can initiate and vote upon statutes or constitutional revisions

organizational culture: the informal relationships, customs and norms that often shape many of the day-to-day decisions made in an organization

parliamentary style systems: common legislative form using the integration of powers; the legislative branch chooses the chief executive such as prime minister or president

patronage: the practice of filling government jobs for political advantage

performance-based budgeting: process for budgeting that links public agency requests for resources with documentation illustrating the outcomes of budget choices made in previous years

pivotal variable: the focal point upon which other factors depend in a given situation; for example, the economic health (growth or recession) of a period is a pivotal variable for the making of many decisions affecting the long-term promotion of sustainability

Plessy v. Ferguson: the 1896 U.S. Supreme Court case ruled that "separate but equal" public facilities were consistent with the equal protection clause of the 14th Amendment to the U.S. Constitution; the Supreme Court's ruling meant that *racial segregation* was acceptable so long as the services provided by government for different races were basically comparable

pluralist theory: an ideal-type democratic theory positing that the American democratic political process is genuinely open to the involvement of any group that wishes to participate; some of the fundamental constitutional principles embedded in the U.S. Constitution (freedom of speech, freedom of assembly, and freedom to petition government for the redress of grievances) constitute core elements of pluralist theory

political culture: combination of attitudes, values, and beliefs about a particular political jurisdiction

political trust: the expectation of a citizen that the rules and practices derived from public institutions are fair and unbiased, that the performance of a political institution is competent and appropriate, and that rules and procedures encourage innovation and produce outcomes that improve governance and society

politicization of courts/judiciary: the situation in which courts function politically and ideologically in decision-making rather than objectively in accordance with legal principle and the norms of fairness and blind justice

pork barrel: government spending for projects that are not necessarily economically viable but are pursued because of their appeal and benefit to particular politicians and their constituents

postindustrial society: a society where the resources of labor and capital have been replaced by knowledge and information as the main sources of wealth creation;

shift in focus from manufacturing industries to service industries; enabled by technological advances

post-materialist needs: a phenomena occurring due to the new wealth accumulated in advanced societies where priorities have shifted from survival to a focus on well-being, self-expression, and quality of life

presidential style systems: common legislative form using the separation of powers between the executive, legislative, and judicial branches

price subsidies: financial assistance granted by the government to a certain person or group whose actions are regarded as being in the public interest

primary election: a preliminary election where voters nominate candidates for office

Progressive Era: period during the late 19th and early 20th century in which economic, political, social, and moral reforms were advocated to deal with changes brought on by the industrial revolution

progressivism: a political and social term that refers to ideologies and movements favoring or advocating progress, changes, improvement, or reform of existing institutions and/or practices

proportional representation: legislative seats are proportionally distributed based on the percentage of the vote a particular party wins at election

protest politics: form of activism in which grassroots organizations and social movements participate in activities such as demonstrations and boycotts to assert their political will

public goods: consumption of a good of service by one individual does not reduce the availability of the good or service for consumption by others; no one can be effectively excluded from using the good

public interest groups: groups that promote issues of general public concern (e.g., environmental protection, human rights, and consumer rights) rather than any specific group or interest

recidivism: a tendency to relapse into a previous condition or mode of behavior; most commonly applied to re-offense by criminal offenders

red tape: forms and procedures required to gain official bureaucratic approval for something; often seen as overly complicated and unnecessary by persons affected while being seen as essential to the effective operation of an official office or agency by persons working in those offices or agencies

referendum: a specific measure put to the voters by the legislature for approval or disapproval

Regents of the University of California v. Bakke: U.S. Supreme Court ruling issued in 1978 that inflexible quota systems in affirmative action were not permissible under the equal protection clause of the 14th Amendment; the court upheld the legality of affirmative action in special cases where historical discrimination can be established and carefully tailored, temporary compensatory preferences are employed to address prior discrimination

reinventing government: attempts by state and local administrators to reorganize their operations to achieve greater efficiency, better program outcomes, better use of resources, and systematically incorporate the input of state-level interests, private sector groups, and the general public so that their services could be made more responsive to consumer preferences

renewable energy portfolios: state utilities must obtain a certain percentage or output (measured in kilowatt-hours) of their power supply from renewable energy sources; renewable energy portfolio standards are benchmarks for the portion of energy used by state consumers that must be supplied by renewable sources

republican government: in this system of government there is separation of powers (executive, legislative, and judicial); government responsibilities can be centralized at one level of government or may be decentralized among multiple layers; the legitimacy of government rests on the principle of popular consent – that is, all levels of government ultimately derive their legitimacy from the consent of the governed through some form of constitutional mandate and elective systems of leadership selection.

reserved powers: based on the 10th Amendment; all governmental powers not explicitly granted to the national government in the U.S. Constitution are reserved to the states and their people

select committee: a temporary legislative committee established for a limited period and for a special purpose

single-member district: the most common electoral system in the United States used to elect House members and many state and local officials; citizens of each district vote on one person to represent them in a legislative body

single-purpose governments: bodies that are responsible for carrying out one specific function, such as education, utilities, irrigation, or transportation services

smart growth: a theory of urban growth and planning that attempts to concentrate growth in the center of a city, thereby avoiding suburban sprawl

social capital: the values and norms held by citizens that reflect trust in others, the active pursuit of engagement in networks of a wide variety, and standards of interchange among people involving the principles of reciprocity (return a favor with a favor) and mutual respect

social movements: group action characterized by focus on a specific political or social issue by individuals who share a common outlook on society and are organized to create social change

social safety net: collectively, the public policies intended to help individuals who suffer the misfortunes of serious disadvantage such as illness, loss of employment, or victimization by natural or manmade disasters

social trust: relates to the ways in which people interact with one another, publicly and privately, and rests on the belief that others will act with honesty, integrity, and reliability

special purpose districts: units of government that serve specific policy functions

standing committee: a permanent committee established in a legislature, usually focusing on a policy area

State Children's Insurance Program (S-CHIP): a state program, cooperatively managed at the state and federal level, intended to meet the healthcare needs of uninsured middle- and low-income children

strong mayor-council: a form of local government consisting of both an elected executive branch and a legislative branch; one of the most significant powers afforded the mayor is that of budget director

sunset provision (or clause): a provision in a statute that terminates or repeals all or portions of the law after a specific date, unless specific legislative action is taken to extend it

supremacy clause: the clause establishing the U.S. Constitution, federal statutes, and U.S. treaties as the supreme law of the land, mandating that state judges uphold them, even if state laws or constitutions conflict with federal legal precedents and holdings in law

sustainability: the manner in which the social, economic, institutional, and environmental needs of a community are met without compromising the ability of future generations to meet their own needs

sustainable community-based eldercare: community-based provision for the needs of elderly residents that seeks to maintain a community's retired population by providing for them within the community

Swann v. Charlotte-Mecklenberg Board of Education: U.S. Supreme Court ruling in 1971 that local education districts across the nation may use mandatory busing as a policy to achieve racial integration in their schools if *de facto* segregation persists in their schools

task force: a temporary group formed to work on a special defined task or activity

tax and expenditure limitation measures (TELs): limits on governmental expenditures on the amount of revenue that can be collected

Temporary Assistance to Needy Families (TANF): formerly known as welfare, TANF provides cash assistance to families with dependent children

tenure: a status of assured continued employment granted after a trial period

term limits: in many states the number of terms, consecutive or otherwise, that a legislator is allowed to serve are limited in number

three-strikes laws: state statute requiring a mandatory and extended sentence to criminals convicted of three or more serious offenses

traditionalistic political culture: school of thought that accepts government as an actor with a positive role to play in the community, but a role limited to maintaining the existing social order; in this system, political parties are not important; rather, political competition is expressed through factions, an extension of the personal politics characteristic of the system their activity, although not necessarily by direct pecuniary gain

trial courts: the courts in which most civil or criminal cases begin; higher courts are termed appellate courts which are generally restricted to the review of the record of the trial court in which the case being appealed was tried

two-party system: a government in which the same two political parties are nearly always elected to dominate the political process and where one party will hold the majority in the legislature

unconstitutional taking: expropriation of private property by government without just compensation

unemployment compensation: a temporary government benefit provided to those persons who become unemployed as a consequence of adverse economic circumstances; these benefits are usually paid from payroll taxes set aside for such circumstances

unfunded mandate: requirement imposed by Congress on state or local governments with no funding to pay for it; term also used by local governments vis-à-vis their respective state governments when state statutes impose requirements upon local government without providing resources to accomplish those requirements

user fees: fee charged for use of a public service or facility

value change: fundamental cultural realignments that lead to significant, widespread, and long-lasting changes in norms and priorities of individuals and groups in a particular society

voucher system: parents receive a predetermined amount of money (depending on the state) to cover tuition at a public or private school of the parents' choice

weak mayor-council: form of local government wherein the mayoralty is a ceremonial position; executive leadership is a cooperative effort on the part of the entire city council, which collectively decides and approves appointments; the budget is a collegial endeavor and the mayor is just one of the council members involved in the budgeting process

Welfare Reform Act of 1996: public assistance is focused less on the recipient of the benefit than it is on the community as a whole; requires work in exchange for temporary relief; limits the benefit period to 2 years, and no recipient can receive more than 5 years of assistance cummulatively

welfare-to-work program: social program instituted in 2004 seeking to encourage those on public assistance to return to work rather than depend on continued assistance

whole building design: design that takes into account the building's purpose, workforce, future, and operations and maintenance costs

xeriscape design: landscaping to maximize water efficiency; xeriscape practices include careful planning and design, practical lawn areas, efficient irrigation, soil improvement, use of mulches, and maximum use of native plants

Notes

Chapter 1

1. J. Hibbing and E. Theiss-Morse, "Civics is Not Enough: Teaching Barbarics in K-12," *PS: Political Science and Politics* 29 (1996): 57–62.

   S. Maced, *Democracy at Risk* (Washington, DC: Brookings Institution Press, 2005).

   S. Mann, "What the Survey of American College Students Tells Us About Their Interest in Politics and Political Science," *PS: Political Science and Politics* 32 (1999): 263–268.

2. K. Kedrowski, "Civic Education by Mandate: A State-by-State Analysis," *PS: Political Science and Politics* 36 (2003): 225–227.

3. R. Dalton, *The Good Citizen: How a Younger Generation is Reshaping American Politics* (Washington, DC: CQ Press, 2008).

4. D. Bell, *The Coming of Postindustrial Society* (New York: Basic Books, 1973).

   R. Bellah, R. Madsen, W. M. Sullivan, A. Swidler, and S. M. Tipton, *Habits of the Heart: Individualism and Commitment in American Life* (New York: Harper and Row, 1985).

   S. Huntington, "Postindustrial Society: How Benign Will it Be?" *Comparative Politics* 6 (1974): 163–191.

5. W. Galston, "Rural America in the 1990s: Trends and Choices," *Policy Studies Journal* 20 (1992): 202–211.

   R. Inglehart, *Modernization and Postmodernization: Cultural, Economic, and Political Change in 43 Societies* (Princeton, NJ: Princeton University Press, 1997).

6. R. L. Kemp, "Cities in the 21st Century: The Forces of Change," *Local Focus* (Salem, OR: League of Oregon Cities, February and April, 2001), p. 1.

7. K. Deavers, "Rural Development in the 1990s: Data and Research." Paper presented at the Rural Social Science Symposium, American Agricultural Economics Association, Baton Rouge, Louisiana, 1989.

8. C. Beale and G. V. Fuguitt. "Decade of Pessimistic Non-metro Population Trends Ends on Optimistic Note," *Rural Development Perspectives* 6 (1990): 14–18.

9. L. Cohen, *A Consumer's Republic: The Politics of Mass Consumption in Postwar America* (New York: Knopf, 2003).

10. R. Louv, *Last Child in the Woods: Saving Our Children from Nature-Deficit Disorder* (Chapel Hill, NC: Algonquin Books, 2006).

11. D. Rusk, *Cities Without Suburbs—Third Edition: A Census 2000 Update* (Washington, DC: Woodrow Wilson Center Press, 2003).

12. A. J. McMichael, "Urbanisation and Urbanism in Industrialized Nations, 1850–Present: Implications for Health." In L. M. Schell and Ulijaszek (eds.), *Urbanism, Health and Human Biology in Industrialized Countries* (Cambridge, UK: Cambridge University Press, 1999), p. 25.

13. M. Carley and I. Christie, *Managing Sustainable Development* (Minneapolis, MN: University of Minnesota Press, 1993).
    J. A. Dunn, *Driving Forces: The Automobile—Its Enemies and the Politics of Mobility* (Washington, DC: Brookings Institution Press, 1998).
14. Organization for Economic Cooperation and Development, *OECD Environmental Data: Compendium – 1999* (Paris: OECD Publications, 1999).
15. K. M. Johnson and C. L. Beale. "The Rural Rebound: Recent Non-metropolitan Demographic Trends in the United States" (2001). Retrieved from Internet at URL: http://www.luc.edu/depts/sociology/johnson/p99webn.html (accessed on November 29, 2008).
16. P. O. Stern, O. Young, and D. Druckman (eds.), *Global Environmental Change: Understanding the Human Dimensions* (Washington, DC: National Academy Press, 1992).
17. M. Steger, *Globalism: The New Market Ideology* (Boulder, CO: Rowman and Little-field Publishers, 2002), p. 9.
18. G. Ritzer, *The McDonaldization of Society: An Investigation into the Changing Character of Contemporary Social Life* (Thousand Oaks, CA: Pine Forge Press, 1999).
19. W. Greider, *One World, Ready or Not* (New York: Simon and Schuster, 1997).
20. A. O'Sullivan, T. A. Sexton, and S. M. Sheffrin, *Property Taxes and Tax Revolts: The Legacy of Proposition 13* (New York: Cambridge University Press, 1995).
21. M. Steger, 2002, op. cit. (see reference 17), p. 4.
22. M. J. Moon, "The Evolution of e-Government Among Municipalities: Rhetoric or Reality?" *Public Administration Review* 62 (2002): 4–24.
23. C. D. Slaton and T. L. Becker, "Increasing the Quality and Quantity of Citizen Participation: New Technologies and New Techniques." In T. J. Johnson, C. E. Hays, and S. P. Hays (eds.), *Engaging the Public: How Government and the Media Can Reinvigorate American Government* (New York: Rowman and Littlefield, 1998).
24. Pew Internet and American Life Project. 2004. Reports: E-Gov and E-Policy. URL: http://www.pewinternet.org/PPF/r/150/report_display.asp (accessed November 29, 2009).
25. J. Scott, "Assessing the Quality of Municipal Government Web Sites," *State and Local Government Review* 37 (2005): 151–165, p. 161.
26. J. C. Pierce, M. A. Steger, B. S. Steel, and N. P. Lovrich, *Citizens, Political Communication and Interest Groups: A Study of Environmental Organizations in Canada and the United States* (New York: Praeger Publishers, 1992).
27. F. Fischer, *Citizens, Experts, and the Environment: The Politics of Local Knowledge* (Durham, NC: Duke University Press, 2000), p. ix.
28. J. S. Nye, P. D. Zelikow, and D. C. King (eds.), *Why People Don't Trust Government* (Cambridge, MA: Harvard University Press, 1997).
29. G. McAvoy, *Controlling Technocracy: Citizen Rationality and the NIMBY Syndrome* (Washington, DC: Georgetown Press, 1999).
30. P. DeLeon, *Democracy and the Policy Sciences* (Albany, NY: State University of New York Press, 1997).
31. R. P. Nathan, *Social Science in Government: The Role of Policy Researchers* (Albany, NY: The Rockefeller Institute Press, 2000).
32. A. Maslow, *New Knowledge in Human Values* (New York: Harper and Row, 1959).
33. R. Inglehart, op. cit. (see reference 5).
34. Ibid.

35. M. Winograd and M.D. Hais, *Millennial Makeover: MySpace, YouTube, and the Future of American Politics* (New Brunswick, NJ: Rutgers University Press, 2008).

36. W. Kempton, W. Boster, and J. A. Hartley, *Environmental Values in American Culture* (Cambridge, MA: MIT Press, 1995).
    B. S. Steel and N. P. Lovrich. "An Introduction to Natural Resource Policy and the Environment: Changing Paradigms and Values." In B. S. Steel (ed.), *Public Lands Management in the West: Citizens, Interest Groups, and Values* (Westport, CT: Praeger Publishers, 1997).

37. R. E. Dunlap and A. G. Mertig, "The Evolution of the U.S. Environmental Movement from 1970 to 1990: An Overview." In R. E. Dunlap and A. G. Mertig (eds.), *American Environmentalism: The U.S. Environmental Movement 1970–1990* (Philadelphia: Taylor and Francis Publishers, 1992).

38. L. W. Milbrath, *Learning to Think Environmentally While There is Still Time* (Albany, NY: State University of New York Press, 1996).
    R. Nash, *Rights of Nature: A History of Environmental Ethics* (Madison: University of Wisconsin Press, 1992).

39. R. W. Kates, P. M. Thomas, and A. A. Leiserowitz, "What is Sustainable Development? Goals, Indicators, Values, and Practice," *Environment* 47 (2005): 9–21.

40. World Commission on the Environment and Development, *Our Common Future* (New York: Oxford University Press, 1987).

41. K. Pezzoli, "Sustainable Development: A Trans-disciplinary Review of the Literature," *Journal of Environmental Planning and Management* 40 (1997): 549–574.
    W. Rees, "Consuming the Earth: The Biophysics of Sustainability," *Ecological Economics* 29 (1999): 23–27.
    W. Sachs, *Planet Dialectics: Explorations in Environment and Development* (London: Zed Books, 1999).

42. D. Halpern, *Social Capital* (Cambridge, UK: Policy Press, 2005).

43. H. Daly and J. Cobb, *For the Common Good* (Boston: Beacon Press, 1989).

44. W. Rees, 1999, op. cit. (see reference 41).

45. R. Prescott-Allen, *The Wellbeing of Nations: A Country-by-Country Index of Quality of Life and the Environment* (Washington, DC: Island Press, 2001).

46. W. Sachs, 1999, op. cit. (see reference 41).

47. Boston Indicator Project, *The Wisdom of Our Choices: Boston Indicators of Progress, Change and Sustainability 2000* (Boston, MA: Boston Foundation, 2000).

48. T. M. Parris and R. W. Kates, "Characterizing and Measuring Sustainable Development," *Annual Review of Environment and Resources* 28 (2003): 559–586.

49. Organization for Economic Cooperation and Development, *Shaping the 21st Century: The Contribution of Development Cooperation* (Paris: OECD, 1996), p. 4.

50. M. Sagoff, "Can Environmentalists Keep Two Ideas in Mind and Still Function?" *Philosophy and Public Policy Quarterly* 27 (2007): 2–7.

51. S. Campbell, "Green Cities, Growing Cities, Just Cities? Urban Planning and the Contradictions of Sustainable Development," *Journal of the American Planning Association* 62 (1996): 296–312.

52. C. M. Duncan, *Worlds Apart: Why Poverty Persists in Rural America* (New Haven, CT: Yale University Press, 1999).
    S. Mendis, S. Mills, and J. Yantz, *Building Community Capacity to Adapt to Climate Change in Resource-Based Communities.* Prepared for the Prince Albert Model Forest, Universtiy of Saskatchewand (Winnipeg: University of Manitoba, 2003).

53. C. C. Harris, G. Brown, and W. J. McLaughlin, "How Resilient are Rural Communities in the Interior Columbia Basin Ecosystem?" *Journal of Forestry* 96 (1998): 11–15.

54. E. Wall and K. Marzall, "Adaptive Capacity for Climate Change in Canadian Rural Communities," *Local Environment* 11 (2006): 373–397.

55. U.S. Global Change Research Program, "U.S. National Assessment of the Potential Consequences of Climate Variability and Change Educational Resources. Regional Paper: Great Plains" (2007). Document retrieved from the Internet at URL: http://www.usgcrp.gov/usgcrp/nacc/education/greatplains/greatplains-edu-6.htm (accessed October 26, 2008).

56. E. Wall and K. Marzall, 2006, op. cit. (see reference 54).

57. S. Mendis, S. Mills, and J. Yantz, 2003, op. cit. (see reference 52), p. 39.

58. R. D. Putnam, "Bowling Alone: America's Declining Social Capital," *Journal of Democracy* 6 (1995): 65–78.
    E. Wall and K. Marzall, 2006, op. cit. (see reference 54).

59. R. D. Brunner, T. A. Steelman, L. Coe-Juell, C. M. Cromley, C. M. Edwards, and D. W. Tucker, *Adaptive Governance: Integrating Science, Policy and Decision Making* (New York: Columbia University Press, 2005).

60. R. Dalton, 2008, op. cit. (see reference 3).
    D. Salt and B. Walker, *Resilience Thinking: Sustaining Ecosystems and People in a Changing World* (Washington, DC: Island Press, 2006).

Chapter 2

1. S. Krislov, "American Federalism as American Exceptionalism," *Publius: The Journal of Federalism* 31 (2001): 9–26.
   A. Wildavsky, "A Bias toward Federalism: Confronting the Conventional Wisdom on the Delivery of Governmental Services," *Publius: The Journal of Federalism* 6 (1976): 95–120.
   J. Yarbrough, "Federalism in the Foundation and Preservation of the American Republic," *Publius: The Journal of Federalism* 6 (1976): 43–60.

2. S. Schechter, "Federalism and Community in Historical Perspective," *Publius: The Journal of Federalism* 5 (1975): 1–14.
   R. L. Watts, "Daniel J. Elazar: Comparative Federalism and Post-Statism," *Publius: The Journal of Federalism* 30 (2000): 155–168.

3. Ibid., Watts, p. 161.

4. J. F. Zimmerman, "National-State Relations: Cooperative Federalism in the Twentieth Century," *Publius: The Journal of Federalism* 31 (2001): 15–30.

5. J. P. Greene, "The Background to the Articles of Confederation," *Publius: The Journal of Federalism* 12 (4) (1982), 15–44.
   J. Rakove, "The Legacy of the Articles of Confederation," *Publius: The Journal of Federalism* 12 (1982): 45–66.

6. See S. Lakoff, "Between Either/or and More or Less: Sovereignty versus Autonomy under Federalism," *Publius: The Journal of Federalism* 24 (1994): 63–78.

7. J. R. Alexander, "State Sovereignty in the Federal System: Constitutional Protections under the Tenth and Eleventh Amendments," *Publius: The Journal of Federalism* 26 (1986): 1–15.

8. For a related discussion see V. Ostrom, "The Study of Federalism at Work," *Publius: The Journal of Federalism* 4 (1974): 1–17.

9. C. Tiebout, "A Pure Theory of Local Expenditures," *Journal of Political Economy* 64 (1956): 416–424.

10. D. Osborne and T. Gaebler, *Reinventing Government* (Reading, MA: Addison-Wesley, 1992).

11. D. B. Rosenthal and J. M. Hoefler, "Competing Approaches to the Study of American Federalism and Intergovernmental Relations," *Publius: The Journal of Federalism* 19 (1989): 1–23.

12. J. Bryce, *The American Commonwealth* (Indianapolis, IN: Liberty Fund, 1995).

13. V. C. Jackson, "State Sovereignty and the Eleventh Amendment in the U.S. Supreme Court: The 1988 Term," *Publius: The Journal of Federalism* 22 (1992): 39–54.

14. The national government tended to focus primary concern in exercising its powers enumerated in the Constitution. One important exception to this general point was the passage of the Northwest Ordinance of 1787, which provided federal government support for the development of grammar schools to provide basic education. The Northwest Ordinance established an important precedent for the national government; early on, the national government undertook to legislate for the provision of some **public goods** (societal benefits) that states could not fully consider.

15. In many ways, the history of dominant dual federalism reflects Hamilton's conjecture in Federalist Paper #36 that in a federal system with weak central government powers, powerful state governments may work to advance their own agenda to the detriment of weaker or smaller states and, ultimately, may lead to the collapse of the federal system as originally instituted.

16. B. Allen, "Alexis de Tocqueville on the Covenanted Tradition of American Federal Democracy," *Publius: The Journal of Federalism* 28 (1998): 1–23.

17. The cooperative federalism model was helped along by major reforms at all three levels of government and within the branches of government, particularly at the national level. Campaigns gave voice to the reformers' opinions in a wide audience, and elections produced progressively minded political leaders. The news media and public interest groups advanced a Progressive policy agenda, detailing the social and economic issues to be addressed at all levels of government. The judiciary focused greater attention on the basic rights and liberties guaranteed in the U.S. Constitution and began the evolutionary process of applying, through legal precedent, nationally guaranteed rights to public policymaking occurring at the state and local level.

18. D. B. Walker, "American Federalism from Johnson to Bush," *Publius: The Journal of Federalism* 21 (1991): 105–119.

19. P. E. Peterson, "The New Politics of Federalism," *Spectrum: The Journal of State Government* 78 (2005): 5–7.

20. See also K. Caruson, S. MacManus, M. Kohen and T. Watson, "Homeland Security Preparedness: The Rebirth of Regionalism," *Publius: The Journal of Federalism*, 34(2005): 143–168.

21. Nathan (1975) discusses how top-down federalism can, through the use of resource provision stipulations and mandates, affect the structural arrangements of state and local government. Structural change may have a more lasting and consequential impact on government than simple resource provision that does not require structural changes.

Richard P. Nathan, "The New Federalism versus the Emerging New Structuralism," *Publius: The Journal of Federalism* 5 (1975): 111–129.

22. R. Barrales, "Federalism in the Bush Administration," *Spectrum: The Journal of State Government* 74 (2001): 5–6.

D. C. Menzel, "The Katrina Aftermath: A Failure of Federalism or Leadership?" *Public Administration Review* 66 (2006): 808–812.

23. C. Rothfeld, "Federalism in a Conservative Supreme Court," *Publius: The Journal of Federalism* 22 (1992): 21–31.

24. D. B. Rosenthal and J. M. Hoefler, "Competing Approaches to the Study of American Federalism and Intergovernmental Relations," *Publius: The Journal of Federalism* 19 (1989): 1–23.

25. Ibid., p. 7.

26. P. N. Glendening and Mavis M. Reeves, *Pragmatic Federalism* (Pacific Palisades, CA: Palisades Publishers, 1984).

See also P. N. Glendening, "Pragmatic Federalism and State-Federal Partnerships," *Spectrum: The Journal of State Government* 74 (2001): 6–8.

27. See Osborne and Gaebler, 1992, op. cit. (see reference 10).

28. D. J. Elazar, *Federalism: A View from the States* (New York: Crowell, 1966).

29. J. J. Montjoy, "National Center for Interstate Compacts: A New Initiative," *Spectrum: The Journal of State Government* 77 (2004): 8–11.

J. F. Zimmerman, "Trends in Interstate Relations," *Spectrum: The Journal of State Government* 77 (2004): 5–11.

D. M. Sprague, "Priority Focus for 2005: Interstate Cooperation," *Spectrum: The Journal of State Government* 77 (2004): 3.

30. R. L. Cole and D. A. Taebel, "The New Federalism: Promises, Programs, and Performance," *Publius: The Journal of Federalism* 16 (1986): 3–10.

T. Conlan, "From Cooperatives to Opportunistic Federalism: Reflections on the Half-Century Anniversary of the Commission on Intergovernmental Relations," *Public Administration Review* 66 (2006): 663–676.

P. Eisinger, "Imperfect Federalism: The Intergovernmental Partnership for Homeland Security," *Public Administration Review* 66 (2006): 537–545.

J. Kincaid, "The Crisis in Fiscal Federalism," *Spectrum: The Journal of State Government* 76 (2003): 5–9.

31. M. Filippov, P. Ordeshook, and O. Shvetsova. *Designing Federalism: A Theory of Self-Sustainable Federal Institutions* (Cambridge, UK: Cambridge Press, 2004).

P. Hobson, and F. St. Hilaire, *Reforming Federal-Provincial Fiscal Arrangements: Toward Sustainable Federalism* (Montreal: The Institute for Research on Public Policy, 1993).

Chapter 3

1. D. F. Kettl, "The Gulf of Government," *Governing* (April, 1998): 12.

2. E. M. Uslaner, *The Moral Foundations of Trust* (New York: Cambridge University Press, 2002).

3. D. J. Elazar, *The American Mosaic: The Impact of Space, Time and Culture on American Politics* (Boulder, CO: Westview Press, 1994).

4. R. Hero, *Faces of Inequality: Social Diversity in American Politics* (New York: Oxford University Press, 1998).

5. R. Middleton, "Streamlining Energy Policy: Working More Efficiently," *Spectrum: The Journal of State Government* 77 (2004): 5–8.

6. L. J. Vale and T. J. Campanella, eds., *The Resilient City: How Modern Cities Recover from Disaster* (New York: Oxford University Press, 2005).

7. See M. Poliakoff, "The Path to Teacher Quality from Regulation to Local Responsibility," *Spectrum: The Journal of State Government* 75 (2002): 5–7.
See also J. E. Norton, "Strengthening Colorado's Families—One Child at a Time," *Spectrum: The Journal of State Government* 78 (2005): 29–34.

8. B. Davis, "Western Growth Trends: Pressure on People and Resources," *Spectrum: The Journal of State Government* 78 (2005): 18–19.

9. See P. V. Fishback and D. Lauszus, "The Quality of Services in Company Towns: Sanitation in Coal Towns During the 1920's," *The Journal of Economic History* 49 (1989): 125–144.
See also K. C. Gaspari and A. G. Woolf, "Income, Public Works, and Mortality in Early Twentieth-Century American Cities," *The Journal of Economic History* 45 (1985): 355–361.
M. Ogle, "Domestic Reform and American Household Plumbing, 1840–1870," *Winterthur Portfolio* 28 (1993): 33–58.

10. S. Schultz, and C. McShane, "To Engineer the Metropolis: Sewers, Sanitation, and City Planning in Late-Nineteenth-Century America," *The Journal of American History* 65 (1989): 389–411.

11. For a good historical background, see:
A. M. Scott, "The Progressive Era in Perspective," *The Journal of Politics* 21 (1959): 685–701.
J. A. Tarr, T. Yosie, and J. McCurley III, "Disputes Over Water Quality Policy: Professional Cultures in Conflict, 1900–1917," *American Journal of Public Health* 70 (1980): 427–435.

12. Many PUCs were initially established to regulate railroads and developed a broader regulatory mission in the early 20th century.
See W. Gormley, J. Hoadley, and C. Williams, "Potential Responsiveness in the Bureaucracy: Views of Public Utility Regulation," *The American Political Science Review* 77 (1983): 704–717.

13. J. A. Lapp, "Public Utilities," *The American Political Science Review* 2 (1908): 595.

14. See O. C. Hormell, "State Legislation on Public Utilities in 1933," *The American Political Science Review* 28 (1934): 84–93.

15. See P. Starr, *The Social Transformation of American Medicine* (New York: Basic Books, 1982): 184.

16. In his classic account, G. Rosen's *A History of Public Health* (Baltimore, MD: John Hopkins Press, 1993) demonstrates that public health and sanitation issues have historically been linked in mission, although the link has varied over time and across cultures.

17. See W. Troesken, "Typhoid Rates and the Public Acquisition of Private Waterworks, 1880–1920," *The Journal of Economic History* 59 (1999): 927–948.
See also G. H. Wolff, and M. Palaniappan, "Public or Private Water Management? Cutting the Gordian Knot," *Journal of Water Resources Planning and Management* (January/February, 2004): 1–3.

18. See R. L. Bish, and P. D. O'Donahue, "A Neglected Issue in Public-Goods Theory: The Monopsony Problem," *The Journal of Political Economy* 78 (1970): 1367–1371.

See also S. Renzetti, "Municipal Water Supply and Sewage Treatment: Costs, Prices, and Distortions," *The Canadian Journal of Economics* 32 (1999): 688–704.

19. See B. Van Vliet and N. Stein, "New Consumer Roles in Waste Water Management," *Local Environment* 9 (2004): 353–366.

20. D. Osborne and T. Gaebler, *Reinventing Government: How the Entrepreneurial Spirit is Transforming the Public Sector* (Reading, MA: Addison-Wesley, 1992).

21. M. S. Anderson, "Governance by Green Taxes: Implementing Clean Water Policies in Europe, 1970–1990," *Environmental Economics and Policy Studies* 2 (1990): 39–63.

    A. K. Biswas, "An Assessment of Future Global Water Issues," *Water Resources Development* 21 (2005): 229–237.

    S. Loranger, "Global Water Management: How Do We Begin to Solve the Problems?" *Global Water Management Conference* (Washington, DC), February 9, 2005.

22. W. Hu, "U.S. Says New York City May Have to Spend $6 Billion on Filtration," *New York Times*, June 1, 2000, pp. B1, B6.

23. K. Fowler and E. Rauch, *Sustainable Building Rating System—Summary (PNNL-15858)* (Richland, WA: Pacific Northwest National Laboratory and the U.S. Department of Energy, 2006), p. v.

24. R. Florida, *Cities and the Creative Class* (New York: Routledge, 2004).

25. R. Florida, *The Rise of the Creative Class* (New York: Basic Books, 2002).

26. J. R. Hipp, and A. Perrin, "Nested Loyalties: Local Networks' Effects on Neighborhood and Community Cohesion," *Urban Studies* 43 (2006): 2503–2523.

27. M. Adams, T. Cox, G. Moore, B. Croxford, M. Refaee, and S. Sharples, "Sustainable Soundscapes: Noise Policy and the Urban Experience," *Urban Studies* 43 (2006): 2385–2398.

28. M. Crang, T. Crosbie, and S. Graham, "Variable Geometries of Connection: Urban Digital Divides and the Uses of Information Technology," *Urban Studies* 43 (2006): 2551–2570.

29. J. Geringer, "The Future of Energy and Supply and Demand in the U.S.," *Spectrum: The Journal of State Government* 76 (2003): 28–32.

    C. A. Simon, *Public Policy: Preferences and Outcomes*, 2nd ed. (New York: Pearson, 2010).

    W. Budd, N. P. Lovrich, J. C. Pierce, and B. Chamberlain, "Cultural Sources of Variation in U.S. Urban Sustainability Attributes," *Cities: The International Journal of Urban Policy and Planning* 25 (2008): 257–267.

30. W. Turner, "Private Investors Selling Wind Power to Utilities," *New York Times*, February 13, 1983, p. A14.

31. M. W. Browne, "New Energy Ideas Emerge as Oil Reserves Dwindle," *New York Times*, December 31, 1985, C1.

32. M. R. Simmons, *Twilight in the Desert: The Coming Saudi Oil Shock and the World Economy* (New York: John Wiley, 2005).

33. J. Finkle, "New Economic Development Strategies for the States," *Spectrum: The Journal of State Government* 75 (2002): 23–25.

34. C. D. Austin, E. DesCamp, D. Flux, R. W. McClelland, and J. Sieppert, "Community Development with Older Adults in their Neighborhoods: The Elder Friendly Communities Program," *Families in Society: The Journal of Contemporary Social Services* 86 (2005): 401–409.

E. J. Bolda, J. I. Lowe, G. L. Maddox, and B. S. Patnaik, "Community Partnerships for Older Adults: A Case Study," *Families and Society: The Journal of Contemporary Social Services* 86 (2005): 411–418.

J. E. Swanberg, T. Kanatzar, M. Mendiondo, and M. McCoskey, "Caring for Our Elders: A Contemporary Conundrum for Working People," *Families and Society: The Journal of Contemporary Social Services* 87 (2006): 417–426.

35. H. Li, D. Edwards, and N. Morrow-Howell, "Informal Care-giving Networks and Use of Formal Services by Inner-City African American Elderly with Dementia," *Families in Society: The Journal of Contemporary Social Services* 85 (2004): 55–62.

J. W. Min, "Cultural Competency: A Key to Effective Future Social Work with Racially and Ethnically Diverse Elders," *Families in Society: The Journal of Contemporary Social Services* 86 (2005): 347–358.

36. R. Putnam, *Bowling Alone: The Collapse and Revival of American Community* (New York: Simon and Schuster, 2002).

R. Putnam, *Making Democracy Work: Civic Traditions in Modern Italy* (Princeton: Princeton University Press, 1993).

37. See historical accounts of successes and failures in societies adapting to changing environments in: J. Diamond, *Guns, Germs, and Steel: The Fates of Human Societies* (New York: W. W. Norton Publishers, 2005).

Chapter 4

1. R. B. Ripley and G. A. Franklin, *Congress, the Bureaucracy, and Public Policy*, 4th ed. (Chicago, IL: Dorsey Press, 1987).

2. J. W. Kingdon, *Bridging Research and Policy: Agendas, Alternatives and Public Policies* (New York: Harper Collins, 1984).

3. R. Dalton, *Citizen Politics in Western Democracies: Public Opinion and Political Parties in the United States, Great Britain, West Germany and France* (Chatham, NJ: Chatham House, 1988).

R. Inglehart and W. Baker, "Modernization, Cultural Change, and the Persistence of Traditional Values," *American Sociological Review* 65 (1999): 19–51.

G. Wilson, *Interest Groups in the United States* (Oxford, UK: Oxford University Press, 1981).

4. A. Ciglar and B. Loomis, "Introduction: The Changing Nature of Interest Group Politics." In A. Ciglar and B. Loomis, eds., *Interest Group Politics* (Washington, DC: Congressional Quarterly, 1983).

R. Inglehart, *Modernization and Postmodernization: Cultural, Economic, and Political Change in 43 Societies* (Princeton: Princeton University Press, 1997).

5. R. Dalton, 1988, op. cit. (see note 3).

S. Szabo, "The Successor Generation in Europe," *Public Opinion* 6 (1983): 9–11.

6. J. C. Pierce, M. A. Steger, B. S. Steel, and N. P. Lovrich, *Citizens, Political Communication, and Interest Groups: Environmental Organizations in Canada and the United States* (New York: Praeger Publishers, 1992).

7. R. E. Dunlap, "Trends in Public Opinion Toward Environmental Issues: 1965–1990." In R.E. Dunlap and A. Mertig, eds., *American Environmentalism: The U.S. Environmental Movement, 1970–1990* (Philadelphia: Taylor and Francis, 1992).

A. M. McCright and R. E. Dunlap, "Social Movement Identity and Belief Systems: An Examination of Beliefs About Environmental Problems within the American Public," *Public Opinion Quarterly* 72 (2008): 651–676.

8. L. Caldwell, "Globalizing Environmentalism: Threshold of a New Phase in International Relations." In R. Dunlap and A. Mertig, eds., *American Environmentalism* (Philadelphia: Taylor and Francis, 1992).

R. E. Dunlap and R. E. Jones, "Environmental Concern: Conceptual and Measurement Issues." In R. E. Dunlap and W. Michelson, eds., *Handbook of Environmental Sociology* (Westport, CT: Greenwood Press, 2002).

9. R. Miliband, *Divided Societies: Class Struggle in Contemporary Capitalism* (Oxford, UK: Oxford University Press, 1989).

10. G. E. McAvoy, *Controlling Technocracy: Citizen Rationality and the NIMBY Syndrome* (Washington, DC: Georgetown University Press, 1999).

G. L. Theodori and A. E. Luloff, "Position on Environmental Issues and Engagement in Proenvironmental Behaviors," *Society and Natural Resources* 15 (2002): 471–482.

11. R. Inglehart, "Changing Paradigms in Comparative Political Behavior." In Ada Finifter, ed., *Political Science: The State of the Discipline* (Washington, DC: American Political Science Association, 1983).

R. Inglehart, 1997, op. cit. (see note 4).

12. S. Cable and C. Cable, *Environmental Problems Grassroots Solutions: The Politics of Grassroots Environmental Conflict* (New York: St. Martin's Press, 1995).

R. Inglehart, 1997, op. cit. (see note 4).

13. W. Gamson, "Constructing Social Protest." In H. Johnson and B. Klandermans, eds., *Social Movements and Culture* (Minneapolis: University of Minnesota Press, 1995).

14. D. Rothenberg, *Hand's End: Technology and the Limits of Nature* (Berkeley: University of California Press, 1992).

15. D. Truman, *The Governmental Process* (New York: Alfred Knopf, 1951).

16. J. Walker, "The Origins and Maintenance of Interest Groups in America," *American Political Science Review* 77 (1983): 390–406.

17. A. McFarland, *Public Interest Lobbies: Decision Making on Energy* (Washington, DC: American Enterprise Institute, 1976).

18. D. King and J. Walker, "The Provision of Benefits by American Interest Groups," paper presented at the Annual Meeting of the Midwest Political Science Association (Chicago, 1989).

19. D. Baer and D. Bositis, *Politics and Linkage in a Democratic Society* (Englewood Cliffs, NJ: Prentice Hall, 1993).

R. D. Beaford, T. B. Gongaware, and D. L. Valadez, "Social Movements." In E. F. Borgatta and R. Montgomery, eds., *Encyclopedia of Sociology* (New York: Macmillan, 2000).

20. M. Olson, *The Logic of Collective Action* (Cambridge, MA: Harvard University Press, 1965).

21. D. Korten, *NGO Strategic Networks: From Community Projects to Global Transformation*, 1990. URL: http://iisd1.iisd.ca/pcdf/1991/stratnet.htm (accessed on August 15, 2009), p. 2.

22. P. Pross, *Group Politics and Public Policy* (Toronto, Ontario: Oxford University Press, 1984).

23. S. Cable and C. Cable, 1995, op. cit. (see note 12).

J. C. Pierce et al., 1992, op. cit. (see note 6).

24. J. Heyman, "Mobilizing Citizens: Citizens' Group Membership and Political Participation," paper presented at the Annual Meeting of the Midwest Political Science Association (Chicago, 1989).

B. S. Steel, J. C. Pierce, and N. P. Lovrich, "Tactics and Strategies of Interest Groups in Federal Forest Policy," *Social Science Journal* 33 (1996): 401–421.

25. D. King and J. Walker, 1989, op cit. (see note 18)

26. R. Salisbury, J. Heinz, E. Lauman, and R. Nelson, "Who Works with Whom?" *American Political Science Review* 81 (1984): 1217–1234.

27. A. McFarland, "Why Interest Groups Organize: A Pluralist Response to Olson," paper presented at the Western Political Science Association Meetings (Seattle, 1989).

28. J. Walker, 1983, op. cit. (see note 16).

29. J. Berry, *The Interest Group Society* (Great Britain: Harper Collins, 1989).

D. Baer and D. Bositis, 1993, op. cit. (see note 19).

30. J. Berry, ibid.

31. R. E. Dunlap and A. Mertig, *American Environmentalism: The U.S. Environmental Movement, 1970–1990* (Philadelphia: Taylor and Francis, 1992).

N. Freudenberg and C. Steinsapir, "Not in our Backyards: The Grassroots Environmental Movement." In R. Dunlap and A. Mertig, eds., *American Environmentalism: The U.S. Environmental Movement, 1970–1990* (Philadelphia: Taylor and Francis, 1992).

C. J. Folke, J. Colding, and F. Berkes. "Synthesis: Building Resilience and Adaptive Capacity in Social-Ecological Systems." In F. Berkes, J. Colding and C. Folke, eds., *Navigating Social-Ecological Systems* (New York: Cambridge University Press, 2003).

32. B. S. Steel, S. Henderson, and R. L. Warner, "NGOs and the Development of Civil Society in Bulgaria and the U.S.: A Comparative Analysis," *Innovation: The European Journal of Social Science Research* 20 (2007): 35–52.

33. J. Gooden and J. Jasper, *The Social Movements Reader: Cases and Concepts* (New York: Blackwell, 2003).

J. McCarthy and M. Zald, "Resource Mobilization and Social Movements: A Partial Theory," *American Journal of Sociology* 82 (1977): 1212–1241.

A. Morris and C. McClurg Mueller, *Frontiers in Social Movement Theory* (New Haven, CT: Yale University Press, 1992).

C. Tilly, *Social Movements, 1768–2004* (Vancouver: University of British Columbia Press, 2004).

34. R. Dalton, 1988, op. cit. (see note 3).

35. U.S. Census, *U.S. Voter Turnout Up in 2004*, U.S. Census Bureau Report CB05–73 (Washington, DC: U.S. Department of Commerce, Census Bureau, 2005).

36. Ibid., p. 5.

37. U.S. Census Bureau, "Voter Turnout Increases by 5 Million in 2008 Presidential Election." URL: http://www.census.gov/Press-Release/www/releases/archives/voting/013995.html (accessed December 16, 2009).

38. H. Hahn and S. Kamieniecki, *Referendum Voting: Social Status and Policy Preferences* (New York: Greenwood Press, 1987).

39. T. Cronin and M. J. Rossant, *Direct Democracy: The Politics of Initiative, Referendum, and Recall* (Cambridge, MA: Harvard University Press, 1999).

T. R. Dye, *Politics in States and Communities*, 10th ed. (Englewood Cliffs, NJ: Prentice Hall, 2000).

40. D. Magleby, *Direct Legislation: Voting on Ballot Propositions in the United States* (Baltimore: Johns Hopkins University Press, 1984).

41. A. Campbell, P. E. Converse, W. E. Miller, and D. E. Stokes, *The American Voter* (New York: Wiley, 1960).

P. E. Converse, "The Nature of Belief Systems in Mass Publics." In D. Apter, ed., *Ideology and Discontent* (New York: Free Press, 1964).

E. R. Smith, *The Unchanging American Voter* (Berkeley: University of California Press, 1989).

42. J. Citrin, "Who's the Boss? Direct Democracy and Popular Control of Government." In S. C. Craig, ed., *Broken Contract: Changing Relationships Between Americans and Their Government* (Boulder, CO: Westview Press, 1996).

B. Gamble, "Putting Civil Rights to a Popular Vote," *American Journal of Political Science* 41 (1997): 245–70.

43. D. Magelby, 1984, op. cit. (see note 39).

44. D. Broder, *Democracy Derailed* (New York: Harcourt, Inc., 2000).

R. Ellis, *Democratic Delusions: The Initiative Process in America* (Lawrence, KS: University Press of Kansas, 2002).

E. Gerber, "Legislative Response to the Threat of Popular Initiatives," *American Journal of Political Science* 40 (1996): 99–128.

45. T. Dye, *Understanding Public Policy*, 9th ed. (Upper Saddle River, NJ: Prentice Hall, 1998).

46. R. Scarce, *Eco-warriors: Understanding the Radical Environmental Movement* (Chicago, IL: The Noble Press, Inc., 1990).

47. Pew Research Center, *Internet's Broader Role in Campaign,* 2008, http://people-press.org (accessed on August 15, 2009).

48. Ibid., p. 1.

49. Pew Research Center, *Public Knowledge of Current Affairs Little Changed by News and Information Revolutions,* 2007, http://people-press.org (accessed on August 15, 2009).

50. C. Lindblom, *Politics and Markets* (New York: Basic Books, 1977).

51. G. Porter, J. Brown, and P. Chasek, *Global Environmental Politics*, 3rd ed. (Boulder, CO: Westview Press, 2000).

52. L. Bennett, *News: The Politics of Illusion*, 7th ed. (New York: Longman, 2007).

53. J. Thurber, C. Nelson and D. Dulio, *Crowded Airwaves: Campaign Advertising in Elections* (Washington, DC: Brookings Institution Press, 2000).

54. R. Dahl, *A Preface to Economic Democracy* (Berkeley: University of California Press, 1985), pp. 54–55.

55. D. Baer and D. Bositis, 1993, op. cit. (see note 19).

56. R. Cayrol and J. Jaffre, "Party Linkages in France: Socialist Leaders, Followers and Voters." In K. Lawson, ed., *Political Parties and Linkage* (New Haven, CT: Yale University Press, 1980).

57. Pew Research Center, *National Security More Linked with Partisan Affiliation,* 2005, http://people-press.org (accessed on August 15, 2009).

58. Pew Research Center, *Independents Take Center Stage in Obama Era,* 2009, http://people-press.org/report/?pageid=1517 (accessed on December 16, 2009).

59. T. Dye, 1998, op. cit. (see note 44), p. 2.

60. Ibid, p. 21.

61. C. W. Mills, *The Power Elite* (London: Oxford University Press, 1956), p. 3–4.

62. M. Edelman, *Politics as Symbolic Action: Mass Arousal and Quiescence* (Chicago: Markham Publishing Co., 1971).

63. R. Miliband. In: *Divided Societies: Class Struggle in Contemporary Capitalism* (Oxford: Clarendon Press, 1989), p. 3.

Chapter 5

1. G. A. Tarr, *Understanding State Constitutions* (Princeton, NJ: Princeton University Press, 1998).
2. Ibid., p. 3.
3. F. D. Wormuth, *The Origins of Modern Constitutionalism* (New York: Harper and Brothers, 1949), p. 3.
4. See J. R. Stoner's classic study *Common Law and Liberal Theory: Coke, Hobbes, and the Origins of American Constitutionalism* (Lawrence, KS: University Press of Kansas, 1992).
5. R. L. Maddex, *State Constitutions of the United States,* 2nd ed. (Washington, DC: Congressional Quarterly, 2006).
6. Council of State Governments, ed., *The Book of the States, 2006* (Lexington, KY: The Council of State Governments, 2006).
7. R. L. Maddex, 2006, op. cit. (see note 5), p. xvi.
8. C. W. Hammons, "Was James Madison Wrong? Rethinking the American Preference for Short, Framework-Oriented Constitutions," *American Political Science Review* 93 (1999): 837–849, p. 840
9. Ibid., p. 840.
10. Ibid., p. 840.
11. A. Blaustein, "Contemporary Trends in Constitution Writing." In D. Elazar, ed., *Constitutionalism: The Israeli and American Experiences* (Baltimore, MD: University Press of America, 1990) and L. M. Friedman, "State Constitutions in Historical Perspective." In *Annals of the American Academy of Political and Social Science* 496 (1988): 33–42.
12. C. W. Hammons, 1999, op. cit. (see note 8), p. 837.
13. Ibid., p. 846.
14. R. L. Maddex, 2006, op. cit. (see note 5), p. xviii.
15. D. S. Lutz, "Toward a Theory of Constitutional Amendment," *American Political Science Review* 88 (1994): 355–370.
16. Oregon Blue Book, "Initiative, Referendum and Recall Introduction." URL: http://bluebook.state.or.us/state/elections/elections09.htm (accessed August 15, 2009).
    J. M. Swarthout and K. R. Gervais, "Oregon: Political Experiment Station." In F. H. Jonas, ed., *Politics in the American West* (Salt Lake City: University of Utah Press, 1969).
17. T. E. Cronin, *Direct Democracy: The Politics of Initiative, Referendum, and Recall* (Cambridge, MA: Harvard University Press, 1989).
18. J. Dinan, "State Constitutional Developments in 2005." In *The Book of the States, 2006* (Lexington, KY: Council of State Governments, 2006).
19. J. C. May, "State Constitutions and Constitutional Revision, 1992–93." In *The Book of the States, 1992–93* (Lexington, KY: The Council of State Governments, 1994).
20. R. M. Alvarez and J. Brehm, *Hard Choices, Easy Answers* (Princeton, NJ: Princeton University Press, 2002).
    P. J. Galie and C. Bopst, "Changing State Constitutions: Dual Constitutionalism and the Amending Process," *Hofstra Law & Policy Symposium, 27* (Hempstead, NY: Hofstra University, 1996).
21. G. Benjamin and T. Gais, "Constitutional Convention Phobia," *Hofstra Law & Policy Symposium, 53* (Hempstead, NY: Hofstra University, 1996).

22. Utah State Law Library, "Research Guide: Utah Constitution." URL: www.utcourts. gov/lawlibrary/docs/constitution_website.pdf (accessed August 15, 2009).

23. Oregon Blue Book 2007, "Constitution of Oregon: 2005 Version." URL: http://bluebook. state.or.us/state/constitution/constitution15.htm (accessed August 15, 2009).

24. G. A. Tarr, 1998, op. cit. (see note 1).

25. Ibid.

26. Ibid.

27. See D. J. Boorstin, *The Genius of American Politics* (Chicago, IL: University of Chicago Press, 1953).

28. R. Seidelman and E. J. Harpham, *Disenchanted Realists: Political Science and the American Crisis, 1884–1984* (Albany, NY: State University of New York Press, 1985).

29. G. Benjamin and T. Gais, 1996, op. cit. (see note 21).

30. G. A. Tarr, 1998, op. cit. (see note 1).

31. P. J. Galie and C. Bopst, 1996, op. cit. (see note 20).

32. L. H. Zeigler, "Interest Groups in the States." In V. Gray, H. Jacob and K. Vines, eds., *Politics in the American States* (Boston, MA: Little, Brown and Co., 1983).

33. C. T. Goodsell, *The Case for Bureaucracy: A Public Administration Polemic, 4th ed.* (Washington, DC: Congressional Quarterly Press, 2004).

34. D. S. Lutz, 1994, op. cit. (see note 15).

35. J. Dinan, 2006, op. cit. (see note 18).

36. J. C. May, "State Constitutional Developments in 2004." In *The Book of the States, 2005* (Vol. 37) (Lexington, KY: The Council of State Governments, 2005).

37. E. Russo, "Follow the Money—The Politics of Embryonic Stem Cell Research," *PLoS Biology* 3 (2005): 1167–1171.

38. P. T. Hampton, "U.S. Stem Cell Research Lagging," *Journal of the American Medical Association* 295 (2006): 2233–2234.
    C. Holden, "U.S. States Offer Asia Stiff Competitions," *Science* 307 (2005), 662–663.

39. Ibid., p. 663.
    M. Delli Carpini and S. Keeter, *What Americans Know About Politics and Why It Matters* (New Haven, CT: Yale University Press, 1996).

40. S. Kelman, *Making Public Policy: A Hopeful View of American Government* (New York: Basic Books, 1987).

41. S. Bowler, T. Donovan, and C. J. Tolbert, eds., *Citizens as Legislators: Direct Democracy in the United States* (Columbus, OH: Ohio State University Press, 1998).

42. R. J. Burby and P. J. May, *Making Governments Plan: State Experiments in Managing Land Use* (Baltimore, MD: The Johns Hopkins Press, 1997).

43. R. A. Dahl and E. R. Tufte, *Size and Democracy* (Palo Alto, CA: Stanford University Press, 1973).

44. B. I. Page and R. Y. Shapiro, *The Rational Public: Fifty Years of Trends in Americans' Policy Preferences* (Chicago, IL: University of Chicago Press, 1992).

Chapter 6

1. A. Lijphart, *Parliamentary Versus Presidential Government* (Oxford, UK: Oxford University Press, 1992).
    R. K. Weaver and B. A. Rockman, *Do Institutions Matter? Government Capabilities in the United States and Abroad* (Washington, DC: Brookings Institution Press, 1993).

2. H. G. Frederickson and K. B. Smith, *The Public Administration Theory Primer* (Boulder, CO: Westview Press, 2003).

3. D. Woodhouse, *Ministers and Parliament: Accountability in Theory and Practice* (Oxford, UK: Oxford University Press, 1994).

4. W. Clarke, "Divided Government and Budget Conflict in the U.S. States," *Legislative Studies Quarterly* 23 (1998): 5–22.

5. K. E. Hamm and R. D. Robertson, "Factors Influencing the Adoption of New Methods of Legislative Oversight in the U.S. States," *Legislative Studies Quarterly* 6 (1981): 133–150.

6. M. J. Gerhardt, *The Federal Impeachment Process: A Constitutional and Historical Analysis* (Chicago, IL: University of Chicago Press, 2000).

7. A. Rosenthal, *Heavy Lifting: The Job of the American Legislature* (Washington, DC: CQ Press, 2004).

8. K. L. Barber, "American Government and Politics," *American Political Science Review* 77 (1983): 1039–1040.

   M. E. Jewell, *Representation in State Legislatures* (Lexington, KY: University Press of Kentucky, 1982).

9. K. Bratton, "The Effect of Legislative Diversity on Agenda Setting: Evidence from Six State Legislatures," *American Politics Research* 30 (2002): 115–142, p. 115.

10. Ibid., p. 127.

11. E. Barrett, "The Policy Priorities of African American Women in State Legislatures," *Legislative Studies Quarterly* 20 (1995): 223–247, p. 223.

12. Ibid.

13. Ibid.

14. K. Bratton and K. Haynie, "Agenda Setting and Legislative Success in State Legislatures: The Effects of Gender and Race," *Journal of Politics* 61 (1999): 658–679, p. 658.

15. Center for American Women in Politics (Eagleton Institute, Rutgers University, 2008): URL: http://www.cawp.rutgers.edu/Facts.html (accessed August 15, 2009).

16. National Conference of Black Mayors, *Mayors of Cities with Populations over 50,000.* URL: http://www.ncbm.org/members_of_NCBM.html (accessed August 15, 2009).

17. K. Arceneaux, "The Gender Gap in State Legislative Representation: New Data to Tackle an Old Question," *Political Research Quarterly* 54 (2001): 143–160.

18. D. Alexander and K. Anderson, "Gender as a Factor in the Attribution of Leadership Traits," *Political Research Quarterly* 46 (1993): 527–545.

19. V. Sapiro, *The Political Integration of Women* (Champaign, IL: University of Illinois Press, 1984).

    S. Welch, "Women as Political Animals? A Test of Some Explanations for Male-Female Political Participation Differences," *American Journal of Political Science* 21 (1977): 711–730.

20. K. Arceneaux, 2001, op. cit. (see note 17), p. 145.

21. R. Darcy and J. Choike, "A Formal Analysis of Legislative Turnover: Women Candidates and Legislative Representation," *American Journal of Political Science* 30 (1986): 237–255.

22. G. Moncrief, J. Thompson, M. Haddon, and R. Hoyer, "For Whom the Bell Tolls: Term Limits and State Legislatures," *Legislative Studies Quarterly* 17 (1992): 37–47.

23. K. Arceneaux, 2001, op. cit. (see note 17), p. 145.

24. R. Darcy, S. Welch, and J. Clark, *Women, Elections and Representation* (New York: Longman, 1987).

25. Ohio Legislative Service Commission, *A Guidebook for Ohio Legislators, 2007.* URL: www.lsc.state.oh.us/guidebook/ (accessed August 15, 2009).

26. L. Braiotta, *The Audit Committee Handbook* (New York: John Wiley & Sons, 2004).

27. Ohio Legislative Service Commission, 2007, op. cit. (see note 25).

28. A. Bowman and R. Kearney, *State and Local Government*, 6th ed. (Boston, MA: Houghton-Mifflin, 2005), p. 160.

29. M. S. Dulaney, *A History and Description of the Nebraska Legislative Process* (Lincoln, NE: Nebraska Council of School Administrators, 2002).

30. G. Tsebelis and J. Money, *Bicameralism* (Cambridge, UK: Cambridge University Press, 1997).

31. A. W. Richards, "Strategic Planning and Budgeting in the New Texas? Putting Service Efforts and Accomplishments to Work," *International Journal of Public Administration* 18 (1995): 409–441.

32. National Conference of State Legislatures, *Full- and Part-Time Legislatures.* URL: http://www.ncsl.org/programs/press/2004/backgrounder_fullandpart.htm (accessed August 15, 2009).

33. Ibid.

34. Ibid.

35. O. Koppel, "Public Good Provision in Legislatures: The Dynamics of Enlargements," *Economics Letters* 83 (2004): 43–47.

36. Council of State Governments, *The Book of the States, 2007* (Lexington, KY: Council of State Governments, 2007).

37. As administrative divisions of a state, counties seldom have power to establish their own taxes, but they are often able to adjust tax rates within fixed maximum and minimum parameters.

38. J. F. Zimmerman, *Subnational Politics; Readings in State and Local Government* (New York: Holt, Rinehart, 1970).

39. H. M. Levin, *An Analysis of the Economic Effects of the New York City Sales Tax* (Washington, DC: Brookings Institution, 1967).
    C. L. Rogers, "Local Option Sales Tax (LOST) Policy on the Urban Fringe," *Regional Analysis and Policy* 34 (2004): 27–50.

40. A. D. Sokolow, *Town and Township Government: Serving Rural and Suburban Communities* (New York: Marcel Dekker, 1996).

41. H. G. Frederickson and G. A. Johnson, "The Adapted American City: A Study of Institutional Dynamics," *Urban Affairs Review* 36 (2001): 872–884, p. 872.

42. K. A. Foster, *The Political Economy of Special-purpose Government* (Washington, DC: Georgetown University Press, 1997).

43. S. Scott and J. C. Bollens, "Special Districts in California Local Government," *Western Political Quarterly* 3 (1950): 233–243.

44. T. Loftus and H. G. Rennie, *Analysis of Enabling Legislation from a Multi-jurisdictional Watershed Perspective.* URL: www.storm.warrenswcd.com/Documents/FinalReport-OSTF-319-Grant-StormWater-MGT-Watershed-Basis.pdf (accessed August 15, 2009).

45. D. A. Austin, "A Positive Model of Special District Formation," *Regional Science and Urban Economics* 28 (1998): 103–122.

46. J. Lang, *New Urban Renewal in Colorado's Front Range*, Issue Paper 2–2007 (Golden, CO: Independence Institute, 2007).

47. H. G. Cisneros, *Regionalism: The New Geography of Opportunity* (Jefferson, NC: McFarland and Company, 1999).

   G. Marks and L. Hooghe, *Contrasting Visions of Multi-level Governance* (Oxford, UK: Oxford University Press, 2004).

48. K. Mizany and A. Manatt, *What's So Special about Special Districts? A Citizen's Guide to Special Districts in California* (Sacramento, CA: California State Legislature, 2002).

   URL: www.csda.net/images/Whatsso.pdf (accessed August 15, 2009).

49. T. Bui and B. Ihrke, *It's Time to Draw the Line: A Citizen's Guide to LAFCOs* (Sacramento, CA: California Senate, 2003).

50. K. Mizany and A. Manatt, 2002, op. cit. (see note 48).

51. U.S. Census Bureau, *2002 Census of Governments*. URL: www.census.gov/govs/www/cog2002.html (accessed August 15, 2009).

52. D. J. Condron and V. J. Roscigno, "Disparities Within: Unequal Spending and Achievement in an Urban School District," *Sociology of Education* 76 (2003): 18–36.

53. A. Feuerstein, "Elections, Voting, and Democracy in Local School District Governance," *Educational Policy* 16 (2002): 15–36.

54. J. P. Danzberger, "Governing the Nation's Schools: The Case for Restructuring Local School Boards," *Phi Delta Kappan* 75 (1994): 367–373.

55. L. Barrow and C. E. Rouse, "Using Market Valuation to Assess Public School Spending," *Journal of Public Economics* 88 (2004): 747–1769.

56. U.S. Census Bureau, 2002, op. cit. (see note 51).

57. United Nations, Department of Economic and Social Affairs, *Local Authorities*. URL: www.un.org/esa/sustdev/documents/agenda21/english/agenda21chapter28.htm (accessed August 15, 2009).

58. B. Evans, M. Joas, S. Sundback, and K. Theobald, *Governing Sustainable Cities*. (London, UK: Earthscan, 2005).

59. B. Evans, M. Joas, S. Sundback, and K. Theobald, "Governing Local Sustainability," *Journal of Environmental Planning and Management* 49 (2006): 849–867.

60. B. Evans, M. Joas, S. Sundback, and K. Theobald, 2005, op. cit. (see note 58).

61. B. Costantinos, "Sustainable Development and Governance Policy Nexus: Bridging the Ecological and Human Dimensions." In G. Mudacumura, D. Mebratu, and M. Shamsul Haque, eds., *Sustainable Development Policy and Administration* (New York: Taylor and Francis, 2006), p. 68.

62. United Nations, 2009, op. cit. (see note 57).

Chapter 7

1. D. Coffey, "Measuring Gubernatorial Ideology: A Content Analysis of State of the State Speeches," *State Politics and Policy Quarterly* 5 (2005): 88–103.

2. J. Barth and M. Ferguson, "The Relationship between Gubernatorial Personality and Public Approval," *State Politics and Policy Quarterly* 2 (2002): 268–282.

3. See R. C. Turner, "The Political Economy of Gubernatorial Smokestack Chasing: Bad Policy and Bad Politics?" *State Politics and Policy Quarterly* 3 (2003): 270–293.

4. J. D. King, "Incumbent Popularity and Vote Choice in Gubernatorial Elections," *The Journal of Politics* 63 (2001): 585–597.

5. R. S. Kravchuk, "The 'New Connecticut:' Lowell Weicker and the Process of Administrative Reform," *Public Administration Review* 53 (1993): 329–339.

6. W. Clarke, "Budget Requests and Agency Head Selection Methods," *Political Research Quarterly* 50 (1997): 301–316.
W. Clarke, "Divided Government and Budget Conflict in the U.S. States," *Legislative Studies Quarterly* 23 (1998): 5–22.
S. M. Morehouse, "Legislative Party Voting for the Governor's Program," *Legislative Studies Quarterly* 21 (1996): 359–381.

7. S. B. Hansen, "Life is Not Fair: Governors' Job Performance Ratings and State Economies," *Political Research Quarterly* 52 (1999): 167–188.

8. J. Soss and D. T. Cannon, "Partisan Divisions and Voting Decisions: U.S. Senators, Governors, and the Rise of Divided Federal Government," *Political Research Quarterly* 48 (1995): 253–274.

9. C. T. Stearns, "A Historical Analysis of the American County Institution and Reform: Values and the Case of the Appointed County Executive," *Administrative Theory and Praxis* 23 (2001): 279–284.
See also A. W. Bromage, *American County Government* (New York: Sears Publishing Company, 1934).

10. J. Dillon, *The Law of Municipal Corporations* (Cornell, NY: Cornell University Press, 2009).

11. C. T. Stearns, 2001, op. cit. (see note 9).

12. S. Nunn, "Urban Infrastructure Policies and Capital Spending in City Manager and Strong Mayor Cities," *The American Review of Public Administration* 26 (1996), 93–112.

13. G. Davis, Sustainable Building Task Force, Executive Order D-16-00. URL: http://www.ciwmb.ca.gov/GreenBuilding/TaskForce/ (accessed December 9, 2009).

14. Oregon Sustainability Act. Available at: http://www.sustainableoregon.net/sust_act/HB3948.cfm (accessed December 9, 2009).

15. Seattle Climate Action Plan. URL: http://www.seattle.gov/environment/ (accessed December 9, 2009).

16. Ibid.

17. U.S. Mayors Climate Protection Agreement. URL: http://www.usmayors.org/climateprotection /agreement.htm (accessed December 9, 2009).

18. Ibid.

Chapter 8

1. A. Hamilton, "The Federalist No. 78: The Judiciary Department," *Independent Journal*, June 14, 1788.

2. D. B. Rottman, "The State Courts in 2005: A Year of Living Dangerously." In *The Book of the States, 2006* (Lexington, KY: The Council of State Governments).

3. G. C. Edwards, M. P. Wattenberg, and Robert L. Lineberry, *Government in America: People, Politics, and Policy*, 8th ed. (New York: Longman, 1998).

4. Administrative Office of the U.S. Courts, *Understanding Federal and State Courts 2007* [cited Dec. 25, 2007]. Available at http://www.uscourts.gov/ outreach/resources/fedstate_lessonplan.htm.

5. H. J. Abraham and Henry Julian, *The Judicial Process: An Introductory Analysis of the Courts of the United States, England, and France* (New York: Oxford University Press, 1998).
   Edwards et al., op. cit. (see note 3).

6. H. R. Glick, R. Henry, and K. N. Vines, "State Court Systems." In W. S. Sayre, ed. *Foundations of State and Local Government* (Englewood Cliffs, NJ: Prentice-Hall, 1973).

7. Ibid.

8. C. McGowan, *The Organization of Judicial Power in the United States* (Evanston, IL: Northwestern University Press, 1967), p. 37.

9. Edwards et al., op. cit. (see note 3).

10. D. B. Rottman and S. M. Strickland, *State Court Organization, 2004.* (Washington, DC: U.S. Department of Justice, 2006).

11. Ibid.

12. Administrative Office of the U.S. Courts, op. cit. (see note 4).

13. G. Bermann and J. Feinblatt, "Problem-Solving Courts: A Brief Primer," *Law and Policy* 23 (2002): 125–140.
    J. Feinblatt and G. Berman, "Community Courts: A Brief Primer," *U.S. Attorney Bulletin* 49 (2001): 33–38.

14. Ibid.

15. V. Flango, "Families and Problem-Solving Courts." URL: http://contentdm.ncsconline.org/ (accessed December 9, 2009).

16. D. Rottman and P. Casey, "Therapeutic Jurisprudence and the Emergence of Problem-Solving Courts," *National Institute of Justice Journal* (1999): 12–20.

17. Bermann and Feinblatt, op. cit. (see note 13), p. 130.

18. National Criminal Justice Reference Service, *Drug Courts.* Office of National Drug Control Policy, Dec. 5, 2007. URL: http://www.ncjrs.gov/spotlight/drug_courts/Summary.html (accessed December 9, 2009).

19. Bermann and Feinblatt, op. cit. (see note 13).

20. S. Belenko, "Research on Drug Courts: A Critical Review, 1999 Update," *National Drug Court Institute Review* 2 (1999): 1–58.

21. Ibid.

22. State of Montana. *Montana Water Court 2007.* URL: http://courts.mt.gov/water/default.asp (accessed December 9, 2009).

23. Colorado Judicial Branch, *Colorado Water Districts: Water Courts.* URL: http://www.courts.state.co.us/supct/ supctwaterctindex.htm (accessed December 9, 2009).

24. D. Schultz, "*Minnesota Republican Party v. White* and the Future of State Judicial Selection," *Albany Law Review* 69 (2006): 985–1011, p. 985.

25. Rottman and Strickland, 2006, op. cit. (see note 10).

26. Ibid.

27. A. Hamilton, op. cit. (see note 1).

28. R. A. Schotland, "To the End Species List, Add: Non-Judicial Elections," *Willamette Law Review* 39 (2003): 1397–1423, p. 1404.

29. M. Scherer, "Is Justice Undermined by Campaign Contributions? Conflicts of Interest and Nasty Ad Campaigns Deepen Public Distrust in State Judicial Elections," *Capital Eye* 3 (2001). URL: http:// www.opensecrets.org/newsletter/ce76/statelines.asp (accessed December 9, 2009).

30. Edwards et al., op. cit. (see note 3).
31. Schultz op. cit. (see note 24).
32. Glick et al., op. cit. (see note 6).
33. Rottman and Strickland, op. cit. (see note 10).
34. Ibid.
35. Glick et al., op. cit. (see note 6).
36. Rottman and Strickland, op. cit. (see note 10).
37. Glick et al., op. cit. (see note 6).
38. Ibid.
39. Rottman and Strickland, op. cit. (see note 10).
40. N. P. Lovrich and Charles Sheldon, "Assessing Judicial Elections: Effects Upon the Electorate of High and Low Articulation Systems," *Western Political Quarterly* 38 (1985): 276–293.
41. Schultz, op. cit. (see note 24).
42. Rottman and Strickland, op. cit. (see note 10).
43. Ibid.
44. D. Sontag, "In Courts, Threats Have Become a Fact of Life," *The New York Times*, March 20, 2005. URL: http://www.nytimes.com/2005/03/20/national/20judges.html (accessed December 9, 2009).
45. A. Goodnough, "In Schiavo Feeding-Tube Case, Notoriety Finds Unlikely Judge," *The New York Times*, March 17, 2005. URL: http://www.nytimes.com/2005/03/17/national/17greer.html (accessed December 9, 2009).
46. Rottman and Strickland, op. cit. (see note 10), p. 237.
47. Ibid.
48. State of Oregon, *Measure 40*. URL: http://www.sos.state.or.us/elections/nov72006/guide/meas/m40_bt.html (accessed December 9, 2009).
49. D. Rottman, "The State Courts in 2006: Surviving Anti-Court Initiatives and Demonstrating High Performance." In *The Book of the States, 2007* (Lexington, KY: The Council of State Governments, 2007).
50. Schultz, op. cit. (see note 24).
51. Ibid.
52. M. Scherer, "Is Justice Undermined by Campaign Contributions? Conflicts of Interest and Nasty Ad Campaigns Deepen Public Distrust in State Judicial Elections," *Capital Eye* 3 (2006). URL: http:// www.opensecrets.org/newsletter/ce76/statelines.asp (accessed December 10, 2009).
53. Rottman, op. cit. (see note 49).
54. Ibid, p. 239.

Chapter 9

1. M. Weber [H. H. Gerth and C. W. Mills, trans.], *From Max Weber: Essays in Sociology* (New York: Oxford University Press, 1958).
2. R. Agranoff and M. McGuire, *Collaborative Public Management: New Strategies for Local Governments* (Washington, DC: Georgetown University Press, 2003).
3. See H. G. Fredericksen, G. Johnson, and C. Wood, "The Changing Structure of American Cities: A Study of the Diffusion of Innovation," *Public Administration Review* 64 (2004), 320–330.

See also T. H. Poister and G. Streib, "Elements of Strategic Planning and Management in Municipal Government: Status after Two Decades," *Public Administration Review* 65 (2005): 45–56.

N. M. Riccucci, M. K. Meyers, I. Lurie, and J.S. Han, "The Implementation of Welfare Reform Policy: The Role of Public Managers in Front-Line Practices," *Public Administration Review* 64 (2004): 438–448.

4. H. Bacot and J. Christine, "What's So 'Special' About Airport Authorities? Assessing the Administrative Structure of U.S. Airports," *Public Administration Review* 66 (2006): 241–251.

5. M. Potoski, "Designing Bureaucratic Responsiveness: Administrative Procedures and Agency Choice in State Environmental Policy," *State Politics and Policy Quarterly* 2 (2002): 1–23.

6. W. M. Lafferty, ed., *Governance for Sustainable Development. The Challenge of Adapting Form to Function* (Northhampton, MA: Edward Elgar Publishing, 2004).

7. C. Bowling, C. Cho, and D. S. Wright. "Establishing a Continuum from Minimizing to Maximizing Bureaucrats: State Agency Head Preferences for Governmental Expansion—A Typology of Administrator Growth Postures, 1964–1998," *Public Administration Review* 64 (2004): 489–499.

8. For good sources on this phenomenon, see:
M. Poole, R. Mansfield, and J. Gould-Williams, "Public and Private Sector Managers Over 20 Years: A Test of the Convergence Thesis," *Public Administration* 84 (2006): 1051–1076.

A. Sapat, "Devolution and Innovation: The Adoption of State Environmental Policy by Administrative Agencies," *Public Administration Review* 64 (2004): 141–151.

C. W. Thomas, *Bureaucratic Landscapes: Interagency Cooperation and the Preservation of Biodiversity* (Cambridge, MA: MIT Press, 2003).

9. H. B. Milward and K. G. Provan, "Governing the Hollow State," *Journal Public Administration: Research and Theory* 10 (2000): 359–379.

D. G. Frederickson and H. G. Frederickson, *Measuring the Performance of the Hollow State* (Washington, DC: Georgetown University Press, 2007).

10. M. Bowens, "Street-Level Resilience," *Public Administration Review* 66 (2006): 780–781.

11. J. Diamond, *Collapse: How Societies Choose to Fail or Succeed* (New York: Viking, 2005).

12. F. S. Berry, R. Brower, S. Choi, W. X. Goa, H. Jang, M. Kwon, and J. Word. "Three Traditions of Network Research: What the Public Management Research Agenda Can Learn from Other Research Communities." *Public Administration Review* 64 (2004): 539–552.

13. M. P. Mandell, ed., *Getting Results through Collaboration: Networks and Network Structures for Public Policy and Management* (Westport, CT: Quorum Books, 2001).

14. W. J. Kickert, E. H. Klijn, and J. Koppenjan, eds., *Managing Complex Networks: Strategies for the Public Sector* (London: Sage Publications, 1997).

C. W. Lewis, "In Pursuit of the Public Interest," *Public Administration Review* 66 (2006): 694–701.

J. Nalbandian, "Politics and Administration in Council-Manager Government: Differences between Newly Elected and Senior Council Members," *Public Administration Review* 64(2004): 200–208.

15. L. O'Toole and K. Meier, "Desperately Seeking Selznick: Cooptation and the Dark Side of Public Management Networks," *Public Administration Review* 64 (2004), 681–693.
S. Page, "Measuring Accountability for Results in Interagency Collaboratives," *Public Administration Review* 64 (2004): 591–606.

16. G. Noble and R. Jones, "The Role of Boundary-Spanning Managers in the Establishment of Public-Private Partnerships," *Public Administration* 84 (2006): 891–917.

17. See contributions to a conference on workplace discrimination held at Rice University in May of 2000, collected into the edited volume Dipboye and Colella, eds., *Discrimination at Work: The Psychological and Organizational Bases* (Mahwah, NJ: Lawrence Erlbaum Associates, 2005).

18. R. Connell, "Glass Ceilings or Gendered Institutions? Mapping the Gender Regimes of Public Sector Worksites," *Public Administration Review* 66 (2006): 837–849.

19. D. F. Norris and M. J. Moon, "Advancing E-Government at the Grassroots: Tortoise or Hare?" *Public Administration Review* 65 (2005): 64–75.
D. M. West, "E-Government and the Transformation of Service Delivery and Citizen Attitudes," *Public Administration Review* 64 (2004): 15–27.

20. B. Gazley and J. Brudney, "Volunteer Involvement in Local Government after September 11: The Continuing Question of Capacity," *Public Administration Review* 65 (2005): 131–142.

21. R. D. Herman, and D. Renz, "Doing Things Right: Effectiveness in Local Nonprofit Organizations: A Panel Study," *Public Administration Review* 64 (2004): 694–704.

22. D. Osborne, and T. Gaebler, *Reinventing Government* (New York: Basic Books, 1993).

23. D. H. Bayley, *Police for the Future* (New York: Oxford University Press, 1994).

24. M. K. Sparrow, *Imposing Duties: Government's Changing Approach to Compliance* (Westport, CT: Praeger, 1994).

25. D. Matthews, *Is There a Public for Public Schools?* (Cleveland, OH: The Kettering Foundation, 1996).

26. E. Bardach and C. Lesser, "Accountability in Human Services Collaboratives— For What? and to Whom?" *Journal of Public Administration Research and Theory* 6(1996): 204–205.

27. See the thoughtful contributions collected in Beryl Radin et al., *New Governance for Rural America: Creating Intergovernmental Partnerships* (Lawrence, KS: University Press of Kansas, 1996).

28. J. Walters, *Measuring Up: Governing Guide for Performance Measurement* (Washington, DC: Urban Institute, 1997), pp. 160–162.

29. M. E. Kraft, and D. Scheberle, "Environmental Federalism at Decade's End: New Approaches and Strategies," *Publius* 28(1998):131–146.

30. U.S. Environmental Protection Agency (EPA), "The Common Sense Initiative: A New Generation of Environmental Protection," *EPA Insight Policy Paper* (August 4, 1994 [EPA 175-N-94-003]).

31. U.S. Congress, "An Assessment of EPA's Reinvention," A Report by the Majority Staff of the Committee on Transportation and Infrastructure, House of Representatives (September 1996), p. 10.

32. B. Bozeman, *Bureaucracy and Red Tape* (Upper Saddle River, NJ: Prentice Hall, 2000), pp. xi–xii.

Chapter 10

1. I. Rubin, "The State of State Budget Research," *Public Budgeting and Finance* 25 (2005): 46–67.

   D. L. Sjoquist, ed., *State and Local Finances Under Pressure* (Northampton, MA: Edward Elgar, 2003).

2. R. L. Bland, *Budgeting: A Budgeting Guide for Local Government*, 2nd ed. (Washington, DC: International City and County Management Association, 2007), pp. 25–26.

3. D. J. Boyd, "The Future of State Fiscal Conditions: Fiscal Boom, Fiscal Bust, Then What?" *Spectrum: The Journal of State Government* 75 (2002): 5–8.

4. J. R. Bartle, "Trends in Local Government Taxation in the 21st Century," *Spectrum: The Journal of State Government* 76 (2003): 26–29.

5. D. R. Mullins and B. A. Wallin, "Tax and Expenditure Limitations: Introduction and Overview," *Public Budgeting and Finance* 24 (2004): 2.

6. B. Edwards and S. Wallace, "State Income Tax Treatment of the Elderly," *Public Budgeting and Finance* 24 (2004): 1–20.

7. A. E. Crabbe, R. Hiatt, S. D. Poliwka, and M. Wachs, "Local Transportation Sales Taxes: California's Experiment in Transportation Finance," *Public Budgeting and Finance* 25 (2005): 91–121.

8. T. P. Lauth, "Budgeting During a Recession Phase of the Business Cycle: The Georgia Experience," *Public Budgeting and Finance* 23 (2003): 26–38.

9. M. Huckabee, "State Budget Shortfalls and Arkansas' Strategies," *Spectrum: The Journal of State Government* 75 (2002): 32–34.

10. K. Willoughby, "Governors' Initiatives in 2005: Facing up to the Problem?" *Spectrum: The Journal of State Government* 78 (2005): 8–13.

11. Ibid.

12. D. Osborne and T. Gaebler, *Reinventing Government* (New York: Addison-Wesley, 1992).

13. D. Osborne and P. Hutchinson, "Budgeting in Tough Times: The Three Decisions and Nine Strategies," *Spectrum: The Journal of State Government* 76 (2003): 18–22, 34.

14. See W. M. Bowen, M. Haynes, and M. S. Rosentraub, "Cities, Tax Revenues, and a State's Fiscal Future: The Value of Major Urban Centers," *Public Budgeting & Finance* 26 (2006): 47–65.

15. K. Augustine, "Effective Debt Collection Efforts in Nevada," *Spectrum: The Journal of State Government* 75 (2002): 36–37.

16. C. Johnson, "The State of the Tobacco Settlement: Are Settlement Funds Being Used to Finance State Government Budget Deficits? A Research Note," *Public Budgeting and Finance* 24 (2004): 113.

17. J. Marlowe, "Fiscal Slack and Counter-Cyclical Expenditure Stabilization: A First Look at the Local Level," *Public Budgeting and Finance* 25 (2005): 48–72.

18. K. V. Byers, and M. A. Pirog, "Local Governments' Fiscal Responses to Welfare Reform." *Public Budgeting and Finance* 23 (2003): 86–107.

    H. Chernick and A. Reschovsky, "State Fiscal Responses to Welfare Reform During Recessions: Lessons for the Future," *Public Budgeting and Finance* 23 (2003): 3–21.

19. J. Musso, E. Graddy, and J. Grizard, "State Budgetary Processes and Reforms: The California Story," *Public Budgeting and Finance* 26 (2006): 1–21.

20. Y. Hou and D. L. Smith, "A Framework for Understanding State Balanced Budget Requirement Systems: Reexamining Distinctive Features and an Operational Definition," *Public Budgeting and Finance* 26 (2006): 22–45.
21. D. Denison, M. Hackbart, and M. Moody, "State Debt Limits: How Many are Enough?" *Public Budgeting and Finance* 26 (2006): 22–39.
22. T. P. Lauth and C. C. Reese, "The Line-Item Veto in Georgia: Fiscal Restraint or Inter-Branch Politics?" *Public Budgeting and Finance* 26 (2006): 1–19.
23. J. M. Kelly and W. C. Rivenbark, *Performance Budgeting for State and Local Government* (Armonk, NY: Sharpe, 2003).
24. L. Friedman, "Performance Budgeting in American Cities," *Public Productivity Review* 3 (1979): 50–62.
25. For a discussion of state level adoption and use, see S. Pattison and N. Samuels, "Trends and Issues in Performance-Based Budgeting," *Spectrum: The Journal of State Government* 75 (2002): 12–13.
26. R. C. Burns, and R. D. Lee, "The Ups and Downs of State Budget Process Reform: Experience of Three Decades," *Public Budgeting and Finance* 24 (2004): 1–19.
    J. E. Melkers, and K. G. Willoughby, "Budgeters' Views of State Performance-Budgeting Systems: Distinctions Across Branches," *Public Administration Review* 61 (2001): 54–64.
27. I. Rubin, "Budgeting for Contracting in Local Government," *Public Budget and Finance* 26 (2006): 1–13.
28. J. W. Kingdon, *Agendas, Alternatives, and Public Policy* (New York: Longman, 2003).

Chapter 11

1. D. A. Super, "The Political Economy of Entitlement," *Columbia Law Review* 104 (2004): 633–656, p. 644.
2. Ibid., p. 648.
3. Ibid., p. 653.
4. Ibid., p. 654.
5. Ibid., p. 655.
6. J. H. Skinner, "Entitlements: What do they Mean?" *Generations* 15 (1991): 16–19.
7. See D. Friedman, "Credit Crisis, Health Costs Threaten States' Economies," *Congress Daily* (December 5, 2007), p. 10.
    D. Malpass, "Monetary Policy and the Growing Fiscal Imbalance," *CATO Journal* 27 (2007): 219–230.
8. A. Meyerson, "Land of Milk and Money," *Policy Review* 56 (1991): 31–35.
9. E. C. Smith, "Moving from Welfare to Work: A Snapshot Survey of Illinois Families," *Child Welfare* 74 (1995): 1091–1106.
10. C. A. Simon, *Public Policy: Preferences and Outcomes*, 2nd ed. (New York: Longman, 2010).
11. G. Rosen, *A History of Public Health*, expanded ed. (Baltimore, MD: Johns Hopkins University Press, 1993).
12. See "Age-Old Wisdom," *Utne Reader* 136 (2006): 12.
13. See "In case you haven't heard…," *Mental Health Weekly* 17 (2007): 8.
14. See R. Murdock, "Drug Use Falls Among Teen, But Increases Among Baby Boomers," *Nation's Mental Health* 36 (2006): 8.

15. Office of Family Assistance, Fact sheet. URL: http://www.acf.hhs.gov/opa/fact_sheets/ tanf_factsheet.html (accessed December 30, 2008).

16. See H. J. Aaron, "Budget Crisis, Entitlement Crisis, Health Care Financing Problem—Which Is It?" *Health Affairs* 26 (2007): 1622–1633.
    L. D. Schaeffer, "The New Architects of Health Care Reform," *Health Affairs* 26 (2007): 1557–1559.

17. See T. S. Bodenheimer, *Understanding Health Policy: A Clinical Approach*, 4th ed. (New York: Lange Medical Books/McGraw-Hill, 2007).
    P. Starr, *The Social Transformation of American Medicine: The Rise of a Sovereign Profession and the Making of a Vast Industry* (New York: Basic Books, 1982).

18. I. Sanz and F. J. Velázquez, "The Role of Aging in the Growth of Government and Social Welfare Spending in the OECD," *European Journal of Political Economy* 23 (2007): 917–931.

19. See S. M. Ross, *American Families: Past and Present* (New Brunswick, NJ: Rutgers University Press, 2006).
    J. M. Wilmoth and C. F. Longino, Jr., "Demographic Trends that will Shape U.S. Policy in the Twenty-First Century," *Research on Aging* 28 (2006): 269–288.

21. C. Simon, *Public Policy: Preferences and Outcomes*, 2nd ed. (New York: Longman, 2010), 192.

22. D. P. Rice and N. Fineman, "Economic Implications of Increased Longevity in the United States," *Annual Review of Public Health* 25 (2004): 466.

23. J. L. Palmer, "Entitlement Programs for the Aged: The Long-Term Fiscal Context," *Research on Aging* 28 (2006): 289–302.

24. Medicaid, "Medicaid Eligibility." URL: http://www.cms.hhs.gov/MedicaidEligibility/ (accessed December 31, 2008).

25. R. Kronick and D. Rousseau, "Is Medicaid Sustainable? Spending Projections for the Program's Second Forty Years," *Health Affairs* Special Issue (2007): 271–287.

26. J. Holohan and A. Weil, "Toward Real Medicaid Reform," *Health Affairs* Special Issue (2007): 254–270.
    C. M. Grogan, and M. K. Gusmano, "Deliberative Democracy in Theory and Practice: Connecticut's Medicaid Managed Care Council," *State Politics and Policy Quarterly* 5 (2005): 126–146.

27. B. Landon, E. C. Schneider, S. L. Normand, S. H. Schoelle, L. Pawlson, L. Gregory, and A. M. Epstein, "Quality of Care in Medicaid Managed Plans and Commercial Health Plans," *Journal of the American Medical Association* 298 (2007): 1674–1681.

28. E. K. Pavalko and K. A. Henderson, "Combining Care Work and Paid Work: Do Workplace Policies Make a Difference?" *Research on Aging* 28 (2006): 359–374.
    P. K. Robins, "Welfare Reform and Child Care: Evidence from 10 Experimental Welfare-to-Work Programs," *Evaluation Review* 31 (2007): 440–468.

29. U.S. Census Bureau, *Statistical Abstract of the United States* (Washington, DC: U.S. Census Bureau, 2008).

30. See V. Feeg, "Why SCHIP is Such a Good Deal for Children's Access to Care," *Pediatric Nursing* 33 (2007): 299, 312.

31. Work Force Security. *Unemployment Insurance Benefits.* URL: http://workforcesecurity.doleta.gov/unemploy/ pdf/partnership.pdf (accessed December 30, 2008).

32. Ibid.

33. J. Quadagno and D. Street, "U.S. Social Welfare Policy: Minor Retrenchment or Major Transformation?" *Research on Aging* 28 (2006): 303–316.

Chapter 12

1. F. Hess, "No Child Left Behind: Trends and Issues." In *The Book of the States, 2006* (Lexington, KY: The Council of State Governments, 2006).
2. R. Clark, *Crime in America* (New York: Simon and Schuster, 1970).
3. E. Banfield, *The Unheavenly City Revisited* (Boston: Little, Brown, 1974).
4. S. A. Shah and L. H. Roth, "Biological and Psychophysiological Factors in Criminality." In Daniel Glaser, ed., *Handbook of Criminology* (Chicago, IL: Rand McNally, 1974).
5. J. Q. Wilson, *Thinking About Crime* (New York: Random House, 1985).
6. Shah and Roth, op. cit. (see note 4).
7. U.S. Department of Justice, "Criminal Victimization, 2006," *Bureau of Justice Statistics Fact Sheet, December 2007* (Washington, DC: U.S. Department of Education, 2007), p. 1.
8. U.S. Department of Justice, "Jail Statistics." URL: http://www.ojp.usdoj.gov/bjs/jails.htm#findings (accessed December 10, 2009).
9. A. Roberts, *Critical Issues in Crime and Justice* (Thousand Oaks, CA: Sage, 1994).
10. The Council of State Legislators, *Book of the States*, 2006 (Lexington, KY: The Council of State Governments, 2006), p. 533.
11. U.S. Department of Justice, "Mandatory Sentencing," *NIJ Research in Action*, (Washington, DC: Office of Justice Programs, 1997), p. 1.
12. Roberts, op. cit. (see note 9).
    H. Ruth and K. Reitz, *The Challenge of Crime: Rethinking Our Response* (Cambridge, MA: Harvard University Press, 2003).
13. U. Bondeson, *Alternatives to Imprisonment: Intentions and Reality* (Boulder, CO: Westview Press, 1994).
14. Ruth and Reitz, op. cit. (see note 12), pp. 285, 287.
15. J. Mooradian, *Disproportionate Confinement of African-American Juvenile Delinquents* (New York: LFB Publishers, 2003).
    T. O'Neill, *Children in Secure Accommodation* (London: Jessica Kingsley Publishers, 2001).
16. The Council of State Legislators, op. cit. (see note 10).
17. S. Baum and K. Payea, *Education Pays: The Benefits of Higher Education for Individuals and Society*. URL: www. collegeboard .com. (accessed December 10, 2009).
18. National Education Association, *The Educational Case Against Vouchers*.
    URL: http://www.nea.org/vouchers/index.html (accessed December 11, 2009).
19. U.S. Department of Education, *The State of Charter Schools 2000: Fourth Year Report*. (Washington, DC: U.S. Department of Education).
20. National Education Association, 2006. *Charter Schools Show No Gains over Public Schools*. URL: http://www.nea.org/charter/naepstudy.html
21. Oyez Project, 2009. *Brown v. Board of Education (II)*, 349 U.S. 294 (1955). URL: www.oyez.org/cases/ (accessed May 25, 2009).
22. J. Kozol, "Still Unequal: America's Educational Apartheid," *Harper's Magazine*, 311 (2005), September: 41–54.
23. Hess, op. cit. (see note 1), p. 474.
24. Ibid.
25. S. Abernathy, *No Child Left Behind and the Public Schools* (Ann Arbor, MI: University of Michigan Press, 2007), p. 130.

26. National Education Association, *No Child Left Behind/ESEA*. URL: http://www.nea.org/esea/policy.html (accessed December 10, 2009).

27. National Council of State Legislatures, *Key Recommendations from the NCSL Task Force on No Child Left Behind* (Washington, DC: National Council of State Legislatures, 2005), pp. 1, 2.

28. U.S. Department of Education, *Building on Results: A Blueprint for Strengthening The No Child Left Behind Act* (Washington, DC: U.S. Department of Education, 2007), p. 2.

29. Hess, op. cit. (see note 1), p. 477.

30. The Council of State Legislators, op. cit. (see note 10).

31. D. Heller, *The States and Public Higher Education* (Baltimore, MD: The John Hopkins Press, 2001).

32. Baum and Payea, op. cit. (see note 17).
R. Inglehart, *Modernization and Postmodernization: Cultural, Economic and Political Change in 43 Societies* (Princeton, NJ: University of Princeton Press, 1997).

33. P. Lingenfelter and T. Flint, *Adult Learners and State Policy* (Denver, CO: State Higher Education Executive Officers, 2003), p. 3.

34. Baum and Payea, op. cit. (see note 17), p. 8.

35. National Center for Public Policy and Higher Education, *Measuring Up 2006: The National Report Card on Higher Education* (Washington, DC: The National Center for Public Policy and Higher Education, 2007).

36. P. Callan, "Colleges, States Increase Financial Burdens for Students and Families." In *Measuring Up 2006: The National Report Card on Higher Education* (Washington, DC: The National Center for Public Policy and Higher Education, 2007), p. 19.

37. Ibid.

38. State Higher Education Executive Officers, *Accountability for Better Results: A National Imperative for Higher Education*. URL: www.sheeo.org (accessed December 10, 2009).

39. Ibid.

40. National Governors Association, *Higher Expectations* (Washington, DC: National Governors Association, 2002), p. 12.

41. Heller, op. cit. (see note 31), p. 243.

42. State Higher Education Executive Officers, op. cit. (see note 38), pp. 6, 7.

43. Governmental Accountability Office, *Highway Finance: States Expanding Use of Tolling Illustrates Diverse Challenges and Strategies* (Washington, DC: Governmental Accounting Office, 2006).

44. Ibid.

45. National Chamber Foundation, *Future Highway and Public Transportation Finance: Phase I: Current Outlook and Short-term Solutions* (Washington, DC: U.S. Chamber of Commerce, 2005), pp. 2, 3.

46. National Governors Association, *State Policy Options for Funding Transportation* (Washington, DC: National Governors Association, 2007).

47. Governmental Accountability Office, *Transforming Transportation for the 21st Century* (Washington, DC: Governmental Accountability Office, 2007).

48. Ibid.
National Governors Association, op. cit. (see note 46).

49. National Governors Association, op. cit. (see note 46), p. 2.

50. Ibid.
   Governmental Accountability Office, op. cit. (see note 47).
51. A. Lakoff, "Social Life of Risk: Preparing for the Next Emergency," *Public Culture* 19 (2007): 247–271.
52. Ibid., p. 253.
   R. Ericson, "Ten Uncertainties of Risk-Management Approaches to Security." *Canadian Journal of Criminology and Criminal Justice* 48 (2006): 345–357.
53. Lakoff, op. cit. (see note 51), p. 250.
54. Ericson, op. cit (see note 52), p. 346.
55. S. Collier, A. Lakoff, and P. Rabinow, "Biosecurity: Toward an Anthropology of the Contemporary," *Anthropology Today* 20 (2004): 3–7.
56. P. Jaeger, B. Shneiderman, and K. Fleischmann, "Community Response Grids: E-government, Social Networks, and Effective Emergency Management," *Telecommunications Policy* 31 (2007): 592–604.
57. Ibid.
58. Ibid.
59. Lakoff, op. cit. (see note 51).
60. Ibid., p. 267.
61. Ibid., p. 261.
62. Ibid, p. 262.
63. A. Katz, A. Stati, and K. McKenzie, "Preparing for the Unknown, Responding to the Unknown: Communities and Public Health Preparedness," *Health Affairs* 25 (2006): 946–957.
64. Collier et al., op. cit. (see note 55).
65. Ibid., p. 5.
66. Katz et al., op. cit. (see note 63).
67. M. Douglas and A. Wildavsky, *Risk and Culture: An Essay on the Selection of Technological and Environmental Dangers* (Berkeley, CA.: University of California Press, 1982).

Index

Note: Endnotes are indicated by n. after the page number. Figures or tables are indicated by page numbers in **bold**.